INVESTMENT
GURUS

ABOUT THE AUTHOR

PETER J. TANOUS is President of Lynx Investment Advisory, Inc. of Washington D.C., a registered investment advisor. Lynx provides consulting services relating to the selection and monitoring of money managers. Its clients include institutions and individuals worldwide. Before founding Lynx, Tanous was Executive Vice President and a director of Bank Audi (U.S.A.) in New York City.

Prior to joining Bank Audi, he was Chairman of Petra Capital Corporation, a New York Stock Exchange member firm, which he co-founded. During his 15 years at Smith Barney, Inc., Tanous served as the International Director. He was also manager of its Paris office and a Director and member of the Executive Committee of Smith Barney, International. He is currently a director of Cedars Bank in Los Angeles, and a director of Interstate Resources Inc., a paper manufacturing company based in Virginia.

Mr. Tanous has written articles on the securities industry which have appeared in French and English publications. In addition, he has authored and co-authored three novels which have been translated into several foreign languages.

Mr. Tanous received a Bachelor of Arts degree in economics from Georgetown University in 1960. He has served as a member of Board of Advisors of Georgetown's College of Arts and Sciences. A long time resident of New York City prior to moving to Washington D.C., he served as a trustee of the Browning School, a private school in Manhattan.

In 1991, Mr. Tanous was the recipient of the American Task Force for Lebanon Philip C. Habib Award for Distinguished Public Service whose prior recipients have included Senator George Mitchell, Governor John Sununu, and Senator Bob Dole. He was awarded the Ellis Island Medal of Honor in 1994.

Peter Tanous is married to the former Ann MacConnell. They have three grown children.

INVESTMENT GURUS

A ROAD MAP TO WEALTH
FROM THE WORLD'S
BEST MONEY MANAGERS

PETER J. TANOUS

FOREWORD BY ANDREW TOBIAS

PREFACE BY RICHARD C. BREEDEN

NEW YORK INSTITUTE OF FINANCE

NEW YORK • TORONTO • SYDNEY • TOKYO • SINGAPORE

Library of Congress Cataloging-in-Publication Data

Tanous, Peter.
    Investment Gurus / Peter Tanous.
        p. cm.
    Includes index.
    ISBN 0-13-260720-4 (cloth)
        1. Investment advisors—United States—Interviews. 2. Stocks. 3. Portfolio
    management. I. Title.
    HG4928.5.T36 1997
    332.6—dc20   96-42939
                                                                         CIP

This publication is designed to provide accurate and authoritative information in regard to the subject matter covered. It is sold with the understanding that the publisher is not engaged in rendering legal, accounting, or other professional service. If legal advice or other expert assistance is required, the services of a competent professional person should be sought.

From a Declaration of Principles Jointly Adapted by a Committee of the American Bar Association and a Committee of Publishers and Associations

Printed in the United States of America

10 9 8 7 6 5 4 3 2 1

ISBN 0-13-260720-4

ATTENTION: CORPORATIONS AND SCHOOLS
NYIF books are available at quantity discounts with bulk purchase for educational, business, or sales promotional use. For information, please write to: Prentice Hall Career & Personal Development Special Sales, 113 Sylvan Avenue, Englewood Cliffs, NJ 07632. Please supply: title of book, ISBN number, quantity, how the book will be used, date needed.

 NEW YORK INSTITUTE OF FINANCE
Englewood Cliffs, NJ 07632

A Simon & Schuster Company

On the World Wide Web at http://www.phdirect.com

Prentice-Hall International (UK) Limited, *London*
Prentice-Hall of Australia Pty. Limited, *Sydney*
Prentice-Hall Canada Inc., *Toronto*
Prentice-Hall Hispanoamericana, S.A., *Mexico*
Prentice-Hall of India Private Limited, *New Delhi*
Prentice-Hall of Japan, Inc., *Tokyo*
Simon & Schuster Asia Pte. Ltd., *Singapore*
Editora Prentice-Hall do Brasil, Ltda., *Rio de Janeiro*

DEDICATION

Most of us recall individuals who influenced our lives early on, perhaps in school or in early career stages. I dedicate this book to five wise men who influenced me not early, but later in my personal and professional life. It just proves that you are never too old to learn.

To: George N. Frem
           Joseph J. Jacobs
           Charles H. Percy
           John H. Sununu
           and the late Philip C. Habib

CONTENTS

PART THREE: THE ROUTE   365

INDEX   405

PREFACE

America's investment markets are the most active and efficient in the world. These markets provide capital to more than 10,000 companies ranging from the tiniest venture-stage company to giant multinationals. Local, state, and national government agencies and a host of trusts, partnerships, and other special purpose entities also seek funds. To a degree strikingly different from most other countries that rely nearly exclusively on their banking system, the United States public securities market is the principal avenue for financing the broader United States economy.

Issuers offer securities ranging from traditional stocks and bonds to highly complex structured instruments and esoteric derivatives. Thousands of different mutual funds offer individual investors both diversification and professional management. For investors, this profusion of issuers represents a world of investment opportunity.

Investor choice in the American capital market extends beyond the type of instrument and the specific issuer to span the spectrum of risk. Under our system, investors have the right to take risks according to their own risk tolerance and to seek out extraordinary gain even at the risk of painful loss. With millions of individual decisions evaluating risk and reward, the market as a whole represents a distillation of economic judgment about risk that is far more accurate than any government body could ever hope to be.

If choice is the dominant characteristic of this extraordinary market, choice also complicates the task facing any particular investor. In *Investment Gurus*, Peter Tanous interviews many of the nation's leading investment managers and some of the academics who have helped establish the intellectual underpinning for today's investment strategies. These interviews present, in their own words, the strategies that some of the best-known professionals have brought to their investing.

These stars of the investment profession express many views on the relative merits of growth and value stocks and on different theories for producing above-average returns. As we listen to what the successful managers say, it becomes clear that choosing risk wisely in order to obtain higher than market returns is in many respects the name of the game. The managers that Peter Tanous interviews excel at that game. The level of return they will achieve—and the wealth they will thereby acquire—is dependent not on how well they avoid risk, but in how sensibly they take risk. The same is true for individual investors.

Some of the investment approaches discussed in *Investment Gurus* involve reviewing the available information concerning a company, its industry, and the overall economy and making accurate value judgments before the rest of the market figures out the same thing (and prices change accordingly!). Other approaches do not rely specifically on faster reactions to significant news developments, but do rely on high quality financial data to permit careful analysis of intrinsic value or likely earnings acceleration.

In the end, we discover that achieving consistent profit requires a wise understanding of risk and the ability to choose exposure to risk prudently. Any individual seeking greater success in the market must understand at the outset what could go wrong (as well as the theories of how to make things go right).

Naturally, both managers and investors tend to focus on the potential for profit through sound investment decisions. It remains a great and enduring hallmark of the United States equities market that astute investors (or very lucky ones) can realize significant profits from successful investing.

At present, I am serving as the trustee in bankruptcy of nine related companies that were the scene of one of history's largest pyramid or "Ponzi scheme" frauds. In a six-year period, the Bennett Funding Group and its affiliates sold more than $2.1 *billion* in unregistered securities. Investors were told these fixed income notes were highly safe and that they were backed by both leases of office equipment to government agencies and private insurance. Unfortunately, many of these notes were backed by nothing more than hot air.

Most investors want to protect themselves against excessive risk, yet prove vulnerable to fast-talking sales personnel. Most investors want to achieve the best return they can get without becoming part of a banquet for con men or vultures. Unfortunately, many people do not have the skill needed to determine how much risk a particular investment or an entire investment strategy may represent. Up to a point, selecting a professional investment manager will help meet the need for understanding and managing risk. (Unfortunately, there have also been cases in recent years of managers becoming involved in frauds as well, so that is not a perfect solution.)

While the role of government efforts to oversee and regulate United States securities markets did not receive much attention in the interviews, the pivotal need investors have for reliable financial reports and other forms of disclosure was apparent. The quality of that information in the market and the mechanisms for maintaining an environment of what the SEC calls "full and fair disclosure" depends significantly on government encouragement and "regulation." Happily, at least at the federal level, the United States regulatory system has for the most part seen its job over generations as combating the worst abuses in the market without trying to go too far in the direction of limiting the market's ability to offer both low and high risk investment.

Those of us who have been on the regulatory side know that the SEC cannot do everything. We always sought to protect investors against fraud and market manipulation, but we also protect their inalienable right to lose money in pursuit of profit.

Readers of this book will be moved by a spirit of curiosity, of inquiry, and also one of skepticism, healthy characteristics to bring to the investment process. *Investment Gurus* demystifies that process while exposing investors to the highest level of investment competence and success.

Richard C. Breeden

FOREWORD

I called my broker to short Ascend Communications, one of the many Internet companies I know nothing about. I just knew it was divided into 110 million shares, each of which was selling for $38, up from $5 a few months earlier. That gave the whole pie about a $4 billion price ($38 a slice times 110 million slices)—which may have been cheap for all I knew. Maybe a *fair* valuation would really have been $10 billion. But it seemed like a lot for a young company with modest sales and earnings that had been priced under $600 million the previous year.

The point of all this is not to knock Ascend—believe me, I knew nothing about it. (When it got up to 65, I shorted some more.) Rather, the point is to tell you what my broker said when I asked him *his* thoughts on the stock.

"I don't want you to think I'm stupid," he said—he's been my broker and friend for 22 years by now, so, no, I don't think he's stupid—"but I don't look at the same kind of stuff you do." Like earnings. "I like to buy stocks when they're going up and short them when they're going down."

Ascend was going up, so, while he wished me luck, it wasn't the sort of stock he would short. Indeed, now that I had brought this craziness to his attention, I knew he was silently contemplating purchase. What kind of nut would buy Ascend at prices like these? My broker, for one.

And do you know what? I'd guess he has done at least as well with his method as I have with mine. I have the self-righteous satisfaction of being "right" about some of these things—for example, I was "right" to short U.S. Surgical at 60 (only to watch it hit $134 before dropping back to $18), because it was overpriced. But he made a lot more money on U.S. Surgical than I did. It was going up, so he bought some.

There is more than one way to skin a cat

But most of us don't want to skin cats at all. It's nasty, unpleasant work. The truth is, neither my broker nor I does the kind of highly disciplined, time-consuming research a prudent man should before investing large sums of money. And neither do most investors. Instead, we tend to rely on the work of others—smart people interviewed in *Barron's,* for example, offering the benefit of *their* research. Why reinvent the wheel?

(Sometimes we rely on the ideas of others we merely assume have done the work, or who are selling what they are recommending we buy.)

Of course, the sensible thing for almost everyone to do is not pick stocks themselves, but simply to make the basic decisions—how much to invest in the market at all, how much in U.S. versus foreign markets—and then do the actual investing through low-expense no-load mutual funds. Just by investing in one of the Vanguard index funds, because their expenses are so low, you are virtually certain over any meaningful stretch of time to outperform most of your friends and neighbors, most other mutual funds, most bank trust departments and pension funds.

Astounding, no? But true. And prudent.

If I weren't so fascinated by this game—and if, pigeon-like, I were not occasionally rewarded with an out-size kernel of corn (I bought 25,000 shares of a Canadian oil company in 1994 at 87 cents that has some sort of deal going in Kuwait and today is $7.33 a share; have you any idea how thrilling that is?)—I would stick with mutual funds myself.

I am, vaguely, a "value" investor, not entirely unlike the first of my friend Peter Tanous's interviewees in this book, Michael Price. Indeed, 20 years ago I invested my IRA in Price's mutual fund, Mutual Shares, and have happily watched him and his late mentor, Max Heine, multiply it several times over.

My broker, by contrast, is more of a "momentum" investor, vaguely akin to Peter's second interviewee, Richard Driehaus. I was bemused to learn from the interview that while I was shorting

Ascend, Driehaus—who actually *did* know a lot about Ascend—was buying it. It is people like me who make opportunities for more serious investors like Driehaus. Why on Earth would someone like me, dabbling at it part-time, unwilling to spend the big bucks to get "First Call" on his computer screen or to spend all day staring at that screen, do as well as Driehaus?

"Everyone wants to be rich," Driehaus tells Peter Tanous, "but few want to work for it."

Peter Lynch, speaking in this book, makes a similar point but with a different twist. People are so persuaded they can't beat the market that they don't bother to try. They either do the sensible thing (mutual funds) *or they just play around as if they were in a big casino, placing bets more or less blindly.* It would be odd if there were no benefit to be had in opening your eyes.

That oddness is a basic paradox of investing. Most securities are priced more or less efficiently. A monkey throwing darts, it has been proven again and again, will outperform most Wall Street professionals.*

But not Peter Tanous's interviewees. Most of them have handily beaten the monkey, and the explanation isn't "chance." It may be hard work and skill. It may be access to superior (or even "inside") information. It may be self-fulfilling prophecy (as a lucky money manager becomes known and then followed by others, who bid up his stocks). It may be the ability to force management to pay greenmail or take some step to realize a higher stock price (when you own a million shares of a stock, you sometimes have that leverage). It may be various combinations of the above. *But it isn't random chance.*

It's true that in any given group of a thousand annual coin-tossers you will have a few "brilliant" ones "able" to toss heads year after year. Indeed, one of them, odds are, would toss heads ten years running. But that's quite different from investors being able to significantly outperform their peers year after year. The people Peter interviewed, and others like them, have not just flipped heads eight or ten times in a row. They've been engaged in a competition where there are typically *hundreds* of tosses—buy/sell/hold decisions—each year.

---

*The monkey wins because, unlike the pros, he pays no transaction costs and charges no fees. The monkey I once did this with cost $700 for the morning, but that's different. We speak here of hypothetical monkeys.

If you had the same thousand coin-tossers tossing not once a year but, say, 500 times a year, guess what? All of them would perform almost identically. All would flip heads almost exactly 50% of the time. And the ones who did flip 52% heads one year would be absolutely no more likely than any of the others to do it again. You'd *never* find a coin-flipper hitting 55% or 60% consistently. But you do find that among a rare few investors.

Why?

The fascination of this book lies largely in trying to figure that out.

The practical benefit of this book is that it will give you a better sense of what you can and cannot achieve with your own investments, and provoke you to reassess your own strategy (or lack of one).

Chances are, you will conclude as I have that steady periodic investment in two or three no-load, low-expense mutual funds—very possibly some of those you'll read about in this book—is your smartest bet. But maybe not. And in any event there's no law that says you have to *make* the smartest bet. If you can afford it, you might want to have the fun and challenge of calling the shots yourself. At least one obstacle to do-it-yourself success has largely disappeared in recent years: with the advent of deep-discount brokers, "transaction costs" are no longer appreciably higher for retail investors like you and me than for the big money.** Indeed, sometimes trading just a few hundred shares you can get better prices than if you were trying to buy or unload tens of thousands.

Still, before you jump into the market as an active investor yourself, or choose to remain in, note this from Michael Steinhardt. When Steinhardt was running his famous hedge fund, he was asked to reveal the most important thing an average investor could learn from him. His answer: "That I'm their competition."

Andrew Tobias

**So why do I still use a full-service broker for some of my trades? Partly because he charges me a relatively low commission (and gives me interest on my shorts); partly because he's got a great sense of humor and makes every effort to accommodate my requests; mainly because we're friends.

ACKNOWLEDGMENTS

It will come as no surprise when I declare that writing a book is a collaborative effort, particularly in the case of a book like *Investment Gurus* which features 18 separate interviews. In addition to the interview subjects, a variety of people, many of whom work with the Gurus, contributed to the timeliness and success of the effort. I am especially grateful to Robert H. Buchen, Irene Diakun, Jane Dubin, Nicholas Gianakouros, Peter A. Greenley, Shirley Guptill, Ziad Malek, John F. Reilly, Debbie Shippee, and Diane Wilke for assistance and help above and beyond, as they say.

Other friends were helpful in identifying potential Gurus and even in providing introductions. My gratitude to J. Carter Beese, Jr. of Alex. Brown & Sons, Tom H. Clark of Smith Barney, Nijad I. Fares, W. Randall Jones of *Worth* magazine, F. Joseph Hallal M.D., and Marlene Jupiter, whose own book on investing is eagerly awaited.

Robert Dintzer of Dimensional Fund Advisors devoted both his time and expertise to help customize and prepare many of the charts we use in the book. David McGrouther of Dean Witter also contributed some excellent charts.

Several of the interviewees proved invaluable beyond their role as Gurus. I am especially grateful to Richard H. Driehaus, Mario J. Gabelli, Peter Lynch, Michael F. Price, and Rex A. Sinquefield.

My children have reached the age where our roles are reversed. It is they who encourage and cajole their father, rather than vice versa. That help and encouragement was meaningful and timely.

Thanks to Christopher Tanous, Helene Tanous, William Tanous, future son-in-law, Paul Bartilucci and to dearest Amber Olsen.

Special thanks are due to several colleagues at Lynx who helped in different aspects of this book. They include Candice O. Atherton, whose investment and analytical skills continue to approach perfection; K. Andrew Sprague, who did research for and attended several interviews; Lara C. Mongini whose investment and editing talents were invaluable; and Peter D. Forbes, who first introduced me to the idea of using indexing as a tool and then introduced me to Rex Sinquefield, which in turn, led to the inclusion of the academics in the book. Special gratitude is due to a special colleague, Ann Tanous, who contributes both work and wisdom in office and personnel management and has the added burden and challenge of going home with the author at night, as she has for 34 years.

In the end, a book is a collaboration between author and editor. My editor, Ellen Schneid Coleman, could teach the course on editing. Her wisdom, knowledge, patience, and encouragement were more than meaningful. Above all, her sheer skill and instincts deserve much of the credit for the value of this work. I hope she writes a book, too.

PART ONE
THE LANDSCAPE

INTRODUCTION

I assume this is not the first investment book you ever read. You may have read some books about the stock market or even one of the recent bestsellers by Peter Lynch, the legendary fund manager who successfully managed the largest mutual fund in America, Fidelity Magellan. Perhaps you were intrigued enough to want to read more about phenomenal money managers and glean from their own stories what it is that makes them great. Perhaps you want to know if there are identifiable common traits or methods used by these top managers that allow them to succeed so brilliantly, and so consistently, while so many others fail or are destined to mediocrity? Well, if I guessed right, you won't be disappointed. And I promise you a lot more.

Here's what I consider it my mission to deliver:

- Informative, revealing, and sometimes passionate discussions with some of the greatest investment minds today.
- An analysis of the investment skills and attributes of the Gurus as we attempt to zero in on what works in stock market investing and, equally importantly, what doesn't.
- A timely and revealing look at the latest, state-of-the-art techniques that we investment consultants use to find and track investment genius and how to use these same techniques in your own investment program.

3

- An investment program you can use to either choose stocks yourself or select your own Guru to do it for you. Again, we will focus on what works.
- One last promise: we will clear the air of some of the annoying noise that is often promulgated under the guise of investment advice. You don't have time for that. I don't either.

This is a mission of financial discovery. We are not only going to talk to great money managers, but also to great academics whose work will help us understand just how investment markets work and what we can realistically expect from them. We will ask the managers tough questions about how they do what they do, and we are going to try to find out not just how, but *why* they succeed. We will delve into the different characteristics of these Gurus and try to isolate those traits that appear to contribute to their success. We will discover if, in fact, there are traits common to all of them, or simply an assortment of characteristics and talents that makes this group of people so successful. In the end, once we identify these special attributes, we will see if it is possible to emulate them in some way to help us in our own investment decisions.

Investment Gurus focuses on one type of investing: common stocks. That's because common stocks are what most of us understand and invest in because they are the best investment over time. I don't want to dazzle you with exotic investment techniques that you will have no use for in your own investing life. (I confess, I've made one exception just to give you a glimpse into the future of investing.) But, in general I take it for granted that you are too busy to spend a lot of time reading about techniques you can't use.

My goal is for you to emerge from the time you spend with me a much better investor. Therefore, you will not find interviews with hedge fund managers, currency traders, arbitrageurs, derivatives specialists, and the like. That's because there is nothing that you and I can learn from those people that we can apply to our own investment strategies. Trust me, you will not learn how to trade currencies like Paul Tudor Jones or do Yen/Deutsche Mark swaps like George Soros by reading a book, but you *can* learn something from managers who buy and sell stocks and do it superbly. That's not to say that some of our Gurus don't use exotic techniques on occasion. A few of them do, and you will end up understanding most of their practices and why they use them.

You may be wondering why I am eager to write this book. As a professional investment consultant, I spend most of my waking hours analyzing investment manager performance as well as manager traits and characteristics. Obviously, of the 20,000 or so registered investment advisors only a handful can be truly great, and I was curious to see what those few were really like. What do they have in common, if anything? What is it about them that propels them to the top of their class? And, most importantly, what can we learn from them?

My firm, Lynx Investment Advisory, Inc., unlike other registered investment advisors, does not manage money. We are part of a small group of advisors who are hired as investment consultants by individuals and institutions, to find and monitor the best money managers in the business. Large institutions hire consultants so they don't have to listen to hundreds of sales pitches from brokers and money managers. Besides, they figure, the really great managers, the Gurus, if you will, are not likely to be out hustling new business. They don't need to!

Why have I been successful at picking managers and making investment decisions, and why do I think I can help you do it, too? Well, I began my career supervising institutional salesmen as head of the international division of Smith Barney; later, as CEO of a New York Stock Exchange investment banking firm, I realized that true investment genius was rare indeed. In starting Lynx, I made it my life's work to analyze and identify the true Gurus, those great investment minds that stand apart from the thousands who offer investment advice to others. Today, my firm advises dozens of institutions, large and small, as well as individuals, some of whose names you would recognize, in creating long term investment strategies.

The investment consulting business has become quite sophisticated. Frequently, new tools appear that help make analysis of risk, returns, and how these important factors interact easier. The Nobel committee has seen fit to recognize these achievements by offering the Nobel Prize to economists in investment disciplines. Two of our Gurus are among the recipients of the Nobel Prize in economics. I want to share some of these tools with you so that you may profit from these advances in our business to enhance your own wealth.

Oh, yes, there is something else. After over thirty years in the financial services business, I have become extremely annoyed at the type of investment advice that is promulgated to the public. There are a number of things that I find difficult to understand and even more difficult to accept. For example, why is it that so many books and articles are intent on misleading investors about the time tested, acknowledged paths to investment success? Why is it that publishers and writers prey on an unsuspecting public by giving them the equivalent of get-rich-quick schemes for making money in stocks? Yes, I'd love to own "Ten Stocks to Double in Three Years," or "The Hottest Growth Stocks for the Nineties." I only wish it were so easy.

How about the books of advice from so-called successful investors? There's a 17 year old whiz kid who wrote an investment book. Is that where you expect to find great investment wisdom? How about investment advice from a barber or a dancer? They've got books on investing out there, too. Let me ask you something: if you heard that a young kid, or maybe a plumber, had come up with a neat way to perform appendectomies, would you buy his book and give it a try? Or would you stick with a medical doctor? Why is it that when it comes to investing, anyone who is a bit successful thinks he or she can tell you how to do it better than the professionals who devote their lives to it? Do you really believe that there is some sort of investment voodoo out there that the millions of professionals who have been working in the field just happened to overlook? Beats me.

In *Investment Gurus,* I will expose you to the greatest minds in investments today and show you how to get rich the safest way possible: with common stocks. You will hear the voices of these great masters and learn from them. I do not want you to fall prey to silly advice. I will teach you to distinguish lucky investors from those with true investment wisdom. We will clear the air of all this nonsense, I promise. I will take you on an excursion to visit the greatest investment minds of the century and then show you how to apply their collective wisdom to insure your own investment success. You will also learn some state-of-the-art techniques now being used to analyze risk and return in stock market investing. At the end, I will offer some specific investment advice using the techniques we have learned from the Gurus.

Common stocks are the single best investment over time in American history. Period. The key phrase is "over time." Since the early twenties, no asset class has performed better than common stocks, including the effects of the 1929 crash, the Great Depression, and more recent calamities like the Crash of 1987.

If you have any doubts about this, take a look at the chart on the next page. Ibbotson Associates calls this chart: "Wealth Indices of Investments in the U.S. Capital Markets." I call it: "The Chart that Hungry Stockbrokers Consider the Greatest Chart in the World." It tracks the performance of Small Company Stocks, Large Company Stocks, Long Term Government Bonds and Treasury Bills back to 1925. It also throws in the Consumer Price Index figure which is a good gauge of inflation. In a nutshell, this chart tells you that if you had invested one single dollar in these different asset classes way back then, this is what you would have at the end of 1995.

To make this exercise a little more interesting, let's assume that Grandpa and Grandma had decided to invest $2,000 for you in 1925. Grandma wanted to invest the money in stocks, because she figured those big companies would keep on growing. Grandpa had a different notion. He was somewhat of a visionary, you see, and he foretold the crash of 1929, which would occur in just a few years, and he even predicted the depression, so the last thing he wanted to do with his grandchild's money was risk it in stocks. No, the only way to assure there would be something left was to put the kid's nest egg in safe U.S. Government Treasury bills. After all, a company could go broke, but the U.S. government wasn't likely to. So, not being able to agree on a course of action, Grandpa and Grandma compromised (which, incidentally, is why they stayed married so long). They decided to split the money: $1,000 to stocks and $1,000 to T-bills. The chart tells you what happened. Grandpa's $1,000 grew to $12,870, at the end of 1995, barely outpacing inflation since the equivalent CPI ending value over the same period was $8,580. Grandma's stocks grew your $1,000 to $1,113,920. So you are now a millionaire. Bless her soul. (Yes, I know the chart shows that if your $1,000 nest egg had been invested in small company stocks, you would now have over $3.8 million, but let's not push the example that far.) You can see why stock brokers and mutual fund salesmen just love this chart.

A couple of postscripts. Grandma's wisdom notwithstanding, she only made one decision and let it rest for 70 years. You and I aren't that patient. We want to do well, and we want to do well a lot faster than that. What's more, Grandma didn't have any gurus to guide her in her investment strategy. She let the market do all the work, and you are about to hear some very convincing voices who

**Wealth Indices of Investments
in the U.S. Capital Markets**

Year-End 1925 = $1.00
From 1925 to 1995

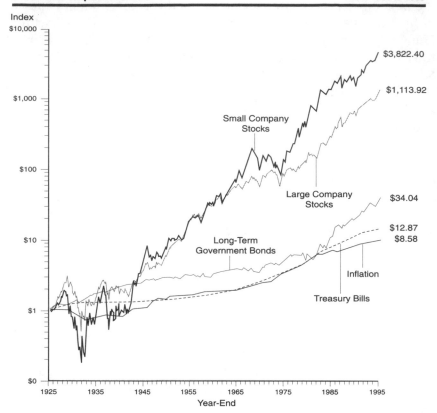

Figure 1

think that Grandma had the right idea all along. But you will also see that most of our Gurus do much better than the market as a whole, and that is what we are going to strive to do as well.

Many of the techniques we use in my investment consulting business to select investment managers for our clients will be disclosed in this book. Indeed, we will put them to work in the process of interviewing the different investment talent. You will learn important risk measures used to analyze the risk investment managers take to achieve their returns, and you will also hear about the importance of style in investing in common stocks. To set the stage, here are the criteria we used to select the Gurus:

AN INVESTMENT APPROACH
THAT MAKES SENSE

That sounds obvious, doesn't it? But so many of the newer approaches in investing may sound good, and even foolproof, but they somehow flunk the test of logic and reason. (I was educated by the Jesuits so this is important to me.) I'm not talking about what the experts think. Is this investment approach sensible for our money? I expect that from the Gurus. I don't have to understand every detail of their complex investing procedures, but it had better make basic good sense to me.

OUTSTANDING INVESTMENT PERFORMANCE
OVER TIME

You will not find any hotshot, young wizards in this work. I really am baffled by people who think that novices with relatively short track records can be great investors by anything other than luck. In this book, you will find only seasoned pros. Great beginners didn't make the cut. This is not a book about individuals who lucked out with two or three great years in a bull market. What can you learn from that?

LOW RELATIVE STANDARD DEVIATION

If you don't know what standard deviation is, you will soon, but the short explanation is that it is a tool we use to measure the volatility of a portfolio. By comparing a specific portfolio's volatility to, say, that of the market as a whole, we can assess the relative risk of the portfolio relative to the market. The theory here is that if your portfolio's volatility—how wide the range of ups and downs in price is over time—is high, your portfolio is riskier than one with lower volatility.

HIGH SHARPE RATIO

This is a relatively new tool used in our profession to measure risk adjusted return. It is named after its creator, Professor William Sharpe, who won the Nobel Prize in economics and is one of our Gurus. In plain English, the Sharpe ratio measures how much extra return you get for the risk you were willing to take. The theory is that if you are prepared to take extra risks, it is because you want extra returns. The Sharpe ratio measures how good a job you or your investment manager did in achieving that goal.

MULTI-DISCIPLINES

We looked at managers who use different styles and size attributes. You'll learn the importance of style in investment management, if you don't know it already. You'll also learn why it is important to look at the size of companies you invest in. Simply put, some managers specialize in small companies, others medium-sized, and, still others, large companies.

These are the criteria used to select the Gurus. We often refer to these criteria as "screens." The analogy is to a screen which sifts data, or particles, or gold for that matter, so that you end up with only those results that conform to the criteria you set. I have purposely not created a mechanical selection environment, one which, for example, might have ruled out managers who had not had an annualized return of, say, 20%. Anyone can do that. We are delving deeper into the risk-adjusted performance of great managers over time. We are searching for the roots of investment genius, the traits and attributes that contribute to greatness, to Guruhood.

You might also be wondering how much prior investment knowledge you will need to enjoy and profit from this book. The answer is not very much. The fact that you have *Investment Gurus* in your hands suggests at the very least you must be interested in investing. I expect that you have probably read one or two other investment books at some point. If you haven't, the best place to start is by reading *The Only Investment Guide You'll Ever Need,* by Andrew Tobias. That's one of the best investment books I have ever read and I turn purple with envy over Andy's writing ability. Likewise, Peter Lynch's books.

Before we blast off on our journey of discovery, we'll start with a little "flight training." To get the most out of these interviews, you need to understand how and why the different managers were chosen and what sort of questions we will be asking them. To make sure we're all talking the same language, I'll take you through a little primer of up-to-date investment terminology complete with examples. So, Part One includes some ground rules and a few definitions. Some of this information will be familiar, but you may not be sure exactly what it all means. I'll provide a refresher and an introduction to some really interesting techniques now being used by consultants and other professionals to analyze returns and risk. There have been great strides in this area, and I think you'll be impressed. I want to quickly add that this is not a book for techies. It is important to me that this book be in English as you and I know it. Throughout this book, we will explain complex and arcane investment terminology in plain English.

In Part Two, get your ticket and grab your pencil and pad. We're off to the first interview. The interviews are really conversations with some of the greatest investment minds of our century, those investment managers who stand out from the crowd and display true investment genius. We will also be speaking with some of the greatest academic investment minds, people who have contributed enormously to the art and science of investments in common stocks. We need to hear these voices to understand the present state of investment thought. As we move from one interview to the next, we will keep in the back of our mind what we have already learned and we will correlate the information we learn from our practitioners and the academics, in our search for clues that lead to the secret of true investment success.

In Part Three, we'll lay our notes out on the table and sift through the data. We will discuss the key points gleaned from our interviews and analyze the results. The questions we seek answers to include:

- Is investing in stocks the most intelligent path to wealth for most of us?
- If we invest in stocks, are we better off doing it ourselves or letting someone else do it for us?
- Is it possible to consistently beat the market?
- Which style of investing is best?
- What are the key characteristics of investment geniuses?
- What did we learn from the Gurus that we can use in our own investment program?
- How can we replicate the Gurus' success?

Having heard what the Gurus have to say, we embark on our mission of discovery, in full possession of the information we have acquired. Have the academics and top money managers discovered the ultimate formula for wealth in common stock investing? Do the precepts of the investment science of today correlate with the actions and behavior of the most successful practicing money managers? If so, we're on to something. Next we'll ask, how can each of us use this information to maximize our own wealth.

One of the key things we will seek to learn is how to avoid mistakes. We will see how to reduce our risk by avoiding dumb investment moves. On the positive side, we will consider investment alternatives, investment styles, and, how to practically apply what we have learned. We will determine what the right investment strategy is for each of us. We will also consider the possibility of having one or more of these (or other) Gurus manage our money for us. We'll examine how professional consultants (like me) select investment talent and put them to work, and how you can put these techniques to use in your own investment program. We will conclude with some specific investment advice and sample portfolios you can actually use, based on the techniques we will have uncovered in the course of our interviews.

One thing I have learned in thirty years: there are very few true investment geniuses. Perhaps that's why so few money managers ever beat the market as a whole for extended periods of time. So unless we throw away all the books and buy an index fund, we had better be very, very careful, and very, very clever in our selection of investment talent or in our own selection of stocks.

By now, you know that I want more than anything for you to emerge from our time together a much wiser investor. Often people think they can be as good an investor as Peter Lynch just by reading his books. Really! (Where are the readers' yachts?) Please don't expect that overnight you will become as good as our Gurus, but you can count on being exposed to some of the greatest talent investing in stocks and bonds, and stocks and bonds are what you and I buy most of the time. Some of the Gurus manage mutual funds we can buy, others have high minimums most of us can't reach. All have something to say that will help us enhance our own knowledge and wealth.

Thanks for coming along.

TOOLS OF THE TRADE

In this chapter, I will review some selected techniques and terminology that will help us communicate with one another and with the managers we interview. Don't worry, this isn't school and you won't have to memorize any of it. In fact, you may know some of this already, but browse through anyway, it will refresh your memory. I've also included some newer techniques which we consultants, and some institutional investors, use to construct portfolios and manage risk. As a bonus, I'll conclude with a little performance measurement trick, which I promise you won't forget, and which will change the way you look at mutual fund performance results from now on.

First, some basics.

ACTIVE VERSUS PASSIVE INVESTING

Your most important decision, after you have decided to invest in stocks, is this: should you try to do better than the market, or should you simply settle for the returns the market has traditionally offered.

ACTIVE INVESTING ▼ Active investing refers to the practice of picking stocks because you think they will do well, for whatever reason. Obviously, to be successful, active management must beat the market on some level. Either we will strive to have greater returns than the market, or we will do as well as the market, but with less risk. Most of the Gurus in this book are active managers who consistently beat the market. But it was important to me to include proponents of passive management, and watch the two sides fight it out.

PASSIVE INVESTING ▼ In passive investing, you are basically buying the market. This is the domain of the index funds, those funds that emulate the performance of the market indexes. Most of the academic Gurus in the book are proponents of passive investing; they simply do not believe that you can beat the market consistently by anything other than luck. Tell that to Peter Lynch and Mario Gabelli! (We will.)

Passive investing has gotten a lot more complex. Firms like Dimensional Fund Advisors use a variety of index funds in different allocations to provide risks and returns that have stood the test of time. Rex Sinquefield will expound on the merits of this type of investing as will Nobel Prize winners Bill Sharpe and Merton Miller and the acclaimed economist Eugene Fama.

Should you invest passively or actively? You and I will take in the arguments on both sides. I will share my conclusions at the end of the book after we hear all of the arguments.

MEASURING RISK

In trying to evaluate investment performance on a level playing field, we must take into account the amount of risk a manager takes in delivering his or her results. Some of us are more comfortable with risk than others. For that reason, we must be aware of the level of risk we are being exposed to. This stands the test of reason since a higher than average return usually entails a higher degree of risk. Put another way, if I told you I could double your money, you might be willing to listen to what I had to say. But if I added that the "risk" in this proposition is that you could lose it all, you would probably think twice. In fact, that is precisely what we do if we go to a casino and bet a wad on the color red at the roulette wheel. If we're right, we double our money; if we are wrong, it's all gone. And the chances are roughly 50/50, forgetting the house percentage. Few of us want to gamble like that with our nest egg.

But how do you measure risk in investments? There is no perfect way. The best the industry has come up with is volatility. In investment parlance, high volatility equates to high risk, low volatility to low risk. Volatility, in this case, is the range of price or value movement in a stock, a portfolio, or the market as a whole. As the theory goes, the wider the range of price movement, the higher your risk.

BETA ▼ Beta measures a stock or portfolio's volatility compared to the market as a whole. In most cases, the Standard & Poor's 500 index is used as the benchmark for measuring the beta of a stock or fund. Thus, if the benchmark is 1.0, a beta of 1.1 indicates that your stock is 10% more volatile than the market. A beta of .85 indicates that your stock's volatility is less than the market's and so forth. You get the idea.

STANDARD DEVIATION ▼ There is another way to measure investment risk. Beta is relative, measuring volatility of the portfolio to the volatility of the market. To measure the volatility of a portfolio, we use standard deviation, which measures the price performance of your portfolio against itself. A low standard deviation means that the month-to-month price performance will fall within a very small range. A high standard deviation indicates that the value of your portfolio may vary greatly from month to month. Here again, that volatility translates into risk. Sounds pretty simple, right?

Maybe, but standard deviation is probably the most misunderstood investment concept out there. Here's one reason: Standard deviation is defined as the square root of the population variance. The second reason is the formula:

$$s = \sqrt{\frac{\sum_{i=1}^{n}(x_i - \overline{x})^2}{n-1}}$$

Where   Equals
  s   Standard deviation
  $\overline{x}$ Sample mean (or average return)
  n   Number of observations

(ARE WE HAVING FUN YET?)

Okay. Let's try to explain this in the kind of language most of us understand. The notion is that the wider the fluctuations in your portfolio, the greater the potential risk. Standard deviation measures the fluctuation, or variance, over time. Possibly the most intelligible explanation I have heard for standard deviation is the following: Suppose you are planning a vacation and, quite naturally, you want to be sure the weather is going to be good. You're traveling next February. You ask for the median (the midpoint between the high and the low) year round temperature in several places and you settle on two: Honolulu and Minneapolis. Honolulu's historic median temperature is 73.5 degrees and Minneapolis' is 75 degrees. Both seem good candidates if you didn't know any better. But if you picked Minneapolis for your February vacation, you would be in for a nasty surprise.

That's where standard deviation comes in. Honolulu's weather standard deviation is very low; Minneapolis' is very high. The very low standard deviation for Honolulu's climate is due to the fact that the temperature in Honolulu has historically ranged from a low of 53 to a high of 94. Minneapolis' temperature, on the other hand, covers a much wider range and has varied between a low of -34 and a high of 105. Yet both cities have median full year temperatures of about 74. Get the picture? (I am indebted to Katherine Burr, president of Hanseatic Advisory Corp. in Albuquerque, for this example.)

By the way, if you think this example is stupid, NBC reported that the Atlanta Olympic Committee told the International Olympic Committee organizers that the average temperature in their lovely city is 70 degrees. That tells you two things: the organizers didn't know much about standard deviation, and they obviously hadn't been to Atlanta in July.

MEASURING RETURN AGAINST RISK

If we want to define the ideal investment strategy, it is probably to achieve the highest return with the lowest risk. But that's like going to Heaven: it's something we all want to do, but we're not real sure how to get there. After all, if I were pretty sure that by taking more risk, I could make more money, then it would be an easy choice. On the other hand, if the risk wasn't real, it wouldn't be risk.

This problem leads people like us to try to analyze the amount of risk we are taking and measure it against the rewards we expect to get and actually achieve. Standard deviation tells us that the higher the standard deviation, the higher the volatility, and the higher the risk that we will lose or make significant amounts of money. What it doesn't tell us is which managers are likely to give us that great combination of a high return and low risk. But never despair: we have tools to measure that, too.

ALPHA ▼ We already know that beta measures the volatility of a stock compared to the volatility of the market as a whole. If we want to analyze performance, it would be awfully nice to know how much of our return was simply due to the market as a whole, and how much was due to our (or our manager's) brilliant ability to select stocks. That's what alpha does. Simply stated, it measures the return that is *not* attributable to the market. In other words, it is the *added value* the manager achieved over and above the results of the market. Thus, an alpha above 0 indicates that the manager has added value. An alpha below 0 indicates he subtracted value.

SHARPE RATIO ▼ A fairly recent measure of risk versus return is the Sharpe ratio, named for economist and Nobel laureate, Bill Sharpe who is interviewed on page 89. The Sharpe ratio measures the risk of the returns in your portfolio. It divides the return earned above the risk-free rate of return (usually what you could have earned if you had put your money in Treasury Bills) by the standard deviation for a given period of time. The resulting number measures excess return per unit of risk.

Did I hear you ask about the difference between alpha and the Sharpe ratio? Remember, alpha measures the portfolio's return above the market return after adjusting for the portfolio's beta. For example, assume a portfolio beta of 1.0 (which means that its volatility is the same as the market's), a portfolio return of 11%, and a market return of 10%. In that case, the alpha is 1%, which is 11%–10%. That, of course, shows that the manager added value. But how much risk did he take to get that extra return? The Sharpe ratio measures how much risk he took.

The Sharpe ratio is interesting because it gives us the ability to determine how much excess return a particular manager can give us for the increase in risk we are taking. Here are a few examples of actual managers' returns, standard deviations and Sharpe ratios for the five year period ended 3/31/96.

Manager	Compound Annualized Return	Standard Deviation	Sharpe Ratio
Private Capital Mgt.	21.8%	6.85	2.55
Dodge & Cox (balanced)	14.2%	5.19	1.90
Bennett Lawrence	32.6%	15.78	1.79
Equitable Asset	26.8%	13.36	1.68
S&P 500 (with Dividends)	**14.65%**	**7.44**	**1.39**

Courtesy: David B. McGrouther, Dean Witter, Palo Alto, California

The first thing you notice about the chart is that the standard deviations of the managers are all over the lot. So you wouldn't necessarily pick a manager by that benchmark alone. The Sharpe ratio number is more consistent. The higher the number, the more return you get for the risk you took, *no matter how high or low the risk.*

In our example, Private Capital Management had a relatively low standard deviation and a high Sharpe ratio which tells us that this manager gave us the best returns for the risk we took. Now look at Bennett Lawrence. That manager had a high standard deviation and a relatively high Sharpe ratio. A look at the return figures show that we made more money with Bennett Lawrence, whose performance was an exceptional 32.6% over the five year period. But Private Capital Management's higher Sharpe ratio tells us that they did the best job on a *risk adjusted basis,* even though the return was less. Note that all of these managers did better than the market (again on a risk adjusted basis).

Another way to look at risk is demonstrated in Figure 1, perhaps one of the most widely used charts in our business. Here, we plot the returns and risk of various managers on a graph. We can then compare returns and betas against a benchmark, usually the Standard & Poor's 500 Index.

In Figure 1, Risk (beta, in this case, but we could also use standard deviation) is measured on the horizontal axis and Return on the vertical. The intersection of the lines is the benchmark, in this case the S&P 500 (including dividends), which is, for all practical purposes, the market as a whole. The dots represent the perfor-

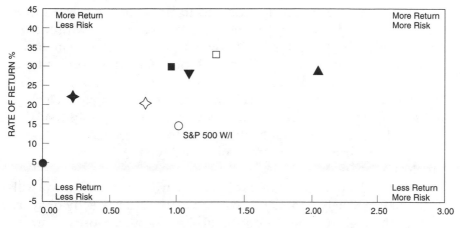

Risk Return Analysis
Five Year Period Ending 3/31/96

Courtesy: David B. McGrouther, Dean Witter, Palo Alto, California

Figure 1

mance of six different money managers over a five year period. You will meet the Gurus from all six of these firms in this book.

You may have heard of the term "Northwest Quadrant." To a money manager, that is the Promised Land. A glance at Figure 1 tells you why. A dot in the Northwest Quadrant means that over the measured period, the manager achieved a *higher* return than the market, but with *lower risk.* And that, of course, is precisely what we all want to do. Note that three of the managers on the chart are in the

Northwest Quadrant. Three other managers gave us a higher return than the market, but with higher volatility, or risk.

Does this mean that all we need to do is find out who those Northwest Quadrant managers are and put our money with them? Not exactly. (You must have known it wouldn't be that easy.) Unfortunately, some managers do well for specified periods of time for a variety of reasons. Perhaps they were very good at a particular style of investing which was itself in vogue for some years. Or perhaps a manager specialized in a particular industry group that did quite well. In fact, consultants often refer to the practice of selecting managers just because they are in the Northwest Quadrant as "chasing dots."

A word about volatility: Managers with high volatility will argue (convincingly, I think) that high volatility is perfectly okay as long as the high volatility is on the upside. In other words, there is nothing wrong with high volatility that results in higher returns. To them, using volatility as a measure of risk is not meaningful unless the discussion is paired with an analysis of the volatility on the way up and the volatility on the way down. We will talk about this subject with Guru Richard Driehaus, whose style is volatile, but whose results are phenomenal.

Not all of the managers we interview will be Northwest Quadrant managers. Some will offer much higher returns than the market, but they will ask you to take more risk in the process. Fair enough. In the course of our interviews, we will raise the issue of risk with the various managers to learn the role risk plays in their investment strategies and how we can apply what we learn to our own investment decisions.

INVESTMENT STYLE

Most of us road warriors who travel a lot use CNN as our beacon from exotic locations around the world. Mention the word "style" and we instantly think of Elsa Klensch and her worldwide fashion show featuring slinky models baring as much as the censors will allow.

To investment professionals charged with the asset allocation of investment portfolios, the word "style" has a very precise meaning and the importance of style is increasing every year. In a word, style refers to the particular type of stocks that a manager chooses to invest in. These, in turn, are distinguished by a set of characteristics that the manager looks for, and is comfortable with.

In this section, we will look at some of the predominant styles of investment and discuss the merits of each. At the outset, let me quickly caution you not to be looking for the "best" investment style. You can make money using any of these styles, if you know what you are doing. Many investment managers diversify their portfolio in their quest for performance results, allocating funds to be managed in each of several investment styles. We will be interviewing outstanding managers who are practitioners of many different investment styles.

While there are a number of different styles, two styles dominate the field and are used and talked about more often than any of the others. These are growth and value, and we will start with them.

GROWTH ▼ We will be interviewing a number of growth managers, including the legendary Peter Lynch, Foster Friess of the Brandywine Fund, John Ballen who runs the MFS Emerging Growth Fund, Van Schreiber, as well as some momentum growth managers I will tell you about in a few minutes.

In seeking stocks to buy, growth managers seek a strong trend in the growth of sales and earnings in the companies in which they are investing. Growth managers generally seek investment vehicles in industries showing strong sustained growth trends as well. This also means that few of these managers would be interested in buying a fast growing company in an otherwise sleepy industry.

What constitutes growth? Well, that's like asking how high is up? Most growth managers agree that growth, at a minimum, must exceed the growth rate of the economy. By how much is the question.

Then there's the question of price. How much can you afford to pay for growth? Companies with high rates of growth sell at high price/earnings ratios, reflecting the expectation that their growth will continue and "catch up" with the high valuations. Sometimes they do, and sometimes they don't, but, hey, that's show business.

One thing is certain: if you buy growth stocks and pay a correspondingly high price for the privilege, if something goes wrong, you are going to suffer swiftly and painfully. A high price-earnings ratio has little tolerance for disappointment. That's why a disappointing earnings report from a growth company often causes a precipitous stock price decline. Investors in growth stocks had better be very sure of their earnings projections. That is why many of the growth stock investors have a habit of staying in constant touch with the managements of the companies they own. If the president of the company has a headache, the portfolio manager may check him into the hospital.

To sum up, here are the principal features of companies that growth managers look for:

- Attractive industry fundamentals
- High rate of earnings and sales growth
- Reasonable price-earnings ratio (but a high price-earnings ratio is okay if everything else is right)
- Strong management

VALUE ▼ Value stock managers are like the people you find at Filene's Basement—forever looking for bargains. Fun, to them, is a going-out-of-business sale. And that's how they manage their portfolios.

The classic definition of a value stock is a stock with a low "BtM," or Book to Market ratio. That means that the stock is trading at a low price compared to its book value. Book value is defined as the company's assets on its balance sheet, less its liabilities. Book value is often figured on a per share basis. So, if a company has a book value of, say, $15 per share, and the stock is trading at $12 per share, it may be perceived as a bargain.

Over time, the definition of value has changed and we will encounter different ways to approach value with our Gurus who specialize in this style. (Our academic Gurus also refer to Value stocks as "distress" stocks, indicating that the underlying companies have some problems.) Among the value managers we interviewed are Wall Street legends like Michael Price and Mario Gabelli; Laura Sloate, and Bruce Sherman. Eric Ryback of the renowned Lindner Fund, who seeks high income from his investments, is another value manager.

Growth is not a big deal to a value stock manager. What value managers are looking for is not the Prom Queen but rather the homely wallflower nobody wants to dance with. Yet there is hidden beauty in this young lady: her character, her values, her future.

Indeed, the value manager seeks those companies whose stocks have fallen on hard times, who have been forgotten by the fickle market, but whose future is brighter than many think. Why? Perhaps because the stock is selling at a discount to the company's *break-up value.* Or, perhaps, the stock trades at below book value. Historically, when this occurs, the market will in time recognize a bargain and the shares will be bid up. Better to get in early, when no one is looking.

One of the problems with value investing is timing. Once you identify one of these forgotten heroines, it is tough to figure out when her fortunes are going to turn around, or if and when others are going to follow you and bid the stock price up. As a result, value investing often takes patience. In our interviews with Mario Gabelli and Laura Sloate, you will discover how these two Gurus arrived at a similar method to address the timing issue.

You might also think that value investing is less risky than other styles. You remember we discussed what happens when a growth stock suffers bad news—you get hurt deep and quick. With value stocks, the bad news is already there, and presumably is reflected in the price. So, if you have done your homework, you are probably buying at or near the bottom. Right? Well, maybe not. Read on.

Here are the key characteristics of value stocks:

- Low price-earnings ratio
- Left behind by the market
- Sells at a discount to book value
- Has hidden assets

GROWTH VERSUS VALUE ▼ Which style is better, value or growth? That's the 64 Dollar Question that I would have preferred you not ask. That question is addressed at some length in the book. Briefly, studies have shown that at least in the past fifty years or so, value stocks have provided higher returns than growth stocks. I realize that this probably surprises you. What's the trade-off? You will hear Guru Rex Sinquefield, the Chairman of Dimensional Fund Advisors, claim that the reason value stocks have outperformed growth stocks is that value stocks are riskier than growth stocks. The theory is that you get paid for the risk you take: if you buy a riskier type of security, you expect both higher risk and higher returns.

Some of our Gurus from the academic community agree with him. Thus, if value stocks are riskier than growth stocks, the returns on value stocks ought to be higher.

But is it true that value stocks are riskier than growth stocks? Get ready for a fight on this subject. Sinquefield insists they are. Another of our Gurus, Nobel Prize winning economist Merton Miller, isn't so sure. Neither is Nobel Prize winner Bill Sharpe. An often cited study by Josef Lakonishok, Andre Shleifer, and Robert Vishny ("Contrarian Investment, Extrapolation, and Risk," *The Journal of Finance,* vol. XLIX, No. 5, December, 1994) claims that over the last fifty years, value stocks have not proven to be riskier than growth stocks.

Value and growth stocks tend to behave differently. There are periods when value stocks outperform growth stocks, and, conversely, there are periods when growth stocks outperform value stocks. That's why we consultants try not to take sides on this issue. We want both styles in most portfolios since that will tend to even out performance over time. When one group is underperforming the market, the other is likely to be outperforming the market.

MOMENTUM INVESTING ▼ This style has been quite popular lately and in the right market environment, the returns can be spectacular. In essence, these managers ride trends, and when the momentum is in their favor, they hop on board. Naturally, in good markets these managers can do very well if they are particularly skillful. Two of our Gurus, Richard Driehaus and Robert Gillam, are momentum managers. Driehaus is a paradigm of momentum investing. We will visit Richard in his mansion in Chicago and Bob Gillam in the scenic surroundings of his home office in Anchorage, Alaska.

Interestingly, some managers shy away from being called momentum managers, including Gillam and another of our Gurus, Scott Johnston. There is, after all, a gunslinger aura about the fellows who employ this technique. Back in the sixties "gunslinger" was the term we used for those managers who bought and sold very aggressively. By nature, in fact, momentum managers must be quick on the draw. When we speak with Gillam, he'll give an example of a conference call on technology stocks which caused him to liquidate a large position before the call was even over.

In essence, momentum managers are avid proponents of Newton's first law of motion which holds that objects in motion tend to stay in motion until another force intervenes. To put it simplisti-cally, to momentum managers, stocks that are hitting new highs are more interesting buys than stocks that are hitting new lows. There are variations and refinements to the approach that you will encounter in the book, but basically, the momentum proponents are interested in a stock with strong upward price momentum.

Before we conclude our little primer, here are two more defin-itions that come up in the book. They relate, too, to style of invest-ing:

Top Down Investing ▼ This style of investing refers to an approach used by the manager in finding a particular stock he wants to buy. The top down manager looks at the big picture first. What's the economy like? Is this a good time to be buying stocks? Then, what industries are attractive to buy now? Having selected the industries, what stocks are attractive within those industries, and so forth. You see how the process works.

Bottom up Investing ▼ This is, of course, the opposite of the top down approach. Here, the analyst looks first at the company, identi-fying it usually because it is so attractively priced on its own merits. Value investors almost invariably use this approach. In essence, they say, I don't care if the world is coming to an end, I know for sure that at this price this stock is a screaming buy, so don't bore me with eco-nomic statistics, because I just don't care. Incidentally, this style is sometimes referred to as "bottoms up" investing, but only by man-agers who have spent too much time in bars.

MEASURING INVESTMENT RETURNS

I think you probably know that measuring investment returns is not as simple as those mutual fund ads would like you to think. "Compound annual return of 15% for ten years!" Or perhaps "22% average annual returns for the past 6 years!" Also: "If you had invested $10,000 in our fund in 1975, you would today have . . . (a Rolls Royce with a lion in the back seat?)" I know you've seen them all. In my business of investment consulting, we use techniques to measure not only the returns of different investments, but also the risk the investment manager is taking to deliver those returns. The trick, of course, is to get all these damn statistics and performance claims on a level playing field. Let's take a look at why this playing field isn't always level.

HOW TO DECEIVE ALMOST ANYONE WITH INVESTMENT RETURN STATISTICS

Here's an investment trick you can use at cocktail parties, although if this makes the party a success, you might want to expand your list of friends. (It will also change forever the way you look at performance statistics.) You ask your friends a hypothetical investment question. Manager A has had an average annual return of 14% per year for the last five years. We have every confidence that this record will continue for the next five years. Your other choice is Manager B, whose average annual return over the last five years was 9% and, likewise, we expect that her return will continue over the next five years. Question: which manager would you want to manage your money for the next five years?

Dumb question, right?

Maybe not. Let's take a look at the year to year record of both managers. Manager A is the one with the 14% average annual return. Here's his record:

Year	Manager A
1	20%
2	40%
3	20%
4	(50%)
5	40%

The first observation here is that this is a pretty wild manager. Note the wide swings from year to year. Everything was going along great until the fourth year when he lost 50%. The following year was much better, however, and he was up again by 40%. Overall, the average annual return for this manager is 14% per year. (Just take the sum of the year-to-year performance and divide by 5.)

Our second manager, Manager B, is the one with the 9% average annual return. Here's her record:

Year	Manager B
1	9%
2	9%
3	9%
4	9%
5	9%

Talk about consistency! And, of course, it is pretty easy to figure out that this record averages out to 9% per year.

So, which of these managers made the most money over the five year period? We assume, of course, that the manager with the 14% average annual return made more money than the manager with the 9% average annual return. But did he? Let's take a look.

To figure out which manager made the most money, we must use a geometric progression. That way, we can measure real money, not just percentages. Let's start with a base of 100 in both cases and see where we go from there, applying the percentage returns each year for each manager. Here are the results:

Year	Manager A	Base 100	Manager B	Base 100
1	20%	120	9%	109
2	40%	168	9%	119
3	20%	202	9%	129.5
4	(50%)	101	9%	141
5	40%	141	9%	154

Hello! Manager B, the one with the 9% average annual return, made more money than Manager A, with the 14% average annual return. Surprise.

This example gives us three things to remember:

- When measuring performance, use the Base 100 method (geometric) to measure real dollars and get real earnings. Don't use "average annual return."

- Look for consistency of performance. Consistency is what saves you from a really bad year. Look again at Manager A. Imagine what would have happened if you put your money with him at the beginning of Year four. You would have lost half your investment by the end of the year. Losses like that are very hard to make up. And with a volatile manager, you just can't predict when those very good and very bad years are going to come along.

- When you look at a manager's record, play it safe: assume that you will be unlucky enough to invest just before his worst year. Then see how you would have done.

Of course, when we meet the Gurus, we will want to know what their performance has been. If we can't use average annual return, what are we supposed to do? Do we have to recalculate everything using the base of 100? That seems pretty awkward, doesn't it? You bet. The difference is that when we calculate returns the right way, we speak of the *compound annual return*. Compound returns simply express geometric progression as a yearly figure.

In the preceding example, the compound annual return for Manager B, who generated a consistent 9% every year, is the same as the average annual return, 9%. But for Manager A, who earned a 14% average annual return, the compound annual return is only 7.1%. In other words, if Manager A had consistently earned 7.1% in each of the five years, he would have ended up with the same amount of money as he did after five years of wildly fluctuating returns.

You can try this on a pocket calculator, by multiplying 100 × 1.071 × 1.071 × 1.071 × 1.071 × 1.071. You'll get something pretty close to 141. There is a formula for figuring out what the compound annual rate of return is if you have the beginning and ending figures and the number of years, but I won't put it here because it is too complicated. However, most computer spreadsheet and accounting programs have this function built in. Thank goodness for computers!

Compound annual returns simply express smooth geometric progressions as a yearly figure. The compound annual return (Manager A's 7.1%) is also called the "geometric" average, whereas the average annual return (Manager A's 14%) is an "arithmetic" average.

Remember this example the next time you see a mutual fund ad touting "average annual returns." (A lot of them still do.) For our purposes, we will use compound annual return exclusively when discussing the performance of the Gurus.

That does it for our review. In this short primer, I have concentrated on many of the advanced techniques used today to evaluate portfolio risk and return. We covered the importance of measuring returns accurately, using compound annual return, not arithmetic average annual return. We also spent time breaking down the different styles of security selection. That way, when we talk to a value manager, you'll know why he or she is different from a growth manager.

Of course, these are the very tools that you should use in your own investment program as well. As you read through the interviews and the concluding chapters, you will learn the value of diversification by style. Diversification is not buying 50 value stocks. You'll hear Peter Lynch say that buying ten emerging growth funds is not diversification. He's right, of course. What you should do is diversify by style and company size, and possibly geography as well. You'll learn the importance of having a portfolio with both value stocks and growth stocks. That's the key to intelligent diversification. You'll also learn the importance of measuring the risk you are assuming with different types of investment, and whether or not the expected returns are worth the risk.

We're now prepared to talk to the Investment Gurus. Let's go out and meet them.

PART TWO
THE GURUS

THE
GURUS

Michael Price, Mutual Shares

Richard H. Driehaus, Driehaus Capital Management, Inc.

Mario Gabelli, Gabelli Funds, Inc.

William F. Sharpe, Nobel Laureate, Professor of Finance, Stanford University Graduate School of Business

Peter Lynch, Retired Manager, Fidelity Magellan Fund

Laura J. Sloate, Sloate, Weisman, Murray & Company

Scott Sterling Johnston, Sterling Johnston Capital Management

Eugene Fama, Professor of Finance, University of Chicago Graduate School of Business

Bruce Sherman, Private Capital Management, Inc.

Eric Ryback, Lindner Funds

Merton Miller, Nobel Laureate, Professor Emeritus of Finance, University of Chicago Graduate School of Business

Foster Friess, The Brandywine Fund

Van Schreiber, Bennett/Lawrence Management

Rex Sinquefield, Chairman, Dimensional Fund Advisors, Inc.

John Ballen, Manager, MFS Emerging Growth Fund

Roger F. Murray, S. Sloan Colt Professor Emeritus of Banking and Finance, Columbia University Graduate School of Business.

Robert B. Gillam, McKinley Capital Management, Inc.

David E. Shaw, D.E. Shaw & Co.

MICHAEL
PRICE

H ere we are in Short Hills, New Jersey, value investing capital of the world. Short Hills, New Jersey? Are you nuts? Not really. You see, Short Hills, previously known primarily for a nifty upscale shopping mall with a Nordstrom and a Neiman Marcus among other high class emporiums, is the chosen home of Mutual Shares, the fund company owned by Michael Price, one of the best known and most successful practitioners of value investing. From his head-quarters, which happens to be right next to the famous shopping mall, Michael Price runs Mutual Shares out of the offices of Heine Securities. That firm is named after Max Heine, who was Michael Price's mentor, and who died tragically in an automobile accident in 1988. Although Michael Price is not exactly a touchy feely kind of guy, his understated but clear devotion to the memory of his mentor is a rather endearing side of his personality.

But no more Mr. Nice Guy. Michael Price is as tough and deci-sive as he is single-minded. He cares a great deal about his share-holders, another Max Heine legacy, and he goes to extraordinary measures to insure that his shareholders get full value for the money they invest with him. If you have any doubts about that, just ask those nice fellows who run Chase Bank about Michael Price. We talk about that in the interview.

Mutual Shares consists of four separate funds—Mutual Shares, Mutual Qualified, Mutual Discovery, and Mutual Beacon—with combined assets of over $16 billion. Yet, despite that impressive total, most people have never heard of Mutual Shares or Michael Price. Why? Because he doesn't advertise. Frankly, he doesn't have to. I can tell you this: some of the savviest financial people on and off Wall Street invest with Michael Price. They know what they are doing.

Mutual Shares, Qualified, and Beacon state their goal as capital appreciation and are virtual clones of one another. Their separate existence arises out of different circumstances. One fund, for example, was acquired when its owners asked Michael Price to run it for them. Mutual Qualified is geared to tax-free accounts. Mutual Discovery is a more global fund than the others.

The four funds have produced total returns over ten years of more than 15% per year with about half the volatility of the average equity fund. Mutual Shares has a 20 year history with annualized returns approaching 20%. No wonder Price's shareholders are happy. As you will see in the interview, Price is not averse to taking huge positions in a company and making things happen. "Rattling cages," he calls it. Chilling.

Tanous: *Michael, how did you first get interested in stocks?*

Price: Well, I was always interested in stocks because the first one I bought, through my dad's broker, tripled. I bought 20 shares of Bandag and it went to 90. My dad sold it at 50 or 60; I kept it even though I didn't know anything about it. I always liked looking at the stock tables. This is, maybe, in junior high.

Then, through some of my dad's friends, I got interested in one little facet of the business which was the risk arbitrage business. I spent a summer observing a small arbitrage department—a woman and three guys sitting around two desks joined together with wires to the floor of the stock exchange and proxies on their desks. They were just trading in the stocks of companies that were about to merge, taking advantage of small discrepancies in the price spread between the two companies. I said, here are three guys, and I knew one of them was making a million dollars a year and this is the late sixties, and I said, if these guys can sit on their butts and make a lot of money by reading various things, there's something to this.

To this day, 25 years later, I have the same approach to running the fund. We have a bunch of people sitting around a trading desk talking to companies and trading in stocks. Some of the companies are involved in mergers, or tender offers, or buybacks and spin-offs; others are cheap based on value investing principles that Max brought to the equation.

We also have a bankruptcy business *[this involves buying securities of bankrupt companies as part of the funds' investment strategy]* which Max and his old friend Hans Jacobsen brought to the business in the thirties, and I picked up on. So we have these three disciplines that together run the same way as my very first experience on Wall Street.

Tanous: *Max Heine comes up in your background and you have credited him generously for a lot of your early training. Can you identify a few of the important principles you learned from him?*

Price: The great things about Max had nothing to do with investing. They had to do with how you live your life as a husband, as a father, as a friend, and as a manager of other people's money. For instance, Max would always return a shareholder's phone call. If he got a letter from a shareholder, he would call him back. I do that to this day. It's great because it shows the shareholders that you're really paying attention. They can't believe you're calling them back, and they realize that you care and that you're working for them. So many managements don't really believe in that. Max had zero arrogance. As successful as he was, and as smart and intellectual as he was, he was able to talk to anyone in the office or building or on the street. He was someone who was not full of himself. He kept an extremely level head. That helps you make better investment decisions in times of crisis.

Tanous: *Do you describe yourself as somebody with zero arrogance?*

Price: Ask other people. I'm sure some people think I'm full of myself and others think I'm okay.

Tanous: *Michael, there's another thing I found, which says more about you than anything else—your loyalty to Max Heine. Your firm* *is still named after him and I noted that there is an endowed chair of finance at NYU. I expect you had something to do with that. Right?*

Price: Yeah. When Max passed away, a group of us got together to raise money for a chair that I had hoped would create a value investing course at NYU. That didn't happen until recently. Now they are starting to structure that.

Tanous: *There's a story out there about how you got interested in buying some metal companies, specifically Fansteel, Kawecki and then International Mining.*

Price: How did you find out about that?

Tanous: *Like you, I do my homework. I'd like you to retell that story because I think it's a good illustration of your investment process.*

Price: In 1976, when valuations were much lower than they are today, I had learned that one of the things you do is watch smart people. This is a business where, especially in our game of bankruptcy and cheap stocks, there are certain people out there who control companies with large amounts of money. These are smart people and you want to be buying what they are buying. You never want to be selling what they're buying. Right? The Pritzkers, Thomas Mellon Evans back in those days; today the Tisches are smart. A Carl Icahn type, a George Soros; you don't want to be on the other side of a trade with people like that. Back in the seventies there were a whole other group of names that I liked to watch. David Murdock, who to this day still controls Dole, and Castle & Cook was one.

One day out of the blue sky, a company called Crane Corp. *[which made plumbing products]*, run by Thomas Mellon Evans, the Pittsburgh financier, made a tender offer for a company called Fansteel. Both were on the New York Stock Exchange. Fansteel was pretty clean.

One of the things I do is look at every merger announcement. What a merger tells you is what businessmen are willing to pay for a business. I think it's the best indication of value. Compare that with what some Wall Street analyst is saying. When an analyst says some radio station is worth twelve times operating cash flow, well, that's not true until someone actually pays twelve times operating cash flow. That's when you know what it is worth. Okay? So when Thomas Mellon Evans says I want to buy all of Fansteel, the first question I ask is why? The second question is: does it make sense? These are the simple basic things you do and we continue to do when there are merger announcements.

Well, I got the S&P tear sheet—we were a lot less sophisticated then, no laser disks or electronic data. I had to go across the street to the Stock Exchange to make copies of the 10Qs and 10Ks. We didn't have a service delivering them to the office. We didn't have a library at all, so I borrowed the annual report from Goldman Sachs in order not to have to wait four days for the company to mail it.

I started reading this stuff and I saw that Fansteel makes refractory metals. I didn't know what refractory metals were so I looked it up in the dictionary. There were four: molybdenum, tantalum, tungsten, and one other, columbium. These metals add strength, conductivity to electricity, and other properties. So I did a little work on each of these metals, and, now, I noticed that one of the metals Fansteel deals in is tantalum. I couldn't find anything on tantalum. So I got out the New York Yellow Pages and sure enough there's a company in the Yellow Pages called Tantalum Corporation of America. I'm not making this up! I called them up and I got some guy on the phone called Larry and I introduce myself. I tell him I'm working at this mutual fund and I'm trying to find something out about tantalum because Crane just made an offer to buy Fansteel. At the other end of the phone I heard: "Crane just made an offer to buy Fansteel!" And I said, yeah, what's so incredible about that?

He said two things. One was, well, "That must be because of all the Thai slag in all their warehouses." Thai slag is what tantalum comes from. And, of course, in the 10K there was no disclosure about a Baltimore warehouse full of Thai slag. But it was a very valuable, off the balance sheet, hidden asset. Okay? It turns out Larry was a metals broker who dealt in tantalum. The second thing he said was, "You ought to take a look at Kawecki Berylco." So, not only did I start buying Fansteel right away because I discovered a hidden asset, and we made some money on that, but I found in Kawecki Berylco a $9 stock with a $15 book value per share and a very clean balance sheet. It was controlled by Molycorp.

And then I looked at Molycorp and found a company that controlled it, called International Mining. So I looked at International Mining and found that they owned a bunch of companies including Kawecki, Molycorp and others. So I laid it all out on a chart and started buying stock in every one of the companies, because, at that time, metals prices were taking off. There were shortages in the government stockpiles of some of these special metals. I figured out that if you bought stock in Molycorp you got all of them. Then I also bought all the others and they all got taken over. Every single one of them.

This is in 1976. I had the chart in my desk. One of the brokers in Max's firm was a friend of Mario Gabelli, whom I had never met. Mario at that time was a broker at Loeb Rhodes. One day, Mario walked over to my desk and took the chart and walked out. I said where are you going with that? He took that chart of the complex of companies. It was so funny. That's how I met Mario.

Tanous: *What was he doing in Max's brokerage firm?*

Price: Just visiting. The broker (his friend) knew I was doing some interesting work. The broker said look at this. So Mario took it. *[For Mario Gabelli's take on this meeting see page 85.]*

Tanous: *One purpose of this book is to explore the riddle of the "efficient market theory."* [The efficient market theory, a stronger form of the "random walk" theory, is the proposition that investment markets fully reflect all available public information almost instantly. The thesis raises doubts about any individual's ability to gain consistent trading advantages by studying publicly available information.] *In addition to active managers, I'm interviewing great academics and passive investors. Now, what you just told us shows a process that goes completely counter to the efficient market theory. You discovered certain facts, by being smart and digging hard, that were not at all reflected in the price of the stocks.*

Price: I think it was in Lowenstein's book on Buffett where he tells about how Buffett first went down to Washington and spent four hours with the chairman of GEICO before he bought his first share of GEICO. He then went on to buy the entire company. Now I'll tell you, you have to do your homework and kick the tires. It's not the answers that make you good in this business, it's the questions you ask. If you ask the right questions you will always find out more than the next guy.

From the '60s when Buffett first visited GEICO, and the '70s when we did the Kawecki deal, to today, a lot has changed to make the markets closer to efficient. The computers and information flows have caused this. We went from the 286 to the 386, the 486, and the Pentium. We used to get Fed filings on some weekly sheet. Now we get them electronically. First Call is a service that eliminates the wait to get hard copy of reports from brokers. Now we get it electronically. The delivery of information is so much faster. That has made the markets somewhat more efficient but markets are not perfectly efficient. The academics are all wrong. 100% wrong. It's black and white.

Tanous: *I suppose you realize that to the academics people like you are just the outliers on the distribution curve.*

Price: Throw the index funds in there. By law they're efficient. But if you take all the index funds out, take out the guys who have no clue as to what they're doing, you're left with a handful of guys who know what they're doing, have a straightforward approach to value investing, and everyone will tell you the market is not efficient. It's least efficient in places like bankruptcy investing. That's why we do it. It's least efficient in the minutes after a tender offer is announced because people don't know about it and the stocks can move above or below what the stock is going to be worth during the deal.

The market gets closer to being efficient when it involves more normal, well-followed large cap stocks. *[Large-cap is short for "large capitalization." Capitalization is the total market value of a company's stock—the stock price × the number of shares, plus other financing. "Large-cap" usually refers to companies with total market value of $2 to $3 billion or more.]* But just because thirty analysts follow Eastman Kodak doesn't mean it's efficiently priced. No one buys a market. There are stocks in the market. Some are fully priced. Does that mean the market is efficient because a stock is fully valued? No. It means the stock is fully valued. Say there are six thousand decent-sized companies in the country. We own stock in two or three hundred of them. We own them because they're too cheap.

Tanous: *Let's talk a bit about investment style. You are probably the quintessential value manager by most standards. You are certainly one of the most successful value managers in the country and maybe in history. You also devote a fair amount of your assets to restructuring, which implies companies with serious problems. Can we talk about why you would want to incur the risk of buying companies with serious problems?*

Price: Because there's less risk, if you do it properly. The New York Stock Exchange used to have a rule that as soon as a company filed Chapter 11 it was delisted. They've taken that rule away and there are Chapter 11 stocks trading on the exchange. But back in the days when those companies were delisted automatically, three market makers, of which we were one, traded not the stocks, but the bonds, over-the-counter. All the people who had margin accounts in these stocks would have to sell them. Any institution that had wanted the dividend or the interest from the bond would sell because these payments would stop when the company did its Chapter 11 filing.

The information flows were very bad. Penn Central *[a prominent early bankruptcy restructuring]* hadn't happened yet. So people didn't know yet, and wouldn't for many years, that you could make money investing in bankruptcies. We learned that the market was very inefficient and that there was a way to create cheap common stocks. To buy "NewCo," the new company that is reorganized around the best businesses the debtor in possession had, you design an appropriate capitalization *[financial structure]* and create the NewCo stock by buying the old claims.

Tanous: *How does that process work?*

Price: The day a company files Chapter 11, lawyers, investment bankers, and the creditors will, through the negotiation process, find parts of that business to restructure. They'll sell off everything else, negotiate and formulate a reorganization plan to pay people out, and at the end of the period, could be a year or ten years as in the case of Penn Central, you're going to have new bonds and new stock and cash distributed. If you buy the old claims cheaply enough, you're going to wind up owning that stock for nothing. In that ten year period, you can get much smarter than you can buying Eastman Kodak on the New York Stock Exchange because Eastman Kodak files quarterly and then annually. A bankrupt company files every month in the bankruptcy court. They file all sorts of things, copies of leases, and other things that a regular company would never disclose.

Tanous: *Is it safe to say that any company that files Chapter 11 gets your attention?*

Price: No. They hit our radar screen well before any filing. Most of the time, when a company files it's because of too much debt. But they also file because of lawsuits, environmental problems, and all sorts of claims against them. So, all those companies are on our radar screen all the time. We look at the securities of "OldCo," the company that is going to go, and there are senior, junior, and preferred securities. We want to buy the seniormost securities so we get protected because we're senior. As we learn more about the case, we'll go down, if the returns are there, to the more junior securities. We try to be one of the biggest investors in the company so we can control the case, but not so large that we are on the committee and prevented from trading. We try to bring the company out with the best and cleanest balance sheet it can get. *[The less debt a company has, and the more equity, the "cleaner" its balance sheet.]*

Tanous: *We're moving toward another aspect of what you do that is a bit peculiar: You not only take a large position in a company, but you become an activist. Your role as the catalyst in the Chase/Chemical merger is almost legendary. I'm curious to know why you would devote your time and energy, since you do run a mutual fund company after all, to getting so involved in a corporate decision.*

Price: The bankruptcy process has evolved today to where there is more competition and you have to get smarter about how you invest your money. Just buying the bonds isn't good enough. In the last five or ten years, we have come up with some pretty creative ways to put money in companies to create new securities.

Tanous: *Do you want to talk about them?*

Price: Yeah. Rights offerings and cash infusions are ways. We go to a company that needs money. Often it's as simple as reading a newspaper to know that if Morrison Knudson doesn't get $150 million by June 30th it has a problem. So you hop on a plane; you go out to Boise.

Tanous: *You did that?*

Price: Yeah. You say to the guys, we read in the paper you need some money. We'll put up the money. Of course, we do all our homework first. We do a lot of homework after, too. We ended up not putting up the money for Morrison Knudson because there was no deal to be done. It ended up being way overpriced in the market at that time and we knew it, but there's a way to say, we'll guarantee you your money. Offer the same right to your shareholders through a rights offering, and if none of them wants it, we'll take it all. But if they want it, you have to guarantee us a third of the deal. And we price it where we love the stock. Say the price is six. We might price it at four.

Tanous: *Okay. Let me understand this transaction. You go to the company. The stock is six. They're in trouble and they need $150 million real soon.*

Price: We say, if you get $150 million and the pressure is off, the stock is now at 6. (I'm not going to pay 6 for 6. It may have been worth 6 or 7 a year ago, based on our research. That was then. Now it's worth 2 because they did a lot of things wrong.) But we say we'll pay 4 bucks a share. So say I buy 40 million shares of stock at 4, for a total of $160 million. But first go offer that deal *[at 4.00/share]* to your shareholders. And if the shareholders don't buy it, I'll buy it. If they do buy it, you've got to guarantee me 30 or 40 million shares at 4. So I'm what's called a standby purchaser. We've done about seven or eight of those deals.

Tanous: *In fact, how could a company say no if they're in trouble?*

Price: What happens is if you get there too early, there's not enough pain so they don't want to give you a bargain. If you get there when things are changing or the bookkeeping is no good, maybe it's too uncertain to buy. This is one of the ways we have found to invest without competing in the marketplace.

Tanous: *Okay. So the shares go into your fund at 4.*

Price: Right. But the stock never trades down at 4. Maybe it trades at 4 1/2 or 5, but it goes right back to 6, because, one, the company now has the money; two, we're a large owner, people know that we're going to make sure the things are done right; three, the company now has a year or two of breathing room to go sell assets, pay down debt, and do all the right things.

Tanous: *At the same time your stock has to be perfectly tradable or it couldn't go into the mutual fund.*

Price: No. If we buy a big block like that, if it's large enough, sometimes we're restricted. Liquidity matters. *["Liquidity" refers to the ability to buy and sell readily. If a stockholder owns too much of the* *total stock outstanding, usually over 5%, trades by that stockholder must be disclosed to the SEC And in bankruptcy cases, there are more legal restrictions. In some circumstances, the buyer of a large block of stock may have to accept restrictions on selling all or part of the block for a period of time.]*

Tanous: *We started to talk about the Chase/Chemical deal.*

Price: You're talking about rattling cages. Our job isn't to rattle cages. Our job is to make money for our shareholders. We can't take our eye off that ball. We never file hostile 13Ds *[the form that must be filed with the SEC when a purchaser acquires 5% or more of a publicly held company]* to get in the press. We only get difficult if we're being screwed. And in the case of a Chase/Chemical and a lot of others, we're not hostile. We're not trying to get control or manage a bank. We're simply trying to get them to allocate their capital in a way that will bring the value out. We thought that structurally Chase was not set up right. The book value was $42 when we bought the stock at $35.

Tanous: *Chase's book value was $42 when you bought it at $35?*

Price: Yep. And it was earning, I don't know, 5 or 6 bucks. And there was another $30 per share of assets, like the credit card business, mortgage business, all sorts of stuff, which was not in the book value. And these guys were using their stock to make an acquisition. That was crazy! The stock is worth $65 and they're using their stock to buy something when the stock was trading at $35. So we had to put a stop to that.

Tanous: *How did you do that?*

Price: Well, we bought 6.8% of the stock. That's over 11 million shares. We came out with a 13D which said we think the stock is worth a lot more. And that started to focus people's attention on what the assets were. Our 13D started to get all the banking analysts to say, hey, let's take a harder look at Chase. Maybe something is going to change. Then what we did, which was very smart, and this was my analyst's idea, Ray Garea, was we went to the top ten holders of Chase stock and we sat down and had lunch with each one of them, and went through our analysis of what Chase was worth. We did that right away, in the month after we filed. We filed on April 6 and by June we had seen six of the top ten holders. One wouldn't see us. We were the largest holder. We laid out our case and within a week or two, Tom Labrecque, Chase's chairman, was doing the same thing. So wherever he went, we had already been there. So what kind of impression is that going to make on him?

Now we didn't say we'd run a proxy fight. We didn't say we were going to do anything other than to say to the board you should focus on getting the shareholders $60 to $65, not on keeping the stock price down at $35.

Tanous: *So what did Chase do at that point?*

Price: They immediately took away the right of a shareholder to call a meeting, which alienated some of the holders. They hired all the top bank takeover lawyers to protect themselves because I was trying to do the same. None of the top lawyers would work for me because they were all working for him. So we hired another firm, and we started the process to get clearance to buy more stock and get seats on the board. The stock at this time was starting to move up, and analysts wrote up not only what the values were but how great it would be if Chase and another money center back would get together and profit from the overhead reductions. In August, they announced the deal with Chemical and the stock got into the low fifties. Today the stock is over $70 because, you know, Wall Street is giving these guys a lot of credit.

Tanous: *Whose idea was Chemical as a merger partner?*

Price: Shipley runs Chemical. He bought Manufacturers Hanover so they had been through a merger four years earlier. It had been successful. We owned two million shares of Chemical. So, now we're going to own 14 million shares of the combined entity. It's our first billion dollar position in one stock. When the merger closes, we'll have one billion dollars in that company.

Tanous: *Let me tell you something that people in my business get excited about. Your funds historically have relatively low standard deviations and yet your performance is, to use one word, exceptional. How do you achieve the returns with such low volatility or risk?*

Price: The goal is to make good returns with less risk. Risk is not the same as volatility. It's very hard to measure risk. It's very simple to measure return. You can't model it. You'd have to go into every company in our portfolio, which is 250, and come up with a discussion about what might happen to the stock if earnings were disappointing. Well, in the case of Florida East Coast, nothing! Cause they're sitting on all the land, it's a debt-free railroad, and at some point it will get taken over. The stock is not going to go down.

So what we did way back when the fund was small, it was $5 million when I got here in 1975, is divide the portfolio into components. Cash is between 5% and 25% always. Well cash doesn't move with the market. Bankruptcies don't really move with the market, they move with the progress of the case. Arbitrage deals, announced tenders, mergers, buybacks, and liquidations, trade as a function of the deal's progress. So if you add up our cash, the bankruptcies and arbitrage and liquidation deals, and some other unusual securities we sometimes carry, it generally will be 40% of the fund. The other 60% will be made up of what I call POCS, Plain Old Common Stocks, and those are value stocks and most are trading if not below book, at least below intrinsic value, so they should go down less than the market. So, if 40% of your portfolio is not really related to the market, you can get a beta of .6 or a real low standard deviation.

We perform well because some of our stocks have these catalysts. You asked why do we spend our time going around to shake some cages? It's because a lot of times you can buy good values. But until there's a catalyst, the value is not going to get realized.

Tanous: *You've been quoted as saying that RJR is your favorite stock.*

Price: Reynolds is interesting now because there's a catalyst in the picture. Ben LeBow and Carl Icahn are trying to push them to do a spinoff.

Tanous: *Are you involved?*

Price: I'm not involved except as a shareholder. I think the stock's too cheap.

Tanous: *Let me tell you something interesting about an interview I did with John Ballen [page 281]. He runs the MFS Emerging Growth Fund. He's a growth guy with an amazing record. I asked him what made him happiest. He said this: the thing that makes me happiest is to know that Michael Price and I own the same stock. He said value and growth investors are looking for the same thing, growth at a reasonable price. If Michael owns the same stock I have, I know I've got a winner.*

Price: *[laughs]* There's probably very little overlap. What's the name of the fund?

Tanous: *MFS Emerging Growth. His turnover last year was very low. Only 20%.*

Price: Our turnover is in the mid 70s, but it is skewed by the arbitrage deals. A lot of our stocks get taken over.

Price: *[At this point Michael calls his assistant.]* Bring me a copy of MFS Emerging Growth portfolio.

Tanous: *I also noticed that one of your funds, Discovery, is essentially a global fund.*

Price: It's mostly Europe. A couple of things in the Far East. Nothing in Latin America.

Tanous: *How do you apply the Michael Price process to finding these European deals?*

Price: We started in Europe in 1984 when I noticed some of the guys buying closed end funds at big discounts. Remember I told you I followed certain smart people? I noticed some very smart guys in New York buying closed end funds at 25% to 30% discounts in London, and all those funds owned were U.S. oil and gas stocks. So we bought one, too. Then it went from closed ended to open ended and we made about 25%.

I then hired a guy in London. We started to buy stocks over there, because from time to time the stocks were much cheaper than comparable companies in the U.S. After ten years, we've got three traders on our foreign desk hedging currencies and doing the trades, and four or five analysts working on foreign situations; one of them just moved to London. We've got $2.6 billion invested in Europe.

I think we're the largest foreign investor in Sweden. We are the largest non-Swedish holder of Swedish stocks. If you can buy a candy company here like Hershey's, Wrigley, those are the best, they're money machines. But they have P/E's around 25. Then we go over there and find Van Mclle's—they make Mentos. We found that company and bought a big block of it at 8 or 9 times earnings and they're in the same business. When you "true up" the accounting, we're trying to buy the same kind of thing much cheaper. Because unless you're buying companies 25% to 30% cheaper, you don't want to take the money outside the United States.

Tanous: *What about the currency exchange risk?*

Price: We don't make currency bets. We hedge all the currency risks.

Tanous: *Why?*

Price: Because we're stock pickers. We don't know anything about currencies.

Tanous: *Let me tell you something I find interesting in interviewing investment Gurus. There's a guy I like a lot called Richard Driehaus [page 53]. He's a momentum investor. I find it very interesting that his approach is totally different from yours. His idea is buy high, sell higher. That's Richard. It's exactly the opposite of what you do, yet both of you do extraordinarily well.*

Price: Look. You're looking at this after a period of a long bull market, whether you measure it from 1990, from 87, from 81, or even 1975. I just think we're all so spoiled. I think you've got to go through a two or three year bear market to see how these guys do. We'll go down, but we'll go down a lot less than these other guys. That's my mission. My mission isn't to make money in bull markets. My mission is to preserve capital.

Tanous: *Has there been a time when you weren't successful in doing that?*

Price: The only time was in 1990 when three things came together all at once, and we were down 9% to 10% when the market was down 3%. We should have been flat. What happened was the Secretary of the Treasury, Nick Brady, and the Fed, stopped money center banks from lending for deals. In 1988, we had a huge year in mergers. 1989 started off that way. Then in the summer of '89, they stopped credit for mergers and hostile tender offers. We owned a few of those positions, since we always have 5% to 10% of the fund in deals. A lot of those stocks went down and a lot of our value stocks, which were subject to rumors of takeovers, came down. We also had a huge position in Time Life. Remember that $200 bid from Paramount that the board didn't take? The stock still hasn't gotten back to it. That stock went from $180 down to $80. 1990 was our only down year.

Tanous: *Michael, I notice you have an interesting set-up here. Can we visit your trading room and see how you are organized?*

Price: This is our only office. At one end we talk to our shareholders. At the far end we have accounting. In the middle we have the trading room, which is a trading desk surrounded by the analysts. I sit on the desk and I can talk to the traders, pick up lines and hear what's going on. The traders' job is to post the analyst with what is going on in the market, rumors they hear and all that. These posts have 800 lines capacity, so each trader has all these wires to all the other desks. If they are bond traders they have lines to bond desks and the stock traders to stock desks and the foreign traders to overseas. So I hear the analysts and traders talking; I'm talking to the analysts, pushing them; I'm talking to the traders asking what's going on; it's a discourse that everyone hears. We don't have meetings here. It's an open dialogue. By sitting here and listening all day, you get to tell people what to do and all that stuff. *[Price's assistant returns with the information on the MFS Emerging Growth Fund. Michael has a look at it and hands it back to her.]* There's very little overlap.

[We leave the conference room and proceed down the corridor to Michael Price's trading room. The large area features a long trading desk in the center of the room around which clusters of analysts and traders speak into phones and monitor information on dozens of screens all competing for attention. Behind and to the sides of the trading desk other analysts sit at desks poring over research reports and other information. A hum of activity hangs over the room and the intense concentration of the mostly young employees creates a tension that seems to permeate the place.]

Tanous: *Who are the people who work in here?*

Price: These are analysts here. Here we do domestic stocks and over there we have foreign securities analysts.

Tanous: *Where do you sit?*

Price: Here. *[Michael points to the chair at the center of the large trading desk. From this vantage point he has traders on his right and left as well as facing him across the desk. He points to one of the many screens at his desk].* These are the funds, priced in real time. As the market changes we see what's going on. *[He points to another screen.]* That's our trading system, which has all our orders in it. I can look up what we've done so far on that screen. First Call is right here. *[He points to yet another screen.]* Up here is our news edge. This is Edgar up here.

Tanous: *What's Edgar?*

Price: Edgar displays SEC filings as they come out. This is all the SEC filings as they are released by the SEC today. I have the computer programmed to take our names *[of the companies Price's funds own or are interested in]* and print them here. You see, Mutual's Edgar files? These are the companies programmed in where there's been a filing. You see this one? Revco filed a five page 14D-9 on their proposed merger with Rite-Aid. And here's the document. *[The screen displays the full image of the document filed with the SEC, in real time.]* In the old days we had to wait to get this in the mail.

Tanous: *In real time?*

Price: Yeah. And it's on both sides of the desk, so you can't miss it. Here's the Bloomberg *[a financial news service]*.

We go over to the analysts' cluster of desks behind the trading desk.

Price: This is Tom Price.

Tanous: *Hi Tom. Any relation?*

Tom Price: No relation!

Price: These analysts have their own computer set-up. Notice the laptop attached to the computer. They go off to visit companies and take the laptop to update their spreadsheets.

Tanous: *Do ideas get generated here?*

Price: The first job of the analyst is to look at what we own. The second job is to work on developments, news, things we need to react to. The third is to come up with ideas.

[Traders are shouting news in the background from the desk.]

Price: *[Michael leads us back to the near side of the trading desk. He addresses one of the traders.]* Here's where we do the foreign securities. Today we have $2.6 billion in what, nine different currencies?

Trader: More, actually.

Price: And the foreign positions are hedged perfectly every day so currency movements don't affect our fund price. How many currencies?

Trader: We've got 15 currencies.

Price:. How could we have that many?

Trader: Some are very small. Let's see Norwegian krone, French franc, Italian lira, they're all there.

Tanous: *It costs money to do all that hedging.*

Price: No.

Tanous: *It doesn't cost money?*

Price: Less than 1% a year. So that's it. *[Michael turns to one of the traders.]* Tell her we're a buyer, you can be a buyer. . .

Tanous: *By most standards, you're a pretty young guy.*

Price: I'm 44.

Tanous: *Do you have any other goals or ambitions?*

Price: No.

Tanous: *This is it?*

Price: Yeah.

Tanous: *Michael, there's one last question I have to ask you. It's a question that's being asked a lot these days, although I think most people are asking the wrong question. We're talking, of course, about reports that you might sell your firm. My observation is, you're very successful, you obviously make a lot of money, in fact, you probably have more money than most people would ever need to do any reasonable thing anyone would want to do. Here's my question: if a very rich uncle died and left you $500 million dollars, what would you do with it?*

Price: Let me say, first of all, that no decisions have been made at all. But there are three reasons to maybe look at deals and, you know, it has nothing to do with money. It has to do with—and this is not BS—one, what complementary products and services could be offered to the Mutual Series shareholders? Are some of them people who might want to trade into bond funds? Well, we don't run a bond fund. Might some of them want a money market fund? We don't have a money market fund. How about those who want more exposure in the Far East? We have very little.

Two, do Mutual Series shareholders deserve to have, not an individual as the owner of the management company, but an institution that could weather any shocks to the financial system?

Three, the Fund Group has grown to $16 billion. It's big, and I think we're doing fine today with the group of people I have. They have evolved into an absolutely first rate team. It's not just the investment talent here, it's a cohesive group effort that is not typical Wall Street competitiveness in a cutthroat environment. We work in a teamwork way, as a team.

Tanous: *I know. I've observed that first hand.*

Price: People here, the 16 or 17 analysts, the dozen or so traders, work so well together. Our back office people work so well together. Taking it to the next level, if we grow and continue to earn our 15% return, the money will double to 30 billion in four or five years, and that's a pressure and a strain.

Tanous: *You'll need a bigger infrastructure to handle that.*

Price: I've invested in the last years a fair bit of money to upgrade all the systems in the house, the hardware, the software, the trading desk, and we've doubled the space of the office. So the infrastructure is not so much the issue. It's all the other things. So we'll see what happens. But the idea is not about money at all.

Tanous: *That's the part I couldn't understand, unless there was something out there that might cost a half billion or billion dollars that Michael Price had his eye on.*

Price: No.

Tanous: *So that's not it at all?*

Price: No sir.

I confess that few of the meetings I had during the course of writing this book stuck with me as long and as vividly as this one with Michael

Price. Think about it. Here is a value investor who doesn't just go out and find cheap stocks. He sees an opportunity in a company that needs a lot of cash, so what does he do? Michael hops on a plane and goes out to make them an offer. I've got all the cash you want, he says. Just sell me some of your stock real cheap. My shareholders will like that. Or he sees that Chase Bank is making acquisitions with its stock when Michael thinks the stock is too cheap. What does Michael do? Just listen to him. "We had to put a stop to that." Scary, isn't it? Well, that depends on your perspective. If you had been one of his shareholders for the past 10 or 20 years, I'll venture to say that you are cheering him on. It takes guts and dedication to go to these lengths to maximize your investment returns. It's plenty of hard work.

Another point. Notice as you continue reading how often the concept of smart people comes up in the different interviews. Early on, Michael Price made it a point to identify the smartest investors and observe what they were doing? He mentions people he doesn't want to be on the other side of a trade with. Of course, that's what we're trying to do, too. We want to find those really smart people and see what they do with their investments, and how they do it. I think you'll agree that there are few better examples to follow than Michael Price.

Postscript: *In late June, 1996, Franklin Resources Inc., the fifth largest mutual fund company and manager of the Franklin and Templeton funds, announced it was purchasing Heine Securities Corp. from Michael Price. Price would stay on for a minimum of 5 years. The acquisition, which involved cash and stock, included a cash payment of $550 million to Price, plus stock and incentives which could raise the ultimate purchase price to $800 million. Michael agreed to invest $150 million of his money in Mutual Series funds the first year. By joining Franklin Resources, Michael fulfilled the criteria he spoke about during our interview to broaden the products and services offered to his present shareholders.*

RICHARD H.
DRIEHAUS

E ven though Richard Driehaus is not well known to the public, he is extremely well known in the investment community. His name is most often associated with the investment style known as momentum investing. A wiry, high energy Chicagoan, Driehaus graduated from DePaul University and went straight to work as a research analyst for a brokerage firm. He started to manage money in 1970 at A.G. Becker, where he was the youngest portfolio manager to be asked to manage a portion of the firm's pension and profit sharing plan. Very early on, his performance ranked him in the top 1% of his peers. He then spent time at two other firms, and never looked back. He began his own firm in 1980.

Driehaus' acknowledged focus has been in small-cap stocks, companies with market capitalizations less than $500 million—some considerably less. The small cap sector of the market is known for the fastest growth and also the most painful declines. This stands to reason, since many small companies which go public in bursts of investor enthusiasm never make it to maturity. Success in this line of business has a price, and vigilance is requisite.

Today, Richard manages $1.9 billion not only in small caps but also in international stocks and mid-cap stocks (typically with market capitalization of $500 million to $3 billion). He is even dabbling *in large companies, where he believes he can consistently beat the S&P 500 and the Dow Jones Averages.*

How about his performance? In his small-cap accounts, Richard's results were up over 34% annualized for the past five years (through 1995) and over 28% for ten years. It takes your breath away. His mid-cap results are almost as good. I need not tell you that this is high volatility investing and so, as one of our other interviewees put it, not for the faint-hearted. But, as Richard might say, it's volatility on the way down that hurts; volatility on the way up feels just right.

Driehaus Capital Management, Inc. is housed in a mansion in downtown Chicago. The offices have become something of an international landmark. The building was constructed in 1885 as the residence of Ransom Cable, then president of the Rock Island and Pacific Railway Company. The house is built of Ashlar, a soft peach colored, rough-faced stone. It has a pitched roof, tall chimneys, dormer windows, and a turret. Inside, Richard Driehaus has decorated the mansion with his favorite artwork and bric-a-brac. The Art Nouveau decor competes with the Victorian furniture for attention. The occasional sounds of intricate, working, antique clocks and a grand piano can be heard. Driehaus has an apparent love of stained glass, and the house is replete with striking and colorful panels and artifacts from which streams of light cast multi-colored hues all around. His collection of Tiffany lamps is exquisite and is complemented by several Tiffany windows. We met at the mansion for our interview. Robert Buchen, one of Driehaus' senior executives joined us.

Tanous: *How did you first get interested in stocks?*

Driehaus: I started as a coin collector. When I had enough money, I invested in the market. Initially, I bought two stocks—a conservative stock and an aggressive stock. The aggressive stock, Sperry Rand, went down and the conservative stock, Union Tank Car Company, was very dull and boring. When those stocks didn't perform, I went to the library and began reading all the magazines, newspaper articles and investment advisory letters that I could. During that time, I subscribed to various investment advisory services. One of those was John Herrold's "America's Fastest Growing Companies."

By subscribing to that service I saw that Herrold had made some recommendations that had gone up several thousand percent—companies like American Home Products, Baxter Labs, Abbott, and Avon Products. He attributed the enormous gains in these stocks in the fifties to their sales and earnings growth. That made a lot of sense to me. He had a chart showing the compound growth rate of the earnings and the stock price over a ten year period. I became very interested in that approach. I wanted stocks that were growing as fast as those companies were when they were originally recommended. Those companies had gone from relatively small companies to relatively large companies. You could take a 20% growth rate for an Avon Products in 1950, with maybe sales under $100 million, and, by the early sixties, sales were over $1 billion. That's how I got very interested in stocks, and in particular smaller, and mid-size companies that were showing sharp earnings gains.

Tanous: *Jeremy Siegel makes the case for stocks in his book,* Stocks for the Long Run, *about as persuasively as anyone. He goes back to 1800.*

Driehaus: That's a good point. What's the long term? A generation? Longer? The 1800s are a good vantage point because the industrial revolution started then. If we went back to the 5th Century, the decline of Rome, to the 12th century, or the beginning of the Renaissance, that was probably the right time for value type investments. If you were born on a farm, you stayed on the farm and you married the girl next door. There was little circulation of ideas.

Man has been on earth for about 200,000 years and it is only in the last 200 years that we have really improved our standard of living. Michael Rothschild, in his book, *Bionomics—Economy as an Ecosystem,* makes a startling comparison. If we collapse these 200,000 years down to a 24 hour day, in the first 23 hours or so, we were just hunters and gatherers. Then from about 11 PM to 11:58 PM, people survived by subsistence, farming and crafts. As Rothschild puts it, all of modern industrial life has unfolded in the last 90 seconds. We are new to change and change is new to us.

Tanous: *Since you mentioned the industrial revolution, some of the managers I talk to, particularly those who follow the technology sector, truly believe that what is happening in technology today is the modern-day equivalent of the industrial revolution. Do you agree with that?*

Driehaus: I absolutely agree. That's why the market has taken off. When I was going to school at DePaul University, we studied the great economists. One of them was Joseph Schumpeter. He asked what caused economic growth. It wasn't governments, it was the entrepreneur and the new industries he was developing that powered growth. The automotive industry stimulated the roaring twenties, which became the engine for America's technological boom. So, I think that if you apply Schumpeter today, the technology sector is the new engine. This industry only began in the late '50s, with the introduction of the transistor, so we're only thirty-five to forty years into it. The point is that the difference between the time of the discovery and the time of the impact was delayed for a while. The real impact of the electronic revolution only started to show up in the 80s when serious computation power became available to the average individual. Then the electronic revolution went from a capital good to a consumer good. And that is what stimulated worldwide growth.

Tanous: *I read an interesting statistic recently. A kid with a Sony Play Station video game today has more computing power than NASA did when it first put a man on the moon.*

Driehaus: Unbelievable, but true.

Tanous: *Richard, to change the subject slightly: What's the key to your investment philosophy?*

Driehaus: Discipline. It's not so much finding and buying the winners, it's the ability to retreat, to sell. That's the hardest thing to do. The question is not how many winners or losers you have, but how much do you make on your winners and how quickly do you cut your losses. Seventy percent of your trades could be losing trades, but if the winning 30% are large enough to overcome the losses you could still show great returns.

So, one of our maxims is cut your losses short. I use a war analogy. If you were engaged in a military campaign, first you try to win philosophically—not mano a mano. Then, if you can't win philosophically, you try to win strategically like the British did when they surprised Napoleon. For example, if I were building tanks, I'd make them with bright back-up lights so if I needed to reverse, I could do it quickly—a strategic retreat. The idea is not to lose men or equipment. This is not a game of muscle, it is a game of survival. Live to fight another day. Long term, battles are won philosophically. Sun-tzu, the famous Chinese military tactician, was always quick to reverse and win in a more intelligent way.

Tanous: *How do you relate this to your investment philosophy?*

Driehaus: On a tactical basis, we are a real bottom-up player. If each stock were like a tank, we'd be quick to reverse and change course if it was not working. In the Iraq war, our generals complained that they wished they had more information on the front line. So we look at each stock like a little tank. We let them be independent but we watch them moment by moment. Things change. So if we need to change course, we do.

Tanous: *This speaks to your information flow. I'd be interested in where you get your ideas.*

Driehaus: We spend a lot on idea flow and information flow. We were probably one of the first to use a local area network system in the mid-80s. This allows us to access information from many different sources and create a central base of information. We've gone from one to six people here who do nothing but information systems. That's about a third of our investment staff. A couple of years ago, when we started marketing, we used to say that we spend a very high percentage of our revenues on information technology. While the percentage has gone down as revenues have increased, the amount we spend on information technology has continued to rise at an accelerating rate.

Buchen: Let me take you back through the history of our information process. Back in the early '70s, Richard, as a research broker, provided ideas to a mutual fund. We had someone come in every Saturday, and sometimes Sunday, to cut and paste information that affected the fund. Every Sunday night Richard would come in and review the portfolio, industry by industry. For example, he would look at the health care industry and review every company for both fundamental and technical information. As a result, on Monday morning he knew in his head where everything was, what the trends were, what was going up and what was going down. And he did that for twenty years.

But technology has changed the entire process. Now, with the punch of one button, he can look at fifteen different pieces of information on one page. We still get all the information, but it has gone from what Richard did early on, which was to outwork everybody, to a technological input that is virtually instantaneous. The work ethic is very strong and remains the same. But technology has made it all happen more quickly.

Tanous: *By reputation you are what people in my business refer to as a momentum investor. In fact, to many professionals, you are considered the father of momentum investing, which might be defined as identifying and buying stocks in a strong upward price move and staying with them as long as the upward move continues. Now, you have all this information at your disposal. What is it exactly that you're looking for?*

Driehaus: We are looking for earnings growth, earnings acceleration. After all, momentum investing is an acknowledgment that things in motion tend to stay in motion. We say that the most successful companies are those which have been able to demonstrate strong, sustained earnings growth. We look for many different variations of earnings growth. We look for accelerating sales and earnings. We look for positive earnings surprises. We look for sharp upward earnings revisions. And, finally, we look for a company that is showing very strong, consistent, sustained earnings growth—like a Starbucks which looks very enduring.

But we don't just look at earnings growth. We have to see how that earnings growth relates to the stock, its group within the market—its sector, and how it relates to other ideas that are out there. It's not an absolute criterion. It's this question: how will this earnings growth, and positive change, impact the stock, especially relative to the market expectations out there? The company could show very strong earnings growth.

Take Oxford Health. Earnings were up about 90% yesterday. Earnings were actually a penny higher for the quarter than expected. But the company also said that their profit margin might start to shrink. So while enrollments were very good, and the top line was very good, there were cost constraints that suggested that investors should focus on the lower end of expectations for the succeeding quarter. So we sold most of our stock yesterday and the rest today. The stock went down from 80 to 69 yesterday and it is off another four points today. That's down 20% in two days.

Tanous: *Your interpretation of that information, if I understand you correctly, is this: the earnings actually came out better than anticipated, but with a little cautionary note that maybe, just maybe, the company would be on the lower end of expectations for the next quarter. And that was it.*

Driehaus: They were guiding the Street lower. Right.

Tanous: *And that sent a clear message to you.*

Driehaus: Right. Obviously, this stock was held by a lot of growth investors. So even though we liked the stock long term, we reacted to what the market environment was saying. We sold.

We react to events much quicker than other investors. That's part of our approach. We like positive surprises and upward earnings revisions and greater than expected gains. This was the opposite: a combination of some deterioration in their cost ratios and the fact that there were probably not going to be any more positive earnings surprises. Since we are active traders, we sold the stock. I think Suntzu would have done the same. Now it could still be an attractive long term situation, but we tend to be more active investors. I would rather err on the side of discretion, even if we miss some of the upside. We can always get back in later.

Tanous: *When you listen to this philosophy it makes a lot of sense. Richard, you make a lot of sense, but so do hundreds of other people who don't have your record. I want you to tell me what you think is different about your approach and why others who try to emulate it don't succeed.*

Driehaus: Could be a number of things. One is my belief that, over the long term, what I am doing will work. Some people, when things get difficult, tend to shift styles, or raise cash, or do things that they consider safer.

Let me give you an example. In 1994, we had a tough first half. We were down over 20% in our small-cap funds. We diversified out.

We bought some stocks that had good futures but were a little more defensive. At the time, all the best names, the high tech stocks, the health care stocks, the retail stocks, which all had good growth rates and were also among the best companies in America, happened to be among the worst performing stocks, so we didn't want to own them. In that environment, a lot of people raised cash, or went real defensive. They bought utilities, for example. But soon after that, right after the June 1994 quarter, the market came back toward technology. We went right back and concentrated on some of the names we had sold earlier that were now recovering. As a result, we recovered dramatically.

Buchen: At the beginning of the second quarter *[of 1994]*, we had 66 stocks in the portfolio. This is a half billion dollar portfolio. So what Richard does when times are bad is spread himself out. We went to 88 stocks at the end of the second quarter. We had a conference call with all of our clients on July 11 *[1994]*. Richard said in that conference call: This market is turning. I sense it turning. I think it will be led by technology. We went from 88 names down to 47 by the end of the third quarter. We went from 25% in technology to 75% in technology.

Driehaus: That's why we recovered so much. We tend to concentrate on our most successful names. The other answer to your question, Peter, is that I'm submersed in the process. You can't look at this academically and just look at the numbers. You really have to be involved and feel what's going on. The time and effort I devote to this allows me to be more sensitive to changes and to react to those changes. Now, since the changes are constantly ongoing, this also requires a lot of stamina.

A couple of observations. People aren't as involved with the market as they should be. It's not just knowing the individual stocks. It's knowing how that stock fits into its group and what's happening within the market as a whole. Too many people are too narrowly focused. I love bigger pictures. I think what makes us successful is knowing what's going on in the larger context.

I've been managing money for over 25 years. I can remember 1973-1974, the worst decline in my thirty years in the business. Everybody thought they needed more information on each company, so the tomes and the research reports kept getting bigger and bigger, and people suffered still bigger losses, because they never reacted to the fact that we were going into a bear market. The point is that you have to have some sense of what kind of market you're in, too. So sometimes there is a time to retreat and let cash build. Markets are often more psychological than they are practical. You can't keep holding onto ideas hoping and praying that they will turn around. There is a time to retreat and sell, even though we are not market timers.

Tanous: *Would it be fair to say, then, that your success is a combination not only of being able to identify earnings growth, but also being able to put this into the context of a market environment? In other words, the July 11, 1994 conference call you told us about was prescient timing. Do you recall what it was that you saw that convinced you that the market was turning?*

Driehaus: It's just my following the market and following individual stocks. It's more the individual stocks; that is the bottom-up approach. We had sold all of the companies that we thought had good outlooks, but were declining in price. 1994 was a very difficult time because it was a year of contradictions. We had the best companies in America, but they were the worst stocks. There are times when our style is out of favor, and this was definitely one of those. After the first half of the year, I could see our style beginning to work again as some of the stocks we had sold earlier started reversing and turning up. And I said, we have to get back in, so that's what we started to do. We reversed our position and bought back stocks we had recently sold. And that's what a lot of money managers don't do.

Tanous: *I suppose that makes your style more volatile than most money managers.*

Driehaus: Yes, we do have volatility, but in general our volatility is on the upside. We're more up than down. And when we're up, we're up in greater measure than when we're down. It is important to understand that upside volatility is not a negative. It works to our advantage.

[Driehaus' July 11 call was prescient, but the record also gives a good example of the volatility in his strategy. In the first half of 1994, his composite performance was down 25.5%. Then, from July 1994 to the end of 1995, his composite rose a stunning 64%.]

Tanous: *Give us some examples of your trading strategy.*

Driehaus: Recently, the technology sector has bifurcated. It's not all going up like it was in the first nine months *[of 1995]*. Some of the semiconductor companies and some of the commodity-type companies have been selling off, even though they have been reporting good numbers and the multiples are relatively low. The stocks haven't been acting well so we sold those stocks.

Now we're concentrating on a few sectors like the internet area, in particular the companies that do the specialized chips—like for video. One is C-Cube, a great situation for us. We held this stock in our mid-cap portfolio. It was our largest holding. They reported a positive earnings surprise. We bought this stock very aggressively within a very short timeframe. We went to a full position within three days. The stock was about 49 and the market volatile. Our average cost is about 51. Today, the stock is up another 2 3/4. So, just two weeks after we bought it, the stock is trading at 75 3/4 while the other tech stocks are getting killed.

Tanous: *Let me go back to my point and my question. What you perceived in this stock is what you perceived in the others. Accelerating earnings growth. . .*

Driehaus: It was accelerating, true, but it was more the positive earnings surprise plus the outlook for this type of chip for which they can't meet demand. The area is just exploding. This was one of the good examples. Oak Technology is another.

Buchen: There is an old investment adage: Buy Low, Sell High. Richard believes that far more money is made by Buying High and Selling Higher.

Driehaus: Exactly.

Tanous: *This leads to the classic debate about the "right" price earnings ratio. What is the "right" price earnings ratio?*

Driehaus: The answer is: there is no right price earnings ratio. It's like asking: how many angels can dance on the head of a pin? It depends on the weather on the pin, how slippery the surface is, you know! And what if the angels want to dance somewhere else? In other words, that is an impossible question. There is no right answer. The market is too dynamic for that. I think when you look at price earnings ratios that way, you are looking at it too statistically. That doesn't mean you ignore valuations completely. All I am saying is that there is no absolute level. That is what creates inefficiencies and opportunities.

There's a popular concept out there known as "GARP," Growth at the Right Price. But we don't always know what the "right" price is. When you are in such an early, embryonic phase of development, you can't pick a right price for the right stock. I remember, years ago, when a company called MCI was finally going from a loss to a profit. We started buying the stock around 9 or 10 for one of our institutional accounts. The client made about 10 times on his money. After the stock doubled, it was trading at 100 times earnings. But these were reported earnings at a very early stage of development. It became a real winner. But you might say 100 times today's earnings could be too high in some cases and, maybe it's too low in other cases. That's what people don't recognize. One hundred times could be high or low depending on where you are in that company's income stream. Then you make a judgment as to the duration and rate of growth of that income stream. We look at these income streams very early. For instance, right now, we are very excited about the internet companies. The internet is becoming a mass consumer item. We're buying companies in that field because they're beginning to show positive earnings surprises, like Spyglass.

Tanous: . . .*and Netscape?*

Driehaus: Actually, we didn't buy Netscape, but it's been a wonderful one. That's one where we said it was too high and we were wrong. That stock's gone 50% higher. But they also came in with positive surprises. Now they make money, rather than lose money. We didn't buy Netscape, but we bought others and we're adding to these positions. We bought Spyglass, which had a positive surprise. This very day we're adding to our position in UUNET Technologies because they reported a strong sequential gain and reported a profit when they were supposed to lose money. Take UUNET as an example *[he shows us a chart]*. This is a $2 billion capitalization company, so it's got pretty good size. As you can see, all the stock trends, monthly, weekly, daily, are positive.

Tanous: *What is the source of this data?*

Driehaus: This is our own internal product *[the page has several charts on it]*. You can't just read one chart. You need to look at several charts from, perhaps, different perspectives: monthly, weekly and daily.

Buchen: We buy the raw data and write programs to break it down into various time frames. That gives us a landscape view rather than a snapshot view. Let me give you another example. Ascend Communications is the largest holding in our small cap portfolio. It's up 850%. We've held it for little over a year.

Driehaus: It lives up to its name!

Buchen: I went to a client presentation recently. Their consultant had put together an analysis of our portfolio. It said that our growth rates were 12% and our average price earnings ratio was 46 times earnings. I said I wanted to comment on that. I said the consultant is doing the right things, but he is doing them differently from the way we do them. If you look at Ascend and its trailing 12 months earnings, it is selling at 175 times those earnings. That would scare anybody! But if you look at the next 12 months, it is selling at 15 times those estimated earnings. Within nine months after our first purchase, the Wall Street estimates for the current year had doubled. There is tremendous drive in this company.

Driehaus: And it still looks like a good buy today. It is making all time highs.

Tanous: *Would you say that this is a particularly good example of your approach?*

Driehaus: This company is not growing at 50% or 70%. It's more like a 200% or 300% rate, compared with the previous year. And even sequentially *[from quarter to quarter]*, it is growing at close to 50%. The sales in the last quarter were about $40 million compared to $10 million. That's incredible.

Tanous: *It seems to me that the price earnings ratio is really a function of the accuracy of your projections. You are not buying on past multiple; you're buying on multiples of future earnings. So the question is: how accurate are your projections of those future earnings?*

Driehaus: It is interesting that when things change they don't change randomly. They change and stay in the new pattern for a while. So when a change occurs—and this is where the momentum theory works—the change tends to be more enduring than the Street, or even the companies, anticipate.

For example, these positive earnings surprises that are occurring in the Internet area are, we think, the very beginning of a long term trend. We think that the estimates on these companies are generally low, and this will lead to positive developments in companies like C-Cube, Oak Technologies, and Trident. When these changes lead to positive earnings surprises, the Street doesn't evaluate it right. The research analysts raise their estimates, but usually only by the amount of the gain or the earnings surprise. They don't really catch the secular change that is going on.

Tanous: *When you say the estimate is too low, Richard, how much are you relying on fundamental analysis by Street analysts, or other analysts? What leads to your convictions?*

Driehaus: Partly my experience. I've seen, in the past, that when companies report very positive surprises the analysts were almost all low. The analysts seem to prefer to be conservative, rather than accurate, although they're improving. But when you are at a fulcrum, or turning point, both the analyst and the companies can underestimate growth. That is what is occurring in the semiconductor area. What's the right price for a D-RAM company? There have been some earnings disappointments at some of these commodity-like companies. We don't know the answer, so we have avoided the conflict. We go to areas where the outlook is more assured. The two things I've learned about the market are that you don't know how high a stock can go, and that you don't know how low a stock can go. That's the point. The market is constantly full of surprises both on the upside and the downside. This is the reality of the market on a day-to-day basis.

To get back to why we are successful, one of the reasons is that we stay abreast of what we are doing. So why am I better? I probably stay in it more. A lot of people like to play the piano. But can you really become a virtuoso? It's like the Olympics. Practice, practice, practice. Remember the old saying: the harder I work the luckier I get? Or: success is 99% perspiration and 1% inspiration? Success requires an addiction to what you are doing and it takes a lot of time. This market demands commitment. That's why some have quit.

Tanous: *I understand you recently married, Richard. Congratulations. The next question is: should your investors start worrying?*

Driehaus: No! Kristyna is very practical and lets me put in my time at work! But I do worry about replicating our success and training younger portfolio managers.

Tanous: *I think it's a fact that there aren't a lot of people like you.*

Driehaus: It does requires stamina and dedication. And the stamina is very important. And discipline is part of the stamina. You can't look at a stock and say everything is okay and it will come back. It doesn't. William Blake said: execution is the chariot of genius. In other words, doing things well day in and day out. And there are others here who manage money and do it well. Bill Andersen manages our international portfolio. He has been here ten years and his performance ranks in the top one percentile. Mark Genovise has been with me 12 years. His small-cap portfolio was up 75% in 1995. And that's with no leverage.

Tanous: *This leads me to a question I wrote down that puzzles me. Keep in mind that, as a consultant, I spend my waking hours searching for investment genius. When people think of the grand masters of our trade, they think of Warren Buffett, Peter Lynch, Mario Gabelli, Michael Price, among others, but the name Richard Driehaus seldom comes up outside purely investment circles. Your record is every bit as good as many of the others, so why are you not better known?*

Driehaus: I had an arrangement with a mutual fund company which, for various reasons, required that I keep a low profile and provide my advice to them on an almost exclusive basis, and I did. It was very profitable, but it was limiting. We all became uncomfortable with the relationship after a time. By the early 1990s, it was time to go our separate ways. The arrangement was discontinued in 1993. Since 1991, I have been building our own advisory business, but focusing on larger clients. Our average account size is around $15 million.

Tanous: *As you know, one of the great debates in our industry is the debate of active versus passive investment management. People like Rex Sinquefield will show you data that suggests it is very difficult to beat the market actively. You're better off just buying the market, whether small-cap, mid-cap, or large-cap.*

Driehaus: We think Rex is looking at the subject academically, and, academically, he is right. But in reality, he's wrong a lot of the time.

Tanous: *But he'll say that Richard Driehaus is the exception to the rule. He and Warren Buffett and a few others are the statistical aberrations that confirm the basic data.*

Buchen: That's right! We don't disagree with that. You look for the aberration because that's where you find the oil!

Driehaus: Okay, we're the anomaly. And that's what people should be looking for—the anomaly. Rex has been finding things like a Jesuit would. In other words, you can't out-argue them because they're speaking the truth. But it's not the whole truth. St. Thomas Aquinas says look for all the truths. There are different ways to look at things. There is not just one truth.

Tanous: *Only St. Thomas Aquinas did it by setting up straw dummies that were pretty easy to topple. I don't think you have that luxury.*

Driehaus: What we are looking for is strong results as part of a strong philosophy and an ability to implement that philosophy. If our philosophy was flawed, it would have failed long ago. You can't keep on doing well if your philosophy is flawed. It has to be correct.

Tanous: *As you know, many of the academics, and also people like Rex Sinquefield, believe in the efficient market hypothesis. Everything known about a stock is in the price. On the other hand, there must be a moment in time after a positive earnings surprise occurs, when the market is temporarily inefficient. After all, it's going to take time to disseminate that information and time before it gets reflected in the price. In this case, it will presumably be a higher stock price, given the good news. Is your philosophy not, in fact, based on being first with that news and acting on it before everybody else does?*

Driehaus: We are quicker to react than most managers.

Tanous: *How much does the Driehaus performance depend on that?*

Driehaus: We put positive surprises in a larger context of the group, the market, and the portfolio. A lot of people have electronics now, but not a lot of people have the same judgment and experience. There are plenty of systems that try to do what we do but don't produce the results.

Tanous: *You're saying it's not just a matter of being there first?*

Driehaus: Most people just can't do it. Everyone has the information, but we seem to make money at it. We look at a bigger perspective: Are these groups in favor? Where is the stock? What's our position? And so forth. It's knowledge, understanding, and wisdom. It's also a belief in my philosophy. It's not mechanical.

Tanous: *How does your philosophy apply to large-cap investing?*

Driehaus: We have a small amount of money in large-cap already and we've beaten the S&P 500 by several hundred basis points. *[A basis point is one one-hundredth of a percent.]* We would look to beat the S&P 500 by 300 to 500 basis points over a full market cycle.

Tanous: *I presume your volatility is not all that high in the large-cap stocks.*

Driehaus: I don't think it has been, but avoiding volatility is not one of our objectives. Edmund Burke said that selection is the ultimate economy. But we do concentrate our portfolios, and we are more active than most managers. We take bigger bets. Like Soros recently— he had a hunch and bet a bunch!

[George Soros, the renowned hedge fund manager, reportedly made a $10 billion bet against the British Pound in September 1992 and netted a profit of $2 billion when the British currency was devalued. Another big bet in early 1994 was less successful—Soros bet wrong on the Japanese markets and lost $600 million.]

Tanous: *To sum up this part, Richard, what are you buying now?*

Driehaus: We're buying networking stocks, internet companies, and specialized chip manufacturers.

Tanous: *Bottom line. What is it that you do that future Richard Driehauses can profit from?*

Driehaus: Time, effort and commitment. Everybody wants to be rich but few want to work for it. It's a lot of work and effort. It's a 24-hour-a-day commitment. I'm always observing. I look for new companies that show the type of growth that the Avons, the Baxters, the Abbott Labs did in the 50s. Earnings are the fountainhead of future stock prices. When these future giants were recommended in the early fifties they were much smaller companies. I want to find new companies with that kind of growth. That's why I focus on small- and mid-cap names.

Then I focus on positive earnings surprises. I remember when American Motors reported a positive earnings surprise and the stock went up 15% in one day, from 8 5/8 to 10 1/8 on record volume. Or when Chrysler reported a positive earnings surprise in the early '60s, and that stock took off. At that time, the electronic revolution was just beginning. I concentrated on technology names since they were showing the most dynamic growth. The '50s were a decade of growth of established companies. The '60s were a decade of growth of new companies—new names and new ideas, the beginning of a new entrepreneurial era for America, not only in technology but in other areas as well.

Tanous: *I think you mentioned earlier that you first started investing not in stocks, but in coins.*

Driehaus: True. But when I was buying coins, I looked not for what dealers were trying to sell, but what they were trying to buy! I would ignore the big display ads showing what they had to sell, and I would look at the bottom of the ad where they listed what they wanted to buy. I remember that American proof sets were very profitable, so I figured this would spill over to Canada and I bought Canadian proof sets. Since the Canadian market was much smaller, it took little demand to move the prices.

Tanous: *Did you make money doing this?*

Driehaus: Oh, yeah. I made a lot of money at age 14. I still have some proof sets from that era.

Tanous: *There is a story that keeps surfacing, which I'd like you to confirm. It's about a clerk at A.G. Becker who gave you $104,000 when you started managing money at that firm. What's the true story?*

Driehaus: It's true, and I'll share the facts with you. The most interesting thing about it is that this happened just before the worst bear market (1973-1974) in years, and the value of her portfolio sank to about $65,000. It recovered a year and a half later, but the noteworthy part of the story is that this woman didn't get cold feet. She stayed with me while the professionals all ran for cover! In the late seventies, I felt that the market was going toward the smaller ideas, and I asked her if she wanted to take the risk. She said, "Fine."

Tanous: *What is her account worth today?*

Driehaus: It was worth $7.8 million at the end of 1995. And she's made some withdrawals over the years for taxes and other things. I think she's 71 now, and her mother is 104. By the way, her mother is still invested! So is her sister. You know, everybody says old people can't take risk. But the real risk is being in all those so-called conservative investments! People think the definition of risk is volatility. We're getting the returns we get because our volatility is on the upside. More up than down, and when we're up, we're up a lot more than we're down.

Tanous: *Let's get a little personal. You're a very generous man. There is a Richard Driehaus Foundation. What does it do?*

Driehaus: It started with a million dollar commitment I made in 1985. That consisted of 40,000 shares of TCBY. My cost on the stock was less than $1 and it was up to $25. I contributed another $2.7 million in the next several years. Now the Foundation is over $30 million.

Tanous: *Tell us about your giving philosophy.*

Driehaus: It's partly entrepreneurial. We've invested in start-ups and plain good causes where we can make an impact. We don't generally contribute to the big organized charities, instead favoring some cultural things, and also education. I contribute to my high school, St. Ignatius. *[A building there has been named after Driehaus.]* In 1982, the school had only a couple hundred thousand dollars in endowment and was in bad shape. Now the school has a $20 million endowment. I am also involved in a project called "Opportunities International" which makes small loans in third world countries. What I like about it is that they require the borrowers to pay interest and there's a 93% payback, so the money gets recycled and helps others. The giving keeps on giving.

Tanous: *If you are agreeable, Richard, I would like to continue the interview upstairs in your trading room. I'll keep the recorder running while we tour the activities. I'd like to create a picture for the reader that will show them how you work in your own environment.*

Driehaus: Okay, we can show you what we're doing today. Here's one example: we took a 200,000 share position in one company and we're adding to our positions in the internet companies.

[Richard Driehaus, Bob Buchen and I leave the Louis XVI sur-
roundings and make our way upstairs in the mansion. Upstairs, the
decor flows consistently, antique originals and copies, heavily influ-
enced by a combination of Victorian and French, complete with elec-
tric sconces, Tiffany lamps, and rich fabrics throughout.
   The stark contrast in the trading room is remarkable. Amid the
ornate furnishings, young traders work at desks replete with the latest,
and, in some cases, proprietary, communications apparatus and com-
puters. Huge screens display myriad data on a single page, a feature
unique to Driehaus—whose programmers have figured out a way to
get all of the information on one screen in real time.]

Tanous: *Where are we now?*

Driehaus: This is the trading room *[points at a large TV screen on*
one of the desks in the trading area]. This is our small-cap portfolio.
It's up 1.5% today. Mid-caps are up 0.6%. As you can see we have
price charts here. These are stocks we are buying. So when the
traders are executing orders, they can look at these price and volume
charts which help their judgment.

Buchen: They also get some fundamental information. Quarter by
quarter earnings for the last four years, for example. *[Buchen points*
to that information on the screen.] Also cash flow numbers on an
absolute and relative basis, so you can track momentum.

Tanous: [I point at one stock position on the screen.] *Tell me about*
C-Cube. You told me earlier, it was up 2 3/4 points today.

Driehaus: That was the price when we started talking downstairs.
Now look at it *[Driehaus finds it on the screen].* It's up 6 1/2.

Tanous: *Maybe your buying is running it up.*

Driehaus: *[Laughs]* No. It's not us! We've got a full position. Other
buyers are coming in now.

Buchen: That's the largest position in our mid-cap portfolio. *[We*
walk to another screen.]

Driehaus: Here's the C-Cube. Here's what happened. On a positive earnings surprise, the stock moved from 42 to around 48. We bought it here *[points to the chart on the screen]*. We owned it when people were getting scared away. Now look at it. *[We move to a series of old fashioned news printers clacking away against a wall.]*

Tanous: *This hardly seems state of the art.*

Buchen: You're right. In fact, you can't buy these anymore. They don't sell Dow tape machines anymore. We had to buy old machines and re-program them. The new machines no longer furnish print-outs. But Richard likes to come out here and browse through the information as it prints off the machine. We have 14 news wires on-line—7 domestic and 7 international. So we see the news as fast as anybody in the country or even in the world. It's no big deal. Anybody can buy them. It's what you do with them. But Richard still likes to read the news on the tape. He was raised on the tape. *[We go back to one of the screens.]*

Tanous: *Let's look at C-Cube again.*

Driehaus: Here's where the positive earnings surprise occurred. *[He is pointing at the price chart.]* Note the huge gain both sequentially *[compared to the previous quarter's earnings]* and versus the estimate *[what the Wall Street research analysts expected the earnings to be].* Here. They were supposed to earn 27 cents. They reported 48. Unbelievable. This was due to strong revenue growth. So the estimates were raised pretty dramatically. The three year growth rate is estimated at about 45% *[per year].* Lehman raised their numbers from $0.87 to $1.01 and from $1.05 to $1.70. *[Here he points to the information which refers to Lehman Brothers' estimate of earnings for the next two years.]* This is classic. Here are the other estimates. Robertson Stephens, Alex. Brown. . .

Buchen: Richard has a very short attention span. When his analysts come to him, they can't come to him with a half-hour story. They get down to key points. He doesn't sit in his office very often. He's always talking to traders, or to analysts, just like we're doing now.

Driehaus: *[He is still focused on the data on the screen. His eyes never left it during our side conversations.]* Here it is. Results were very much better than expected as a result of very strong revenue growth for this video process. This is it. All our small cap stocks are making new highs today! Look at Oak. I told you about it downstairs. It's in a similar area. Now we've got to look at what's down. *[Points at a stock on the screen.]* This one is down because somebody downgraded its evaluation, but we like it a lot.

Tanous: *Let's talk about that. Somebody downgraded that stock because they thought the price earnings ratio was too high?*

Driehaus: We often found that they are too early in the downgrading. They are too conservative and we should let things play out. In other words, this stock is up about 50%, but it's up because of very strong underlying fundamentals. But they're saying it is too high short term. Short term they may be right, but over the intermediate term, it's going higher. They are trying to be too cute by saying it's not going to work. It is going to work over the long term based on the information we have.

Tanous: [Pointing at the bottom of the screen] *What's this down here that looks like it is down four points. Davidson & Associates.*

Driehaus: Davidson? Down four? That's one we're selling!

Tanous: *A technical point. Because you're so well known in the business, do you disguise your trading?*

Driehaus: We try to be anonymous, but it's not perfect. Here's the Oxford. We sold most of that yesterday and sold a little more today. This is a typical day.

Tanous: *I notice that the holdings that are down are down fractionally, but the ones that are up are up dramatically.*

Driehaus: That's how we make our extra return. We're adding to Bay Networks. Sun Microsystems is up to a full position . . . Notice that the red numbers are those that are down. Wait a minute . . . this one is not acting well. Altera. *[Driehaus focuses intently on the screen, oblivious to everything else momentarily.]*

Tanous: *Now, you say, it is not acting well. Do you mean in the last few days, or hours?*

Driehaus: It's a combination of things. Here's another one that isn't acting well. MU is Micron Technology. Everybody says it's a big stock. *[We move back to the trading desk. Traders are monitoring screens and barking orders into the telephone. An analyst joins us. He gives Richard a list of stocks he thinks ought to be sold, and explains the reasons why. But Richard is still obsessed with what he saw earlier.]*

Driehaus: The only trouble is I'm more concerned about Altera, that's A-L-T-R. It's selling off again. The Macromedia I think is still okay. How much are we over?

Analyst: We need to raise $20 million in cash.

Driehaus: We're being forced into a situation here.

Tanous: *Why?*

Driehaus: Because of other Buy ideas. *[Driehaus turns to the trader on the phone.]* I'll tell you what I want to sell today. Altera A-L-T-R from the small-cap fund.

Trader: All of it?

Driehaus: Yeah.

Trader: Okay. Altera is trading well. It just traded over a million.

Driehaus: See, the Macromedia looks to me like it could break out on the upside. *[Driehaus points at the chart.]*

Tanous: *Interesting chart.*

Driehaus: It's got a 100% growth rate. And the market is going toward heavy growth. Now look at this, Mark *[Genovise]*. That's the Xilinx again. That doesn't look so great either. I think we should lighten here, too, in the mid-caps. This is our day-to-day work. Here's the U.S. Robotics. There should be a positive surprise here. Note that the local area networking companies are doing better as a group. We'd rather find a company that has less powerful numbers, but is in a better group, where the industry estimates of the growth rate are increasing, than buy something with very strong earnings but where the group is going down. See, one of the most important things is, we want to buy stocks that are going . . . up! *[Laughter all around.]*

Buchen: Richard does focus heavily on the group. Fifty-three percent of our portfolio is in the four top performing groups—out of 195 groups.

Tanous: *The CIA would probably be envious of these data banks. At the end of the day, where do you get your best ideas?*

Driehaus: Actually, I get my best ideas from *The Wall Street Journal* and *Investor's Business Daily.*

Well, maybe. But several recurring themes in our day with Richard Driehaus provide very valuable clues to his success. Remember how often the phrase "positive earnings surprise" reoccurred in our conversation? That is clearly the single most important criterion that Driehaus looks for. He also likes accelerating earnings trends. Like many other managers, Driehaus subscribes to First Call, a sophisticated and expensive service that provides on-line research information from a variety of sources. If an earnings estimate comes out that beats most, or even all, of the Wall Street estimates, that's a positive earnings surprise. Driehaus looks not just for surprises, but dramatic surprises.

But perhaps the most important personal trait that he brings to the process is his personal dedication. His comment about the piano player stuck with me long after our conversation. How many people who like to play the piano ever become virtuosos? Not many. But those that do have something in common—they practice a whole lot. That is precisely what Richard Driehaus does. He practices a great deal. He is consumed by his business and he is totally immersed in it. For those who do not plan to spend upwards of 15 hours a day at this craft, we may do well to remember the discipline that Richard Driehaus brings to his successful strategy. And for investors who are prepared to accept the volatility of small-cap stocks, the notion of accelerating earnings trends and positive earnings surprises is something to keep in mind.

Postscript: *Six months after our initial interview, we asked Bob Buchen for an update on the stocks that were mentioned during our visit. Buchen reported that every stock holding mentioned at the time had been sold during the following six months, with one exception, Ascend. Driehaus bought 3 million shares between July and October of 1994. The average cost was $3. At this writing, the stock is trading in the mid-60s.*

GABELLI

They call him "Super Mario," and why not? He is one of the most visible, ubiquitous figures on Wall Street. A legendary stock-picker who must now divide his time between managing his rather large empire and doing what he loves most, managing money, Mario Gabelli does not appear poised to slow down. Ask him about leadership and he'll give you an interesting analogy. He doesn't see himself as a dark-suited corporate president, or even the coach of a basketball team. Rather, Mario visualizes himself as a jet fighter pilot at the controls of his plane, hands on the stick, ready to blast off—which says something about the dynamic nature of this high-powered individual. A perennial member of the prestigious Barron's roundtable, Gabelli's investment style has always been value. But he has modified the traditional value approach with some interesting wrinkles of his own, including a "catalyst" dimension which we discuss in the interview. I think you will find that twist quite compelling.

    Gabelli's firm is divided into three activities. One is an institutional brokerage firm, which also has some specialized arbitrage and venture capital funds; the second is the mutual fund management company, which oversees a dozen separate funds including the flagship Gabelli Asset Fund which Gabelli personally manages; and third is the money management business, which caters to institutions *and well-heeled private investors. Add it all up, and you quickly come to a total under management that exceeds $10 billion. Not bad for a nice Italian kid from the Bronx. Okay, this was a real smart kid.*

Mario Gabelli moved his headquarters to suburban Rye, New York, a few years ago, but we met in his New York City office and continued our conversation in his car as we were driven down to Wall Street where he headed to a board meeting of the American Stock Exchange.

Tanous: *How did you first get interested in stocks?*

Gabelli: My first investment experience was somewhere around 1956. I was working in the Catskill mountains as a waiter and they were financing the ski resort. I looked at the offering, but I was not a qualified investor. So I didn't invest in it. The ski resort then went bust, which was kind of fascinating. I must have been between 13 and 15, I forget. Also, I used to caddy at Sunningdale Country Club. I shared in the enthusiasm for investing that the floor brokers I worked for had.

Tanous: *That ski resort experience does not seem to be an experience that would lead to a career in investments.*

Gabelli: I think if you look at Warren Buffett, Peter Lynch, and Mario Gabelli, we all caddied, and we all invested in the stock market very early in life. There must be something about caddying.

Tanous: *As a matter of fact, I discussed the caddie experience with Peter Lynch* [page 113]. *Like Peter, you certainly qualify as one of the best known and visible fund managers out there.*

Gabelli: I've been doing it a long time. It's called survivability.

Tanous: *But the other thing I find interesting about you is probably not as well known. I'm referring to your academic credentials. You're a CFA* [Chartered Financial Analyst, a designation earned by taking a series of 3 qualifying exams]. *Not many of the fund managers I've spoken to are, and it's an important discipline. You also have an MBA from Columbia. You're obviously smart.*

Gabelli: A lot of people are smart. I was summa cum laude from Fordham. I went to a Jesuit undergraduate high school and a parochial grammar school. But it's tough to get into this business these days without an MBA. There have been gaps in talent coming into Wall Street, like in the '50s due to the lackluster market. There was also a gap in the seventies, predictably, given the market at the time. I'm on the board at the Columbia Graduate School of Business, so we're actively involved in the curriculum and how we mentor students. Obviously this is a part of America that is important to money managers. The competitive advantage we have is entrepreneurialism and ingenuity. Education is an important springboard to that.

Tanous: *There are, of course, lots of different approaches to investing. What is there in your background that led you to choose the value style?*

Gabelli: Very simple. I was at Columbia in 1965. Roger Murray taught security analysis. I wanted to take security analysis, and I took his course because he was the best. He basically is an extension of Graham and Dodd and actually co-authored the fifth edition of the Graham and Dodd book, *Security Analysis. [The value style of investment is sometimes called "Graham and Dodd" because of their pioneering role articulating it.]*

Professor Murray, who is 85 today, is wonderfully focused and still talks about stocks in more than just an academic way. About four years ago, our firm, in part to create a living legend, asked Roger Murray to give lectures on value investing. He gave four lectures, 120 minutes each, non-stop, at the Museum of Television and Radio. We invited Columbia Business School to participate. Dean Meyer Feldberg joined Professor Greenwald. Based on that, Professor Greenwald brought back to the curriculum a value investing course.

I think if I trace the roots of Gabelli, Cooperman, Samberg, and a whole array of mid-'60s-vintage investors, you'll find that many of them have one thing in common, and that is value investing. It was a fundamental approach to the investment process driven by a Graham and Dodd academic background. We were not University of Chicago, we were not University of Pennsylvania, or Harvard. We were driven into this style by virtue of the discipline that we learned in graduate school.

Tanous: *One of the things we're doing in this book that I think you'll appreciate is bringing academics into the discussion. The academics don't think that people like you are predictable. You're the lucky orangutans.*

Gabelli: I think your selection of academics is the problem. You should have Roger Murray. *[I decided to take Mario Gabelli's advice; you'll find my conversation with Roger Murray on page 301.]*

Tanous: *Let's talk about your investment strategy. The Gabelli Value Fund is structured to allow you to take big bets by buying substantial positions in companies. How do you justify that amount of concentration since, with more concentration, you have potentially more risk?*

Gabelli: Within the framework of concentration, if you read Berkshire Hathaway's annual report for the last 20 years, you'll find that, if you understand a business, buying the business has less risk. So your assumption is not valid. It goes to the notion of what you're doing. Are we buying a piece of paper? Concentration in a portfolio could be 33 stocks at 3% each as opposed to 100 stocks at 1%. But I suppose somebody would also argue that that gives you diversification.

We're buying a business and a business has certain attributes. We're not buying a piece of paper and we're not buying soybeans. As surrogate owners, there are certain characteristics with regard to the value of the franchise, the cash generating capabilities of the franchise, and the quality of the management. So you have quantitative and qualitative measures. You also have a notion of price. Where are you buying that stock within the context of what I call "private market value"—what others might call intrinsic value? And within that framework, Mr. Market gives you opportunities to buy above that price and below that price, that intrinsic value. So risk can come in because you're buying a great franchise, a great business, run by wonderful people, but at too high a price. It's kind of the blending of a series of judgments with some mechanical and arithmetic exercises.

Tanous: *So clearly you're not an efficient market proponent.*

Gabelli: There are lots of ways to make money. I don't think fundamental analysts, who do disciplined bottom-up research, believe there are no bargains. The harder you look, the more you find them. They are uncovered in strange ways.

Tanous: *Could we talk a bit more about private market value and some of the criteria you use to zero in on companies that you ultimately buy?*

Gabelli: The "private market value" approach is the terminology I coined in the late 1970s coming out of the bear market of 1973-74. We went back to fundamentals to determine what a business is worth. If it's selling on the stock market for $10 a share, I will look for the private market value, the summation of the pieces of its business, by looking at cash, receivables, inventory, off-balance sheet assets like goodwill, franchise values, earnings power. Then I'll ask: what would an informed industrialist pay to own this enterprise? What is the value of the company if it were privately owned? What would somebody pay and why? Of course, private market value multiples change. They are a function of interest rates, capitalization structures, taxes, all of which have an indirect impact on the value of the franchise. So private market value investing does change over time.

I developed this approach in the mid-1970s for a practical reason. I wanted to convince people that it was okay to buy stocks. I actually took an ad out in *The Wall Street Journal* congratulating my friends at Houdaille, and to Kohlberg, Kravis and Roberts for doing the Houdaille transaction. I believe it was in 1979. It was the second LBO *[leveraged buyout]* that was done by KKR. It was a perfect example of the private market value principle, since the LBO took Houdaille private. As a result of my knowledge of how to do these "private market value" transactions, I became the leading guru in the early eighties on the leveraged buyout business.

Tanous: *So, is the idea that you're putting these stocks into your funds and accounts, and then anticipating that something is going to happen?*

Gabelli: No, that's backwards. What you do is identify a company in the public markets that is selling well below a channel called "intrinsic private market value." That gives you a margin of safety, and helps protect the downside by providing a cushion, because it is selling at a significant discount to the underlying value.

The other element that I added to the investment process was a need for a rate of return and a definable time period. So I added the element called the "catalyst." What would be the element that would help narrow the spread between "the private market value" and the stock price? That catalyst was important. It could be a 13D filing, it could be a split-up of a company. All the things I talked about in 1979 are back in 1996. Nothing changes. *Plus ça change, plus c'est la même chose.*

Tanous: *What are some of the other examples of catalysts, Mario?*

Gabelli: A divorce of a founder, the death of a founder, a family block that wants a change in their tax situation. A change in regulation. For example, right now, in 1996, you have a major structural change in the way the telephone industry is being regulated. That is the new Telecom act. That is a major catalyst for certain industries.

Tanous: *The identification of the catalyst is important as part of the process of identifying the companies.*

Gabelli: The first thing you do is examine 100 companies, and you'll find 15 of them that fit your criteria regarding price, cost, margin of safety. The second element, before you buy them for the portfolio, is that you want to have a catalyst.

Tanous: *So the catalyst is part of the investment process?*

Gabelli: It's not part of the research process, but it is part of the total investment process—including pulling the investment trigger.

Tanous: *Most managers who are identified with a style, as you are with value, stay wedded to it. But your firm has expanded beyond the value style and has been very successful. You've grown a lot.*

Gabelli: You're getting confused. But it's not you alone; it's the Street, too. I wear two hats. Mario Gabelli, the fighter pilot; that is, the person at the throttles running the value style of investment our firm has. Secondly, Mario Gabelli, the Ned Johnson *[Fidelity]*, the John Bogle *[Vanguard]*—I'm Bogle and Johnson put together. That is, I'm the business guy running a firm, who has a moral responsibility to his professional staff to make sure that their business of investing stays healthy in all markets at all times, and, also, gives them a continuing challenge. As a result, the Gabelli brand is preeminent in value and has certain other niches—we think we do a marvelous job in arbitrage; we think we do a marvelous job in convertible bonds; etc. We also have a wonderful individual in the gold fund; a wonderful individual in the growth area, Howard Ward, who is a world class professional under the mantra of growth. That's part of the other mantra of the firm, which is to take the Gabelli brand and leverage it to create niches.

Tanous: *Here's a softball question. Which activity do you like better?*

Gabelli: The ideal world is a growth stock selling at below its intrinsic value. That's what we look for. There's no virtue in buying a company that's selling at a dollar when it's worth two dollars if ten years later it's selling at a dollar fifty and it's still worth two dollars. What you want to do, within the mix of private market value investing, is find the company that's selling for a dollar and is worth two dollars where the two dollars will grow at least faster than inflation plus our hurdle rate. *[The hurdle rate is the minimum risk-adjusted rate of return that makes an investment worth the bother.]*

Tanous: *Are we talking "catalyst" again?*

Gabelli: No! You're talking fundamental valuations. You're talking about when you value an enterprise and you say it's worth two dollars, and that's the private market value, but it's selling at one dollar. That's a snapshot. Then you need a motion picture. What will that two dollar value be in five years? That is, will the value grow? So, getting back, a value investor like myself wants a business franchise that will grow in value over time. Revenues will grow, EBITDA *[earnings before interest, taxes, depreciation, and amortization also sometimes loosely referred to as "cash flow." Most private market purchasers look at EBITDA multiples in preference to price-earnings multiples]* will grow. Ideally, EBITDA margins will grow, but you don't need that. In that framework, cash flow is used to reduce debt, enhancing the enterprise value. You go from a dollar value, to a two dollar value, to four dollars of value, and, in theory, from one dollar in the public price to four dollars.

Tanous: *So here we're not talking about "catalyst," we're talking about fundamental improvement in earnings; fundamental improvement in other financial measures.*

Gabelli: Yes! It is the microeconomic variables that go into making the intrinsic value of the enterprise. Going back to your question,

Peter, there was a quant and an index guy at a conference like the ones your academics attend, and they were debating which style was a better virtue, in terms of investment process, and the debate was getting very heated. All of a sudden the ground shook, and they saw a piece of paper gently floating down from the sky. They looked at it and it said: Quants and indexers are equal. Signed: God, Value Investor *[lots of laughter]*.

Anyone who buys a stock based on earnings dynamics alone without looking at it from a price point of view is a momentum investor.

Tanous: *I've got one in the book, Richard Driehaus.*

Gabelli: Richard is one of them. His shop is very good at it.

Tanous: *You also have bred "personalities" within the Gabelli empire, if I can call it that. Elizabeth Bramwell, who used to run your growth fund, comes to mind. But there are pluses and minuses to creating personalities, aren't there? You create a personality, and then they leave.*

Gabelli: That's okay. I mean, I left Loeb Rhodes. Driehaus left A.G. Becker to start his own company. Everyone leaves sometime. Dick Strong, who founded the Strong Funds, left. But basically the answer is simple. I hired Elizabeth Bramwell as an analyst, and then I made her my research director. She was my classmate at Columbia and we also worked together at William D. Witter. As a result, I knew her investment skills.

But the point is that you need personalities to compete against Fidelity, Dreyfus, and Vanguard. As a result, we also believe that people run money, and they are part of an organization and a process. I launched Elizabeth as a personality. And she was a growth investor just like Howard Ward is. Within that framework, we like personalities. I will continue to help advertise personalities. Caesar Bryan is a wonderful personality. He's a Brit, lawyer, good background. He loves stocks, and he loves precious metals and golds, and he is world class. We think Hart Woodson is one of the best in the convertible bond area. It's a niche that few people understand. It's like fly fishing.

Tanous: *Can I tell you a funny story?*

Gabelli: Go ahead.

Tanous: *I interviewed Michael Price and we went through this whole business about International Mining, and Kawecki, and Fansteel, and he told me about how he put together this great chart back in 1976 about the relationships between all these companies. Let me quote from the interview: "One of the brokers in Max's brokerage firm was this guy who is a friend of Mario Gabelli, whom I had never met. Mario at that time was a broker at Loeb Rhodes. Mario walked over to my desk and took the chart and walked out. I said where are you going with that? He took that chart of the complex of companies. It was so funny. That's how I met Mario."*

Gabelli: Well, maybe the story is backwards. I think we met because I was looking to buy furniture cheap and his firm was going out of business. I bought three desks from, I believe, Heine Geduld, for a hundred dollars each when they were going out of business, and I was starting my firm in 1976. I couldn't afford to buy them whole-sale, so I bought them below wholesale.

The report Mike refers to is basically the same report that Mutual Shares used without paying me a commission on it. But Michael's a good guy. Michael comes to research dinners I sponsor, and I go to Michael's dinners, and we share a lot of stories, and he's a friend. He's a good value investor and we've been on Barron's panels for the last 12 or 13 years.

Here's another insight. Two professors from Tulane did a study to determine who picked the best stocks on the Barron's panels for ten years. I'm obviously mentioning this because I was number one!

Tanous: *You have an intriguing and whimsically named fund called "Gabelli Global Interactive Couch Potato Fund™." Tell us about it.*

Gabelli: A couch potato is a guy who went home with a six pack, four for him, two for his wife, and he sat on the couch and watched television. Then the remote control came along, and that started changing America's appetite. Instead of just sitting down and turning on channel 2 and watching it for a four hour block, the couch potato started grazing and surfing—all thanks to the remote. But then what happened about five years ago was that the advertisers started trying to get the TV viewer to interact with the TV set. For example, scratch off something and look at it while Coca-Cola is running an ad during the Super Bowl.

Because we have an area of competence in global entertainment and media, which is one of the strong suits of our firm, we just coined the term "Interactive Couch Potato™", but that is strictly an American phenomenon. Europeans don't know what it is yet.

Tanous: *As an investor, what am I looking for in that fund?*

Gabelli: If you look back over the last ten years, and look forward to the next 20, one of my great themes of investing is the concept of the notion of time and place. Wireless communication has changed, unshackled and uncoupled man from a place. You can be anywhere, any time. It is wonderful. It is changing the way humanity communicates, the way humanity functions, where people live and work. You still need food, but you can have it FedEx-ed! So we're looking at the world in terms of cable, which is televisions, voice and video, data, and we're also looking at it from an unwired point of view. The distribution of information is going through a major change. Some countries are getting it for the first time; other countries are finding new ways to communicate.

On the copyright side, taking ideas putting them together, it's the same thing. So we're looking on a global basis for things that travel well around the world—like music, MTV, jazz, films, sports, news, entertainment. Then, we're looking for the facilitators, like Microsoft that can put devices together to allow it to happen in multimedia. Our fund is doing this on a global basis. I think we're good at it and unique. We bring to the table a knowledge of all of these disciplines that no other firm has. If markets around the world grow 10% per year over the next ten years, we think this fund should be able to do about 15% per year.

Tanous: *This is why I wanted to spend some time on it. Mario, what does the future hold for you? Are you going to do this forever?*

Gabelli: About ten years ago, the Harmonie Club had a breakfast on a Saturday morning in the middle of February, a very snowy day, and there were four panelists: Seth Glickenhaus *[Glickenhaus & Co.],* Roy Neuberger *[Neuberger and Berman],* Tubby Burnham *[Drexel Burnham & Co.],* and me. Tubby gcts up there and says "I'm Tubby Burnham, I've been in this business 50 years, Roy Neuberger's in this business 60 years, Seth Glickenhaus 60 years, and here's Mr. Gabelli, only 25 years." So I said, I thought I was invited to this club because it was politically correct to invite me! A sign of the

Harmonie Club's affirmative action! But it was really basically because of my age! *[The Harmonie Club is a prestigious, largely Jewish, club.]* And it was a lot of fun. What I'm getting at is that every one of us didn't have to be there. We loved the market, we loved what we were doing, and this is over ten years ago! So, if I'm doing this forty years from now, I'll be 95, it'll be 2036, and we'll still be debating value versus growth, and which has the greater virtue.

I wonder if Gabelli's hyper energy came through in the interview? I suspect it did. One has the sense of an individual who would rise to any challenge. Mario, have you tried bungee jumping? I came away dutifully impressed by his enthusiasm and energy level. There seems little doubt that Gabelli also oversees every aspect of his business. You wonder when he finds time to sit back and do the analysis of companies and stocks that has historically been his forte. Yet he does continue to do that, while building a firm that has expanded well beyond the original value mantra that its founder espouses.

Gabelli's philosophy on companies is also very interesting. His "catalyst" notion is an intelligent and sensible approach to the market, wouldn't you agree? After all, it's one thing to find an undervalued company. It's quite another to find one that is not going to stay undervalued indefinitely. The difference, of course, is the catalyst— that factor that will cause the stock price to rise—and Gabelli intelligently includes it in the analytical process. Gabelli's notions about the future of telecommunications in a wireless world also bear watching. So here we have a value investor with a twist. He finds undervalued companies, as do most value managers, but he also tries very hard to find the ones that aren't going to stay undervalued very long, the ones with a "catalyst." Makes sense to me.

WILLIAM F.
SHARPE

*D*oes anybody start out to be an economist? That reminds me of the old joke: an economist is someone who didn't have the personality to become an accountant. Yuk Yuk. Bill Sharpe didn't start out to become an economist either. He really thought he wanted to be a doctor, but quickly changed his mind. Instead, he earned his B.A. and M.A. in economics at UCLA.

His association with Harry Markowitz, who became his mentor, began in 1960 when Bill Sharpe undertook his graduate work on the relationship between the movement of individual stock prices and the movement of the stock market as a whole. The breakthrough came in 1964 with the publication of the Capital Asset Pricing Model, known as CAPM, which, among other things, concludes that you can't really beat the market without taking undue risk—exactly what legions of Wall Street analysts and brokers did not want to hear. Thirty years after they first began working together, Harry Markowitz and Bill Sharpe shared the Nobel Prize for economic sciences with Dr. Merton Miller of the University of Chicago.

Bill Sharpe is about as close as anyone can come to being a household name on Wall Street, at least among the academics who utter pronouncements on matters affecting the stock market. He contributed beta to the investment vocabulary, as well as the eponymous

Sharpe ratio, a widely used measure of risk-adjusted investment return.

Talking to Nobel prize winners is something one might understandably approach with a sense of trepidation, but I found Bill Sharpe unusually easy to talk to. You will too. He offers some interesting advice on investing, which we will tuck away for future discussion.

Tanous: *How did you first get interested in stocks?*

Sharpe: As an undergraduate economics major, I thought that if I learned something about the stock market, I could make a lot of money. So, I took a course in investments, which I found totally opaque. It was taught by a very nice man, but it was really old fashioned and had no structure or theory. That was just the way we used to approach investments: you learn how to read a balance sheet; you compute all these ratios; you think about the management; and you do some kind of mumbo jumbo. I thought that was very uninteresting. I was an economics major and I was used to logic and structure and theory, and I didn't see any in this process. So, that was that. I went on to a research firm, and then went back and got a Ph.D. in economics.

But here's the key thing: When I was doing my masters in economics I was a research assistant for J. Fred Weston who was not in investments, but in corporate finance. Weston was a very smart guy and solid as a rock. So I got interested in finance—not so much in investments per se, but in finance. I took my Ph.D. in economics, and I took a field in finance—which was unusual, but allowed under the rules.

Along the way, I learned about Harry Markowitz's work, which I thought was really nifty because it had all the great theory and structure that I liked. When my first dissertation project didn't excite the faculty member who would have been the supervisor, Fred suggested that I talk to Harry Markowitz, who was not on the faculty, but was working at the same research firm I was working at. See if maybe there was something there. We chatted, and I got excited about some ideas. I did a dissertation on portfolio theory, extended it to *equilibrium and the capital markets,* and the rest is history.

Tanous: *I was very interested in your 1990 Darden School* [The University of Virginia's business school] *lecture on asset allocation. You mentioned Fidelity Magellan's superior performance from '86 to '89. Fact is, you cited its great performance, indicating that Peter Lynch had, in fact, demonstrated outstanding stock selection ability.* [See our next interview on page 111, which is with Peter—who became a legend as the extremely successful manager of Fidelity Magellan.]

Sharpe: I define selection as total return, minus style return. *[For example, growth stock returns versus value stock returns, since they behave differently.]* Yes, he beat the benchmark that style analysis, run through time, would put him against.

Tanous: *The interesting thing to me is that* [I don't know if your study has been updated since '89] *in the case of Fidelity Magellan, it seems to me that the outstanding performance continued.*

Sharpe: Hold on a second. I'll look it up. *[Sharpe turns to his computer and begins punching keys to search for the relevant data.]* This is a commercial data service so I'm not implicated! Let's see . . . this is it . . . Okay. Fidelity Magellan. Found it. We'll do a sample and we'll analyze style . . . we'll do out of sample . . . we'll update quarterly . . . how about that?

Tanous: *Perfect.*

Sharpe: Let's see. Starting in early 1993 *[the years Jeff Vinik was managing Magellan],* it shows "outperformance" then flat, then down a little—this is relative to the benchmark—then flat, then down a little again, then basically they had only added about 5% in '93 and '94. But, then, in the first part of '95 they did so well. That was the big move into tech stocks we all read about.

Tanous: *The question is; is Peter Lynch a great manager or is he the millionth monkey?*

Sharpe: Morris Smith was the second Magellan manager, and he actually had a better style-adjusted record in the Fidelity OTC Fund—which he ran before he took over Magellan—than Lynch had in Magellan at that time. If you look at Fidelity equity funds in general you'll find that they're not bad. There seems to be a little something there.

Tanous: *How do we rationalize the "little something"?*

Sharpe: Some of the competitors used to say that the way they did it was to run up the prices by buying such huge amounts! Maybe that's why Lynch resigned because he didn't want to have to sell any of that stuff! But I don't think we have a lot of evidence that that's it. We're not talking about blowing out the lights. The good performance isn't in every Fidelity fund. Some of their funds underperform and some overperform. I haven't done this, but I'll bet if you took a dollar-weighted portfolio of the Fidelity equity funds—before load fees at least—you probably would be in pretty good shape. You would probably get close to, or maybe even beat, the indexes.

Tanous: *But who else can I ask but you? Why and how do we pick these funds?*

Sharpe: In any negative sum game, the average is going to be negative because of cost, relative to benchmarks. There will be some that win and some that lose. Recently a number of us have turned up some evidence of persistence in fund returns.

Tanous: *Aha!*

Sharpe: Marty Gruber has *[Gruber is a professor at the NYU Stern School of Business];* I have. If you look on my web site you'll see a study I did. *[Bill Sharpe's home page web address is: http://gsb-www.stanford.edu/~wfsharpe/home.htm]*

Tanous: *What all of this comes down to is a couple of investment mysteries. One is the predictability of future performance. This is what it's about, isn't it?*

Sharpe: Of course. There are two issues. One is: Are you getting the asset allocation you wanted? If you decide you want a value tilt, you hire some managers. Do you get a value tilt? That's an issue of style and aggregation. That's independent of performance. The second is: You pay managers more than if you invested in Vanguard Index funds. So, you've got added risk and cost. But have you gotten enough added return to warrant doing it?

Tanous: *Fair enough. I read a piece you wrote in which you very elegantly make the case that after costs, the return on the average actively managed portfolio must be less than the return on the average passively managed portfolio. A wonderful piece.*

Sharpe: When I speak in front of an audience that hasn't been exposed to much of this, I like to play a game. I do this little routine in which we divide the room and a third of the audience are passive managers, and two thirds are active managers. And they collectively have all the money in some market—French equities, whatever. I announce what the return was on the market last year, last month, or yesterday, it doesn't matter. Then I ask them, before costs, how did the passive guys do? Well, they did so much. How about the active guys? Well, gee, I guess they had to do the same, and, after costs, they had to do worse.

I usually dramatize it by saying the passive people are really boring, all they really know how to do is count to 500 *[Sharpe is referring to the S&P 500, which is often used as the benchmark for passive investors]*, or look up how many shares are outstanding. Hope you never get stuck at a cocktail party with them. On the other hand, the active managers are fascinating and charming, they know all about the latest products. They're so interesting and so intelligent. It makes the point pretty well.

Tanous: *It certainly does. I guess it points out that among the active managers, some are going to be lousy and some are going to be good. But in the end, if the market's return is 10%, then the aggregate of the passive managers and active managers must equal 10% before costs. Of course it must!*

Sharpe: The active managers have to be better than average to be good enough to beat the passives. That's because of costs *[the fees that active managers charge]*.

Tanous: *Therefore, the name of our game is to try to identify those people who either have been, are likely to be, or continue to be, in the upper bracket.*

Sharpe: This is very preliminary but there's some work that I've done, that Marty Gruber has done, that Mark Carhart has done— he's an academic at USC who worked under Gene Fama and did his dissertation in this area. He is doing some really nice work. What I get out of this work, and it needs a lot more investigation, suggests that funds that have done well—that have beaten their style benchmarks, meaning they've done well relative to what they do—have added value.

Funds that have done well in that sense, in the relatively recent past, meaning one, two, or three years, will be slightly more likely to do well next year than those that have done badly. A lot of this, of course, is because the bad ones are the ones with high costs and high turnover. But if it were just that, you'd expect that the best performers in the past would still underperform the benchmarks. But there is some evidence that they don't. They actually outperform them a little, net of costs, except loads. I'm leaving loads out. *[A "load" is a fee charged to purchase a mutual fund.]*

Mark's work suggests that the funds that did well last period were the ones that tended to pick stocks that had done well in the prior period. We know that stocks in the U.S., although not in every country, tend to have short term persistence. So if you buy stocks that outperformed last year, they tend to do better in the near term. You tend to do okay if you keep buying the very recent winners. Mark's work, if I read it correctly, is suggesting that the funds that did well recently were doing that. To the extent that they keep doing it, they'll outperform.

On the other hand, Marty's work, and mine also, suggests that whatever it is that makes a fund successful, has a relatively short half-life. So you don't want to buy the fund that did well five years ago, but you may want to buy the one that did well last year. This may be because managers move on; or raise their salaries so high after they've done well that all the benefit is gone; or a fund has too much money and can't do it any more. *[Funds that are very large become illiquid—their stock purchases move stock prices up; their stock sales move that stock's price down just because they are so big.]* Could be any or all of the above.

We're learning more about this process. But, it remains true that it's really hard to beat a passive strategy with active managers, although we see some evidence of people who do it. I work with some pension funds that manage to get managers who on average, more often than not, collectively beat an appropriate set of benchmarks. I won't say all the funds I work with do! And I won't tell you which ones are which!

Tanous: *When you refer to the persistence of positive-style adjusted returns, are you talking about very style-specific managers, who tend to stick to the four corners of the stylebox?* [A stylebox is a chart which shows how true a manager's portfolio is to his stated style. Managers whose portfolios are in the corners are consistent with their respective styles. The corners are value, growth, large and small.]

Sharpe: People have told me that the ones who seem to win, relative to style, tend to be fairly consistent in their style BUT, I've never done that analysis directly myself and I haven't seen any papers on it.

Tanous: *Let's talk about value stocks and growth stocks. Isn't it widely acknowledged today that value stocks outperform growth stocks over time?*

Sharpe: That's not widely acknowledged! A number of us have found that, in various places, value stocks have outperformed growth stocks over time. The issue of whether or not they will in the future is still very much debatable.

Tanous: *But is the statement true historically? Value stocks have outperformed growth stocks?*

Sharpe: That obviously depends on where you are and what the time period is. Nothing is universal in this world of investments. But the work Fama and French have done, the work I've done on other countries and what Fama and French have now done on other countries, the results people have found in various models over the years, seem to indicate that over the long term, that it has been the case. Again, there's still a lot of dispute on how persistent this is and, if it's going to occur, why it's going to occur and all the rest. It's not uncontroversial.

Tanous: *Yet so many people believe that the case for value stock performance is rock solid.*

Sharpe: Some people will tell you, oh yeah, it's proven. But it's not.

Tanous: *The question I'm leading to is, if you accept that value stocks, under whatever conditions, outperform growth stocks, many of the passive theorists claim that the reason they do is that value stocks are riskier. Is that true?*

Sharpe: They're not riskier historically, with the possible exception of the '29 and '30 period in the U.S. There is some work, although it's never been published, that suggests that so-called value stocks, low price-to-book stocks they are also called, took a real bath in the '29-

'30 period, but for virtually any other period when the studies have been done (except maybe in Switzerland), you find that they have lower standard deviations; they have lower betas. The Fama-French position is this kind of bizarre metaphysic that says: "value stocks do better; but we know in an efficient market things that do better ought to, in some sense, be riskier, ergo, value stocks are riskier! Now we don't happen to have seen the manifestation of the risk *[laughter all around]*, but it must be so, therefore the market is efficient." End of discussion.

Tanous: *So are you saying that you don't think that value or distress stocks, are, in fact, riskier than growth stocks?*

Sharpe: This might be what we generically call a peso problem. You get something that has a very small probability of a real disaster; you can look at 20, 30, 40 years and never see the manifestation of the disaster *[because the probability is so small]*. As a result, you won't see evidence of the risk, but it's still there. A lot of people say, well, if value stocks have done better it's because when you buy value stocks, you take this gamble: There is a small probability of a total wipeout. For the last fifty years people who have taken that gamble have gotten lucky. If you say that, there is no way to test that theory.

Tanous: *But that statement is intellectually very unsatisfying.*

Sharpe: Absolutely. Jeremy Grantham, a money manager in Boston, did some work which I believe shows that if you owned low price-to-book stocks *[value stocks]* in 1929 you would have had to wait until 1939 before you were made whole.

Tanous: *The study we saw is the Lakonishok, Shleifer and Vishny work ["Contrarian Investment, Extrapolation, and Risk," The* Journal of Finance, *vol. XLIX, No. 5, December 1994].*

Sharpe: Yes. That shows value stocks doing better, without a manifestation of higher risk. That's post-war. There are various studies out there, but the only one I've seen or heard of that seems to show some evidence of a risk that goes with value stocks is Jeremy Grantham's.

Tanous: *Interesting. Put your investor hat on. Faced with all of this data, wouldn't you want to own a lot of value stocks?*

Sharpe: Well, probably not if I were paying taxes on it. Value stocks have high dividend yields. Some of this may be just the tax effect. In an economy where a fair number of people pay higher taxes on dividends than on capital gains, you'd expect that stocks that give more of their return in tax disadvantaged ways, i.e. high yield, i.e. value, would have to do better before tax to make them competitive after tax.

Tanous: *Fair enough. But the vast majority of institutional stock buyers, like pension funds, don't have a tax problem.*

Sharpe: What I would do is put the value stocks in my tax deferred account and the growth stocks in my other account. But I wouldn't go all value. I don't go all value. I tilt toward value, but if I have to do it in taxable accounts, I don't tilt a lot.

Tanous: *A few minutes ago, you spoke about the persistence of returns with certain funds. There is a style of investing based on that theory— momentum investing. I interviewed Richard Driehaus who is a proponent of that style. Richard and people like him believe they are exploiting inefficiencies in the market through what they call "positive earnings surprises."*

Sharpe: Langdon Wheeler of Numeric Investors is another one. He has a remarkable record. He has capped that strategy and won't take any more money. There is evidence, and try as they might, the accountants and financial people can't make it go away, that when you get an earnings surprise, somehow or other the market doesn't seem to absorb it all right away.

Tanous: *Exactly. It takes time. And for those who are on top of the information, that may present an advantage. Right?*

Sharpe: It's not hard to get the information. You have to worry about liquidity, and have a good trading desk, and all that.

Tanous: *But it can happen.*

Sharpe: There have been a lot of studies of it and some people have done well with that strategy.

Tanous: *Are we poking holes in the efficient market theory here?*

Sharpe: Well, you'll have to ask the accountants who study that phenomenon.

Tanous: *What do you think?*

Sharpe: Yeah, I think that that is one of the anomalies which suggests that, if your costs are low and your trading efficiency is high, there are some things you can do to gain a little advantage.

Tanous: *To people like us, one of your great contributions to the investment industry is the Sharpe ratio. Everybody in the business uses it.* [The Sharpe ratio is a widely used statistic which measures risk-adjusted portfolio performance. In other words, did the returns justify the risk taken? For an expanded discussion, see page 17.]

Sharpe: It's funny how that lay fallow for so long, then all of a sudden it's come to the fore.

Tanous: *It's amazing. This is the one of the sexiest tools we consultants have!*

Sharpe: Probably misused, of course!

Tanous: *Maybe so. In fact, my question relates to that. It is interesting to me that a ratio named after you, a Nobel laureate and passive investment proponent, is used by us to show an investment manager's risk-adjusted contribution to return. That means, of course, that we use this ratio to help select active managers. Where did we, or you, for that matter, go wrong?*

Sharpe: If you want to take on active management and add active risk in the hope of active returns, you ought to be thinking about how much active return you're expecting to get per unit of active risk you're expecting to add. That's the measure, as you say.

I'm agnostic as to how you form those expectations. If you're a real believer in passive management and efficient markets, you'll assume that the active managers will add on average *negative* amounts per unit of risk and then you won't give them any money at all! *[Laughter]*

Again, I'm interested in the normative aspects as well. I certainly work with people who believe that their active managers have an expected positive added value. The question is, how do we put that information together and come up with an appropriate mix, not only of active and passive, but also how we allocate the active money among them?

Tanous: *But look at the contribution you've made to active management. The Sharpe Ratio is one of the most important tools we have to evaluate a manager's risk-adjusted value based on his management history. Those are the guys we want to hire.*

Sharpe: The manager's added risk in the past is a pretty good predictor of added risk in the future. The added return in the past, because of a relatively small degree of persistence, is a pretty rotten indicator unless it is big and negative. Most of the studies over time have said: Give me a manager with a positive alpha *[a measure of excess return]* and a manager with a negative alpha, and the probability is 50/50 that they'll be above whatever the average alpha is next period, whether they've been positive in the past or negative in the past.

We're now beginning to find that it is not quite that stark. The kind of number that I have found over the years is something like this: Give me the manager who was the very best in terms of average return alpha or Sharpe ratio, for that matter, in the last five years, the 100th percentile manager. Then ask me to make my prediction as to what percentile he or she will be in over the next five years. I wouldn't say 50th, but I probably wouldn't say more than 55th. And that's to a major extent because I have some assurance that the guys in the bottom are going to be more likely to be in the bottom in the future. I'm talking, of course, about the high expense ratio, high turnover managers.

Tanous: *So, if we set out as an objective to consistently have the managers we select as being, say, top third, are we kidding ourselves?*

Sharpe: You bet. But let me be careful before I answer your question. You're going to select, what, ten managers?

Tanous: *Say.*

Sharpe: Okay, ten managers. The question is what's the probability that all of them will be in the top third? Or that the weighted average will be in the top third?

Tanous: *Say all of them.*

Sharpe: I would say that the probability is, basically, zero.

Tanous: *Over the next five years?*

Sharpe: Yeah.

Tanous: *How about 80%? Eight out of ten of the managers will be in the top third.*

Sharpe: I would say, still, pretty small. The question you want to ask is, assuming you give 10% of your money to each of these ten guys, will that portfolio of ten managers be in the top third?

Tanous: *Thank you. What's the answer?*

Sharpe: We have to decide what measure we're going to use for the ranking. If you mean value added, or value added per unit of risk, the Sharpe ratio.

Tanous: *Let's use the Sharpe Ratio.*

Sharpe: My ten guys, compared to random combinations of ten other guys—because you've got some diversification benefits by having ten. So we're going to, basically, take all the managers in the universe and make random combinations of ten of them. Now we're going to rank those combinations. Then we're going to take our guys and see where we are.

Tanous: *That's perfect.*

Sharpe: Okay. And the question is, what's the probability you're going to end up in the top third of the group?

Tanous: *Exactly.*

Sharpe: Well, unless you're a whole lot better than most people are at doing this, I would say that the probability is certainly going to be less than 50%.

Tanous: *Statistically, the chance would be one out of three, right?*

Sharpe: Well, yes. If you're no better than anybody else. If you're the average consultant, it's going to be one out of three. If you're below average, the probability will be less than one out of three.

Tanous: *A very sobering thought, Bill. Shall we move on to another topic? Let's talk about your non-academic activities. Do you have a consulting practice? I know you sit on a number of boards and you advise people. Could you tell us a bit about all this?*

Sharpe: I took some time off to set up a consulting firm, and did consulting. I had a two year R&D phase and then four years of full time, full staff, and all the rest. Basically, what I wanted to do was deal with the problems of the pension sponsor. Asset allocation, manager performance, manager selection, liability, asset/liability analysis and what have you. I knew there were big holes in the research on how you should analyze these things. One of my goals was to develop techniques and databases to fill those holes, and make it all practical.

Tanous: *Did you?*

Sharpe: Yes, I think so. Style analysis came out of that and some other work, liability analysis and such. The first two years it was R&D. Then it was real consulting, where we had to deliver or they wouldn't pay us! Now, what I'm doing is standard academic consulting with a few clients. Which is to say you call me and I'll definitely get back to you within a month! I don't travel much. If they want to talk to me in person they have to come here most of the time. So it's a different level. I work with a small number of funds, mostly pension funds, and one private family with a lot of marketable investments. I work with Union Bank of Switzerland, as a strategic advisor on the money management side. I'm over there a week every year.

Tanous: *What do you talk about?*

Sharpe: I talk about the study we did on the value stock effect in France, Germany, Switzerland, the U.K. and Japan. I'm not a research director, although I kibbitz there to some extent. The rest of the things I do as a consultant are with *[the Pension Fund]* sponsor side. I work with Calpers *[the California Public Employees Retirement System]* and AT&T, so I've got some fairly big clients, but I'm not the main-line consultant by any means. Episodically, I do style analysis of all their managers, and risk/return trade-offs, and Sharpe ratios and that sort of thing. It's analytic work. They do all the hard work. They have to get the data all ready. I just run it through various models. I also get involved in special studies. I don't do them typically, but I kibbitz or contribute or discuss with them how they ought to be done. It's a higher level consulting function. I'm not on-the-line consulting.

Tanous: *I have this vision of a pension fund in which you are a consultant and all the guys are waiting for you to leave the room before they dare ask about active managers!*

Sharpe: You probably think that I'm much harsher on that than I am. I'm skeptical, and I want to hold my clients' feet to the fire. I want them to look very carefully at just what they've been getting and look at it in a way that is as revealing as possible. I have clients who have very heavy passive stances and I have clients who have, basically, none. With the private family we are free to do anything we want—we don't have a committee, we don't have ERISA—this is all private money. I'm definitely bringing in some of my friends who do active management.

Tanous: *You actually have friends who do active management?*

Sharpe: Sure. Barr Rosenberg, Lang Wheeler, Martingale, Boston International Advisors, Rob Arnott at First Quadrant. We've got some money we want to invest, so we look around the world for very, very smart people who have a very well-developed story to tell. Therefore, we have reason to believe that whatever they're doing might persist.

Tanous: *Imagine sitting where I'm sitting and speculating on what it takes to get Bill Sharpe to recommend entrusting money to an active manager.*

Sharpe: First of all, I want a very well-defined product. I want a product to be defined relative to a benchmark. I want that benchmark very explicit. It can be a combination of standard benchmarks. In most cases it makes sense for it to be. But I want the manager to say, for example, we will manage relative to 60% this index and 40% that index. That's the benchmark. And we will control the process so that the difference between us and that benchmark will remain within bounds. And I want those bounds to be reasonably tight. The basic idea is, I want to know what it is they're doing and the benchmark, or a combination thereof, is a good way to focus on that. I want to know that they're controlling the process, so we're not taking wild bets. Then, I want to hear an awful lot about what the process is that leads to the risk they do take.

Tanous: *The methodology. . .?*

Sharpe: Absolutely. Back tests are always wonderful, we know that. I want some history of success, but you only see the people who have a history of success. You only see the products that have been successful. I also want a very convincing story as to why they are able, or that they have some information that either others don't have, or that they use information in ways that others don't.

Tanous: *Like a black box?* ["Black box" is Wall Street jargon for a computer program or formula that comes up with ways to beat the market. There hasn't been a completely successful one yet.]

Sharpe: No. It doesn't have to be a black box. But it has to be a story, for example, we are looking at the following things that most people don't look at. Or, we're looking at this—lots of people look at it, but we have done an analysis and know how to look at it in ways that other people haven't caught on to yet. You've got to have a very strong story.

Tanous: *Are there any intangibles like something about an individual you can't quite put your finger on?*

Sharpe: Well, they have to be swift and really smart. Active managers are by and large pretty smart people. And these people have got to be smarter than the average active manager, so that means they've got to be really smart. If somebody comes along and says what we do is we buy high yield stocks . . . Well, I can buy high yield stocks myself. I don't need them for that. Now, maybe that's a good strategy, but I'm not going to pay active fees for them to do it.

Tanous: *I think it's fascinating to hear someone as universally known in the industry as you describe what it takes to pick active managers.*

Sharpe: Well, it doesn't mean that even if you do all that, you're going to add value! But that's the way I do it.

Tanous: *How have you done?*

Sharpe: I don't usually pick active managers myself. Remember, in my view, active management is something you do with your "mad money." For my client, I came in and kibbitzed the managers they picked. I also try to slow them down from firing managers, since we know that costs money. I tend to get involved more on the firing side. On the hiring side, I tend to focus on the style issues. In other words, if they say we'd like to hire X, then I look at X's style and see if X is all growth stocks, then they're up to their ears in growth stocks *[i.e., they are not style diversified]*.

Tanous: *What is the practical application of this process?*

Sharpe: Here's an example: I've got a client who wants to put more money in active management. I'm trying to push a long/short strategy, which is my favorite active strategy.

Tanous: *Please tell us about that.*

Sharpe: In my best of all possible worlds, and if we get the costs in line, I would do all asset allocation with either index funds or futures—because you know what you've done—and there's no question as to what you've got. Then, if somebody comes along and says, "I'm really great at growth stocks. I can tell the good ones and the bad ones," I might say fine, you've convinced me. I want you to go long the ones you think are really good and short the ones you think are really bad. That means that, net-net, you bring me no exposure to growth stocks, or any other stocks. Basically, what you're bringing to me is T-Bills plus, we hope, something in addition. That's the only kind of active manager I'd ever hire in the best of all worlds.

Now, the problem is that, except in U.S. equities and some of the fixed income classes, the cost of going short is fairly high. As a result that's probably not the way to operate in all asset classes. I've given talks about this which I sometimes call "a modest proposal to revolutionize the investment management industry." It has another advantage. If you did this, and you wanted the typical multiply-managed pension fund in terms of risk and returns, you'd only put about 20% of your total money with active managers. That's because most active managers give you mostly passive returns plus a little bit of sizzle around the edge. And you're paying active fees for the whole thing.

So, if I give a hundred dollars to some highly diversified active manager, what I'm really doing is giving eighty or ninety dollars to an index fund with that style and the rest to a long/short strategy around that index fund. If I give a manager ten dollars, he might charge me twice the fee that he used to charge, but not ten times the fee. That's too blatant. That will also cut the cost of management fees, which is always helpful.

Tanous: *I want to understand the long/short strategy in terms of expected returns and risk.*

Sharpe: Basically you get the return on cash, plus selection returns. You add precisely the selection return and selection risk.

Tanous: *But there are some extraordinary risks in being short anything.*

Sharpe: Not if you're long the other thing. You don't get hammered if growth stocks go down because you've got them on both sides. In other words, the risk is the spread risk between your good growth stocks and your bad ones.

Tanous: *I see. The idea is that in the same style, in this case growth, you take the ones you think are terrible and the ones you think are good, and then go long the good ones and short the bad ones.*

Sharpe: Most managers, whatever domain they look at, growth stocks or whatever, have a list, and at the top of the list are the ones they think are really underpriced and great buys. Somewhere down at the bottom of the list are the ones they think are real dogs and are wildly overpriced. They don't hold those bad ones, but they could get more mileage out their information, if it is good, if they went short those bad ones and they're stopped out at zero.

Tanous: *Has this been back-tested?*

Sharpe: Well, it's been done, but it's hard to back-test because you don't really know the cost of being short. But there are managers who have done this and have strategies which have been long/short for several years.

Tanous: *Have you seen this new scheme that has been published in several magazines, where you buy the ten highest yielding stocks of the thirty in the Dow Jones Average once a year. They've back-tested it and it shows great results. It's called the Dow Dog theory.*

Sharpe: Let's see, you buy the highest yielding, so it's a value strategy. That's consistent with the value stock results. Remember the old Bob Newhart routine? He reads a news article which says that if you put a thousand monkeys to work on a thousand typewriters for a thousand days one of them will type the Gettysburg Address, and Newhart is saying: "Let's see, doctor, let's see. Wait a minute . . . look at this one: 'Four score and seven . . . bananas . . .'" *[lots of laughter].* If you put enough monkeys to work with enough computers and enough data one of them is going to find some strategy that would have just made you a fortune.

You can do that with random numbers, too. But on the other hand, the substance of your example could be the value stock effect and you've read Lakonishok. I do not dismiss the behavioral aspects that Joe *[Lakonishok]* and others have argued which is to say that there are all kinds of reasons from cognitive psychology that suggest that a real dog is likely to get underpriced, and maybe people know it's underpriced and they still don't want to hold it. It's hard socially. You think about going to your clients and saying I want you to buy this fund which holds the worst stocks in the world. We all like to hold stocks of great companies, what some people call admired stocks of admired companies. It's a cognitive error that people make over and over again in experiments. They identify something—it's called a representation error—and there are various experimental settings for this, but it basically says "great company, great stock." And if you think about that, and survey investment people, CFOs and CEOs, they make that assumption: it's a great company, it's a great stock. That's the growth stock story.

In an efficient market, you'd say: "great company, so-so stock." If the market is pricing stocks correctly, great company stocks are priced to be just as attractive, but no more so, than bad company stocks. Thus, an efficient market. People generally say "great company, great stock." Efficient market people would say "great company, average stock," and to the extent that people are making the error of saying "great company, great stock," it would follow that sometimes it would be true then that "great company, rotten stock." That is, it's over-priced. That's the value phenomenon.

Tanous: *Earlier you described asset allocation in the best of all worlds. You mentioned using derivatives* [futures], *which I found rather intriguing. Can you elaborate?*

Sharpe: I think derivatives, properly used, can be very helpful. *[Any security which is dependent on another is, technically, a derivative. That includes puts and calls, futures and other fairly straightforward securities as well as the very complex securities which have given derivatives a scary reputation.]* They can give you liquidity at low cost. For whatever reason, I want to be able, if need be, to change from stocks to bonds. It's a lot more efficient for me to hold a stock future and sell it and buy a bond future. At the same time you don't want to switch from bonds to stocks so we'll just trade our futures, and nobody has to move all the securities around and do all the recordkeeping and whatever. So there is a role for these types of contracts that allow you to buy big diversified portfolios in a very liquid and very low cost manner. You can go beyond that and ask what if, for whatever reason, I want 80% of the upside of the market but want to be assured that I won't take more than, say, ten percent of a downturn.

Tanous: *Sounds good to me.*

Sharpe: Well, if that proportion is right, I'll sell it to you. Remember, you're giving up some of the upside.

Tanous: *But if you're talking about an upside/downside ratio of 80% on the upside and only 10% on the downside, that sounds pretty good.*

Sharpe: I'm not saying that we'll floor you at a loss of ten percent. Basically, what happens is that if there's any upside, I keep 20%, and if there is a downside below 90%, I'll make up the difference to you. There are numbers that make it profitable for me to sell this to you. For everybody who buys one of those deals, somebody has got to sell it. There is an argument that there are people who will want to buy that insurance and there are people who, for the right price, will be willing to sell it.

Derivatives are a very efficient way to do this. So, despite all the brouhaha about derivatives, you have to know what the derivative is, and you have to know how much leverage there is, and you have to know what is going to happen to you in various places in the world, but once you get past that disclosure issue, these can be very valuable things.

There is also the credit issue. You have to know that the guy you're doing it with is going to make good if it goes against him. I do think these contracts are really very useful, but need to be used correctly with disclosure of the terms and the creditworthiness of the counter-party. There are a lot of issues there. It's all happened so fast that we haven't quite gotten all the pieces in place to make these as useful as they should be. But the futures markets are fine. Futures markets are not a problem. They've been doing that for a couple of hundred years and we know how to do it.

Tanous: *It's just that they are so complicated that most people, except people who are selling them, can't possibly understand them.*

Sharpe: If you don't understand what it is, don't buy it! But that's a burning issue and I think we are going to see a continuing move in this business toward separating the asset allocation decision and the active management decision. Ultimately you'll end up using index funds, futures and derivatives for the asset allocation. Active managers will be basically factor neutral, asset neutral, long/short, what have you. You don't have to get all the way there. In many contexts it will cost too much in transaction costs to do it.

Tanous: *At the end of the day, given all you are saying, are you looking to get better than market returns?*

Sharpe: The average dollar can never get better than market returns.

Tanous: *Then why are you doing all this?*

Sharpe: You're doing it (a) to make sure that you've got the asset allocation you want, and (b) to make sure you know just how much mad money you've put with active managers and how big your bets are. It's nice and clear. Here's our asset allocation. We've got this much in this index fund, that much in that one, that much in S&P futures. We know exactly what our asset allocation is and we know we're going to get it. We've taken twenty percent of our money and put it in the bank as margin, as collateral, for these guys who are making bets out here, and we know exactly how much we've got there, and we have at least some reasonable notion of how big the bets are. It's much better for your mental health than the situation you might have with a bunch of active managers. You don't really know what your asset allocation is. You estimate it as best you can, but it's not all that good. You're not absolutely certain how big your bets are. And there are other problems.

Tanous: *What advice might you have for our readers who invest in stocks?*

Sharpe: Decide how much risk you are willing to take. Choose an asset allocation that makes sense, given the level of risk. Try to select managers and funds that will give you that asset allocation. Keep your costs low, and be realistic about the extent to which even a brilliant active manager can add value over a comparable passive strategy. Nothing to it!

Investment advice from the winner of the Nobel Prize in economics! Remember, most of our academic community friends are proponents of efficient markets. If they believe that the market can be beaten at all, they are equally certain that it is rare and hard to do. Now Bill Sharpe does like a few active managers. He gave some examples. I was particularly taken by his long/short strategy. It essentially takes the market out of the picture and leaves you with rewards (if any) based on stock selection ability, which is the only thing you ought to pay a manager for. We'll discuss this again in the concluding chapters of the book.

Note the emphasis on keeping costs low. This is consistent with the theory that it is very difficult to beat the market, so every dollar you spend on fees, commissions, and other costs are dollars you have to make up just to be even with the market. That increases the challenge and the difficulty. This is good advice no matter what you believe in. I came away from the conversation with Bill Sharpe somewhat awed over how someone as brilliant and accomplished as he could still manage to make his work—specifically his important contributions to our knowledge of risk, style, and how the markets work—accessible to most people interested in the markets. Nice going, Bill.

PETER
LYNCH

What can I tell you about Peter Lynch? That if you had put
$10,000 in the Magellan Fund in 1977, the year he began to manage
it, your stake would have grown to $280,000 when he retired 13
years later? That's close to 30% per year. That under his steward-
ship, Magellan Fund was the top fund in America? That even after
Magellan's size kept roaring ahead to become the largest fund of all
time, Peter Lynch's performance did not falter? I could tell you all
this, but you probably already know it. After all, we are talking
about the most legendary mutual fund manager in history.

So, let's talk about some things you may not know. In my consulting business, consistency is one of the key traits we look for in
picking managers. Why? Because if I told you that a manager had a
30% return over ten years, that would be great. But what if most of
the performance came in the first two years when he had spectacular
results, and the last eight years were mediocre? Well, if you happened to buy the fund in the last eight years, you were out of luck
and your returns would be considerably lower than the ten year
average. But if a manager displays consistency in performance,
you've got a much better chance of making money with that fellow
no matter when you sign on.

Let's reintroduce Peter Lynch. Not only are his numbers extra-ordinary, but there were virtually no bad times to hop on board. Of such stuff legends are made.

If there is a single difficulty in interviewing Peter Lynch it is this: he is genuinely modest and unassuming. This is not an individual obsessed with himself or imbued with his self-importance. While that makes for one awfully nice human being, the trick is to scrape away the modesty to get at the underlying wisdom without making him feel that he is thumping his own chest, something he clearly doesn't like doing. In this interview, I tried hard to break some new ground with Peter Lynch, by provoking ideas and thoughts not nec-essarily covered in the three very successful books he's written. I think we succeeded. There are pearls of wisdom here, and all of us can profit from the advice of the master.

I interviewed Peter twice, the second time in Boston. Peter Lynch works in the picturesque setting of downtown Boston's financial dis-trict, where winding, cobblestone streets evoke the early history of the United States. The stately Federal period building in which he main-tains his office proudly flies the green flag of Fidelity Investments. In the small lobby of the building, a discreet directory lists the nine floors and their occupants. But one floor is not listed at all. That one, of course, is his. Anonymity is the price of great celebrity.

At the entry to Peter's office, the telltale signs of a security setup are visible, another legacy of fame. I am buzzed in and greeted by Peter's assistant, Shirley Guptill. Peter comes out to say hello and a few minutes later, we are seated on opposite sides of his desk. The office is small and functional; there are no trappings of great success here. Papers are scattered around the desktop in no discernible order. It is high noon and I am offered a sandwich. Peter has brought his from home in a little brown bag. Old habits die hard.

Tanous: *How did you first get interested in stocks? I recall a story about you as a teenage caddie.*

Lynch: I grew up in the '50s. Except for the decade of the '80s, which was slightly better, the '50s were the best decade in this century *[in the market]*. The Dow Jones Industrial Average tripled over the '50s. I grew up in an environment when stocks were going up. Somebody would talk about a stock and you'd look it up later and it would be higher. You'd look two years later and it was higher still. If somebody grew up in the '30s, I guess they'd have a different outlook on life.

Tanous: *So did you start investing right off the golf course?*

Lynch: No. I didn't have any money. My father took sick when I was seven. He died when I was ten. My mother went out to work. I had to help pay my way. There were scholarship jobs as caddies for students who needed financial aid. Tuition was only a thousand dollars and I got a three hundred dollar a year scholarship. I could earn more than seven hundred dollars a year in my part time jobs, so I had a little bit of extra money. So, when I was in college, I bought my first stock.

Tanous: *Do you remember what stock it was?*

Lynch: Yes. Flying Tiger. How could I not remember that one!

Tanous: *How did you do?*

Lynch: It's funny. I bought on the premise that air freight was going to be a big market. It's funny how things work out—something else happens and you get lucky. What actually made the stock a huge hit was that the Vietnam War came along. Not only did that change the air cargo market, but they used every plane they could find in the world to transport troops. It was a unique war. Everybody who went to Vietnam went there by airplane. They didn't go there by boat. The company wound up with an unbelievable amount of business, so the stock went up for a different reason than the one I bought it for. It went up from about 10 to about 80.

Tanous: *If you'd lost money, is there a chance we might not be talking today?*

Lynch: Well, I guess if I'd lost money over and over again then maybe I would have gone into another field. How do you know where your life is going to go in the end? You have no choice who your parents are; you have no choice where you grow up. I was lucky enough to have great public schools and go on to Boston College. It was only three or four miles away, so I could be a commuter. That's a lot of good fortune.

Tanous: *Peter, since you are arguably the most successful, as well as the most famous, fund manager of all time, and given the focus of this book, I want to zero in on process and methodology, especially on areas that I think will fascinate readers of this book. My first question relates to style. From my analysis, I'd say you have a growth bias, but you really can't be pegged to one style, unlike so many of the others in this book. In fact, in* Beating the Street, *you said: "I never had an overall strategy. My stockpicking was entirely empirical." That was some stockpicking! Apart from hanging around at malls, could you tell us a little bit about the selection process?*

Lynch: I guess I was always upset by the fact that they called Magellan a growth fund. I think that is a mistake. If you pigeonhole somebody and all they can buy are the best available growth companies, what happens if all the growth companies are overpriced? You end up buying the least overpriced ones. If you can find growth companies at very low valuations and with great balance sheets and great futures, that's where you invest. Only sometimes you find that these companies are terrific, but they are selling at 50 times earnings.

My premise has always been that there are good stocks everywhere. Some people say you can't buy companies with unions, or you can't buy companies in dying industries; for instance, who would ever buy a textile company? I mean, I didn't buy it but a company called Unifi went up, I think, a hundred fold in the textile industry. I missed it. But look at all the money I made with Chrysler and with Boeing. I also lost money with a few airlines and I made money with airlines. But you hear this concept that you can't make money if you ever buy a company that has a union, because the union will kill it. These are prejudices and biases that prevent people from looking at a lot of different industries. I never had that. I think there are good and bad stocks everywhere.

Tanous: *But in zeroing in on the process, one of the things that mystifies me is this: How much of your personal ability just can't be defined? I mean, how much of it is simply the keen, even instinctive, judgment that you have, and maybe that a lot of other people don't?*

Or is there some methodology that you hang your hat on that you, and maybe our readers, can turn to for process?

Lynch: I think that if you take my great stocks, and you ask a hundred people to visit them and spend a reasonable amount of time at it, 99 of them, assuming they had no prejudices and biases, would have bought those same stocks. I disagree with a part of your question. I don't think that with great stocks you need a Cray super-computer or an advanced Sun microstation to figure out the math.

Take this example of a company I missed: Wal-Mart. You could have bought Wal-Mart ten years after it went public. Let's say you're a very cautious person. You wait. Now ten years after it went public, it was a twenty-year-old company. This was not a startup. So it's now ten years after the public offering. You could have bought Wal-Mart and made 30 times your money. If you bought it the day it went public you would have made 500 times your money. But you could have made 30 times your money ten years after it went public.

The reason you could have done that is that ten years after it went public, it was only in 15% of the United States. And they hadn't even saturated that 15%. So you could say to yourself, now what kind of intelligence does this take? You could say, this company has minimal costs; they're efficient, everybody who competes with them says they're great, the products are terrific, the service is terrific, the balance sheet is fine, and they're self-funding. So you say to yourself, why can't they go to 17% *[saturation]*? Why can't they go to 21%? Let's take a huge leap of faith: why can't they go to 23%? All they did for the next two decades was roll it out. They didn't change it. I only wish they had started out in Connecticut instead of in Arkansas. I bought Stop & Shop because I saw it here in New England. I also bought Dunkin' Donuts because they were a local company.

Tanous: *You're touching on what I call the Great Peter Lynch Investment Theorem, which is to observe early business success as it occurs around you. I suppose it helps when the great companies happen to be in your own backyard and you see them every day. Of course, you've done well with other companies, too.*

Lynch: Yes, but I wish Home Depot had started here in Boston instead of in Atlanta. You could have bought Toys R Us after they had 20 stores open and made a fortune on it the next fifteen years.

You have to ask: why can't this company go from 20 stores to 400 stores?

Tanous: *There was something in one of your books that addresses your legendary stockpicking that rang a bell. Fidelity started inviting various corporations in for lunch or breakfast so that you could hear their stories firsthand. But then you contrasted those you invited with the companies who wanted to invite themselves over. Those companies were telling you the same story that they were telling everyone around the Street. Peter, you talk a lot in your books about communications, meetings, information sharing, and so forth, and that starts to give me a picture.*

Lynch: Again, I've always said that if you look at ten companies you'll find one that's interesting. If you look at 20, you'll find, two; if you look at 100, you'll find ten. The person that turns over the most rocks wins the game. That's the issue. If you look at ten companies that are doing poorly, you'll probably find nine companies that there is not much hope for. But maybe in one of them, one of their competitors has gone out of business, or the plant that caused them a lot of problems has been closed, or they got rid of the division that was losing money. You'll find one out of ten where something concrete has happened and the stock hasn't caught up with it. If you look at 20, you'll find two. It's about keeping an open mind and doing a lot of work. The more industries you look at, the more companies you look at, the more opportunity you have of finding something that's mispriced.

The theory is that the market is perfect and that all companies are fairly priced. And that is true in a majority of cases. If you find a company whose stock is on the new high list, generally they're doing well and they have a good future. You might also find companies where the stock is depressed and they're doing poorly, and you'll also find out that the company is having problems.

But maybe you'll find a company where the stock's gone from 40 to 4, it has no debt, it has two dollars per share of cash, and they might be losing money but, remember, they have no debt. It's a real challenge to go bankrupt if you have no debt. I find it interesting that people will buy a bunch of companies that are losing money. If you do, you might as well buy the company that has the good balance sheet and also has something going on that they can show—

maybe a new product that is working out well, or something else. Each story is different.

Tanous: *In fact, one of the people I interviewed, who is one of my favorite managers, is a guy called Richard Driehaus in Chicago. The way he put it is that a lot of people play the piano but how many become virtuosos? The point is to become a virtuoso you've got to practice a lot.*

Lynch: And what I'm saying is that you could have bought Microsoft three years after it went public and made 30 times your money. Now I didn't buy it. I don't own a computer. I can't turn on a computer. My kids can do it, my wife can do it, but there are millions and millions of people who know about software. Now maybe you don't know who's going to win the hardware game. Is Compaq going to win? Is Acer going to win? Is it going to be Dell or IBM? There are lots of guys selling PCs. But somebody should have been able to figure out that Microsoft was the one that had the operating system that was going to win.

Well, people could have bought Microsoft but, instead, many people were buying biotechnology companies, which are very hard to understand. That doesn't make any sense to me. What I'm saying is that there's a 100% correlation between what happens to the company and what happens to the stock. The trick is that it doesn't happen that way over one week, or even over six or nine months, and that's terrific. Sometimes the fundamentals are getting better and the stock is going down. That's what you're looking for. The stock market and the stock price don't always run in synch.

There are two basic things. First, there can be a mistake that applies just to this company. Or second, you'll have the occasional corrections where the whole market goes down. These great companies, where everything is fine, get back to a price where you get a chance to buy them again just because the market dropped sharply. So you can either have a general market correction that gives you this opportunity, or you'll have ten companies that are depressed and you just might find one of them where the market is wrong. So that's what you're trying to find.

If you look at the electric utility industry, you might find two or three that are mispriced. If you look at the insurance industry or the retailing industry, which is out of favor—I mean, it used to be really in favor three or four years ago, now it's out of favor—but you don't want to get pigheaded. Take banking. In the early nineties, that industry was quickly going south. You had to wait till it got better. I don't buy things just because they're depressed. I wait until the fundamentals get better. That's what happened in the banking system. You can't wait until everything is dramatically improved. But you have to wait for symptoms, signs, even some evidence that things are getting better, and not just the hope that it's getting better.

Tanous: *You said that you don't operate a computer. That thing behind your desk looks like a fancy computer to me.*

Lynch: All that gives is stock quotes. It's a dumb terminal.

Tanous: *It's getting hard to function without knowing how to operate a computer, isn't it?*

Lynch: Warren Buffett uses his to get in on a bridge game. He's done pretty well the last ten years without a computer. I had dinner with him last week and he doesn't have a computer in his office. He just uses one to play bridge. You can play bridge with somebody in Washington, or Arizona, or France.

Tanous: *Speaking of banking, I interviewed Michael Price. His Chase story is real interesting.*

Lynch: Mine was Bank of America. I bought two percent of it. I think I started buying it at 16 and it went down to 8. But it was getting better and it wasn't going to go bankrupt.

Tanous: *You bought it at 16 and it went down to 8? And you stuck with it?*

Lynch: Yeah. Here's the example of a case where Bank of America wasn't doing very well. But it was over 100% retail-funded. A lot of banks get their money by selling money to money market funds or commercial paper to businesses. Bank of America's loans were all backed up by retail deposits. With some of the banks like Bank of New England or Continental Illinois, if you're half wholesale-funded, and people hear you've got problems, not only will they probably not renew your paper, but if they renew it, they want 200 basis points more. So your cost of money goes up because you have problems, and now you've got more problems.

But Bank of America didn't have to pay more for their deposits because all their deposits were FDIC insured. The public didn't care about the headlines that Bank of America wasn't doing well. There wasn't going to be a run on this bank. They had more branches, I think, than there were post offices in California. They may even have had more branches than McDonalds. So, if you looked at the company and said this is not the same situation as some of those banks in Texas, or some of those banks in New England (where they are basically wholesale-funded and the deposits are going to disappear, or they're going to have to pay 200 or 300 basis points more, and they're going to get squeezed), you would have realized that this bank did not have that kind of problem.

Tanous: *I'm on the board of a bank. Why didn't I figure this out?*

Lynch: That's one of my arguments. People who've been in the restaurant industry should have seen Taco Bell, they should have seen Pizza Hut, they should have seen Kentucky Fried Chicken, they should have seen Chili's, they should have seen Dunkin' Donuts, they should have seen McDonalds, Applebee's and many more. And when the companies lose their edge, these same people will see the slippage months ahead of the professional investors. Fundamentals deteriorate and the people in the business could sell six months or a year ahead of the professionals. They see the industry; they have great information. But they throw it away.

Tanous: *Peter, you really do make sense when you articulate this commonsense approach to investing. Now let's go to the heart of the issue. In this book, I'm trying to engage the debate on something you alluded to earlier, the efficient market theory. This is where your opinion is so important, because you and Warren Buffett are the two people whose names always come up as examples of very successful active managers. Let me start my question by quoting from* One Up on Wall Street. *"It's very hard to support the academic theory that the market is irrational when you know somebody who just made a twenty fold profit in Kentucky Fried Chicken and who explained in advance why the stock was going to rise. My distrust of theorizers and prognosticators continues to the present day."*

Now the academics say the market is efficient. Everything that is known about a stock is in the price, and you just can't predict what stocks are going to go up except by chance. So, of course, people with opposing viewpoints say, what about Peter Lynch, what about Warren Buffett, and a few other great names. The academics say, look, these guys are the outliers on a normal distribution curve. Okay. To them, the Peter Lynches and Warren Buffetts are the outliers on the right tail of the distribution curve, the lucky orangutans that write Romeo and Juliet *by pure luck. How do we answer that?*

Lynch: Well, you could answer by saying that there are going to be one million tennis matches this weekend. And there are going to be 500,000 people who lose and 500,000 people who win. Therefore, should people not practice tennis, should they not practice their serve? Should they not practice their backhand? The question is; why not be the winner rather than the loser? You could be a better investor if you looked at the balance sheet, if you knew what the company did, if you use the information you have. You would simply do a better job. Just like you would be a better tennis player if you worked on your weaknesses and improved your strengths. The concept is that maybe we should ban tennis, since half the people are going to lose so the other half can win.

What the academics are saying is that people have done a bad job investing, therefore they shouldn't invest. As a result, people become convinced by the academics and the media that the large investors all have the edge with their large computers and their MBA degrees, and that the small investor—I don't know what that means except maybe all the people under five foot two—the small investor doesn't have a chance. But what happens is the small investor buys this bill of goods that they don't have a chance. He or she goes in and maybe buys an option on the stock. Or they do one minute of research, or no research, and buy a piece of junk. Or they buy a company with no sales or no earnings and they lose more. And when they lose money, do you know who they blame? They blame the institutions because of program trading, or some other excuse.

When they shop for a car, and they buy a clunker, they don't blame institutions. No! They say, my God, I should have done some research. When they buy a refrigerator, they ask their neighbors, what's a good refrigerator? They get *Consumer Reports.* In all phases of their life, if they make a mistake and they buy a stupid house at the wrong price, they're not going to blame institutions. But when it comes to investing, they're looking for a scapegoat and all this stuff is feeding on itself. These people are being told they don't have a chance, its a big casino, and they act accordingly. Then they get bad results. It's sort of a self-fulfilling prophecy. You convince the public that the odds are against them so they behave like they're in a casino. They go in there and buy options—which is like betting on number twenty-six. It's like playing poker without looking at your cards.

Tanous: *You once said a share of stock is not a lottery ticket.*

Lynch: True. But a better example is that people play cards, bridge, or poker. Now suppose they don't look at their cards. What kind of results will they get? That's like investing without doing research. I don't mean just reading the annual reports or the quarterly reports. I'm saying if you own Chrysler, you ought to find out if somebody is coming up with a better Jeep, or somebody is coming up with a better minivan. You don't get that from reading stuff, you get that by driving the new vehicle that's coming out.

Tanous: *I guess the appropriate expression here would be "kicking the tires."*

Lynch: Literally ten years after Chrysler came out with the minivan, they still have a 60% share of the minivan market. This is a stock that in 1982 you could have bought and made ten times or twenty times your money. You could have bought it in 1990 and made six times your money. In 1990, they were upgrading Jeep which no one had done much with over the years. They bought AMC to get Jeep. They've been turning Jeep around ever since. If you were a car dealer in 1982 and 1983, or in 1990 and 1991, you should have said, wow, this company has got a lot going for it.

Chrysler wasn't the only one. When Ford introduced Taurus/Sable, which was an enormous hit, I think Ford went up five times. So you could have made money in Ford. There may be only a few times a decade when you make a lot of money. How many times in your lifetime are you going to make five times on your money? I'm not saying these stocks are available every week. I think that's what people are missing. I'm not saying that you can wake up today and look around and the average person is going to find a good stock. Maybe once every year, or once every two years, or maybe once every six months you want to be able to find one of these. The average person ought to be able to follow five or six companies. Remember, there are 15,000 public companies. So follow five or six companies, and know these companies very well. But if none of them is attractive, don't own any of them.

Tanous: *Wouldn't you agree that for most people mutual funds are the way to go? And, if we use that as a premise, it still leads to another mystery in the selection process. That mystery, of course, is the great active versus passive debate. You recognized this in one of your books. In* Beating the Street, *you stated that 75% of all mutual funds don't beat the market.*

Lynch: That was true in the eighties. I didn't say that was going to last for the next 25 years. I said in the '80s, 75% of funds didn't beat the market.

Tanous: *You don't think we're stuck with that number forever?*

Lynch: No.

Tanous: *My question is, whether it's 75% or some other percentage, what sort of criteria would you recommend we use to pick funds? Most of us only have past performance to look at. In your book, you cite a lot of the dangers of only using past performance.*

Lynch: Particularly the last quarter or last six month's performance. If you buy the hottest fund of the last three months, I don't think that's a good formula.

Tanous: *There are different studies on this.*

Lynch: Before you get to that step, you've got to understand what kind of funds you have. If you buy ten emerging growth funds and all these companies have small sales and are very volatile companies, buying ten of those is not diversification.

Tanous: *Of course not. You're not diversified by style.*

Lynch: What I'm saying is people have to say: What do I want? Do I want to have five funds, with one fund in international markets because I think over the next ten to twenty years those markets are going to grow faster than the United States? Maybe in the near future gold is going to be the place to be. Inflation is going to heat up. They have to decide what they want, and then put together a portfolio they are happy with. And that's what some firms will do for them, even over the telephone. They'll explain this like a waiter. They'll say in our fund group this fund is a very conservative fund.

It's a third in bonds, it's two thirds in stocks that pay dividends, very large mature companies. But, in addition, we have this other fund that just buys very rapidly growing, high octane small companies. Then we have one that just buys quality blue chip growth stocks. Then we have another one that buys emerging market stocks. It buys in 40 emerging markets that are growing at twice the rate of the ten largest countries in the world. The point is: this is a more important question than who the hot fund manager is over the next year.

Tanous: *That's absolutely right. But that is exactly the point the academics are making. They'll say you're absolutely right. The way to diversify and do this intelligently is to pick style and size. In fact, Gene Fama's three factor model [page 171] is based on these components of risk and returns. But the academics will also quickly add: Decide how much you want in small-cap. Decide how much you want in value stocks. Decide how much you want in growth or international stocks. And then go out and pick the corresponding index funds. Stop worrying about which manager is better or worse than the other guy. Does that make sense to you?*

Lynch: I think if people aren't willing to do homework and they're not willing to do research, maybe they should buy an index fund of the Russell 2000 or the Wilshire 5000, and buy an S&P 500 index fund. Those people should just say, I think over time historically small-cap stocks do better than big-cap stocks and I'll put half my money in big stocks, half my money in small stocks and so forth.

Tanous: *Okay. But I say, that's not good enough for me. I appreciate that advice. It's very nice. It sounds sort of safe. But I want to do better. I'll tell you what I want: I want to find another Peter Lynch! Can you help me do that?*

Lynch: There's no such thing as a hereditary talent for picking stocks. What helped me the most is logic, because it taught me to identify the inherent illogic of Wall Street. I believe I mentioned in my book that Wall Street thinks like some of the ancient Greeks did. They'd sit around for days and debate how many teeth a horse had. The right answer is to go check a horse.

In picking funds, just using past performance doesn't seem to work. Here's an approach I used: several colleagues and I undertook an assignment to pick money managers for a nonprofit organization.

We figured that in a changing market, different styles of investing go in and out of favor. If you own only one fund, you might wind up with a manager who lost his touch or your fund's style may be out of favor. A value fund, for example, can do well for three years and relatively poorly for the next couple of years. So the first idea is to diversify by style and pick funds in the basic categories. One is capital appreciation. Magellan is one of these. Value funds are another. There are quality growth funds, emerging growth funds, special situation funds and also international funds. But you have to stay with them for the long term. If value funds are out of favor and growth is in favor, Mario Gabelli and Michael Price can't be expected to perform as well as a growth fund.

In deciding which managers to pick, it helps to look for a consistent and steady performer. Look at the fund's performance in different markets. Some funds lose more than others in a bear market but gain more on the rebound. The ones to avoid are the funds that lose more and gain less. In our search, we picked one value manager, two quality growth managers, two special situation funds, three capital appreciation funds, a fund that invests in companies that consistently raise their dividends, three convertible securities funds, and one emerging growth fund. Out of this group, our hope is to produce a different star performer who beats the market every year. If we have enough all-stars to counteract the poor performers, we hope to beat the dreaded market averages.

Tanous: *What is your opinion of technical analysis?*

Lynch: The problem with technical analysis is that somebody could love the stock at 12 and hate it at 6. In pure technical analysis, the stock itself will show what's going on. You just have to watch the movement of the stock price. But to be fair, it doesn't apply to all the stocks. Technical analysts will look at maybe ten formations *[stock price graphs]* and one will tell them something. So they might like something at 12 and hate it at 6 because the formation has changed. That bothers me.

But, with that as the background, I have traditionally liked a certain formation. It's what I call the electrocardiogram of a rock. The stock goes from, say, 50 to 8. It has an incredible crater. Then it goes sideways for a few years between 8 and 11. That's why I call it the EKG of a rock. It's never changing. Now you know if something goes right with this company, the stock is going north. In reality, it's probably just going to go sideways forever. So if you're right it goes north and if you're wrong it goes sideways. These stocks make for a nice research list. You look at stocks that have bottomed out.

It's like trying to catch a falling knife. When it's going from 50 to 8, it looks cheap at 15; it looks cheap at 12. So you want the knife to stick in the wood. When it stops vibrating, then you can pick it up. That's how I see it on a purely technical basis. If you look at the fundamentals, you say, wow, at 15 it's selling at 3 times earning power. It's got 12 dollars a share in cash. You can show fundamental reasons why you should jump in at 15. But if you were a technician, you wouldn't see it that way. From a technical standpoint, this is the only formation that would show me something.

Tanous: *But the problem with that formation is that that flat EKG could go on forever. What makes it go up?*

Lynch: That's why the stock is on your research list, not on your buy list. You investigate and you find that of these ten stories, this one has something going on. They're getting rid of a losing division, one of their competitors is going under, or something else.

Tanous: *So we're back to fundamental analysis.*

Lynch: The process cuts 15,000 public companies down to 20.

Tanous: *An interesting screening technique.*

Lynch: Yes.

Tanous: *I'm interviewing one quant, David Shaw, who has a reputation for being mysterious and secretive. Do you have any experience with or opinion about quants and the use of super computers to find inefficiencies in the market?*

Lynch: Yes. 20th Century Growth has had a good record. Brad Lewis at Fidelity went to Annapolis, then Wharton, and was a basic fundamental analyst and loved quantitative things. Now he's running Disciplined Equity and Stock Selector using artificial intelligence with an incredible amount of variables. He's really in the forefront of quantitative methods. He runs a high speed computer to chew out hundreds and hundreds of variables.

Tanous: *What do you think of it?*

Lynch: It works. I've seen the results. This is a very objective business. That's not true in everything. For example, people might say, I'm dealing with the top urologist or the top cardiovascular surgeon. But who's in the bottom quartile of cardiovascular surgeons? Did you ever hear anybody say I'm going to a bottom quartile orthopedic surgeon? I mean, everybody thinks they're dealing with the top neurosurgeon. Have you ever heard anybody say, I'm going to see this person and he or she is at the bottom? But our business is objective. We measure everybody. So I'm saying that this guy, Brad Lewis, has done a terrific job.

Your question was what's my opinion of quants? When I see a quant who has done a good job over a period of time, I say there must be a method to this. There's been a long enough period to prove it. But it has to make sense. I mean, if they sit in the park with 23 varieties of trees and the method involves observing which leaves come off and that worked, I still wouldn't put my money in it. But the quantitative method has made sense, dealing with profit margins, inventory turnover, balance sheet changes and hundreds of variables that you can't possibly balance in your head. They might say, right now the market is pricing earnings momentum, so they give more weight to that. They might say that at certain moments in time, certain factors are more important than others, and that makes sense to me. There are a certain number of variables that are impossible for a human being to deal with and process all together.

I do it both ways. If the results are positive, I ask if it makes sense. If the answer is yes, then I would invest on it.

Tanous: *I want to share with you an excerpt from an interview I did with Bill Sharpe, who won the Nobel Prize in Economics. Like most academics, he's a believer in passive management. At a lecture at University of Virginia's Darden School in 1990, he specifically cited your great performance and your outstanding selection ability. When I discussed this with him, he also said: "If you take the Fidelity funds as a group, I haven't done this, but I'll bet if you took a dollar-weighted portfolio of the Fidelity equity funds—before load fees at least— you would probably be in pretty good shape. You probably got close to or maybe even beat the indexes." That's quite a compliment.*

Lynch: We've had so many good funds. There were the Destiny I and Destiny II Funds which have been incredible funds. Equity Income I,

Equity Income II, Growth and Income, Contrafund, New Millennium, Stock Selector, which we just mentioned, Puritan, we're loaded with good funds. Our Fidelity Growth Fund has beaten its peers and the market by a wide margin over the last ten years. I've said that in the '80s, 75% of the funds didn't beat the market. The same is true if you take the last ten years. We've had lots of funds that have beaten the heck out of the market the last ten years.

Tanous: *On another subject, Peter, I thought your piece in* Worth *magazine* [published by Fidelity] *in which you defended corporate downsizing and layoffs was rather courageous.*

Lynch: The wrong people are being blamed. In the last 30 years, we've added 54 million jobs in America. Europe, which has a third more people, has added 10 million jobs. Ten! They're just starting to downsize in Europe. There are 20 million people out of work in Europe. That's 11% of the workforce. We're at 5 percent. The United Kingdom hasn't added a job in over thirty years. The workforce is exactly the same as it was in 1965. In the '80s, the five hundred largest American companies eliminated three million jobs. But the country added 18 million jobs. In the so-called "greed decade," we added 18 million jobs! That's because all these little companies started up and medium-sized companies grew. Together they added 21 million jobs. They don't have that in Europe. You don't have small and medium-sized companies growing there. So if you blame all of business for layoffs, you miss the fact that there are a lot of people creating jobs. You don't hear about those folks. You know, there were 2.1 million businesses started in the '80s. At an average of ten jobs each, that's 21 million new jobs. You never hear about these folks. If you, me, and Shirley start a business, you never hear about it.

When United Technologies lays off 5,000 people or AT&T lays off 30,000, you hear about that. If you put together AT&T and their spin-offs, at the time they broke up the company they had a million employees. One out of every 100 American employees worked for the telephone company. If you put it back together now, they'd have less than 700,000 employees. They process twice the telephone calls, fifty times the data communications, a hundred times the faxes, a millionfold of cellular calls, with 30% fewer employees. Now, would America be better off if they had gone to two million employees? I would argue no. What you hope would happen is that most of the reduction was from a lot of people who retired, while those who did get laid off had a good training program and help finding other jobs. You don't want to be harsh about this, but America is better off with a great telecommunication system that is efficient and low cost. If they had three million workers, we'd be paying more for telephone calls.

Tanous: *The overall unemployment rate didn't go up. So can you even argue that most people didn't find work?*

Lynch: Well, obviously some of them didn't. But nobody likes to lay workers off. This theory that they're a bunch of Scrooges who enjoy saying "whom can we fire this week? Maybe we can find some people whose children are having medical problems and lay them off. That would really be bad," is not the way it is. No one likes to lay off employees. It's either you cut your workforce by 10 percent and survive, or the whole hundred percent lose their jobs, like the Pan Ams of the world.

Tanous: *Peter, why is everybody picking on your old fund, Magellan? It seems to be constantly in the press these days.*

Lynch: I guess because it's the biggest and I think there are now five people at *The Wall Street Journal* who cover mutual funds. There used to be nobody. More people own mutual funds than own stocks now, so there's a lot more coverage. And Magellan is the biggest fund. So it's not surprising that it gets coverage. If you watch a basketball game and at the end of the game the score is 105 to 95, no one says, wait a second, in the third quarter, you lost 28 to 18, what was the story in the third quarter, before you won the game 105 to 95? Since Jeff Vinik has been running the fund it's beaten the market and it's beaten 80% of all funds. That's the game. He's run it for four years, and that's the game. *[Days after this interview, Jeff Vinik resigned to form his own investment management company. Fidelity Magellan is now managed by Robert Stansky, who delivered an outstanding record for ten years with the Fidelity Growth Fund.]*

Tanous: *The rap today on Magellan is that, with 56 billion dollars under management, beating the market is not only very difficult but it involves making major bets.*

Lynch: That was true at 10 billion and 20 billion too. You can have a 100 million dollar fund and have 80 stocks exactly clone the market. You put a couple of energy stocks in, a couple of drug stocks, and others. You can have a small fund with 80 stocks and clone the market, or a big fund with 2,000 stocks. But people sometimes miss the point. If the airlines are one percent of the S&P 500, you might want nine percent in your fund. Energy is 13% of the index; but you say we'll have zero. If you have certain things that make up the index, the index might have, say, two percent in banking, but if you love banking, you make it 14% of the fund. If you're right, you beat the hell out of the index. If you're wrong, you're wrong.

Tanous: *Isn't that what you're being paid to do?*

Lynch: That's right. But here's the point. The New York Stock Exchange is, I think, close to $6 trillion *[in market capitalization]*. If you look at the 200 largest stocks outside the U.S., you're looking at a couple of trillion dollars. Look at NASDAQ and you're talking a couple of trillion. It's not like Fidelity is $500 billion or a trillion. All of our equity assets are, I believe, less than $300 billion.

Tanous: *That's for all of Fidelity?*

Lynch: Yes. Fidelity is around $400 billion but the equity assets are less than $300 billion, or only five percent of the New York Stock Exchange. So its not like we're managing $4 trillion and the world market is $8 trillion.

Tanous: *As they say, it's a nice problem to have.*

Lynch: If you want to beat the market by a lot, you'll have to buy a small fund and take bigger risks. But which small fund do you buy? If you went and picked one, the odds are four out of five that you would not have done as well as Magellan.

Tanous: *I see. That's because, to bring it back to the point you just made, Magellan beat four out of five, or 80%, of all the funds.*

Lynch: Exactly. And it's pretty much the same over time.

Tanous: *You're not managing a fund any more. I must tell you that I loved your quote that nobody on their deathbed ever said "I wish I had spent more time at the office." I'm aware of the charities you're involved in and the things that interest you, but I want to know if you* *have any plans to get back in the business beyond what you're doing now.*

Lynch: No. I'm done running a fund. I did it for thirteen years. And it was a wonderful thing. One out of every hundred Americans was in my fund.

Tanous: *One out of a hundred?*

Lynch: For many of these people, $5,000 is half their assets other than their house. And there are people you meet who say we sent our kids to college, or we paid off the mortgage. What I'm saying is that it's very rewarding to have a fund where you really made a difference in a lot of people's lives. A lot of people manage lots of money, but if it's for some state pension fund or for a huge company, the manager probably has 20 customers. It's amazing when you make a difference in a lot of peoples lives. It's comforting and it's a lot of responsibility, and when it works out you're very pleased.

Tanous: *But now that you're not managing a fund anymore, what do you do with your life?*

Lynch: I used to leave for the office at 6 A.M. six days a week. The last ten years I ran Magellan, I got home late and traveled twelve days a month. Now I leave for the office around eight, four or five days a week. I see my wife; I see my kids. I haven't worked a Saturday in six years. I do about two days a week of Fidelity stuff and about three days a week of not-for-profit stuff. At Fidelity, I work with young analysts. We bring in six new ones a year and I work with them one-on-one. I write four or five times a year for *Worth* magazine and I'm a trustee of the funds.

Tanous: *Since you stopped managing the fund actively, have you seen anything in the markets that has changed your views about either the way the market works or the value of investing in stocks over the long term?*

Lynch: Zero. Human nature hasn't changed much in about 40,000 years. Corporate profits have their ups and downs. Markets have their ups and downs. Companies turn around; companies deteriorate. I don't think these things are going to change in the next hundred years.

The lingering thought you come away with after speaking with Peter Lynch is how simple he makes it all sound. For generations, people have spent millions of dollars devising theories and schemes to invest successfully. Today, quants use Cray super computers and state-of-the-art mathematics with algorithms that will unlock the key to successful investing. Peter Lynch's alternative advice: hang out at the mall. See what stores and products are doing well. Do your own research.

The very logic of his approach is difficult to refute. "There's a hundred percent correlation between what happens to the company and what happens to the stock," he told us. That phrase sticks. In other words, if you are successful at identifying good companies, you have also identified good stocks. The examples he cited to back up this theory are compelling.

Of course, for most of us, the way to invest is to pick a manager or a mutual fund and let them do the picking. After all, Peter also stressed the importance of doing your homework. Do you have the desire and the time to do the homework? He's probably right when he suggests that most Americans do more research when buying a refrigerator than they do in buying a stock. There's no question, logic is Peter's long suit. Maybe he's got the right idea. Maybe we have just overcomplicated the whole process of picking successful stock market investments. Maybe a return to common sense is the best approach. It sure worked for him.

LAURA J. SLOATE

Laura Sloate is no novice at the craft of investing. She has been running her firm, Sloate, Weisman, Murray & Company since 1974. She earned her B.A. from Barnard College and an M.A. from Columbia. She is also a Chartered Financial Analyst. Although Laura has been blind since the age of six, nothing in her schedule or work activity reflects any disadvantages she might have. In fact, she told The New York Times that nowadays, with a guide dog and some electronic equipment, it's a level playing field.

Level or not, Laura does quite well on that playing field. Her distinguished performance record over time earns her Guru status. She is widely admired by her peers, and especially by her clients, for whom she manages over $1 billion. The firm's net annualized returns for the five years ended in 1995 were in excess of 24% and the seven year returns were 20%, exceeding the S&P 500 by a considerable margin.

Another exciting feature of her performance is that Laura's up-market capture ratio is consistently over 100, while her down-market ratio is often negative. In plain English, she does better than the market when the market is going up but when the market is going down, she either loses less than the market or actually makes money even though the averages are down.

133

We met in Laura Sloate's midtown Manhattan office. The office is equipped technologically to allow Laura to work unconstrained. An electronic voice chants the latest news off the tape and quotes can be called up in the same manner. During our meeting, Laura shared some very precise advice on selecting stocks and what to look for.

Tanous: *How did you first get interested in stocks?*

Sloate: I guess there are two parts to that question. How I got interested in stocks, and then how I got interested in going into the business. My dad was an investor since the '50s. He always had annual reports around, and every New Year's Eve, early in the evening when the market closed, he'd call me in and let me add up his portfolio. I'd do it in my head and he'd do it by pencil and often I'd beat him.

Tanous: *How old were you then?*

Sloate: Oh, ten or eleven. In those days I knew the annual reports by how the covers felt. I lost my sight when I was six.

Tanous: *You knew the reports by how the covers felt?*

Sloate: Every annual *[report]* has a different feel. I'll give you an example. *[Laura shuffles through a stack of papers and documents on her desk and picks one up.]* This here is Harrah's annual. I remember that on Friday I put the Diebold annual down here. I remember it's smooth . . . *[She shuffles through some more papers and quickly picks one report out of the stack. She hands it to me.]* See. *[It was the Diebold annual report.]*

Tanous: *That's remarkable.*

Sloate: And if you come back three days from now I'll do the same thing. This is the Saks Fifth Avenue prospectus. I remember putting it in here and that it was fat. *[Laura "reads" in several ways. Sometimes she has readers come in and record information on cassettes. More often, she scans written material into her computer which digitizes it and, then, using special software, reads it back to her.]* I'll feel one of these once and remember it forever. Here's *Business Week.* I guess I started this kind of young. That's how I knew about stocks.

Getting back to how I got interested in the business, I went to high school and college. In fact, the other day my brother sent me an article about me from the *New York Journal* of 1963. I was eighteen. The article said that I was an intense listener, that I read 12 hours a day, and I was going to have my Ph.D. by the time I was 26. What ended up happening was that I did go to college and finished in three-and-a-half years. Then I got my master's in six months. After that, I went to law school for a year, and decided I didn't like it. So I left after a year and went to Columbia to study history. I finished my course work and my orals for a Ph.D. in 18 months, but, by then, I was kind of burnt out academically. It was the time of the Columbia riots.

I decided I wanted to get a job. I was ill-equipped to get one because all my work was as an academic and I had no working skills. In those days, there were no computers. I read about some go-go fund manager named Fred Mates who was going to build his firm by taking ordinary people who knew nothing about the market. So I went down there. He was a charitable individual; he hired me to be an analyst for his fund.

Tanous: *What was his fund?*

Sloate: It was called the Mates Fund. It was one of these go-go stock funds of the late '60s. I started to read things. I was living at home and I hired a secretary to read to me. After paying her salary I was making, like, forty dollars a week. Mates laid me off four months later. The fund soon went out of business. I ran around looking for work, and finally found somebody who hired me for $200 a week as a junior analyst in the research department. I paid $140 to my secretary and lived on $60 dollars a week. I started to read accounting and financial books and tried to learn how to pick stocks. That's how it all started. I never went back to Columbia.

Tanous: *What were you going to get your Ph.D. in?*

Sloate: American History. The reason it was going to be American history is that my Master's was in modern European. It was much more practical to get readers to read English than French or Italian. If you got into European history you were definitely getting into languages.

Instead, I got into the market and I never left. I was a research analyst for a rising star named Meyer Berman. Then we went over to Neuberger Berman in 1970. I was there for about a year. I went to Burnham and Company. During this period, I had 22 stock recommendations in a row that went up. Starting in 1973, I was pulling back on my recommendations because I couldn't find any stocks that were cheap enough. Management was on my case because we were paid through commissions. At that point, I realized that if you worked for a big firm, you would be controlled by the management. *[Since Laura could not find stocks she liked, she was unable to generate commissions for the firm through her recommendations. Of course, 1973 was the beginning of one of the worst bear markets in history, so it was a good time* not *to be buying stocks.]*

Tanous: *What happened after that?*

Sloate: I met a fellow named Neil Weisman in 1971. We became very friendly. We decided we had one shot to go out and start our own thing. We were 29 years old. So we started Sloate, Weisman in 1974 as an equity research boutique.

Tanous: *I want to get into your approach to investing, Laura. Yours is a value approach. Could you describe your approach to value investing and how it might differ from some other managers.*

Sloate: We believe that every situation, at some point in time, presents value. In order for value to be brought out there has to be a catalyst. Sears sat with value wrapped in it for about 20 years.

Now value, in my mind, is a mirage. If you look at many of the statistical screens used by value managers, many of the companies listed are bankruptcy candidates. They may look attractive relative to book value and inventory value, but the numbers only tell one side of the story.

We look for a catalyst to bring out the value. It could be a management change, like George Fisher leaving Motorola to go over to Kodak. Or a restructuring, like the Federated *[Department Stores]* management coming in and turning around Federated initially, then integrating the Macy's and Broadway Stores acquisitions—bringing the operating margins from the low single digits to the low double digits. The catalyst could also be a secular event. For instance, two or three years ago, we invested in retail drug store stocks because we recognized that the delivery of prescription drugs was becoming a very important part of medical care.

Tanous: *Was that the catalyst?*

Sloate: The secular catalysts were the expansion of the prescription drug benefit and the change in the delivery of prescription drugs. The drug stores were computerizing and preparing to deal with third party payers, such as managed care companies. We bought Revco, Rite-Aid and Eckerd. We still own Rite-Aid.

Clinton's proposed revitalization of the health care system was the catalyst for the drug stocks. That knocked down drug stock prices to valuations not seen since the early 1980s. We bought a couple of them. In retrospect, we sold too early, but the stocks had reached our price objective.

We find our ideas through fundamental research. We read a lot of trade journals—over 100 a month. We also read 7 or 8 daily newspapers, company documents, and, of course, we get tons of Wall Street research. In our line of work, we get two feet of material a day from the Street. But, the problem with Street research is its agenda. It's investment banking agenda-ed. It's not very innovative, but it is very informative. We read Street research for background and to understand consensus, because consensus is reflected in the price of the stock.

Tanous: *Are you making the point that Street research might be a little bit tinged by who the firm's investment banking clients are?*

Sloate: I would like to think it's only a little bit. But it isn't a little bit. It's a lotta bit.

Tanous: *But you also said that the research is chock full of information. So it's not the opinion you're looking for as much as the facts.*

Sloate: Right. But you must know the facts and the opinion, and you must know the consensus earnings estimates, because that's what the broad range of portfolio managers are buying.

Tanous: *Isn't it too late then?*

Sloate: Well, it may or may not be. You could have an epileptic fit every time you miss something. You have to know what the Street is saying. But you don't necessarily follow what they say. We use Street research as an information source. Our process is much less quantitative than that of the traditional value manager. We get to the situation conceptually. The traditional value manager looks at P/E, looks at the relationship of price to book value or cash flow. We create financial models to help us determine where the stock should sell based on its valuation relative to its growth rate, its peer group, or its assets. I never look at the market because I believe I know zero about the market.

Tanous: *Going back to your approach and process, you mentioned that you're not so quantitatively-oriented as other managers. As you correctly say, value managers are essentially quantitatively oriented because they look at book value, they look at assets, and other things that are measurable. So I need to delve into your approach a little more. Presumably you look at these other factors too, but is it the catalyst that is more important? Are there other factors in your approach that are more important?*

Sloate: First of all, book value today is an illusion. Between restructuring, write-downs, and share buybacks, book value has little value. Assets are important, particularly in manufacturing businesses, but in service companies they don't have a great deal of importance. Then you get into accelerated depreciation. Are they long-lived assets or short-lived assets? When we look at manufacturing companies, we have begun to calculate EVA.

Tanous: *What's EVA?*

Sloate: Economic Value Added. You take the average capital employed and the cost of that capital. If the return on the capital investment is not greater *[than the cost of capital]*, or if it's negative, clearly the company is under-earning or poorly managed. That puts a damper on its value.

Tanous: *When you're looking at the cost of capital, I assume you're not looking at the specific cost, but what the capital costs are generally?*

Sloate: Each company has a borrowing cost. So it's the specific cost. EVA is a very hot measure now on Wall Street. It was developed by the consulting firm, Stern, Stewart, and the first place I saw it used in financial analysis was in First Boston research. Now there are seminars on EVA. It's becoming important in business schools. It has a lot of validity because it includes factors that help reflect true profitability, such as the cost of all capital employed including working capital, inventories, etc., so you can't just build inventory. It doesn't permit companies to show positive returns and earnings if management is not meeting its capital cost hurdles.

Tanous: *Your catalyst approach is especially interesting to me because one of the other people I interviewed, Mario Gabelli, uses an approach which is also very much catalyst-oriented. It's value plus a catalyst. I find that interesting.*

Sloate: Well, if you don't have a catalyst, things will just sit around. The trucking industry hasn't had a catalyst in years and it's been among the worst performing groups in the market for two years. We bought a trucker recently. The catalyst here is restructuring, which they started to do, along with adding new services, but all that produced was a sea of red ink. The industry is not willing to bite the bullet and restructure or downsize to drive for profitability. That's why we decided to sell our position.

Tanous: *Laura, your returns are very impressive. Your net returns for the seven years ended in 1995 were 20% per year. That's about five points better than the S&P 500 in an environment where the S&P 500 has been very tough to beat. What do say about this?*

Sloate: I think it's related to a couple of things. We try to have a discipline, and we study every mistake we make. We never study a victory. If we're right, what's the point in studying it? It's why I never read about scandal. I'm never going to be a crook, so why should I waste my time reading about a scandal? What am I going to learn? My view is you study your mistakes.

We have a research lunch every Friday at which we all get together and talk about stocks. I give a little monologue about something topical. The two things I mentioned last week were the hatchet job on Julian Robertson in *Business Week* and Warren Buffett's annual letter to shareholders, which I had everybody read. *[Julian Robertson is a renowned hedge fund manager whose performance fell on hard times. Warren Buffett's annual letter to the shareholders of his company, Berkshire Hathaway, is legendary.]*

I said, in my opinion, here is what you can learn from the Julian Robertson story. It's focus. Focus is the key to success. Why do Warren Buffett and Peter Lynch *[page 111]* do well? Because they are focused. They have their niches and they stick to them. They may evolve them over time. Buffett writes about how his preferred stock investments weren't a good idea, and he discusses why.

Again he's looking at his mistakes. But it's the focus on how the investor makes the long term, rainmaker bet on the quality management companies with a franchise. If you look at most people who have been successful, and most companies that have been successful, you find they're focused, very disciplined, about how they conduct business. Therefore, focus is very important. Julian Robertson may have temporary problems because he is trying to be a global manager rather than a stock picker when picking stocks is what he does best.

I know I can't play commodities or options. Somebody asked me once, would I hedge the portfolio with some S&P puts? I said, I wouldn't know what to do. I wouldn't know what the premiums meant. You could show me these programs and, to me, all these programs work until they don't. The day they don't work is the day you really needed them. That's what happened in 1987. Portfolio insurance worked until the day everybody needed insurance. Then it failed. I think derivatives are fine for those who understand them and know how to work within the system.

Tanous: *You say, stay with what you know.*

Sloate: Right. Improve what you know, always keep improving, but stay with it. 1990 was a rough year and we learned some things. One is, don't let your losses run.

Tanous: *I was about to ask you about your sell discipline. You have said, basically, that if a stock goes down 15%, it's gone. That's got to be controversial.*

Sloate: I'll tell you what we did. We've modified that a little bit. We looked at fifteen stocks we sold from 1991 to 1994. The original reason for that discipline was that if you look at individual portfolios, they generally have one or two meltdowns—stocks that collapse. What a meltdown does is divert your energy and your focus. It erodes your confidence and it kills your performance—wonderful characteristics! So, we try to prevent meltdowns.

In 1990, before our sell discipline was in place, I bought Broad, *[named after Eli Broad]*, which became Sun America. It went from 11 to 4 and I owned it. *[That's what inspired my decision to sell stocks that went down 15%.]* We had a fairly large position, so it really hurt our performance. It went back up and we sold it between 17 and 20. It then proceeded to go significantly higher. The bottom line is, when we look at our '91 to '94 stocks, out of fifteen stocks that we sold because of our sell discipline, twelve of them were higher six months later than where we originally bought them. And a couple were real winners. We said, okay, this could be a timing phenomenon and we never know. There's no way we're going to be the perfect timers.

What we do now is, barring an October '87 crash, or a Gulf War kind of situation, if a stock goes down 15%, we look at it and rethink our assumptions. We ask why it is down. We ask whether or not we should increase the position by 50% or 100%. Maybe we don't quite love it as much as we did, but maybe it has gotten too cheap to sell. That's how we've modified the sell discipline. We just don't let it go down and not do anything.

Tanous: *That's a pretty drastic change of heart. Instead of selling it you are buying more, even twice as much.*

Sloate: It's not a change of heart. It's an evolution of process based on a close examination of results. Statistically, we found out that in 80% of the cases, if we had kept the stocks we sold six more months, we would have made money.

Tanous: *But how much fundamental analysis goes into this decision? Maybe the stock went down for a reason.*

Sloate: That's right. If it goes down for a fundamental reason, it's gone. We look at all the fundamentals. We call the company; we redo our earnings models. We go through the whole process all over again. We decide yes or no.

When these things are on the bottom, you wish you never owned them. You kind of hate them. It's like a kid who's had a temper tantrum. You've had enough. I look at my portfolio as little puppy dogs. Some days they're well, some days they're sick, some days they leave you alone. But every day there's something going on. An example is our initial purchase of Marvel Entertainment at 14, which we thought was pretty cheap. Ron Perelman *[the billionaire owner of Revlon and Marvel among other companies]* was buying it pretty aggressively at that price.

Tanous: *I thought he sold the company?*

Sloate: Well, he sold a chunk in the 17 to 25 range, and he bought back a big piece of that around 14 3/4 to 15 1/2. That was for tax consolidation reasons, but I'm sure he would rather pay 10 1/2 than 15. I think there's value there. The company had many problems with its principal businesses—trading cards and comics—and now it's come down to the $11 area. We looked at the cash flows; we looked at the underlying values of the company's divisions, including Toy Biz *[Marvel owns 37% of the company]*. The baseball season should be better than last year—no strike—which will help their trading card business. Ron Perelman is a resourceful guy. He's got his right-hand man at Marvel, and it's my guess that at 10 1/2 bucks it's probably bottomed. So we increased our position. The market won't believe their story until the company turnaround is evident. But in the spring, these guys got up at a meeting and gave EBIT *[earnings before interest and taxes]* and earnings projections by division. Either they want to hang themselves, or they banked those numbers, and they're pretty certain they'll hit them.

Tanous: *They gave estimates by division?*

Sloate: I said either those numbers are almost certain or those guys are nuts. Would I buy it today *[April 1, 1996]*? Probably not. I don't think it'll do anything till July *[1996]*. The bottom line is, if I sell it, I know I'll see the stock at 15, and that's almost a 50% move from its current level.

Tanous: *So, why did you say you wouldn't buy it?*

Sloate: Because we already own it. This is one we doubled up on. At this point I'm so worn out with all the problems and the aggravation I've had with it, and I've been wrong about it before. Most of the bad stuff is in the price; we bought it prematurely. There are a lot of positive elements in this company's turnaround and Perelman is down two-and-a-half billion dollars in his stake in the last two and a half years. I still think there's a lot of value there. I realize I spent a lot of time on this, but I wanted to give you an example of the discipline.

Tanous: *Laura, many of the managers I talk to have investing themes or areas that they latch on to that are particularly important to them. How about you?*

Sloate: I can tell you two we don't do. One, we don't invest in technology stocks.

Tanous: *Of course, technology is tough for a value investor.*

Sloate: Well, a lot of value investors do buy technology. Value investors bought Digital Equipment because the cash flow is this and the balance sheet is that. But we don't buy tech stocks because we believe we know nothing about technology. The creators of technology have their own network and you really have to understand it. We don't know who is going to come down the pike tomorrow morning with a better widget or gizmo, and our stock will be down 30%, and we'll have no idea what to do. So we don't buy technology.

Second, we don't buy foreign stocks because, although we may understand the business, we don't know the political or currency risks.

Tanous: *Any other themes you like or dislike?*

Sloate: We like managers. Good management is key. We'll buy some companies with secondary managements and great asset values, but we obviously prefer having a good manager.

Tanous: *Let's talk about that for a second. It's interesting because I talked to another investment manager with almost the opposite approach. It makes sense when you say you like good management, but this other value manager, Eric Ryback [page 197], who runs the Lindner Funds, doesn't talk to companies at all. He doesn't even want to talk to them. I found that strange. He said that they're now starting to talk to them on the phone under certain circumstances. Problem is, Eric says, all the companies are trying to put a spin on things and give the answers they think we want to hear. That raises this question: If evaluating management is very important, how do you do that? How do you know who the good ones are?*

Sloate: You do and you don't. Part of it is the track record. What have they done? You know that Jack Welch *[GE]* is a good manager. Look at his record. Larry Bossidy *[AlliedSignal]* is a good manager. You know by their track records. You know if a management is good or not by their responsiveness to changing scenery. I'm not sure that I agree that most of what they tell you is party line.

Yes, the annual report is P.R. for the most part, but you can often find some elements within it that make sense if you've read enough of them. For example, read Coca-Cola's annual report—by the way, I don't own Coke. To me the stock is at a bizarre multiple. It may have the greatest franchise in the world, but I get acrophobia at 40 times earnings. If you read the annual, you will find a very disciplined approach to growth. You can see how logical it is. This company is well-run, well-focused. It's not like reading a report from a company where management is talking about shareholder value, but the returns have been down for the last three years, plus it has four different unrelated businesses with no synergy.

Here's an example. We just bought FMC. Let's see where it's trading. *[Laura's fingers find the keyboard on her desk and she punches in the symbol FMC. A squawk box speaks mechanically in response: "F . . . M . . . C . . . closed at 76 . . ." She switches it off.]* It closed at 76. We paid 74 1/2 last week. I read a lot of stuff. I became interested in it after I read several Merrill Lynch reports over the last few months. We sent one of our analysts over to a Merrill Lynch Chemical Conference and told him to be sure to see the FMC people. What we discovered was that this had been a public LBO *[leveraged buyout]* by Goldman Sachs in the '80s. Management did it to avoid a takeover, leveraging the balance sheet in the process. Sixty percent of the company is in chemicals, 30% is machinery equipment, of which about half is in the underwater platform business. The gold mining business is up for sale. We did some quantitative analysis and the earnings estimate looked like $7 to $8.50 *[per share]*, which sounded very attractive for a 74 dollar stock.

Tanous: *Seven dollars was the estimate per share for what year?*

Sloate: Seven for '96 and $8.50 per share in '97. Next, we looked at its peer groups and discovered that if you broke the company up into the pieces, and the pieces traded at comparable multiples to their peer groups, the stock would be worth over $100. We looked at where the conglomerates are selling and FMC is selling at 3 or 4 multiples below the bottom of the range. FMCs capital expenditures were over $60 a share and R&D was more than $15 over the last five years. Then we looked at management's age and they were only 54— that was a negative. And, they own 22% of the company.

Tanous: *What's negative about being 54?*

Sloate: Well, management has done a sub-par job and, at 54, they could conceivably be around for another ten years. Al Costello, CEO of W.R. Grace, is on the FMC board. He knows a lot about companies being broken up and sold, and he understands the chemical business. The long and the short of it is, we thought this was an undiscovered value on an asset discount basis. We just didn't think there was a lot of downside at ten times earnings.

Tanous: *That example really speaks to your investment approach. I also noticed that you manage one of the Strong Funds, not surprisingly, the Strong Value Fund. How did that come about?*

Sloate: That's new. I've known Dick Strong for 28 years. We were talking last summer and he said, would you run a fund for me? I thought about it, and said I'd love to. The fund opened on December 29, 1995. And the fund is run like all the other accounts. We were up over 8.5% in the first quarter of 1996. It's a little baby fund though. The reason we wanted a fund was to get into the 401(k) business and the variable annuity business. Also, we were turning down a lot of money, since our account minimum is $500,000. We wanted to be with a large, reputable organization that would handle the distribution and marketing functions. We just want to manage the fund.

Tanous: *Laura, I want to give you a chance to revert to your academic background for a second. One of the things I'm doing in this book, that I don't think has been done before, is juxtaposing the opinions of great money managers and great academics. The academics I interview generally believe that you can't beat the market consistently. People like you, they say, exist in any distribution, but the identity of the outperformers is inherently unpredictable. How do you respond to the thesis that the market is efficient—that everything about the company is known and therefore you can't beat the market? How do you respond to the contention that future predictability of performance based on the past performance of the manager is not possible?*

Sloate: I'd agree with the second part of that. I think the past gives you an example of what the future could be. But past results shouldn't be over-stressed. Of course, if a manager has a terrible past, it may mean a lack of talent. If they've had a past that is totally off the edge of the curve, you should be careful because that may be luck or maybe they took some very high risk, some rainmaker bet. For example, they might have had 30% of their portfolio in a stock that got taken over or the manager bought 22 new issues and made money. That's just getting lucky.

But there is value in information. A couple of weekends ago, Hilton's stock was getting murdered. It was down like three points, and my guys say they hadn't heard anything. I said, they probably had a lousy weekend at the baccarat table. So I swear, five minutes later C.J. Lawrence comes out on the tape and lowers their estimates. Two minutes later they said it was due to gaming shortfalls. I said to my traders: "I told you it was the baccarat table! You didn't believe me!" I know Hilton's business. They're in the high roller gaming business. If they have a lousy weekend at baccarat it could cost them three cents a share. Look, maybe you can't beat the market if you're playing the market. We're not playing the market; We're playing 60 stocks. We should be able to beat the market with 60 stocks.

Tanous: *Well said.*

Sloate: So the bottom line is, yeah, I agree with the academics. If I try to play the whole market I can't beat the whole market. That's why size is important. That's why $50 billion is totally inefficient to run in one portfolio.

Tanous: *Yeah, because you have to make big bets, which is what Jeff Vinik did at Magellan.*

Sloate: And you have to make too many of them—and be right. But if you're dealing with 50, 60, or 70 stocks, you should be right. You should be able to be right enough to beat the market.

Tanous: *Because you picked the 60 where your information is superior and thorough?*

Sloate: We have an insight. I call it vision, an insight that's beyond what's there. A perfect example is Comsat, which I own. It's probably selling at a third of its real value.

Tanous: *What's it selling at today?*

Sloate: 23 1/2. The company has been misrun. It was the original U.S. commercial entry in the satellite business. If we did it all over again today, and satellites were where they were and wireless communication was where it is, we'd have no cable. It's much cheaper and much more efficient to use satellites. Only one fourth of the world has telephones. Probably 10% of the world has cable, and the way the rest are going to get communications is by satellite. This company is leading the effort to privatize the Intelsat and Inmarsat Satellite Systems, which is probably worth the value of the company.

Tanous: *What do you mean by that?*

Sloate: Comsat is the U.S. representative of a 136-country consortium that was set up in the 1960s. The consortium owns Intelsat. And Inmarsat has 75–80 country participants. Intelsat and Inmarsat have announced initiatives to privatize over the next 18 months to make each a commercial, profit-driven corporation. Comsat has several other ventures. They have a stated book value of $17. It pays a 3.5% dividend. Analysts think this is an earnings story. But this is an asset redeployment story. Comsat has an entertainment business they'll sell. They own Command Video and two Denver sports teams, the Avalanche *[NHL hockey]* and the Nuggets *[NBA basketball]*, plus the arena.

Tanous: *That sounds dumb.*

Sloate: It's stupid for Comsat to own these other businesses! I told you they were dumb. Comsat is an example of poor management. Well, has the dumb management suddenly gotten smart? I don't know. But I do know that Bruce Crockett *[the CEO]* has several hundred thousand options at 20.

Tanous: *That's called incentive!*

Sloate: And he understands the satellite business. Comsat understands the satellite business better than everyone else because they've been at it for 33 years. We have a different vision on this stock versus the world.

Tanous: *You own it, I assume.*

Sloate: We've owned it for a year. We just doubled up our position.

Tanous: *This is fun. As soon as everybody gets this book the first thing they'll do is look up the price of Comsat! That was brave of you! Laura, you're young, you've got the world ahead of you, what is in your personal future?*

Sloate: Well, I'm going to teach a bit at Columbia next year.

Tanous: *In the business school? Are you going to teach value investing?*

Sloate: I did a lecture this year and I've been invited back to do that. I'm going to teach a seminar with Bruce Greenwald.

Tanous: *Gabelli also mentioned Greenwald. He replaced Roger Murray at Columbia.*

Sloate: I'm going to teach the seminar course next spring. Teaching is something I enjoy. I love what I do, so I do it seven days a week. There's nothing else I'd do right now.

There's no question that Laura Sloate is a master of her craft. What was it in her background that made her so good? She mentioned focus. She cited it as the quality that distinguished Peter Lynch and Warren Buffett and led to the downfall of others who may have had it, became distracted, and lost it. She is smart, of course, the common characteristic of all the successful managers. Discipline, focus, tenacity, and judgment are all qualities Laura Sloate seems to have in abundance.

Her technique is interesting. You can see from the interview that she really latches on to a story once it has captured her attention. And it is a piece-by-piece, detail-by-detail process. Once Laura Sloate has decided to buy a company, I dare say there is not a single rational question you can ask her about the company that she can't answer. It is interesting that Laura follows the same value precept that Mario Gabelli does: Good value in a company is not enough. If the stockholders are going to make money, you also need a catalyst to shake things up and get the value realized.

Another manager, another lesson. Laura Sloate reinforces the rules for finding the hidden values in certain stocks, either by analyzing the sum of the parts, or through a clear vision of what the future may hold for a company or an industry, a vision which may not yet be apparent to others. For those who want to invest on their own, these pathways are worth following. For the readers who would like to let Laura invest for them, she runs the Strong Value Fund.

SCOTT STERLING
JOHNSTON

The quest for investment gurus takes us to strange places. In this case, Scott Johnston and I got together at a private meeting room in the United Airlines Red Carpet Club at Washington's Dulles Airport. I would have preferred to meet him on his home turf, San Francisco. Just try to catch up with this guy, and you'll know why I met him at the airport in our nation's capital. He is one of a new breed of managers who are constantly on the move. The breed may be new; Scott Johnston is not. He's been around for a few years and qualifies, although just barely, for membership in the AARP. You'd never know it from his schedule.

Scott Johnston, a former institutional broker turned money manager, founded Sterling Financial Group, a predecessor company, in 1985, after nine years turning around the investment results of two major bank trust departments. In 1992, the company became Apodaca-Johnston Capital Management Inc., which specializes in small-capitalization emerging growth stocks—stocks with future earnings growth of a minimum of 35% and with a maximum of $750 million in market capitalization.

Successful money managers, as we know, come from a variety of backgrounds. Scott's is particularly unusual. After receiving a degree in zoology at U.C. Berkeley, and an MBA from the

University of Southern California, he began his career as a consul-
tant. He was an auditor with Arthur Andersen & Co. before becom-
ing an institutional salesman with Smith Barney. Securities salesmen
don't usually have the temperament or patience to do the detailed
investigations required when analyzing potential companies to buy.
But Scott says that being a salesman actually helped him become a
successful portfolio manager.

How do we define success? Scott's five-year annualized perfor-
mance record is 38.2% for the period ended June 30, 1996, and his
ten-year record 25.6%. His 20-year record is 27.2%. I'll wait until
you catch your breath. The Wall Street Journal *recognized his*
accomplishments as a money manager as early as 1981, and he was
profiled in Money Magazine *in 1984. Let's settle in and find out*
how he does it.

Tanous: *How did you first get interested in stocks?*

Johnston: I never was so much interested in stock per se; it's always
the great story that fires me up. I get excited when I discover some
great product or unique service, a dynamic management, something
that's got a competitive advantage. It's almost like you want to be
part of that company. You want it to grow. If you can discover it
early on, and understand what makes it tick, that's the fun part. I
love the creative aspect of the investment process. I love the hunt.
But, I also get bored with a company once I've discovered it. I want
to go on to another company and find another exciting story. The
maintenance part is not that interesting to me. I have people who do
that for me.

Tanous: *You and I have a common investment heritage in that we*
were both early alumni of the old Smith Barney.

Johnston: That's where a lot of this came from.

Tanous: *One of the interesting things about you, unlike most of the*
other managers I talk to, is that you come from the sales side of the
Street. Has that helped or hurt?

Johnston: It's a major help. But let's step back.

First, the degree in the sciences is an important foundation. The scientific method is a way of thinking, a formal approach to investigation. It's the essence of what analysts do. Second, my Arthur Andersen background out of graduate school also helped. I spent a year-and-a-half consulting, so I understood systems real well. Then I went into the small business division of Arthur Andersen, which audits only small companies. Within a one-to-two-month period you audit a whole company. During my time, I probably audited thirty different companies in a myriad of businesses. I talked to senior managements and did the complete audit. That gave me a firm foundation in systems and in audit. Look at it this way: The entire stock market valuation mechanism revolves around one simple number which is the bottom line of all publicly traded companies—earnings per share. So you damn well better be able to read a financial statement. Most research analysts just look at snapshots when they look at balance sheets and income statements every quarter. They don't really understand cash flow and inventory turnover. But if you have actually audited a company, as I have, you understand these things.

Then I went to Smith Barney, and that experience did a number of things. One, working on the sell side gave me an edge. I learned how Wall Street research departments worked, how they put together a story, how they put an idea together, how they marketed the idea.

Wall Street's research engine is what drives stocks. Think about it. One way or another, 80% maybe 90% of all the ideas we investment money managers purchase come from the brokerage side. That's because we have outsourced most of that activity to the Street. So, if you once worked in the canyons of Wall Street, it gives you one hell of an edge.

Tanous: *You had other useful experiences, I believe, in addition to having worked for Arthur Andersen and Smith Barney.*

Johnston: In 1976, I joined San Diego Trust and Savings Bank as chief of investments, and stayed there until 1981. I worked for Oliver James, who headed up the trust department and was my mentor. Our investment team was one of the earliest clients of the William O'Neil Company. I met Bill O'Neil in 1976 and his investment principles contributed to the development of my style of investing. I headed up Security Pacific's investment activities from 1981 to 1985, and I ran about $5 billion there. My mission was to turn around the lagging performance results. I took my former right-hand-man, Art Nicholas, with me, and we hit the deck running. Our style quickly produced the returns the bank was after.

Tanous: *One of the things that we are looking for in this book is what the academics call "persistence." I'm not interviewing any manager who hasn't been managing money for a long time because lots of managers have two or three great years. They can, arguably, be called lucky. Lots of mutual funds are on lists of top performers and then you never hear from them again. You're one of the precious few who are there consistently. Follow these numbers with me: You were up 21% in 1994, compared to the Russell 2000 index, which was off 1.8%. You were up 41% in 1995. Your five year annualized record was 37.5%. Your ten year record is 27.7%. These are amazing numbers, Scott. What's the process?*

Johnston: The principal thing that makes stocks go, in my opinion, is early discovery. A lot of companies will meet our small-cap growth style, but the difference is the great story. We are looking for companies, products, services, that have huge upside potential. You're after the big home run. To do this, you need a company that is so exciting, it will capture the imagination of other investors. You could look at ten stocks that have the same damn profile, the same big percentage increases in earnings, etc., but the ones that will really move early on are the ones that have the great story.

The typical institutional salesperson on the desk is competing with about two hundred other firms trying to get the buy side's attention. To be good at it, you've got to be able to process a huge amount of information and synthesize the very best names and stories. If you've done that for four years, like I did, you get damn good at encapsulating the essence of a story. So when you go over to the buy side, you're good at recognizing whether a story has all the elements to be a winner.

On the buy side, you're hearing from 150 brokers. They're calling you all the time, and they're giving you stocks, so you develop a sixth sense to pick out the best story. If you can get into that story before anybody else does, you know that other people are going to hear the same thing and they're going to say, wow, that's a great story! Sure it's a great company, great fundamentals, but, boy, is that ever a great story! And that is what drives stocks. Because in my opinion, the old adage that stocks are sold, they're not bought, is true.

Tanous: *Let's talk about the "great story" concept. By the time you hear this great story, isn't it almost certainly all over the Street already?*

Johnston: Wrong. It may not be all over the Street. There are over 10,000 publicly traded stocks in the U.S. Even if the new idea is all over the Street, it takes time for firms to do their homework, especially the large banks, advisors, mutual funds and others with huge bureaucracies. Or their sheer buying power requires weeks to establish a meaningful position, moving the price up in the process.

We are very nimble and responsive to brokers' calls. About 20% of the ideas we get are off our own screens and database. Most of the names we are buying are between $100 million and $750 million in market capitalization. The median is usually about $300 million. We are generally initiating our positions at about $150 to $200 million. At that stage, you've only got two or three brokers covering them, and sometimes only one. We do most of our business with regional firms who are closest to that kind of information. The major firms do an excellent job, but by the time the Smith Barney's of the world pick a stock up, it's got to have enough trading liquidity to make it worth their while. By then you've probably got a company that's worth $500 million market cap, with five or six firms following it.

Our job is to capture the companies early-on in that huge growth phase, when you've got only two or three regional firms following it. Now, if they have a great product, great management, you've got a company that could become a Microsoft. You've got company after company that have grown to be $1 billion to $5 billion market cap companies because the product is great and you were able to pick them up at the $250 million level on the way to $600 million—in the early phases. And that stock can keep going to $5 billion.

Tanous: *How does the discovery process break down? You mentioned you were looking at screens. You might, presumably, find a company before the sell side broker even calls you, right? Then, at other times, the salesman calls you and says, Scott, check this one out: Here's the story in two-and-a-half minutes.*

Johnston: Right. We do business with 150 brokerage firms. That's a massive information flow of ideas to our firm. We try not to miss a thing.

Tanous: *That's a lot of calls.*

Johnston: A lot of calls. Now these people don't talk to me every day. Some I might talk to every three months or so. Maybe I talk to 30 or 40 regularly. I run screens to look for stocks with the earnings profiles and the technical profiles. Then I pick up the phone and call the company and ask "who covers you" [on Wall Street]? Usually you find two or three firms that do. That's one way.

Also, when you use screens, you might notice that energy stocks, for example, are really beginning to move. And you look at the new highs every day and you notice, boy, this group is hitting new highs. It might be the medical or the technology stocks. You dig a little deeper and you might find that this company is a driller and the oil drillers have been strong for the last four or five months, and they all have big forecasted earnings. So then you ask, okay, who else is in the drilling group? Next, I do a screen of all the stocks in the oilfield service machinery and related areas, and then hone in on the ones with the best profiles. Then, I get on the phone and call brokers. That's maybe the source of 20% or 25% of the ideas.

The vast majority of ideas, though, comes from regional brokers who I've been doing business with for 10 to 20 years. These people know exactly what my style is, so it's an efficient call for both of us. I've had relationships with these people for a long time. When the market is really moving and you're overwhelmed with information, and you have more calls than you can possibly return, you don't have the time to check out a name as thoroughly as you'd like. How do you prioritize? You take the call from the guy or gal who has always been there for you, who consistently made you money. These pros are so good they could be managing money themselves. They've got the instincts and judgment, and they know who the best analysts in their firms are. In my opinion, the better institutional salesman wants to do business with your three-or-four-man shops, because they want to talk to decisionmakers. In the largest firms, like Smith Barney, Goldman Sachs, or Morgan Stanley, where they've got so much product, the institutional salesman just can't know all the stories. You go to a regional firm, and the institutional salesman knows the story almost as well as the analyst. So when he picks up the phone, he is much more effective than his counterpart at the larger firm.

Also, the larger firms have younger salesmen who are coming up the ranks. They act as social secretaries, taking investment banking deals or research analysts around. There's a lot of maintenance-type coverage, which is not so much idea-driven. So the key here is, when the great salesman calls, one who is "Street smart" from years of experience, and says, Johnston, you've just got to get into this thing, you get into it. You focus your attention very quickly because this guy is so good. That's what happens.

Tanous: *Let's get a summary of your investment criteria, which I presume these salesmen you're talking about know by heart.*

Johnston: You bet. First of all, we're basically a bottoms-up, stock-picker manager. We stay fully invested at all times. In terms of the academicians, for 20 years I haven't known of anyone who can consistently and accurately time the market. They might exist out there, but I've never met one. Therefore, I stay fully invested. You want to focus on the strongest industry sectors and the strongest stocks, because the better, stronger companies should decline less in a bear market and come out of the starting blocks faster during the rebound in a bull market.

Second, I want to be in the sweet spot of the "S curve," which is the point of maximum rate-of-change, acceleration, momentum. I want to own companies that are undergoing the greatest upward rate of change in earnings, sales, discovery, ownership change, brokerage sponsorship, and relative price strength.

There are five things that I specifically look for in stocks and a sixth kind of overview theme if I can get it. You don't have to have every one of these, but you need most of them:

One, I want dramatically accelerating earnings. I am not interested in a company growing trendline 30%. Most money managers would love to own those things. I don't. I want something going from 30% growth to 60% growth. Conversely, you might have a stock that's growing 15% or 20%, but all of a sudden—because you've got the big product, the big management change, the great service—this is going to drive those earnings so powerfully that it will substantially change the nature of the company. If you can capture that, you've got two things going for you. One, you have the increased price of the stock, because the earnings are going to go up 60% instead of 30%. So you get 100% greater price appreciation because the earnings are going up higher. And two, if you're right in your assessment of the company's growth, you're going to get a multiple expansion. The market is going to say, wow, this isn't a 30% grower anymore, this is a 50% grower. So you get a higher multiple *[price-earnings ratio].* Two bangs for your buck. Our typical companies have been growing maybe 10% annualized for the last five years, which is nothing to write home about. But next year's earnings should be up 50% to 60% on average for the companies in my portfolio.

Second, I want a strong balance sheet. No debt or virtually no debt. If there's any debt, there'd better be good cash flow. Why do I want this? It comes from my Arthur Andersen experience. Young companies have a tendency to get in trouble. They're growing so fast that they have an insatiable appetite for working capital to fund their growth. As a result, they sometimes leverage up their balance sheets and management gets in trouble. So, I want the operating leverage but not the financial risk. That at least helps keep me out of trouble.

Third, I want a strong relative price strength. The concept is how well is that stock acting in the market relative to all other stocks? Let's say the median stock in the market has a relative strength of 50. Most of the companies that I own are 80 and above, meaning that they are outperforming 80% of all stocks in the market.

Tanous: *How do you measure that?*

Johnston: There are services that can give you these measurements. But, basically, we're not bottom fishers. We want stocks that are acting well and breaking out to new highs. The importance of this is that we think that the market is remarkably efficient at ferreting out good companies. The market seems to know. If a stock is acting well, it's probably acting well for a reason—positive earnings surprises coming, new product announcement, etc.

Fourth, I want companies in industries that are doing well in the market pricewise. If you look at the industry's group rank, its industry's relative price strength, you want that to be doing well too, because it's awfully difficult for any company to be doing well in an industry that is doing poorly. I mean, you might have the lone ranger out there, but you really want your industry to be performing well. Remember, stocks are sold; they aren't bought. It's hard enough to find companies that are interesting and exciting. If you have a sector that's flat on its back, it might be the greatest company with the greatest story ever, but when the institutional salesmen are out there calling around trying to get your interest, the answer is likely to be, hey, forget it. I don't want to own semiconductors; it's a dead group.

Fifth is low institutional ownership. We want to be in the first wave of institutional buying, long before the majors are buying these names. We want the company's sponsorship to be young and small with limited brokerage coverage. We want to be ahead of the big buying programs of the majors that will undoubtedly follow, as other investors discover what we already know—a potentially great company, a great investment opportunity in the making.

Sixth, we like to focus on dominant investment themes—the dynamic trends we identify early. This is not a criterion, since it's not company specific, but it is important. We uncover a rapidly growing company that is exploiting an industry niche—maybe it's an invention, perhaps a change in government regulations. Other companies will respond by altering their growth strategies to profit from the new opportunity and new companies will emerge funded by venture capitalists. Before you know it, an entirely new industry is created before your very eyes. These mini-industries have such powerful dynamics that they are essentially insulated from the broader economic changes impacting the overall economy. These micro-industries are often recession-proof. The economy moves on the waves of innovation and lifestyle changes.

Tanous: *Can you give us some examples?*

Johnston: There are numerous, mini-industry niches experiencing dramatic growth. Starting with technology: the machine vision industry, supply chain management software, data warehousing software, wireless cable, video conferencing, caller ID, flat panel display. In the health industry you have the kidney dialysis industry, gene therapy, orthopedic devices, bone growth stimulation, clinical research organizations, group practice management, patient care computing, emergency room outsourcing, and so forth. In the consumer area, the rent-to-own industry, the pawn shops, book retailers, craft beer brewing, in-line skating, snowboards, temporary staffing, privatization of correction facilities. As you can see, the opportunities are still there.

Tanous: *You know, as I heard you rattle off your criteria, Scott, you sounded suspiciously like a momentum investor. Would you call yourself a momentum investor?*

Johnston: Define momentum investor and I'll be able to answer the question. I began implementing this investment style in 1976, over

20 years ago. The elements of style have remained unchanged since inception. You know, I doubt the term "momentum investing" was even around back then. If I am a momentum investor, I must have been one of the very earliest ones. You know, momentum investing has the connotation of quickly jumping on and off trends. You have to be mindful of the big picture, the long term secular trends. It was the inflation of the 1970s, it was the consumer disinflation of the 1980s. I believe the themes for the '90s and the 2000s are the information age and the graying of America. You don't need to be a hotshot, gunslinging portfolio manager flitting from one idea to another to produce good returns, if you're mindful of the big picture.

Tanous: *Let me ask you a hypothetical. Let's say you find a company that has all the things you're looking for. I'm the salesman and I know exactly what you want so I'm pitching you this story and, bang, bang, bang, we're hitting all your criteria. Then at the end I say, Scott, by the way, it's selling at 42 times earnings. Do you care?*

Johnston: No. The price-earnings ratio is not real important to us. How the hell do you put the right price-earnings ratio on a company that is growing 50% or 60% a year? As long as that stock is acting well and the earnings are coming through, it's okay. Of course, there are always cases where the price is beyond all reason, and we'll stay away from those. But don't worry about the P/E. Great companies deserve great earnings multiples.

Tanous: *Okay. What else is important?*

Johnston: We rarely buy a company without talking to management. That comes from my audit experience. First, you tap into the great minds at the research firms, who have known the company for years. But by talking to the company, too, you get an undertone. How positive or negative are they? You might discover that the last time the analyst talked to them was three months ago, in which case you might rethink your analysis. So you always talk to the management of the company first, usually the CEO or the CFO or both.

In terms of visiting companies, we see maybe 30% or 40% of them because they come through San Francisco, where we are, but it's not that critical. If you know how to ask the right questions of management, and you do that as part of your business, you don't need to visit the company. What you're doing is confirming what the analyst is telling you.

Tanous: *Let's talk about your sell discipline.*

Johnston: We have three criteria. First, we sell the stock if the reason for purchasing the stock is no longer valid. That's generally because the company has lost its "window of opportunity." You might have a company that's got the greatest widget of all time—smaller, cheaper, faster, better. But you find out that they've got a glitch in their production process, or maybe there's a new competitor coming in, so they don't own the market anymore. We sell the stock because these concerns generally lead to earnings disappointments.

Second, we sell if it gets way overvalued. Certainly, there is a strong correlation between a company's underlying growth rate and the stock market's valuation via the price-earnings ratio or the market cap-to-sales ratio. Clearly, we try to find growth companies before other investors do, hopefully before the company's prospects are fully reflected in a high stock price. But if a big mutual fund loads up and shoots the stock price up, it may become way overvalued. We'll sell into the buying frenzy, capture the profit, and come back later.

Third, and generally most important, we sell the stock if the relative price strength begins to diminish. If the relative strength begins to roll over, or if the industry group rank starts to get weak, that's telling us that something might be going wrong. We found out that stuff leaks out of companies. Analysts or other investors may suspect some problems arising. The purchasing agent might be playing golf with a broker or something like that. If there's going to be some disappointment, the market will know that things aren't going well. That would be a reason for us to investigate, call the analyst, call the company. If it continues, we know the market is smarter than we are, so we'll sell out.

Also the industry might come under a dark cloud. For instance, the health care stocks were very powerful until the Clinton Administration came in. When they started looking at health care, all those stocks really underperformed. The concern was for the future profitability of the industry. Those earnings came through magnificently in 1993, but still the stocks performed very poorly. So, we were out of all of them until the cloud passed.

Tanous: *Did you get back in?*

Johnston: You bet. Big time. But not until the industry strength began to lift, evidencing investors' willingness to accumulate the stocks again. Regardless of your specific disciplines, the key point when you run money, is that you have to be decisive. Whether it's a buy discipline or a sell discipline, make a decision and act on it. There's a terrific scene in the movie *Wall Street* that epitomizes this point. It captures the essence of what we are faced with every day—the rush, the adrenaline, the mandatory decisiveness, the urge to take action, don't look back, and go on to the next one. In the movie, Gordon Gekko, played by Michael Douglas, has been buying millions of shares of Bluestar Airlines at the $22 level, believing the stock is going to 30. But the stock has been drifting down all day. Gekko is in his big trading room office, high above Gotham City, and his broker on the deal, Bud Fox, played by Charlie Sheen, calls him when the stock is at 16 1/2, representing an enormous loss, and says: "Two minutes to close, Gordon. What do you want to do? You decide." Gekko knows he's been had. He replies almost immediately: "Dump it!"

I loved that. He's got balls!

Tanous: *I understand you'll also sell a stock if the company gets too big. Why would you sell a company that's a great company with great earnings that you've been right on, just because it got too big?*

Johnston: Your value-added diminishes once a company gets that large. At the larger size, its inherent growth rate has to drop; it's a law of nature. By then, if it's a great company, it's now an "institutional darling" and you've got seven or eight brokerage firms covering it. We concentrate on finding the small company before it's been discovered. I know that some small-cap managers keep their winners going even as they grow to large-caps. We sell them when they get too large. Why? Because, as I said before, we want to be in the sweet spot of the "S curve"—the discovery, the momentum, the period of biggest change. Those are characteristics of smaller companies. Companies with a billion dollar market cap are generally not as dynamic as the younger companies. So we'll sell them out even though their prospects may be excellent.

Tanous: *Let me ask about the firm. How much money do you have under management?*

Johnston: About $540 million in small-cap assets. We're looking at managing about $750 million in small-cap, and then closing that product. We want to stay a focused boutique. We want it to be fun and not have a lot of administration. That will ensure client service. That's as important to us as performance. Your clients should understand how and why you are managing their money. That needs to be communicated from a principal of the firm.

Tanous: *What's your minimum account size?*

Johnston: It's $20 million now. A micro-cap limited partnership fund will be introduced with a $1 million minimum.

Tanous: *The risk side of the equation is the other part of the story. As we all know, there is no free lunch, and one of the things about your management style is that it does appear to be volatile. What's your average turnover?*

Johnston: About 150%, which is in line with most other small-cap managers. We are very, very active, but we have held positions for several years as long as earnings keep coming through. Our companies are growing so fast that the market caps quickly rise beyond our buy zone. Our $1 billion maximum market cap mandate forces the sell decision.

Tanous: *On a standard deviation basis, your volatility is about double the market's. I suppose that is consistent with aggressive small-cap investing, but that's the price you pay for this kind of performance, wouldn't you say?*

Johnston: Here's the thing. If you're after companies with great exciting products that are growing three or four times the rate of the market, with big expectations, you're going to have disappointments. Small companies are prone to erratic earnings swings. It's the nature of the beast. They are about discovery. They are under-owned, under-followed, thinly capitalized, and subject to big moves when institutions find out about them. Conversely, when something goes wrong, most everyone rushes to get out the doorway at the same time. Need I remind you that it's a very narrow passageway? Higher risk equates to higher returns. Now over long periods of time—and I'll note that investors must have a long-term investment horizon to participate in this sector—the small-cap indexes have shown very meaningful incremental returns over the large-cap indexes. But the point is that small-cap stocks, by their nature, are volatile. It's inherent in that sector of the market, and investors are well-rewarded by this sector.

Tanous: *What are some of the other tenets of your investment discipline?*

Johnston: Here's a big one: If you've established a successful investment discipline, don't change it. Many money managers get into a rough market period and they modify their strategy or make excuses, like we're going to make this one exception. I say, don't violate your rules. If you strictly adhere to your discipline year-in and year-out, you ought to be successful. That's how you stay on the right side of the distribution curve. Remember, we are operating in an inefficient area of the market, which is small-caps. To me, large-cap stocks are boring as hell. They're efficient and they're boring! You've got to make the macro call to be right. If you have information sources that are adept at discovering interesting stories early on, you will find great companies early and you can consistently beat the market.

Tanous: *I see. So small-cap stocks aren't as well known as large-caps, nor as widely followed, and that, presumably, creates the inefficiencies. How many stocks do you keep in your portfolio?*

Johnston: We maintain 75 names in our portfolio. We don't expand that number. A lot of money managers put their toe in the water. By that I mean, instead of buying a full position for their portfolios, which for us is 1 1/2% of the portfolio, they'll buy half-positions or quarter-positions. That's going into it halfheartedly. I don't subscribe to that. I think you own it and you love it, or you don't buy it. And you're constantly reevaluating your 75 names. In order to buy a new name, you've got to kick out an old name. That imposes a discipline—to always focus on the strongest names in your portfolio. That helps keep the performance up. You're forced to make the buy and sell decision.

Tanous: *Another manager I interviewed has the identical philosophy, Foster Friess [page 229] who runs the Brandywine Fund. He has a very colorful way of describing this philosophy. His analogy is to "pigs in the trough." Fifteen pigs fit at the trough. The sixteenth comes along and nudges himself in. In the process, one of the original pigs is displaced and wanders off, presumably fat and happy.*

Johnston: That's great. What you're doing all the time is focusing on the very best companies, the very best names.

Tanous: *What are some of your future plans?*

Johnston: Simply keep my head down, stick to my knitting. No grandiose expansion plans. Let things evolve in a timely manner. Our singular focus is on providing the best returns for our clients and maintaining strong communications with them, so that they understand our process. The rest should take care of itself.

Tanous: *Before we conclude, I want to go back to the six investment criteria, plus the overview, that we talked about. I keep wondering if there isn't something else involved?*

Johnston: Yes, there is. It's that the very best managers develop a sixth sense where they just know that a stock is going to move.

Tanous: *I asked that question of a lot of managers. I asked Peter Lynch, for example, since his approach is so logical and simple. If that's the case, though, why isn't everybody rich? I often wonder what role instinct plays.*

Johnston: You develop a sixth sense, an instinct. We're talking art here, not science. Many have the ability, the training, the commitment, but few have the touch.

Tanous: *When you go home at night, can you identify what it is that makes you feel that way?*

Johnston: I have no idea. It's visceral. You just sense it. You know that a stock's got all the elements to be a winner. It feels right; it's ready to move.

Tanous: *But where did that sense come from?*

Johnston: The story, the catalyst, the trading pattern.

Tanous: *Let me ask the question another way, because we've got to get to the bottom of this. Ten years ago, did you have this sense?*

Johnston: Yes.

Tanous: *Did you have it 20 years ago, when you started?*

Johnston: I had it 15 years ago. It took me five years to develop it. You want fresh names and fresh stories. I don't want to hear a story and have to say, yeah, we know that story. It was around a year ago. Give me freshness.

But you have to be open-minded to opportunities and listen for changes. Look at oil stocks and energy exploration stocks. Most people who have been in the business a long time will say, I don't want to own them. But the industry has changed. The typical growth stock manager doesn't own energy stocks now. But what about all this new technology in the industry? It's worth looking at. Fresh names. Fresh stories.

One final comment about purpose. This is a humbling profession, with minefields all over the place capable of destroying a good performance record built on years of hard work. Investment legends come and go; you could be history before you even know it. We all know that if we consistently produce exceptional returns for our clients, we can make an unconscionable amount of money in the investment business. Whether the Guru was born with the gift, learned the gift, or perhaps some higher power intervened, one must ask, for what purpose? Is there more to life than making a lot of money for oneself and others in this world? The Gurus are among the fortunate few. I asked the question of purpose a long time ago. There is a source on that subject that is right on the money, *God Owns my Business,* by Stanley Tam. For me, the answer is in *Malachi* 3:10: [*Malachi 3:10 "Bring the full tithe into the storehouse, so that there may be food in my house, and thus put me to the test, says the Lord of hosts; see if I will not open the windows of heaven for you and pour down for you an overflowing blessing."* (The New Oxford Annotated Bible)]

An interesting story and an interesting fellow. I kept thinking about the fact that Scott Johnston started as a broker, so he knows good salesmen from bad, and more importantly, he knows a good story when he hears one. I also thought a lot about his notion of a sixth sense. Okay, do you have it? And if so, how important is it? Keep that in mind as you read through the other interviews. Is the sixth sense something we should look for, either in ourselves or in a money manager?

In one sense, it is great to have somebody like Scott Johnston to talk to about investments. In another sense, it's a little frustrating, because only institutional investors will be able to use him, given his high minimums. I keep waiting for him to announce a new Johnston mutual fund which most investors could buy.

But, for those who are interested in doing some homework, I think that Scott's ideas and management philosophy are so clear-cut and inviolable that many of you, especially those among you who like to pick stocks yourselves, would be able to glean some useful ideas from him. For example, an amateur investor, guided by the principles Scott articulates in this interview, might be able to find some of these outstanding companies and invest in them on his or her own. True, it wouldn't be easy. You'd have to buy some research, and maybe develop a contact or two at a regional brokerage firm. But the criteria he shared with us are easy enough to follow, if you have the patience and persistence to do it. Of one thing there is no doubt: Scott Johnston's prescription for buying undiscovered small-cap growth stocks has stood the test of time, making him one of the premier investors of this genre in the country.

Postscript: *Not long after our interview, Scott Johnston left Apodaca-Johnston and reactivated Sterling Johnston Capital Management, a company he founded in 1985. With headquarters in San Francisco, the firm specializes in small-cap emerging growth equity management. The firm will dedicate 10% of its profits to religious and philanthropic organizations.*

EUGENE
FAMA

Eugene Fama grew up in Boston, a third generation Italian-American. While an undergraduate at Tufts University, he excelled in athletics and majored in French— an inauspicious beginning for a future giant in the field of economics. But he also worked for a professor who was trying to develop "buy" and "sell" signals based on price momentum. Although the theories the professor devised worked well when applied to the past, they worked poorly when Fama tested them in real time. That puzzle, plus the skills that he acquired evaluating stock market data, drew Gene Fama to business school. After earning his doctorate at the University of Chicago, he joined the faculty there in 1963.

A simplified version of his dissertation, "Random Walks in Stock Market Prices," was published in Institutional Investor *magazine, provoking a stir. It was Gene's article that introduced the still-controversial efficient market theory to the investment community. (There are many variations of the efficient market theory, but they all postulate that stock prices promptly and fully reflect all public information.) Very few academics specializing in investment research have any audience in the investment community, but that article made Gene Fama very well-known on Wall Street. But he is an academic and technical terms are used in this interview. We covered some of these terms earlier in the book, but here's a quick, but non-scientific, refresher course on some of the lingo:*

Efficient market theory: *The theory that holds that stocks are always correctly priced since everything that is publicly known about the stock is reflected in its market price.*

Random walk theory: *One element of the efficient market theory. The thesis that stock price variations are not predictable.*

Active management: *The practice of picking individual stocks based on fundamental research and analysis in the expectation that a portfolio of selected stocks can consistently outperform market averages.*

Passive management: *The practice of buying a portfolio that is a proxy for the market as a whole on the theory that it is so difficult to outperform the market that it is cheaper and less risky to just buy the market.*

Outliers and fat tails: *In a normal, bell-shaped distribution of returns on investment portfolios, the majority of the returns, or data, can be found in the "bell," or bulge, which centers around the weighted average return for the entire market. At the ends, both right and left, we find what are known as "outliers," those returns which are either very bad (left side) or very good (right side). Of course, few managers are either very good or very bad. Those returns on the right and left tails are known as outliers since they live on the outlying fringes of the curve. Similarly, "fat tails" refers to larger than normal tails of the curve, meaning that there are more data on the extremes than you might expect.*

Tanous: *How did you first get interested in stocks?*

Fama As an undergraduate, I worked for a professor at Tufts University. He had a "Beat the Market" service. He figured out trading rules to beat the market, and they always did!

Tanous: *I beg your pardon?*

Fama: They always did, in the old data. They never did in the new data *[laughter]*.

Tanous: *I see. Are you saying that when you back-tested the trading rules on the historic data, the rules always worked, but once you applied them to a real trading program, they stopped working?*

Fama: Right. That's when I became an efficient markets person.

Tanous: *Okay. Let's get into it. You're known for your work on efficient capital markets. In fact, on Wall Street, the phrase "efficient market" is often attributed to you. I believe you and Ken French made the point that stock market returns are, in fact, predictable over time. How does that jibe with the random walk theory?*

Fama: The efficient market theory and the random walk theory aren't the same thing. The efficient market theory is much more powerful than the random walk theory, which merely postulates that the future price movements can't be predicted from past price movements alone. One extreme version of the efficient market theory says, not only is the market continually adjusting all prices to reflect new information but, for whatever reason, the expected returns—the returns investors require to hold stocks—are constant through time. *[For example, we know that, since the '20s, returns on the New York Stock Exchange common stocks have averaged a little over 10% per year.]* I don't believe that. Economically, there is no reason why the expected return on the stock market has to be the same through time. It could be higher in bad times if people become more risk-averse; it could be lower in good times when people become less risk-averse.

Tanous: *So risk is the component that leads to how much you get paid?*

Fama: It could be just taste, too, you know. People's taste for holding stocks can change with time. None of that is inconsistent with market efficiency and it can give rise to some predictability in returns. The predictability is simply based on the returns people require to hold securities.

Tanous: *But, in one of your papers, you did refer to the predictability of returns over time. Is that just the investor getting paid for the risk he was willing to take? Is that the point?*

Fama: It could be that or it could be that people are simply more risk-averse in bad times.

Tanous: *On a related subject, I think you also said that fundamental analysis is of value only when the analyst has new information, which was not fully considered in forming current market prices. When I hear that I say: Hey Gene, that's the point! The analyst believes he knows something, or infers something, that other analysts don't see. He sees an evolution taking place or he believes this company is doing better than people think, and that's why he gets paid millions of dollars on Wall Street to pick stocks. What's wrong with this thesis?*

Fama: Well, not everybody can have that talent. In fact, as far as I can tell, not many do. The system is designed to make that very difficult. By that, I mean that under U.S. accounting *[and regulatory]* systems, if you reveal anything, you have to reveal it to everybody.

Tanous: *Fair enough, but what if the analyst is making a judgment on the future prospects of the company. For example, the analyst might say; "the Street says this company is going to earn $0.82 per share and I say it's going to earn $1.10 because I'm seeing order flow, consumer demand, customers' tastes for the product and what have you. Now, if the analyst is right, he's worth the millions he gets paid. My question is: in your thesis, if he's right, is he right because he's so smart or just because he's lucky?*

Fama: For the most part, I think it is luck. The evidence is pretty strong that active management doesn't really do better than passive management.

Tanous: *Except, of course, when we start talking about the so-called outliers, those managers, like the Gurus in this book, who have persistently outperformed the market. That, in turn, leads to the other great exercise in our business, particularly with mutual funds, which is the predictability of future investment success based on past success. I know you've done some work on that, too.*

Fama: One of my students just finished his thesis on that subject, actually. What he found was that performance does repeat when it's on the negative end! In other words, funds that do poorly, tend to do poorly persistently.

Tanous: *Why couldn't one postulate that the same would be true at the other end of the spectrum?*

Fama: One could postulate it, but it doesn't seem to be true. On the negative end of the spectrum, you have things like turnover and fees and all that kind of stuff, which can explain why you have negative persistence in poor returns.

Tanous: *Yes, but good managers trade and charge fees, too. They might even deserve them more!*

Fama: Poorly performing funds tend to be higher fee and higher expense funds. In fact, when my student adjusted for fees and expenses he could explain most of the persistent under-performance.

One thing I did a couple of years back was take all the funds that survived from the beginning of the Morningstar tapes, which is 1976. Now, funds that survive that long will have a survivor bias built into the test, because only the successful funds survive. So I split the sample period in half and took the 20 biggest winners of the first 10 years, or the first half of the period, and I asked how did they do in the second half of the period? Well, in the second half of the period, half of them were up and half of them were down.

Tanous: *Wow. Half were up and half were down?* [That indicates that there was no predictive value in the fact that these managers all finished in the top half in the first ten year period.]

Fama: Exactly half, relative to a risk-corrected model.

Tanous: *How did you adjust for risk?*

Fama: I used the three-factor model.

Tanous: *The three-factor model takes into account market risk; value versus growth styles; and also size, which is the large-cap stocks versus small-cap distinction, right?*

Fama: Yes. But since most retail funds have a bias toward growth stocks, the adjustment helped them.

Tanous: *So even risk tested, the data came out 50/50 which means that the mutual funds that did the best for ten years only had a 50/50 chance of repeating their success. I'm curious to know who the biggest winner was in both periods?*

Fama: Fidelity Magellan.

Tanous: *What's the reason for that?*

Fama: Obviously, the performance of that fund has been really good.

Tanous: *It has, to Peter Lynch's credit. Another issue you have addressed: that old subject, value stocks versus growth stocks. Are stocks of good companies good stocks to invest in?*

Fama: They're good stocks, they just don't have high expected returns.

Tanous: *Then growth stocks are stocks of good companies, not good stocks, right?*

Fama: To me stock prices are just the prices that produce the expected returns that people require to hold them. If they are growth companies, people are willing to hold them at a lower expected return.

Tanous: *As we get into this, I think our readers are going to be surprised to read that value stocks are riskier than growth stocks. That is counterintuitive.*

Fama: I don't know why it's counterintuitive.

Tanous: *Well, we used to think of value stocks as stocks that may have already had a decline, that are languishing. We believe we're buying value stocks at the bottom and waiting for them to go back up again.*

Fama: Value stocks may continue to take their knocks. Their prices reflect the fact that they are in poor times. As a result, because people don't want to hold them—in our view because they are riskier—they have higher expected returns. The way we define risk, it has to be associated with something that can't be diversified away. Everybody relates to a market risk. If you hold stocks, you bear stock market risk. But the stock market is more complicated than that. There are multiple sources of risk.

Tanous: *In our business, we usually associate growth stocks with high earnings multiples, and value stocks with low earnings multiples. Multiples are themselves usually an element of risk. So, if a growth stock falters on its anticipated growth path, it declines precipitously because it no longer deserves the multiple that had previously been awarded to it when its prospects were better. Therefore, a lot of people think that growth stocks, in fact, are riskier. What's wrong with that thesis?*

Fama: Just look at the data. It's true that growth stocks vary together, and it's true that value stocks vary together. In other words, their returns tend to vary together which means that there is a common element of risk there. Now, for growth stocks that seems to be a risk that people are willing to bear at a lesser return than the return they require for the market as a whole. Whereas, if I look at the value stocks, which we also call distressed stocks, their returns vary together, but people aren't willing to hold those except at a premium to market returns.

Tanous: *So you're saying that I expect to make more money when I buy value stocks than I do when I buy growth stocks.*

Fama: Right. On average. Of course, sometimes you get clobbered.

Tanous: *We've always associated the risk of getting clobbered more with growth stocks than with value stocks that have already taken their lumps.*

Fama: The data don't support that.

Tanous: *The other dimension, of course, is size. Now the size effect is very easy for those of us in the investment community to accept. The notion that small companies are riskier than large companies seems obvious.*

Fama: That's not the reason the community accepts it. What they think is that small companies pay higher returns because they're unknown, or something like that. It's not because they're more risky. The risk, in my terms, can't be explained by the market. It means that, because they move together, there is something about these small stocks that creates an undiversifiable risk. That undiversifiable risk is why you get paid for holding them.

Tanous: *What causes that risk?*

Fama: You know, that's an embarrassing question because I don't know.

Tanous: *Fascinating. I would assume that the risk is that small companies have a lower survival rate than large companies.*

Fama: No. That's not it at all. The good news and the bad news about that is that the reason small companies don't survive is because some of them fail, others get merged; that's bad news and good news.

Here's a fact I always use. First I say I don't know, but then I say it's fair. Here's my example. The 1980s were, supposedly, the longest period of continuous growth the country's seen since the second world war. Yet, in that decade, small stocks were in a depression. Small stock earnings never recovered from the '80-'81 recession. They were low the whole decade. The market was fooled every year by that, because in every previous recession, the small companies came back. Why did that happen in the '80s? I don't know. But it happened. And it tells you there is something about small stocks that makes them more risky.

Tanous: *Another question that comes up frequently is if markets are correctly priced, how do you explain crashes when they go down twenty percent in one day?*

Fama: Take your example of growth stocks. If their prospects don't go as well as expected, then there will be a big decline. The same thing can happen for the market as a whole. It can also be a mistake. I think the crash in '87 was a mistake.

Tanous: *But if '87 was a mistake, doesn't that suggest that there are moments in time when markets are not efficiently priced?*

Fama: Well, no. Take the previous crash in 1929. That one wasn't big enough. So you have two crashes. One was too big *[1987]* and one was too small *[1929]*!

Tanous: *But in an efficient market context, how are these crashes accounted for in terms of "correct pricing"? I mean, if the market was correctly priced on Friday, why did we need a crash on Monday?*

Fama: That's why I gave the example of two crashes. Half the time, the crashes should be too little, and half the time they should be too big.

Tanous: *That's not doing it for me. What am I missing?*

Fama: Think of a distribution of errors. Unpredictable economic outcomes generate price changes. The distribution is around a mean—the expected return that people require to hold stocks. Now that distribution, in fact, has fat tails. That means that big pluses and big minuses are much more frequent than they are under a normal distribution. So we observe crashes way too frequently, but as long as they are half the time under-reactions and half the time over-reactions, there is nothing inefficient about it.

Tanous: *Let's go back to value stocks versus growth, and large versus small stocks. Tell us why the three-factor model contributes to our knowledge of risk in investments.*

Fama: The three factors are the market factor, the size factor, and the distress *[value]* factor. We distinguish between distress and growth. What we find is that, in addition to the market factor in returns, in other words the fact that stocks move together, it's also true that small stocks move together, and big stocks move together, but not in the same way. The value stocks move together and the growth stocks move together but the two groups are different from each other. There are at least three dimensions of risk: market risk, small stock versus big stock risk, and distress stock versus growth stock risk. When I say risk, I mean that these groups move together. We could have found that they didn't move together, and then it would have been market inefficiency.

Tanous: *What would that have told us?*

Fama: It would have told you that you could get a diversified portfolio of small stocks, and a diversified portfolio of big stocks, short the big stocks and buy the small stocks, and get a positive return with no risk.

Tanous: *Why would that be true?*

Fama: It would only be true if there weren't a common factor in the return on small stocks that caused them to have randomness that wasn't shared with big stocks.

Tanous: *I'm not sure I follow.*

Fama: If there's no small stock risk, and I take a diversified small stock portfolio, I would be able to explain its return entirely in terms of the market risk. So there's nothing left over.

Tanous: *I see. We're comparing small stock returns to the market as a whole. What you're saying is that small stock returns have risk that's not explained by the market. And this higher risk is the size risk you talk about in the three-factor model? Is that correct?*

Fama: Right. Take a diversified portfolio of value stocks. Those stocks will move together. That portfolio's return will not be perfectly explained by the market even if it has a few thousand stocks in it.

Tanous: *If that's the case, wouldn't growth stocks mirror the market as a whole?*

Fama: Growth stocks do come closer to mirroring the market as a whole.

Tanous: *So once you've decided to take the market risk, creating your portfolio seems to come down to deciding what your overall risk level is, and then you allocate by size, and between growth and value, to achieve your risk/reward goals.*

Have there been any studies that have ever impressed you about active management in any capacity? I mean, has there been any evidence that would suggest to you that all of the Wall Street analysts, gurus, salesmen, and research departments are anything but a complete waste of time?

Fama: You used the key word: salesmen. I might be willing to say that the people who get pointed at consistently, who have shown consistent performance even after they have been pointed at, really do have something. These are always the same people, Warren Buffett, Peter Lynch, and then who?

Tanous: *Okay. You talk to Rex Sinquefield, and he'll tell you that in any normal distribution you're going to get those outlying orangutans.*

Fama: I put it carefully. I said if you identify them, and in the future they continue to do well, then I'm starting to believe it. This sounds like the frustrations of my college days when I found that the system that worked on the old data didn't work with the new data!

Tanous: *So, in fact, there may be a Lynch and a Buffett effect out there somewhere?*

Fama: There may be, but the *non sequiturs* that people jump to after that is to say, aha! Active management pays!

Tanous: *No, it means that Peter Lynch and Warren Buffett pay! And what is it about them that we can clone? Where's the next one?*

Fama: Yeah. I don't think that's something you can teach anybody or anything like that. The Magellan Fund *[once managed by Peter Lynch]* by any risk-adjusted model, is off the map. But there are only one or two like that.

Tanous: *Isn't it interesting that the last three years' performance at Magellan Fund isn't Peter Lynch's? Jeff Vinik's performance was also good. I presume because he made a big bet on technology stocks and won.*

Fama: Another thing I found when I looked at Magellan was that it had a greater small stock bias when it was a smaller fund.

Tanous: *Are you working on anything now that you could share with us?*

Fama: We're trying to extend the three-factor model internationally. The scientific approach is always to say: does it work out of sample? In other words, does it work on new data, in this case, foreign stocks? So, what we are doing is trying to use international data to see if we can come up with a global view of risk and return.

Tanous: *How does it look so far?*

Fama: The problem is that the international data stink. You can't get the kind of data we can get here in the U.S. going back to 1926. We also have good accounting data going back to the early sixties. Internationally, you don't really have returns before 1988. And you only have a sub-sample of stocks.

Tanous: *How much data do you need to get a valid sample?*

Fama: You never know that until you do it, because it's a function of how variable the returns are. The problem with stock returns is the variability is so high. It takes long samples to really document anything. But, so far, the new data turn up the same kind of risk factors.

Tanous: *I guess we still haven't found a way to predict the future.*

Fama: That kind of reasoning will get you closer to my way of thinking!

Tanous: *The trouble with you academic guys is that you all approach this with such religious zeal that I feel like a heretic if I disagree with any of you. Like I'm going to be excommunicated any second.*

Fama: No. We'll just throw you out of the scientific community. You get to stay in the active management community.

Tanous: *Gene, you're very well known in our business for your work on returns. Do you do much work in the private sector?*

Fama: Not a lot. I'm a little lazy! Most of the outside work I do is in a forum framework. I mean how am I going to manage to do all that if I go windsurfing every afternoon?

Tanous: *How's your windsurfing coming along?*

Fama: I'm probably the best in the world over age fifty!

Tanous: *Who knows, Gene, maybe you're the millionth orangutan on the surfboard, the fifty-year-old outlier who wins the world championship.*

A couple of things struck me about this discussion. You might or might not agree, but I thought I sensed a much more open attitude from Gene about market efficiency, the concept he developed. I felt that his was not the extreme version of the efficient market theory that some others adopt, but rather an open-minded attitude which says that, yes, market efficiency is there and chances are you will never do better than the markets, and as a rule, active management just doesn't pay.

On the other hand, the door seemed open a crack to the reality that there are the occasional Peter Lynches and others who achieve truly great performance records over extended periods of time. The term the academics like to use for this is "persistence." Yes, these guys exist, but there aren't that many. Still, the sobering example Fama used that throws cold water on the performance expectations is the study he did on mutual fund performance over a ten year period since 1976. He then took the top performing funds in the group and analyzed them for the following ten years. The result: the top performing group only had a 50/50 chance of staying in the top half in the second ten year period. What are you going to do? I think it's time we talked to another active manager.

BRUCE
SHERMAN

Private Capital Management which is run by Bruce Sherman is not a typical money manager. The firm started out as the family office of the wealthy Collier family, at one time among the largest landowners in Florida. Besides their sage real estate purchases, the family also was lucky and smart enough to attract Bruce Sherman, a CPA born and bred in New York, to join the family business and, eventually, manage money. Originally intent on a career in accounting, Bruce was so successful at managing the Colliers' money, that he and they decided to expand their scope to include outside clients who might benefit from Bruce's successful style of investment management. Thus, was born Private Capital Management.

How successful is his style? For the five years ended in 1995, Private Capital Management's returns were 25% per year, versus 17% for the S&P 500 over the same period. All right, you say, I'm getting jaded. You've already shown me managers who do that well or even better. Right. But Sherman achieved these remarkable results without incurring any more risk than holding the S&P 500 would. To put it in perspective, over those five years Private Capital Management's standard deviation was 9.6 while the S&P 500's was 9.1. That, my friends, is a real achievement.

Private Capital Management is located in Naples, Florida, a bucolic, not to say sleepy, town on the west coast of Florida, where retirement is a growth industry. We met at the company's offices, located in one of the Collier family's office buildings, on U.S. 41.

Tanous: *How did you first get interested in stocks?*

Sherman: My father, whom I lost a couple of years ago, was an engineer. For my Bar Mitzvah present, he gave me 10 shares of Polaroid. By the time I turned 21, Polaroid had grown from about $20 a share to $180. It was at that point that my father gave me possession of the shares. I sold it all the day I got it. My father asked why? I said, I read the annual report; I had taken a business course in college; I took some accounting, obviously; and I sold it. I asked myself why should something sell at 50 to 60 times earnings, let alone 100 times cash flow? I don't think it ever saw that price again.

A better indication of my interest in the stock market: I used to go with my dad to the Dupont Glore Forgon office in Great Neck even though I lived in Little Neck, to watch the tape. That got me interested.

Tanous: *You have a background as a CPA, don't you?*

Sherman: My brother was the one who went to the Ivy League school and became a doctor. I was the third son. My mother said, if we're going to pay for business school for you, you have to take an accounting degree so you can become somebody when you get out. So I went to a good accounting school, became a CPA, and it was a great experience. Most young people on the Street think they know accounting, but they really don't. When you start talking to them about management's fungibility in making earnings per share, it may be a little like Greek to them. They don't worry about the deferred tax liabilities on balance sheets; they don't worry about companies trading revenue for prepaid advertising and some of the incongruent accounting artifacts that can make or break earnings.

At Arthur Young *[the accounting firm],* I was diligently doing the audits for a lot of big public companies, like a good manager. Sometimes the partner would come down and say, we're going to take a reserve of $100 million. They used to call that "big bath" accounting. And I'd say, well, what's it for? He'd say, well, we have a list but we can't show it to you. And then, over the next five years,

I saw how the company would live off the reserve by charges against the reserve, thereby inflating earnings.

The best experience, and I don't want to ramble on, was in my twenties, when I spent about two years in the report review department at Arthur Young.

Tanous: *What's report review?*

Sherman: All you did was read annual reports, proxies, and 10Ks. I did very well in there. I loved doing it. My job was to look at the hard numbers to see if everything reconciled. Did the fund statement reconcile to the balance sheet? If the inventory went from 100 days to 125 days, you could ask the partner: Did you really audit the inventory? You had the ability to ask any question you wanted about those financial statements and you had as much time as you needed to do the work. In essence, you were auditing and reviewing and asking things like, is the fully diluted earnings per share calculation right? Why isn't there disclosure on the preferred stock issue? These were all disclosure-type questions, which ultimately led to what I love today—which is discretionary cash flow analysis.

Tanous: *At some point in your life, you made a jump to where you are now. Tell me about that. Also, about Private Capital Management, which also has an unusual history.*

Sherman: I've only had two jobs. When I hire people, I try not to hire people who have had a lot of jobs. I was a principal in the New York office of Arthur Young and, one day, a search firm called. I was an impressionable 29-year-old and the person said, a large asset-based company with a small staff is looking for a chief financial officer, experienced in venture capital, investments, real estate, tax planning, etc. I had a lot of real estate experience with clients, albeit I didn't know what I didn't know. I had always been around taxes. I had a lot of investment experience.

The client turned out to be the Collier family, so I went to meet them. Miles Collier had been looking for somebody for about a year. We're very different. I went to Rhode Island; he went to Yale. I got my MBA at night at Baruch; he went to Columbia during the day. He's a brilliant, hardworking individual, who just has a different background than I do. I invested a considerable amount of time and effort getting to know him, and he did likewise. So I came to Florida, and to Collier County.

Tanous: *I presume the name is not a coincidence.*

Sherman: Not a coincidence. The county is named after the Collier family who, at one time, owned almost all of Collier County—which is bigger than the State of Delaware. They owned over a million acres. This was the third generation.

I soon realized that the staff at their company was very small and the asset base was very large. Miles has a lot of experience hiring professional money managers. I had to earn my stripes. I sat on the *Naples Daily News* board of directors, and I sold the company to Scripps Howard. I was on a couple of their venture capital boards, too. I wasn't afraid to take an aggressive stance about where I thought they should put their money and where they shouldn't. I did some investing alongside their professional money managers in New York, and earned the opportunity to become a money manager and grow our operation internally. If you grow a money management firm successfully enough, you can have it for almost nothing, because the fees you get for managing outside money cover your costs. So, in 1985, we founded Private Capital Management.

Tanous: *You've expanded the company to take outside clients.*

Sherman: Right. We started out running $50 million. We never had more than one marketing person. I don't do a lot of marketing, because I think that would take away from what we're attempting to do. Now we're up to an organization of 15 people—4 security analysts, the rest support staff—managing $1 billion.

Tanous: *Let's talk about your approach. Yours is a small-cap, value style. Right?*

Sherman: I would say small- to medium-cap depending on your definitions. Up to $1.5 billion in market capitalization would be midcap. Small-cap for us starts at $50 million in capitalization.

Tanous: *Most small-cap and mid-cap managers are growth managers. You happen to be a value manager. As you know, most managers define value stocks as high book-to-market stocks. I suspect your definition is broader.*

Sherman: Good question. Book, to us, is a starting place. It is meaningless. America has written off book value left and right. Property, plant and equipment may show under-utilization of assets and returns. So our definition of value is intrinsic value—the private market value that someone would pay for the business, coupled with the discretionary cash flow that the business generates. I can put all businesses on a discretionary free cash flow generation basis, whereas earnings per share are different in different industries. A bank and a thrift generate discretionary free cash flow, if reserves are stated properly. A media company doesn't have a lot of capital requirements, at least in the television media. A manufacturer has heavy capital requirements. The market, using Value Line statistics *[as simplistic as that may sound]*, sells at about 30 × to 35 × free cash flow.

Tanous: *Now might be a good time to define free cash flow.*

Sherman: It's defined as cash from operations, minus capital expenditures. That's after all expenses and everything that working capital has to absorb, like inventory, receivables, whatever. That's free cash flow. It's right on the company's financial statement.

You can take a cable company, and someone may say that the cable company is selling at 12 × cash flow. Well, if they have to spend $100 per subscriber to upgrade their wire, you've got to take that number out. Now, maybe it's selling at 15 × to 16 × cash flow. If something is selling at 15 × to 16 × cash flow, and it's a 6% yield, that means I can have a business that's going to grow, yielding 6%. That might be attractive.

Conversely, there may be companies that are selling at low earnings multiples, but the capital expenditures requirements are so high that the company may not have any ability to generate free cash flow over a three year period. Free cash flow allows a company to buy back its own stock, pay down debt, or buy incremental new businesses. So, in any business, I evaluate how much free cash flow a company can generate over the next three, five, or ten years. We measure our own personal lives by how much free cash we have in the bank; we should evaluate companies the same way. We will pass up companies that have good earnings momentum and a good earnings story if all the cash is getting sucked up by capital expenditures unrelated to expansion, or being sucked up by receivables, inventories, or prepaids. You can fudge it on the income statement just so long. Eventually the problems start to show up on the balance sheet.

Tanous: *So every company you look at goes through this evaluation process?*

Sherman: Yes. And my associates know to look for it. Just the other day someone brought me an idea, Mikasa china. It's selling at 11 × earnings; it's been beaten up. It went public a year or two ago. My problem is, why are they building a $70 million distribution facility? What's wrong with the one they have? Isn't that going to suck up cash?

It reminds me of Haggar, which was a good non-buy when the stock was 20. It had just earned two or three bucks; it looked cheap; so I went to visit the company. I said, if you could generate all that free cash, why would you sell the business and go public? *[Companies often go public to raise capital, but sometimes go public for other reasons.]* Finally, management indicated that, if they could generate levels of cash flow equal to earnings, they wouldn't have.

Tanous: *Some of the other value managers I talked to, Mario Gabelli [page 77] and Laura Sloate [page 133] come to mind, have a precept about value stocks and the kind of analysis you go through. But both of them add a factor they call the catalyst. In other words, it's great to have all these cheap stocks, but aren't you worried they're going to stay cheap forever? Do you look for a catalyst?*

Sherman: Not necessarily. There are a lot of lousy companies selling below book value. Unitel Video is a great example. The stock is six bucks; we've never owned a share. It had $12 or $13 per share book value before their recent write-off. That looks cheap. And they make a little money! But it's all video post-production editing equipment. The reality is that the technology changes every three or four years. Guess what, fellas? They're under-depreciating their assets.

Most of America under-depreciates their assets. Twenty-five years ago, one of my clients, American Standard, had a big foreign operation. They made their units report *replacement* cost depreciation on their internal financial statements even though, for the public, they were reporting economic depreciation *[which was much less]*. I don't think accounting standards have improved that much in this country over 25 years. The quality of auditing certainly hasn't.

But you asked about a catalyst. Free cash flow will become a catalyst. The money will pile up. The company will use those funds for something good. If nobody recognizes the stock value, they will use that cash to buy their own stock.

Tanous: *Your approach is grounded in what you grew up with, which is accounting. It's obviously been successful, but I also happen to* *know that you frequently visit companies. I would have thought that somebody with your background would be so comfortable with the numbers and so comfortable in doing these analysis, that you probably wouldn't care about visiting the companies.*

I'll give you an example: one of the people I interviewed, who is a very successful young fund manager, is Eric Ryback [page 197]. He manages the Lindner Dividend Fund. He follows the precepts of his mentor, the late Kurt Lindner, who approached investing in almost the same way you do, with one difference. They never visited companies! They never talked to managements! They don't care about visiting companies because, they say, all those guys are going to do is snow you, and put their own spin on things.

Sherman: As an auditor, by definition, you visit companies. In the last ten years, I probably visited 250 companies. I like several things about company visits. One, you are totally immersed in that company. In the motel the night before, if you're traveling with an associate, all you're thinking and talking about is that company. No phones, no Bloomberg screens, no trading calls, nothing.

Tanous: *There's always HBO.*

Sherman: I'd rather read my stuff. When you spend a few hours at the company the next morning, you are totally immersed. You are not seeing the people on a road show, not seeing them with charts in front of a hundred analysts. You're seeing the CEO in his office. You ask to spend a half-hour with the CFO. You're seeing the cars in the parking lot. You're asking the in-your-face questions that he doesn't want to answer.

I just took a big position in International Game Technology. I wanted to own that stock five or six years ago. It's always been too expensive. It was never close to being a value stock. They dominate their industry; they're a casino without walls, because they have these link progressive machines. But the stock disappointed. They had flat earnings instead of up 25%. They promptly lost half of their market capitalization. The company was buying back their stock. The stock had gone from 25 to 12, and I established about a two million share position between 12 and 12 1/2. But before I did that, I had to find out what I didn't know; I had to go visit the company. Here they are in the casino business, the world's largest slot machine manufacturer, and I want to know what these people are like. I was supposed to meet the CEO, but the chairman terminated him about a week before I got there. But, in speaking to all the other people up and down the organization, I was able to come away with things I never would have deduced without a company visit.

Tanous: *How about an example?*

Sherman: I asked: Tell me about the people who are talking negatively about your company. Tell me about the new technology that your competitors have. I don't want to read it in Bear Stearns research. I want to see it myself.

Now here we are in Reno, Nevada in winter, and I get a call that my daughter at Northwestern is sick, so I had to fly to Chicago, but I didn't have a coat. So I asked this fellow, the investor relations guy who was schlepping me around, to drive me to a store to buy a coat. We get there. He tries to take me to the fancy coat section, and I go to the cheap coat section. But I found more out in the 45-minute drive to the clothing store where I bought an overcoat than I did anywhere else.

Most important, on the way to the airport, I ask him, what does the chairman do? And he says all he does is keep busy managing the buyback of the stock. Now I really wanted to hear that they were still buying the stock back before I bought it. My original premise for possibly buying it was: You're getting the manufacturing of the slot machines for free if you pay $12 for the stock. That gives you the value of the cash flow generation from their megabucks, their link progressive machines. They link up machines around the country *[and create giant jackpots].* So I was glad to hear that the chairman apparently agreed, and was still buying the stock.

Tanous: *Is the point of this that you learned about the buyback as a result of the detour to buy the coat?*

Sherman: The point is, that when you take somebody out of their element and you're not sitting in their office in a formal structure, you can relax. I was on the fence about the stock situation. That detour helped me learn things I would not have learned in my office analyzing numbers.

Tanous: *How's your daughter?*

Sherman: Oh, she's fine now.

Tanous: *Any other examples?*

Sherman: I also went to *Brinkers International,* a stock I didn't buy.

Tanous: *Those are the Chili's people?*

Sherman: Yes, the Chili's restaurant chain. I was sitting in their offices, actually on the same trip, and the CFO has a Bloomberg *[a financial newswire and data terminal].* Why does a CFO need a Bloomberg in his office? Is he worried about stock quotes for the restaurants' accounts? Not with my money!

Tanous: *Let's get a little deeper into your style. I want to quote something from your brochure. In bold letters, which jump out at you, it says: "One inviolable standard is DON'T LOSE MONEY." That's a tough thing to do with your record. Your five year returns average 25% on your composite portfolio, and your risk, measured by standard deviation, is the same, or less, than the market as a whole. That's pretty amazing.*

Sherman: *Money Manager Review* came out with us in it. SEI *[a large investment management and financial consulting firm]* just came in and looked at us sixteen-ways-to-Sunday. And I get really bored because I don't know how they do what they do. I really don't care because, to me, all this is about absolute dollars. What counts to me is comparing net worth in period A to net worth in period B. I also want to adjust for taxes in taxable accounts. *Money Manager Review* said we were in the top 7% of value managers for the five years ended December 1995, and number one out of 641 on a risk-adjusted basis. If you ask me how they got to that, I don't know. It probably has to do with portfolio volatility against the mean, by quarter.

Tanous: *But Bruce, you can't ignore that! Surely you appreciate the value of a risk-adjusted performance. Your performance, as great as it is, is enhanced by the fact that your investors, for some reason which you may or may not be conscious of, are not taking the same kinds of risk to get these returns as they might have to with another manager. I think that's an important point.*

Sherman: I'll bet that 90% of today's investment managers have never experienced a bear market. There really hasn't been much of a bear market since 1985. The year of the crash *[1987]* we were up 18% and the overall market was up slightly. In the last four or five days, we've been pretty heavy sellers of some of our positions. Why?

Because a lot of the stocks we bought at 50 cents on the intrinsic dollar, are now trading at 80 or 90 cents on the dollar. It's hard to kiss them good-bye, but you have to.

But the answer to your question about our emphasis on never losing money, is that the bulk of our money is private capital. Private money is a precious, irreplaceable commodity. With confiscatory taxation, it's very hard to earn it.

Remember the old line, what's the definition of a good investment for a doctor? Answer: He gets his money back. It's the same for my own account. It's the only thing we know how to do. For example, Coca-Cola is a great company. The market capitalization, as I sit here looking at a Coke can, is greater than the capitalization of the bottom 100 companies in the Standard & Poor's 500 *combined*. Coke probably sells at 40 × to 45 × free cash flow, and it's a great product. But to me, that's an inversion of a 2% yield. And I don't know why people would pay that.

Tanous: *Please explain that.*

Sherman: Well, it's probably selling at 30 × to 35 × earnings, and Coke does have capital expenditures. If you adjust the numbers, you would see that it is probably selling at 40 × free cash flow, by our definition. If something is 40 × free cash flow, inverting that is a 2.5% yield on that cash. *[In other words, for every $100 spent to purchase stock, the company generates $2.50 of free cash.]* And why do I need to hold something at 2.5%? Having said that, it's been a wonderful holding for some people. But no bell is going to go off when it's over. Let me get back to your question. Your question was about our intense antagonism to losing money.

Tanous: *Also, the one you haven't answered yet about volatility. Maybe there is no answer. Are you saying that you don't manage with volatility in mind? Does it just happen?*

Sherman: We do not manage with volatility in mind. We are the first, second, or third largest shareholder in about 50% of the names in our portfolio. I want to know more about the companies than anybody. I want to be thinking like an owner. I want to be thinking like a CEO. And our names are companies that are traditionally sleepy. No one on the Street follows them. They're not out selling stock. They want to be off the radar screens. They may be public for some of the strangest reasons. Maybe they were public for 25 years and they have since disappointed investors, but they have inherently good, strong cash flow characteristics.

Nirvana, to me, is a stock like BHC Communications, which is a Gabelli *[page 77]* stock. The company is Herb Siegel's company. I'm oversimplifying, but it's the company that was created when he became the white knight for Time Warner. It owns the third or fourth largest group of independent TV stations in the country, including a TV station in New York and a TV station in L.A. It pukes out cash flow. It has about $65 to $70 a share in cash. No debt. It sells at about 93, and it's run by smart people. It started the UPN network which, is trying to become the fifth network. Of the 12 million shares that were publicly floated four years ago, there are now only 6 million shares of public float. Siegel is a patient man. He bought 6 million shares back in the open market.

Tanous: *How much of that do you own?*

Sherman: We own about 12% of the 6 million share float. *[The float is that portion of the stock that can trade in the open market.]* It's a big position. Remember, there were 30 million shares outstanding. Chris Craft Industries owns 18 million shares *[not part of the float]*. That left 12 million shares outstanding. The company retired 6 million shares of the stock and now that's down to only 6 million outstanding. Theoretically, I want to own the last share. I want to see management face-to-face. If I think it's worth 50 cents on the dollar, and they don't think it's worth 50 cents on the dollar and they're not buying the stock back, then I'm making a mistake. So I want to be in-their-face and ask them, why?

Software Spectrum is a classic example. The stock has done well in the past two or three years. It started showing up on our radar screen at 9 or 10 and the stock recently got over 20. We're the biggest shareholder of the company. They're the world's largest corporate reseller of software products. They've gone to electronic distribution, as opposed to hard, shrink-wrapped software distribution. Most of their employees around the world work out of their homes. They provide service to people. So when this stock got down to 10, my associate kept asking, why aren't they buying the stock back? It's selling below book value; it's got $3.00 a share in cash; it's trading at 7 × cash flow; so why aren't they buying back the stock? We wrote letters to the board. In the end, we find out that they've been working on a strategic acquisition for two years which consumes all the cash. That's a good answer. I don't want to invest in cash for cash's sake, because I can do that myself. Our clients can hold cash. I want to see stock buybacks or I want to see that cash utilized. *[A secretary comes in with an important phone message and shows it to Bruce Sherman. He replies that he'll have to return the call.]*

Sherman: That guy who just called is the CFO of Albank Financial Corp. It's a $3 billion bank. I'm the largest shareholder. When the stock was about $18, I wrote a check for 600,000 shares. The stock is now 28. They just turned down an offer of $35 a share for the company. I am leaping out of my chair! Not only did I write the management a letter, I sent a copy to all the directors. I got the directors' addresses by having somebody look them up. I wanted them to get the letters at their home addresses. They have a fiduciary obligation! If they turned down the offer, I want to ask them: Why did you turn it down? What other alternatives do you have? They said, "If we sell, now is not the right time and we're not sure they're the right purchaser." My question is, who is the right purchaser, and when is the right time? They have an obligation. At least the company just announced a buyback of stock.

Money managers don't like to get in there and mix it up. It's my obligation, if somebody pays me compensation, to get in there and protect their interests. Shareholders have rights and they need to be protected. Michael Price *[page 33]* did it with Chase. We can do it on a smaller scale.

Tanous: *Let's talk about your sell discipline.*

Sherman: It's much harder to sell than to buy because, before you buy you can crunch numbers, visit management, understand the dynamics, and you don't have to think about what the economy is doing. Of course, you ought to know what's going on in the industry, whether it's media, health care, or software.

The sell side is difficult. You have to sell not when they're fully valued, but when they're close to fully valued. To be candid, most sales in a bull market have been good intellectual sales, but the stocks really haven't gone down. So I'm really converting a piece of paper to cash.

The discipline is, if I buy and I think it's trading at 50 to 60 cents on the dollar, or 8 × to 10 × free cash flow *[which is a good multiple of free cash flow]*, and then it goes up to 15 × or 16 × free cash flow, and I think management is about to announce a secondary stock offering, I run for the hills. If you think management's going to build a new corporate headquarters, you'd better run for the hills. (I'm oversimplifying.) And you need to read those proxies, read those footnotes. Where is the value accruing to? Is it accruing to management as compensation? Is it accruing to the shareholders? So it becomes intuitive, but it all goes into the mix. It's hard to be a seller, other than a disciplined seller. We sell on a graduated basis.

Rio Hotel. We went out and visited them. RHC is the symbol. It's a Las Vegas stock. Rio Hotel & Casino is extremely well run. It always wins the Best of Vegas awards. It's an all-suite hotel, great property. All of sudden, they had a flat quarter. Stock was hit down to about $11 or $12 a share. What an opportunity. Now it's only 5 × or 6 × EBITDA *[Earnings before Interest, Taxes, Depreciation, and Amortization]*, 8 × or 9 × cash flow. I'm looking for a reason to buy, but management hasn't bought a share. All of a sudden Marnell, the chairman, buys 150,000 shares in the open market. He's already a rich guy. He thinks the same way I do. That's unusual. This is 3 months ago. Stock went right up to 18. You want to be lucky rather than smart sometime? I can't tell you why it happened, other than Bear Stearns picked up coverage and started writing about the stock. It's gone from 12 to 18.

Tanous: *How did you find it originally?*

Sherman: It showed up on the computer screens. The company's EBITDA and multiples against residual market value got our attention. We have formulas to calculate this. Gregg Powers, a valued associate, does a tremendous job. I say, give me a listing of all companies in this order: percentage of outstanding stock they bought back, rated by EBITDA multiple, compared to residual market value. Then take free cash flow, by lumping all capital expenditures against the number, without analyzing it. Then run the computer screens. Sometimes you get garbage. Half of it is junk, but you'll find some oddball companies which were once followed by the Street but are no longer followed. Those might become great ideas.

That's the starting point. You read the material; make a lot of phone calls. You talk to the company's customers; get the investor relations people; get the management on the phone, see how they respond. Now you don't go into a meeting and ask: What's your next quarter going to look like? That's what Wall Street does. Understand what your two-to-five year time horizon is, and then go visit the company. The company visit is half of it.

Tanous: *It's interesting when you talk about doing this work. As you know, some of the people I'm interviewing are efficient market theorists. Their view is that everything about a company is reflected in the price of the stock at all times. So they think the idea of running these screens and finding stuff is a waste of time because, as the theory goes, anything you might be able to figure out is already in the price of the stock.*

Sherman: I had a client call up who gave us about $3 million and now it's worth $11 or $12 million. I don't remember the timeframe, but it's been about 7 or 8 years. He wants to put some money in large-cap stocks. This happened last Friday. He thinks that we've been great. At the time we represented about 50% of his net worth; now it's about 80% of his net worth. And he thinks it's reasonable for him to want to go large-cap. So he asks if we can recommend a large-cap manager. I said, I'm going to save you some money. Don't buy a manager, buy the index. You can own the index by buying "spiders" *[so-called because the abbreviation is "SPDR," which stands for Standard & Poor's Depository Receipts]* on the American Stock Exchange. Symbol SPY. You'll own the index; you won't pay taxes; and you can own it forever, if that's what you want. And, if I don't outperform that index from here forward, fire me, and maybe I'll put my money with you.

Tanous: *In essence, you are challenging the efficient market crowd by putting your money where your mouth is. Your message is, if I can't beat the market, don't pay me; in fact, fire me. That certainly seems fair. But in your case, Bruce, you go beyond what most managers do in their investment strategy. Of all the managers I'm interviewing for this book, you are the only one who uses short sales, albeit to a limited extent. I deliberately avoided interviewing hedge fund managers because I want the readers of this book to be able to identify with managers who invest the way they do. You don't call yourself a hedge fund manager, and I don't think you identify with them. So please explain. Give us examples of stocks you've shorted and how those shorts fit in with your philosophy.*

Sherman: I think the best way to describe shorting is, if you believe in value, by definition you believe in anti-value. If you're looking for companies that have certain characteristics, you can make money on the long side. The same is true on the short side for companies that have the following characteristics: no free cash flow, heavy insider selling, no franchise value, poor to average management, and fungible accounting. Remember, I spent ten years of my early professional life making earnings per share. I know you can be pretty creative in making earnings. If you had those characteristics, at least up until this crazy momentum market of 1996, it was a great vehicle for us. We identified four or five accounting shenanigans, where we were among the first to identify them. I think of Delmed and Media Vision, for example. We made a lot of money for our clients that way.

But, so far in 1996, that's not possible. Every Monday morning, mutual fund companies are pouring money into names like Iomega. The stock has quadrupled. I wouldn't be in business if we had shorted a lot of that. I can tell you that, in the first quarter of 1996, anything that had sex-appeal and a story behind it, even if it met my short criteria, was going up in your face. So first, we want to be right, like in 1994 when the market was flat and we had an overall return of 14%. The shorts paid off handsomely. I think it's going to happen again in 1996.

Tanous: *What are you shorting now, with all these stocks going crazy?*

Sherman: You want names?

Tanous: *Sure.*

Sherman: Okay. We have a company called Just for Feet which has 22 (going to 30) sneaker super stores. It has a market capitalization of about $850 million, or about $30 million per store. You can put one of these stores up for about $1.5 million. In the proxy statement, not the annual report—always read the proxy first—the president has personally guaranteed $17 million worth of vendor payables. That's for a company with a market capitalization of $850 million. Why did he have to guarantee those payables? Their format is a superstore selling sneakers. Now, at last count, there are about 25,000 mall units around the country selling sneakers. According to the proxy statement, the company borrowed $50 million on January 28th, and paid it back on February 2nd, so they could show good cash per share in their annual report (their fiscal year-end is January 31st). They have ten months of inventory, but they don't take mark-downs *[on their balance sheet]*. They got through their audit this year; we don't think they'll get through their audit next year.

Tanous: *Where's the stock now?*

Sherman: The stock is around 50. Management has cashed out about $200 million worth of stock. We've visited seven or eight stores. They're good merchants. The guy had one shoe store for about fifteen years. He probably took home half a million dollars a year. Now, only in America, in two short years he's probably worth about $300 million.

Tanous: *Short sales are risky, of course, because if the stock keeps going up, there's no theoretical limit to your losses. How do you assess the risk in this situation?*

Sherman: The risk is if you believe there will be, maybe, 3,000 super sneaker stores around the country. Or, if you believe what they told us, and I quote, "We've invented entertainment retailing." They have a popcorn stand and a hot dog stand and, they say, "We taught Barnes and Noble how to do it." I think it's a phenomenal short idea. I should point out that it's gone up since we shorted it.

Tanous: *That does sound like a great idea. But I presume these shorts are a small percentage of your portfolio.*

Sherman: Typically, we have two types of accounts. We have long-only accounts, and we have long-and-short accounts. We let the client make that decision. In the long/short account, the shorts will be a small portion of the total account.

Tanous: *What are your minimums?*

Sherman: Minimums are $1.0 million. Fees start at 1.5%.

Tanous: *What advice would you have for investors who might not be able to put money with you?*

Sherman: The stock market has offered higher returns than almost any other vehicle since early in the century. It is an efficient mechanism over time. But a lot of people don't have the patience and don't look at it over a five year horizon. I think people who get into the market should stay in the market and understand what they own.

Peter Lynch *[page 119]* puts it pretty simplistically, "Know what you own." I would buy a mutual fund and find out who is really running it. I would also open a discount brokerage account somewhere and buy one or two stocks. Figure out a reason you want to own them, and don't just say, I've been to the Gap and my kids spend all their money there. It's not that simple. Understand how much you're paying for it, because in our business: price paid, quality received. Mercedes at a Cadillac price, or a Cadillac at a Chevy price. That allows room for error. If you can't find that, there's nothing wrong with cash.

The bottom line of the whole process is doing work. One magazine reporter asked me once, what do you do in your spare time? I said, I read 10Ks in the Jacuzzi. So he asked, could we take a picture of you doing that? I said my body doesn't warrant taking a picture in the Jacuzzi. But you've got to have a passion. The thing that differentiates good managers from mediocre managers is, you've got to have a passion.

You can take the man out of New York, but you can't take New York out of the man. Welcome to in-your-face investing! But personality aside, it's interesting how your individual background and interests will find their way into whatever it is you decide to do. If I hadn't told you that Bruce Sherman was a professional accountant, could you have guessed? Of course you could, because his investment philosophy is rooted in value and, boy, does he know how to read those financial statements! His success in investing proves that his approach really makes sense, too.

Let's review some of the Bruce Sherman basics. You want to own a company that has a lot of free cash flow—that's cash flow after all the company's expenses, but also allowing for any necessary capital expenditures the company might have, or is planning to have, which will also use that cash flow. The search for the free cash flow is valuable because companies that have extra cash can do interesting things, like buy back their own stock (something else that Bruce likes to see), or retire debt. Then there's the management. Bruce Sherman wants to make sure that the management is up to the task, *so he visits them and sees them in their own environment. This, of course, is something that's a lot harder for the rest of us to do, since when Bruce calls up, they know he might be prepared to invest $50 million or so in their company.*

If any of this has a familiar ring, let me help you out. The common element is what the lawyers call "due diligence" and you and I call "hard work." Fortunately, Bruce Sherman actually enjoys what he does. Poring over financial statements is major recreation to him. But as we consider how he invests, we begin to see the elements of his success. Research is the key to finding value, particularly undiscovered value. You may not be able to do everything that Bruce Sherman does, either because you may not be a professional accountant or have instant access to corporate managements, but there are a number of clues in this investing approach that each of us can learn from. Just remember to take those 10Ks into the Jacuzzi with you.

RYBACK

The Lindner Funds—named after legendary investment manager Kurt Lindner, who died in 1995—are managed by Lindner's protégé, Eric Ryback. Based in St. Louis, Missouri, the fund group today comprises six mutual funds: the Lindner Growth, Lindner Dividend, Lindner Utility, Lindner/Ryback Small-Cap, Lindner Bulwark, and Lindner International. A nice collection, but we're here because of just one of them: the legendary Lindner Dividend Fund, which has, arguably, the best risk-adjusted performance of any fund in America. This fund was started in 1976. Since then, it has compiled a record of 17% annual growth (through the end of 1995). Yes, you can find a few others that have done that well, but you won't find another fund, or I daresay another manager, with that kind of return in a very low-risk investment style. In fact, the Lindner Dividend Fund states that "capital appreciation is a secondary goal." The fund, long a favorite of very conservative investors, continues to compile an enviable record year after year.

Eric Ryback has been managing the Lindner Dividend Fund since 1982. If we were looking for clues and common background traits which lead to successful investment management, here's another one to add to our list: backpacking. Eric Ryback's claim to fame, prior to joining the money management community, was that while still in college, he became the first person to complete backpacking's *"triple crown" by hiking 8,000 miles, over three summer vacations, thereby completing all three cross country routes: the Appalachian Trail, the Pacific Crest Trail, and the Continental Divide Trail. Imagine the kind of discipline, perseverance, and character that exploit takes! We were eager to speak with Eric Ryback about how he does it.*

Tanous: *How did you first get interested in stocks?*

Ryback: I think it goes back to high school. My mother was trying to get me interested in reading, so she bought me this book on J. Paul Getty. It was a paperback. I remember reading about this man who made millions in the oil industry. I was very impressed with that. I then gravitated away from the investment side of things and more toward the outdoor life. I had an outfitting and guide business.

Tanous: *So I heard! Your hiking record is quite impressive.*

Ryback: That's what Kurt *[Lindner]* was impressed with, believe it or not! He had done a lot of hiking, and I think he related to the fact that it took a lot of planning, perseverance, and foresight to accomplish one of these major hiking events. I've applied that to the investing I do.

Tanous: *Indeed you have. In fact, Eric, you're the only manager I'm interviewing who focuses on yield* [dividend per share as a percent of stock price and interest as a percent of bond price]. *Would it be correct to say that a manager who is very interested in yield uses selection criteria similar to that of most value managers?*

Ryback: I would think so, particularly if, like us, you're going after higher yield. Higher yield traditionally equates to higher risk. Since we are seeking high yield, we have to overcome that risk factor. If we apply a value approach to it, or a fundamental approach, we hope we can define what we call "the intrinsic value" of an entity or a company. If we can define value correctly, we know what the company is worth, and then we attempt to buy that security at a discount. If we can apply that same kind of analysis when we're going after yield, we can overcome the risk factor—that is, the higher the yield, the higher the risk. I think we've proven that with our long-term track record.

Tanous: *Yes. I'll get to your performance record later—I certainly want to talk about it—doesn't the process we're discussing involve finding overlooked securities?*

Ryback: Definitely.

Tanous: *This brings up the other interesting theoretical discussion. You know that the efficient market theorists don't believe that over-looked securities exist. To them, as you know, everything that is known about a stock is in its price now. How has your experience been different from that?*

Ryback: I agree with the efficient market theorists up to a point, but I'll give you a prime example that occurs almost every day where the theory doesn't always work—that's new issues. New issues are brought out, traditionally, through brokerage firms. They're well disseminated, even touted, to the public. Obviously, the more information these firms disseminate while they tell the story, the higher the price they can get for the company and the more the brokerage or investment banking firms will make. As a result, the public perception of new issues is quite high. There are other factors, of course. Is the issue hot? Is it an internet-related company, since they're hot today? The public has been well informed by the press about how great the internet is, so that's an easier sale than trying to sell an oil stock today, or even a retail stock, since they're down in the dumps. So, there's generally a high *[investing]* public perception of new issues.

But what happens if an issue falls by the wayside very quickly? That could be the result of a number of factors, particularly if you're bringing out a new issue when the market is near a top. Even in a good market, when you get a few 100 point down days, those new issues can fall by the wayside very quickly. They come out, they get caught up in the general market, and they get lost. That's when the inefficiency comes into play. These issues are quickly forgotten by the public because the public is focused on the overall market. So these new issues can come out quickly, sell off, and be forgotten.

Tanous: *Interesting point. You're saying that sometimes, a new stock is overlooked because investors are distracted from the stock itself by the market in general. That, of course, is the opposite of market efficiency.*

Moving on, another thing that I find interesting about your process is your rather unique sinking fund strategy. Could you tell us about it?

Ryback: I'd be happy to. A sinking fund pertains mainly to convertible bonds or convertible preferred stocks. That's a different class of security issued by corporations. What happens, typically, is that convertible bonds have a maturity date. A company goes out and issues a 10-year bond. After five years, the company can start to buy back the bond. It can buy the bond in the open market.

Tanous: *Does the company have to buy it back?*

Ryback: Yes. It's mandatory.

Tanous: *Okay. So the buyback is part of the indenture. They might typically have to buy back a certain part of the issue after, say, five years?*

Ryback: Right. I'm using five years as an example. It does depend on what the indenture says. Traditionally, it's about five years. I should also mention that this applies not just to convertibles, but also straight bonds. The company is generally buying back 10% to 15% of the issue, so that within five or seven years, the entire issue is redeemed.

Obviously, the company is not going to pay more than par when it starts buying its securities back, because the indenture says all they have to do is offer to pay par plus the accrued interest. On the other hand, if their bond is perceived to be weak, and it is trading at a discount, it's really an advantage to the company and its shareholders that the company can buy its own bonds at a discount. Actuarially, they're putting dollars to the bottom line of the income statement by buying their own bonds at a discount.

From our point of view, if we've done our homework and we own this issue, we want to own all of it. The intent is for the company to make only one phone call every year when it wants to buy its bonds back, and that's to us.

Tanous: *I have a feeling, Eric, that you make it an expensive phone call.*

Ryback: We do. We say, yes, your bonds are trading at a discount, but guess what? The price is par.

Tanous: *This tactic seems analogous to squeezing the shorts, doesn't it?*

Ryback: It is. It's called "cornering the sinker." I learned that in the very early days of the Milken era of peddling what were later called junk bonds. *[Milken called them high-yield bonds.]* I can't say that I came up with this idea. It was a very eye-opening experience when, one day, I identified a bond in the market that I really wanted to own and I called up and told my Drexel broker to buy these bonds. *[Michael Milken developed the junk bond business at the now defunct firm, Drexel Burnham.]* They came back and said, well, you can't buy any. I asked, why not? They said, because there's just one person who controls the whole issue and he's not selling! I said, boy, I would love to be able to do that. And I made it a personal goal from then on. I wanted to own an entire issue.

Tanous: *Let me suggest an example. You buy up the entire issue when the bonds are trading around 82, because in today's market, that's what they're worth. Right?*

Ryback: Right.

Tanous: *And the guy calls you up and says, you know, we'll make you a bid. And you say fine. I'll sell at 100—par.*

Ryback: That's right. I don't want to belabor the point, but for the Dividend Fund in particular, which holds a lot of these securities, that really reduces the beta *[volatility]*. Here we have an instrument, the bond, that has maybe five or seven years left to run. If we own the whole thing, there is no volatility. Since we own the entire issue, all we're doing is peeling off a certain percentage every year back to the company. It's wonderful.

Tanous: *Utilities, dividends and income go in lock-step don't they?*

Ryback: They do.

Tanous: *Yet you know better than I that almost every other manager just hates utilities. Let me give you an example: One of the people I interviewed, who is a terrific manager, is Foster Friess of the Brandywine Fund.* [See page 229.]

Ryback: I know who he is.

Tanous: *I asked Foster, in our interview, what sorts of things he never buys. I'll quote him. Foster says, "We have a hard time getting excited* *about utility companies because that's a politically-driven profit picture. You cannot grow beyond the demographics of a given area, except if you're able to get good pricing. If you start showing too much profit, the political process will take those prices away." Which of you guys is right?*

Ryback: There's a lot of truth to all that. The other side to that argument is that the utility industry is becoming deregulated, and through deregulation there is the opportunity to downsize the number of utilities or merge utilities, the bad with the good. Ultimately the good will prevail. Now there's always an interest rate factor that influences the price of the stocks. That's undeniable. So there is a tendency, over the long haul, to trade utilities.

Two years ago, the Dividend Fund had minor exposure to utilities because rates continued to drop. When utility regulators go up in front of the *[public service]* commission, their case to raise rates is weak when interest rates are declining. Obviously it works to their benefit when rates are rising, because then they can go and say, look, the fixed costs are such and the cost of borrowed money is such, and we need to raise rates. Under those circumstances, the commissions usually look the other way and say, go ahead. So, yes, there is that factor: utilities tend to be proactive on declining rates and reactive on rising rates. There's a lag effect, and it hurts utilities. But there's also consolidation going on now, which, I think, is a positive, an advantage to owning them.

Tanous: *As you pointed out, deregulation is an important part of that.*

Ryback: Yes, it is.

Tanous: *Eric, you've been so successful in your strategy that the readers of this book are going to be very interested in your process. Could you walk us through, from the way a stock gets discovered, to the time you push the button and it gets into your portfolio?*

Ryback: The initial process involves screening for yield. We look for the highest yield possible—higher than the yield on the S&P 500. We'd like to get yield at least 200 basis points higher than the yield on the long bond *[30-year treasuries]*. We screen on a wide basis for that. The candidates we screen then go through our fundamental value process. We're looking for a strong balance sheet, income is secondary. The company doesn't really have to be earning money, but it has to be covering the interest and dividend payments. We look on a historical basis, at least five years, and we project forward about three years or more, based on the historical five-year average of their revenues and income stream. If there is no income stream, we look at cash flow. We plot this information in graphic form. I'm going to be a little bit vague here because it is a proprietary process.

Tanous: *Aha! In that case, we'll sharpen our questions.*

Ryback: Right. Kurt developed the process back in the early fifties as a CPA, and it's a numbers-driven formula.

Tanous: *But it is a formula?*

Ryback: Oh yes!

Tanous: *Wait a minute. There's a formula that is proprietary that guides your selection process?*

Ryback: Yes. Absolutely.

Tanous: *That's interesting.*

Ryback: I would be lying if I told you otherwise.

Tanous: *It's not a black box, is it?* ["Black box" is Wall Street jargon for a computer program or formula that comes up with ways to beat the market. There hasn't been a completely successful one yet.]

Ryback: It's kind of a black box. We put the numbers through. All the companies go through that screening process. We did it by hand until I bought the company three years ago, and then we put it on a computer. Kurt was very concerned that if it went on a computer, anybody could get access to it. We've tried to alleviate that problem.

Tanous: *But it's obviously not so complex, since it used to be done with a bunch of calculators.*

Ryback: Calculators and by hand. Anyway, once we get this earnings stream, we can then arrive at the intrinsic value of a company. Since we're going to invest in common stocks, we're also going to try to get a time value of the money; basically what we would earn if the money was invested in, say, treasury bills, instead, or some other government instrument. That will lead us to the intrinsic value of the company over the period of time we think we'll be holding it. The next step is to arrive at the sell target-price. Then we discount that to what we might want to make in that company, say, a 30% or 40% return, and we back into our buy-target-price.

Tanous: *Presumably these are moving targets, are they not?*

Ryback: You're absolutely correct. Because as the company earns more money every quarter, which we hope for, then that profit target will move upwards. If the company remains the same, the target goes nowhere, unless interest rates are doing something that would lead to another adjustment. Or, if the company is earning less than what our model perceived, that would cause a downward adjustment.

Tanous: *This sounds like it's part of the formula.*

Ryback: It is.

Tanous: *It does start to make sense.*

Ryback: Right. We're trying to stay ahead of the curve here. That's why we've got this interest rate factor in there. Because, with our low beta and our safety factor, if we decide that we can go into treasury bills and make money ... I mean wouldn't it be lovely if we could be all in treasury bills and the market cracked 20%? Well, that's kind of what we're hoping the model will do for us, although it's not perfect.

Tanous: *But the model presumably is not predicting overall market movement, is it?*

Ryback: It's not a market-driven model. But there is a high correlation between interest rates and markets. We've seen that in this market.

Tanous: *Does your model attempt to predict interest rates?*

Ryback: No, but it has an interest rate influence that, we hope, anticipates these moves in a broad sense. That should mean that we are selling while everybody is in a climactic buying stage.

Tanous: *That's interesting.*

Ryback: It's not foolproof, by any means. But that's the real intent.

Tanous: *How much does this process contribute to your success?*

Ryback: It's the foundation of the whole firm.

Tanous: *Has it evolved since Kurt died?*

Ryback: No. We still use it and we will always use it. We were all indoctrinated into this approach and we are highly influenced by it.

We believe in it very strongly, so it's really the main driver for all the managers here.

Tanous: *Eric, I understand you don't bother visiting companies or talking to managements. That strikes me as bizarre.*

Ryback: Some would say that, yes. If there's been any loosening up, it's probably been in that area. We still do not visit companies. But we do talk to them over the phone.

Tanous: *I noticed that one of your largest holdings is an Occidental Petroleum preferred stock issue. It is 1.6% of your portfolio. I mention that in part because I'm on the board of Cedars Bank in Los Angeles and Ray Irani, Occidental's dynamic chairman, is also a director. Are you saying you never spoke to him?*

Ryback: I've never talked to the company. It's a highly liquid issue. There's a lot of stock out. The yield is quite attractive. I bought it down in the low fifties and it closed today at sixty and change. You know, I'll stay with it until it starts looking at me funny. Then I'll get rid of it. For now, I'm very content with it.

Tanous: *Please define: "looking at me funny."*

Ryback: Well, if it starts acting a little strange. Not the way I think it ought to act.

Tanous: *Why aren't you eager to visit companies?*

Ryback: This goes back to Kurt's days of going out and auditing companies as a CPA. It's hard to really cover up things in an audit. Part of it, I think, was his awareness that any company would do things if they could get away with them, to a certain extent.

Tanous: *Do what?*

Ryback: Well, you know, inventory . . . Back in the '50s, they might have put the auditors up in the top floor without air conditioning to do an inventory count. And you know, their attitude might be, let's forget the rest of this. Get me down from here! So a little bit of skepticism and realism emerged. Companies will tell you anything you want to hear. I'm not trying to paint them as unethical, but it's human nature.

Tanous: *I've run into another side of that argument in my interviews with other managers. Many investment fund managers have a sort of* *sixth sense, a hard-to-define feeling, or very good people instincts. They want to meet company managers to get a sense of their aggressiveness, their forcefulness, their sincerity. Fund-managers want to judge whether or not company executives are good managers, and a lot of that has to do with the human dimension. Now, your approach is different, yet very successful. Yours is more quantitative than theirs, but do you see how this other approach might be useful, too?*

Ryback: Yes I do. I can concur with some of that. It really comes down to two human beings meeting, and being able to size one another up and, hopefully, you as a portfolio manager, have the innate abilities to be able to judge the managers of the business you're going to visit.

Tanous: *But you, Eric, don't get that opportunity.*

Ryback: No we don't. We have, on rare occasions, but, yes, I would say the far majority of the time we don't. We do pick up the phone now and talk to them.

Tanous: *That's a change in your strategy. What do you get out of that that you didn't get before?*

Ryback: More communication. Not just strictly going by the numbers like a racehorse with the blinders on. Sometimes we've found it helpful to just pick up the phone and get an explanation. If it sounds reasonable, it does affect what we do with the stock.

Tanous: *Getting back to process, can you summarize your approach to the Dividend Fund. What is it that makes this approach so successful?*

Ryback: What makes the Dividend Fund unique is its four components. It has a cash component, which we put in treasury bills while we're waiting to buy a security. It has a bond component, and a common stock component, and a convertible component. The real success of the fund is the four different components and the percentage allocation, which is dictated by what interest rates are and where we think they are going. We juggle these four components over a long term view of what interest rates may be doing. By long term, we mean three or four years.

Tanous: *And the secret formula aids in this process, right?*

Ryback: The secret formula is the foundation that it sits on. I think the key to our success, our long-term record picking out the fallen angels in bonds and convertible preferred, is that we are buying yield-to-maturity for very long periods of time. So our turnover is very low. We ride through overreactions in those issues. By-and-large, we're buyers when there are panic sellers out there.

Tanous: *I presume your expense ratio is pretty low, too.*

Ryback: Very low.

Tanous: *What is it?*

Ryback: Zero point six one percent.

Tanous: *That is low. Part of that must be because your turnover is so low.* [The transaction costs are reduced.]

Let's talk a little bit about your performance. The Lindner Dividend Fund is a nice, conservative, yield fund. We're not trying to shoot the lights out here, yet the five-year performance is over 15%. The ten-year performance is 12%. The performance since inception is 17%. I don't know what to say. I've been in this business a long time and I've never seen anything like this. I'm not sure what question I ought to ask you? Help me out.

Ryback: We do it with low volatility.

Tanous: *I know. You're just making my job a little bit harder. My next question was volatility. I remember a few years ago, one of the big magazines picked the best mutual fund of all times, and it was yours! Remember that?*

Ryback: Yes. We've been the number one Best Buy stock fund in the *Forbes* list since they started their ranking back in 1992. The only year we were not number one was the year the fund was closed.

Tanous: *That's right. You closed it for a while, didn't you?*

Ryback: Yes, we did.

Tanous: *I think I know why you closed it.* [It was growing too fast.] *Why did you reopen it?*

Ryback: Well, because we perceived that there were some great buying opportunities. We had closed it *[The Lindner Dividend Fund was* *closed from March 4, 1993 to November 8, 1993. Minimum invest-ment is $2,000.]* because we had grown a billion dollars in a year. It was getting out of hand. You know, I'm not going to knock the cover off the ball, as you mentioned earlier. I just want consistent, very low-risk growth for the shareholders. I built up a very loyal core of investors. I continue to get new investors daily, and I think it's at market times like this that we will outshine our competition. We're not going to be number one in a bull market, but we are certainly going to do well in down markets. We're quite resilient. Believe it or not, I do try to enhance the performance. Hey, I would love to have done 35% last year and keep it all and do better, but that's hard to do on a consistent basis and still have the low volatility. So I'm going to continue to give the investors what they want. What I think they really want is to go home and sleep every night; they want to get their nice dividend on a quarterly basis and not have to worry about the fund.

Tanous: *But the performance is awesome because it exceeds the barometers you set for yourself—which is to provide, what, 200 basis points above long bonds? I mean, you're way over that. . .*

Ryback: Yes, we are.

Tanous: *I believe that your performance competes with the S&P 500 even in the bull market we've been in for so long.*

Ryback: My personal goal is to do 20% per year, if I can. However, some markets don't allow me to do that. I try like bejesus to do it, but it doesn't happen. I've rigged this fund to be extremely defensive right now, probably the most defensive it's been in a long time.

Tanous: *Is that a reflection of your view of the market?*

Ryback: Yes. The bond portion of the portfolio is three years dura-tion. And the average yield is 10.5%. With the long bond rising dra-matically, to about 6.75%, it's not even close to where my return is. But I'm very uncomfortable at this time. I'm very happy on one side, but uncomfortable on the other.

Tanous: *You've expanded your business, Eric, to include a lot of dif-ferent kinds of funds. For instance, the farthest thing I can think of from what you do is small-cap. Talk to us about that strategy and tell us how you have done with it.*

Ryback: Last year the Small-Cap Fund lagged the Russell 2000. This year *[1996]* it's outperforming it. We started the Small-Cap because the Lindner Growth Fund grew to $1.5 billion. The Growth Fund had tremendous performance through the '80s and then started lagging. About two years ago, we took a close look at it. We decided we had too many issues in there, too many different names. We were up to about 240 names. A fund this size shouldn't have that many names. We were still applying our fundamental approach, but we were getting too cute. We had names in there that represented only 0.2% of the total portfolio. These things could double and triple and it still wouldn't have any effect on the fund overall, because the positions were so small. So, we've taken about two years to whittle it down to about 160 names. The fund is now starting to perform the way we want it to.

Tanous: *Now which fund are we talking about?*

Ryback: The Lindner Growth Fund. I know you asked me about the Small-Cap Fund. We started the Small-Cap to absorb the names that we could no longer buy for the Lindner Growth Fund.

Tanous: *I see.*

Ryback: Last year I had my hands full. In January of this year, we finally got a co-manager for the Small-Cap. I'm happy about that and it's already doing quite well.

Tanous: *Another peculiarity, if I can call it that, is that your rather considerable success—your Lindner Dividend Fund has $2.2 billion in it—has come without the benefit of advertising. I mean, pick up any of the dozen or more magazines devoted to investments, and every other ad is for a mutual fund. But not yours. Why?*

Ryback: We do not advertise. We want to keep our expense ratio low. Kurt always believed that if you perform well people will invest. We want to adhere to that. It's certainly not our intent to advertise.

Tanous: *That's not going to change.*

Ryback: No.

Tanous: *There's no chance I might pick up an issue of* Forbes *or* Fortune *and see a full page ad for your fund.*

Ryback: No.

Tanous: *I think you have a total of $4 billion under management in all the funds? Do you manage any private accounts?*

Ryback: No. I got rid of them when I took over the business. It was like having 60 more mutual funds. I didn't need it.

Tanous: *I know. And sometimes they call every day!*

Ryback: It was just too much for the managers here.

Tanous: *Let's go back to the subject of process one last time. Your forte, and this is the way you were brought up, is manifested in your extraordinary success with the Dividend Fund. But a small-cap is a completely different animal and requires a very different investment approach. What skills will help you succeed with that fund?*

Ryback: That's a fair question. When I came here, I worked on the Dividend Fund and the Growth Fund. Now it's just a matter of applying our value approach to smaller issues. I used to contribute a lot of small names to the Growth Fund over the course of the years, and I will direct the Small-Cap Fund in the same fashion. I've got all the confidence in the world that it will really be a duplicate of the Growth Fund during its heyday in the '70s and '80s, when it well outperformed the S&P 500. I think I lost some focus last year because I may have had my hands too full, but I think that focus has been regained with our new person.

Tanous: *Would it be safe to say that the majority of the investors in the Lindner Dividend Fund are tax-free accounts, like retirement and pension accounts?*

Ryback: Oh boy. Surprisingly, we do have IRAs, but we don't have as many as you might think, given the type of fund that it is. The fund has attracted a lot of older people. We were just out at the Louis Rukeyser investment conference in Las Vegas.

Tanous: *I heard there were 9,000 people there!*

Ryback: It was just amazing. People wanted my tie! It had a bull and a bear on it. They thought we were giving it away. Talk about the herd instinct. I spoke in the auditorium where they hold the prize fights, where Tyson's going to be. So they had this elaborate projection system, where the speaker's image was displayed on these huge screens. They could see this tie. When they came running out of the conference after that session, they came up to me and said, oh, look at the tie! Where can we get one? I said, my six year old daughter bought it for me for Christmas, so you can't have it!

Tanous: *Now you know what it feels like to be a rock star, right?*

Ryback: Oh, man. I guess.

Tanous: *You're a relatively young guy. You've been very successful. I don't know what they teach at Idaho State* [where Ryback went to school], *but it must be pretty good. Your hiking experience is something that people like me who have lived in large cities all their lives are in awe of. What tempts you down the road as you look to the next phase of your life?*

Ryback: I just want to win. I come to work every day to try to win.

That sums it up all right. First, I have to tell you that I tried real hard to get the formula out of him, but I didn't succeed. I never was a big fan of black boxes, but here is a case where the investment process really shines.

Let's look at two issues that come to mind after spending time with Eric Ryback. First, if you and I think that there is a particular type of person who has a better chance to succeed as a money manager than others, I think we can quickly disabuse ourselves of that notion. Certainly being smart helps a lot, but do you have to go to the right schools? Apparently not. Eric Ryback didn't need a prestigious business school, high-powered connections, or a Wall Street environment to learn to be a great money manager. In fact, he is the most un-Wall Street-like person I think I have ever met, maybe because he never worked in New York. But he is smart. And disciplined.

Now look at the process. He uses a well-defined, thorough process taught to him by his mentor, Kurt Lindner. When Eric Ryback took over the business, he continued applying the very same precepts and principles he had learned from Lindner. He expanded the business to include other investment vehicles, and, while they have done well, the shining star in this Missouri firmament is the Lindner Dividend Fund. Using their famous formula, and the investment skills of Eric Ryback and his team, they continue to deliver a very low-risk, high-return investment vehicle. We learned about as much as anyone knows about the process and how they do it, black boxes aside. The process is clear and sensible. I honestly think that this is one type of investing that most of us could do on our own, if we were willing to apply ourselves and rigorously follow the procedures you just read about. Of course, why bother? We can just buy the fund and let them do the work. Happy trails.

MERTON

MILLER

Merton Miller's illustrious academic career started at Harvard, from which he graduated in 1943. He spent the next few years in Washington, D.C. working at the U.S. Treasury and the Federal Reserve. He earned his Ph.D. from Johns Hopkins in 1952. The following year, he joined Carnegie Tech, in Pittsburgh, where he taught economic history. At Carnegie Tech, Merton Miller first encountered another, somewhat older, economist, Franco Modigliani. Their subsequent collaboration was destined to become part of economic history. Modigliani won the Nobel Prize in Economic Sciences in 1985. In turn, Merton Miller won his in 1990. The product of their collaboration, which was quickly dubbed the "M&M theorem," is still widely discussed and argued among economists and corporate finance types.

If you thought economists were dull, Merton Miller will change your mind. He has a well-known sense of humor, and we'll put it to the test. While the M&M theorem is not directly about investing in stocks, it does have some very real application to valuing a company. By the time we're finished, I think you'll agree that everyone interested in the field should know something about it. We ask about his views on market efficiency and investing generally, and we get into areas few people have ever explored with Professor Miller. Here we go.

213

Tanous: *How did you first get interested in stocks?*

Miller: Well, I don't know, because it was so long ago! They are part of the atmosphere. I was in economics even as an undergraduate. Stocks were part of the environment. How did *you* get interested in stocks?

Tanous: *I was an economics major at Georgetown. In my first economics class as a freshman, our professor, Dr. Gunther Ruff, asked the students why they were taking the course. I said, because I thought I might learn how to make money. He said, "My dear fellow, I have a Ph.D. in economics, and if I knew how to make money, I wouldn't be here."*

Miller: When I started worrying about stocks, it was the late 1930s and early 1940s and it didn't seem like a good way to make money then, either. Stocks were in bad repute after 1929. A variety of questions were being raised everywhere about the role of the stock market crash in bringing on the depression. There were also congressional hearings and investigations, not only into the crash, but on the role of the corporation in American economic life. The subject of stocks was very much in the news. As an economics undergraduate, I also worked on a part-time basis in Cambridge, Massachusetts, for a company that was advising customers about portfolio decisions, writing reports. So I was constantly exposed to stocks, if only by reading through Moody's and transcribing numbers for the customer reports.

As far as personal investing was concerned, I was more concerned with my savings account than with stocks.

Tanous: *I guess that was appropriate to the '30s.*

Miller: Yes, it was. You could get an interest-paying savings account in Harvard Square, providing there wasn't too much activity in your account. I would get my monthly allowance and put it in one of the local banks, making small withdrawals every day to pay expenses. After awhile, I would get a notice from the bank saying that there was too much activity in my account and they were closing it out. So, I would walk my money across the street to one of the other banks. There were four of them, one on each corner. I just put the money in the next bank. That way, I managed to have a checking account without paying transaction fees. I didn't feel guilty, because I knew that the banks had gotten the government to ban interest on checking accounts. I was just doing to them what they were doing to me.

Tanous: *I see the beginning of an economic theory here. As you know, Professor, our book focuses on interviews with great investment managers, but I also wanted to get some top academic points-of-view on markets. I thought it might be interesting to begin our conversation by talking about your celebrated work with Franco Modigliani in the area of corporate capital structure. I am referring, of course, to your combined work, amusingly known as "the M&M theorem." As I recall, instead of asking investors how they might determine which of a corporation's securities they might want to buy, you looked at it from the opposite perspective. You asked, how should corporations decide what securities to sell.*

Miller: Yes. That was certainly part of it. Early on, I had to teach a course on corporate finance. I had never had a course in finance, or at least a business school variety course. My expertise was in public finance, particularly corporate taxation, since I had worked at the U.S. Treasury. At first, I worked in the corporate tax unit of the Division of Tax Research at Treasury, later in the government finance unit at the Federal Reserve. So, I knew the tax side of corporate finance, and the economics of public finance, but not the standard finance stuff.

In 1954 or so, before they let me teach a business school finance course, at Carnegie Tech *[now Carnegie Mellon]*, they said, you must sit in on the class of someone who is teaching it the proper Harvard Business School way. So, I sat in the class. When we took up case number one in the case book, I remember being struck that the solution was not obvious to me. After the instructor explained it, however, I said, Yeah. That's right; that makes sense. Then we came to case two, and I said, Okay, I remember how we solved case one, so the answer must be this. And, of course, it was different. I couldn't sense any connection from one case to the next. Everything was, as they say on railway tickets, good for this train and this day only. For me, as an economist, it was frustrating to have no sense of a theory of corporate finance to tie all this material together.

Tanous: *Do I sense the origins of M&M theory here? I think you are saying that there wasn't just one right solution to the cases you studied. Likewise, in M&M, you were seeking the optimal capital structure* *for a corporation; in other words, how much debt, and how much equity a company should have. Then you found out it didn't matter. There wasn't just one right answer.*

Miller: That's down the road a bit. First, the problem was to figure out what determines these choices. There are various analogous models in economics that could have been applied in this area, but none of them seemed to work very well. Franco and I were both working on the problem, but from somewhat different perspectives—he from macroeconomics and me from corporate finance. I had some of the students in my finance class actually do some empirical work on capital structures, to see if we could find any obvious patterns in the data, but we couldn't see any. We couldn't find any consistent patterns and certainly no evidence of an optimal structure. We said, you know something, maybe there isn't any optimum! *[For example, in the proportions of debt and equity.]* Franco and I then tried to prove our suspicion that there is no optimal capital structure.

People often ask: Can you summarize your theory quickly? Well, I say, you understand the M&M theorem, if you know why this is a joke: The pizza delivery man comes to Yogi Berra after the game and says, Yogi, how do you want this pizza cut, into quarters or eighths? And Yogi says, cut it in eight pieces. I'm feeling hungry tonight.

Everyone recognizes that's a joke because obviously the number and shape of the pieces doesn't affect the size of the pizza. And similarly, the stocks, bonds, warrants, etc., issued don't affect the aggregate value of the firm. They just slice up the underlying earnings in different ways.

Tanous: *I recall a story that, after word got out that you had won the Nobel Prize in Economics, the media tracked you down and asked you to explain your theorem in a way their audience might understand. Like in ten seconds.*

Miller: The pizza story is one I often use. Another is, if you take money out of your left pocket and put it in your right pocket, you're no richer. Reporters would say, you mean they gave you guys a Nobel Prize for something as obvious as that? *[Lots of laughter.]* And I'd add, Yes, but remember, we proved it rigorously. *[More laughter.]* Actually, we did use a new form of rigorous proof known as "arbitrage" proof. Arbitrage proof has since been widely used throughout finance and economics.

Tanous: *If I'm summarizing the M&M theorem correctly, the market value of any firm is independent of its capital structure, so the proportions of stock [equity] and bonds [debt] doesn't affect the value of the corporation. Now if that's the case, are all these highly paid corporate chief financial officers wasting their time trying to figure out how much preferred stock to issue, or how many bonds, or how much common stock?*

Miller: To some extent. But remember, the M&M proposition is the beginning of wisdom; its not the end of it. To really utilize it best, you have to tip the proposition on its head. You say, look, in order to make this proposition true, you must make the following 15 or so assumptions. So if people out there say, aha, the M&M theorem doesn't hold true in the real world, then we say, it must be because one or more of the 15 assumptions must be failing. And that has provided the research agenda for the profession.

. What happened after publication of our paper was that, for the next 40 years, people said, all right, we now know the answer to the capital structure question under ideal conditions. Let's now drop, or relax, some of these assumptions and see how it affects some of the conclusions. That's not the kind of undisciplined Harvard Business School, each case on its own, approach. It's systematic. You can say, for example, as we did even in our first paper, suppose there's a big corporate income tax with a 50% rate? That's going to affect the optimal choice between debt and equity. In fact, it's going to make issuing debt, rather than equity, extremely desirable *[since interest is deductible for tax purposes]*. Next, you go on from there and say, yeah, but firms don't have 100% debt. Then you have to start to explain why and think up additional reasons, such as agency costs or offsetting taxes, that will keep them from going to extremes. That's what the profession has been doing for 40 years.

Tanous: *It occurs to me that the great junk bond revolution might have had the effect of confirming or disproving the M&M theorem since so many companies opted to go heavily in debt. Did the popularity of junk bonds affect corporate values?*

Miller: The junk bond revolution fits right in with M&M. Junk bonds prove there's nothing magical in a Aaa bond rating. Don't pass up big profit opportunities, or tax savings, just because of your credit rating. What counts is what you do with your money, not where it came from.

I also want to mention the one example where the original M&M theorem can actually be seen holding in the real world. It comes from the field of options, where it is known as the put-call parity. It holds to three decimal places. Options, of course, bring Myron Scholes, one of my former students, to mind as well as my good friend Fischer Black.

Tanous: *Their reputations are well established. These fellows developed the famous Black-Scholes model. Could you explain it briefly?*

Miller: I don't have a pizza story, but I do want to go on the record saying that I regard their Black-Sholes formula as one of the major intellectual breakthroughs of the latter part of the 20th century in this field. It was not only an intellectual achievement, but it spawned a whole new industry. Their model was an amazing development because it is one of the few cases in finance where you can actually compute what a security is worth, not just in abstract terms, but in actual dollars.

Black and Scholes developed a formula which priced options as a function of observables. By observables, I mean that the warranted option price is a function of the strike price, the price of the underlying security, the interest rate, the time to maturity, and the volatility of the underlying security. The only thing that isn't directly observable is the volatility, but that can be very closely approximated. Much better to approximate the volatility of something than the mean expected return, which is what stock pickers have to do. You can always get a pretty good fix on the volatility, even though it's not perfect. It's still a lot easier than estimating the expected rate of return on shares. Incidentally, if you read the original Black-Scholes paper *["The Pricing of Options and Corporate Liabilities,"* Journal of Political Economy, *vol. 81, May-June, pages 637-659]*, you would note that they generously acknowledge the influence of the arbitrage proof from the M&M capital structure paper, which was earlier.

Tanous: *Since Fischer Black and Myron Scholes were able to determine option pricing by using all of the surrounding variables, might it be possible to do the same thing for stocks?*

Miller: No, you can't really, except, perhaps, in some extreme cases. If a share is super highly leveraged, so that you just got this little thin sliver of equity over the debt, then Fischer and Myron pointed out that it's basically a call option, not a share. And you can, to some extent, price it that way. You can also do that with some kinds of bonds. But, by and large, options are the only case in finance where you can successfully price something as a function of observables.

Tanous: *That's very interesting. Now let's turn to the subject that is a focal point of this book: active versus passive management. Let me ask you right off the bat, do you believe in active management in any form?*

Miller: Not really. That's based on my study of finance and my belief that markets know much more as markets than an individual does as an individual. This is, of course, the subject we talked about a couple of weeks ago. I should mention that I am a member of the board of directors of Dimensional Fund Advisors.

Tanous: *I had a long talk with Rex Sinquefield* [page 257].

Miller: Rex is one of my students, too. Almost everybody is because I've been around so long!

Tanous: *I spoke to another one of your students, Gene Fama* [page 167].

Miller: Of course. I favor passive investing for most investors, because markets are amazingly successful devices for incorporating information into stock prices. I believe, along with Friedrich Hayek *[also a Nobel laureate, and a contemporary of John Maynard Keynes]* and others, that information is not some big thing that's locked in a safe somewhere. It exists in bits and pieces scattered all over the world.

Everybody has a little piece of the total information. Even the dentist from Peoria, I always say, at least he knows whether or not his patients are paying on time. So everybody has some information. The function of the markets is to aggregate that information, evaluate it, and get it incorporated into prices. But if information, as I insist, is widely scattered and diffuse, most individuals are not going to have much information relative to the total. Most people might just as well buy a share of the whole market, which pools all the information, than delude themselves into thinking they know something the market doesn't. They can't be hurt by doing that, because the price they pay will indeed reflect society's best current information.

Tanous: *I've tried to approach this as open-mindedly as possible and I've talked to top-tier academics, you among them. I've also talked to people in the business, like Rex Sinquefield, who is dogmatic on this subject. Yet, when I talk to the active managers, especially those who have a fairly long performance history—what the academics call "persistence"—I keep running into anecdotes. . .*

Miller: That's all they are. . .

Tanous: *But you keep running into these stories about information, seemingly previously unknown, that gets uncovered, with a certain amount of research. Isn't it true that, until somebody does that research, it really wasn't widely known?*

Here's an example: Michael Price, who runs Mutual Shares, had a wonderful story about a metal, tantalum, that was going up in price [page 37]. He did some research to find out which companies were involved in tantalum, and, in fact, managed to discover them before the effect of the price rise was generally reflected in the prices of those stocks. I expect there are many other stories like this.

Miller: Let me back up and say one thing more clearly, I hope. There are really two different groups of investors. One group, the overwhelming majority, and the group I've been talking about, has no significant private information not already in prices, and they should invest passively. They aren't going to make above-normal returns, except by accident. But there's another group that can hope to make money by careful research in the market. How much money can they expect to make? Taking the group as a whole, they make just enough, on average, to cover the cost of their research.

This distinction I've been making, between traders with significant nonpublic information and those without it—which includes most investors, including pension fund and mutual fund managers—is known as the Grossman/Stiglitz theorem. Sandy Grossman is a brilliant young economist at Wharton (and a former student of mine, needless to say). He was here at Chicago, and then went on to Stanford, Princeton, and now Wharton. Joe Stiglitz went from Yale to Stanford, and is now the President's chairman of the Council of

Economic Advisors. They wrote a famous paper on rational expectations and prices *["On the Impossibility of Informationally Efficient
Markets,"* American Economic Review, *Vol. 70, 1980, pp 393-408].*
Their proof that both the informed, and the uninformed, investors
can expect to make the same return, on average, is neat.

The essence of the efficient market thing is, after all, as we in
economics have always held: There's no free lunch. You can't just sit
back in your office scanning the newspapers, reading research
reports, and listening to "Wall Street Week," and hope to earn
above-normal rates of return. To beat the market you'll have to
invest serious bucks to dig up information *no one else has yet.*
Because it looks easy, many people may be tempted to try it. But
there's no automatic reward from investing in trying to dig up important non-public information. It's like gold mining. A few lucky ones
may strike it rich, but most "active" investors are just wasting their
time and money. Once they realize that average returns on investment in information are zero or less, if the industry becomes over-
crowded, the smart ones will stop trying and will leave the search
industry. They become indexers.

Tanous: *Isn't the research and the hard work you do the price you pay
for the reward you achieve?*

Miller: Yes, but it just compensates you for the expenses. Of course,
I don't mean you, personally. I mean you, on the average. Remember,
as economists, not psychologists, we deal with behavior on the average. This is just my view, of course. It's not the opinion of everybody
in the finance or economics profession, needless to say.

Tanous: *I sensed that even Gene Fama* [page 167] *and Bill Sharpe*
[page 89] *believe that a very few managers, like Peter Lynch at Fidelity
Magellan, have persistently outperformed the market, and that is
borne out by the data.*

Miller: Well, we've heard many of these tales. We used to hear, for
example, that Value Line had some kind of an edge. These tales
come and go. They don't usually stand up forever, although sometimes they seem to last for many years. You can make a huge living
in the investment field, moreover, if you can once get the reputation
of being a winner. It's going to take a long time to reverse it.

I always use an example that dates back to the '30s. The big
name then was Bernard Baruch. A genius. He was everybody's

favorite pundit. There wasn't any economic issue where the press didn't go to see Barney. When you study his fabulous record, however, I think he was right once. But, he was right in a big way. If you make a big score way out on the right hand tail of the distribution, then the probabilities you face from then on are mostly the little moves to the left and to the right in the center of the distribution. You're not going to get that first big gain removed. You only need to make one big score in finance to be a hero forever.

Tanous: *I see your point. That one score will keep your average gain high for years. But take the whole outlier theory—the right tail of the distribution curve where you find the Peter Lynches and Warren Buffetts. What separates the men from the boys, so to speak, is persistence, isn't it?*

Miller: Perhaps it would be, if we could measure persistence accurately. But in practice, it often comes down to not suffering a loss as big as the huge gain you made a while ago. Thus, a fellow like George Soros may be skating on thin ice. You see, he made a big killing and if he would now just do modest investments, he would never lose it. He'd be a winner on balance over any time horizon. But if he insists on plunging again, he's just as likely to take a bigger loss. He may wind up giving it all back.

Tanous: *It's funny. One of the managers I'm interviewing, Richard Driehaus, said about Soros, "He had a hunch and bet a bunch!"*

Miller: Right. And he'll have another hunch, and he'll bet another bunch, and this time he'll lose. But if he doesn't do it that way, if he has a hunch and bets a bunch and wins, and thereafter plays the conservative game, he'll go down in history as the genius of all time. The gains and losses average out, but only in the very, very long run.

Tanous: *To me, the name of the game is finding the people who show persistence at beating the market.*

Miller: Well, let me tell you one of my favorite stories. I once asked a pension fund manager, why don't you just index your funds instead of doing all this churning you're doing there? And he said, I can't index the fund because then I wouldn't be worth $400,000 dollars a year! If you ask people in the trade, how come you make so much money? What do you want them to say? Oh, it was just dumb luck, Professor. I don't think you'll get that response very often.

Tanous: *The more typical answer is that it was our brilliant deductive analysis that got you that great performance.*

Miller: Yeah. There are people like Bill Sharpe and Gene Fama who are working all the time to test various hypotheses about it, but to me the sample is way too small to judge "persistence," that is, to be able to tell luck from skill. There's another story I love to tell: The bursar of a British college, at Oxford, had members who were pounding on him that they weren't earning enough. He answered by saying, I admit our returns have been down recently but you must remember that the last two hundred years have been very unusual!

Tanous: *Big consolation!*

Miller: I don't know how long is long enough to get rid of the influence of sample flukes.

Tanous: *I have no doubt that Bill Sharpe and Gene Fama's work all supports the efficient market theory.*

Miller: I can't speak for them, of course, but I believe that most economists would accept the view that, while you sometimes can make a score by sheer luck, you can't do it constantly, unless you're willing to put the resources in. One way or another, you have to get significant *non-public* information, which most fund managers don't have.

Tanous: *In fact, I thought the most convincing of Gene Fama's points was that he took ten years of mutual fund data from The Top 20 Morningstar funds and looked at their performance for the following ten years.*

Miller: And there was no correlation. It has all the earmarks of a random process. One amusing thing that the SEC once did was, they said you can't bring out a new commodity fund unless you've got five years of experience. So what do you do? You run your fund on the small until you manage to hit five good years. Then you've got a track record, and you say we've done it five years in a row! And then you go public, of course. All the studies have found that there is no correlation between the results of the previous five years and the subsequent five years. Virtually no correlation. But that's a mass statistical test. There may be one fund that was high in both periods. But remember, in economics, we work with statistical aggregates, not individuals, so that is bound to happen sometimes. Individuals, quite naturally, resent our pointing that out. They say, don't treat me as a statistical aggregate. I'm an individual!

Tanous: *I've got to tell you, I spoke to Peter Lynch, who was absolutely wonderful. I said, Peter, you've got to realize that to the great academicians, and we're talking Nobel Prize winners, you are the millionth monkey, the lucky orangutan at the typewriter who wrote* Romeo and Juliet. *And Peter is not the only one with a great record.*

Miller: That's why they're where they are and I'm where I am. It's a tough argument to counter. He did have success. Anything we say sounds like sour grapes. If we're so smart, why aren't we rich?

Tanous: *No. They don't talk like that. That would be very inelegant. They wouldn't do that. The point they do make is, wait a minute, let me tell you how I did it! I mean, this is the process that I use, and continue to use, and guess what? It's not magic. It's just common sense, and it works.*

Miller: Here's the way to look at it. There's a famous trader in the bond market at the board of trade—I'm getting so old, I can't remember his name—but he made huge amounts of money trading bonds and bond futures. He said, I've got a foolproof trading system here. But here's the acid test of whether I really have a winning system. I will accept a few hand-picked students and teach it to them. The test is whether they make money. Can you explain it to a third person, and if that third person trades, does he make money? He set up a little school and he trained these people. You know what happened? He's now out of the business and so are the students. Maybe Peter Lynch can do it, but can he teach another person to do it? If he could, we'd have some evidence that it's more than just luck.

Tanous: *Well, he says he can in his books. The way I put it to Peter Lynch was, if I read both of your books, which I have several times, I'd find the answer to getting rich is to hang out at the mall and see what's selling.*

Miller: I don't read the books. But that's the thing that makes us academics so skeptical. If it's a teachable skill, then perhaps you can teach it to many others. That may generate enough data to tell skill from luck. After all, when a 15 handicap golfer breaks par, which can happen, you know it's just dumb luck. But to be considered a real champ, you have to break par in hundreds of matches. My point is that you can't tell skill from luck unless you have large samples. We just don't have them for testing skill in stock picking.

Tanous: *I have to ask you a favor.*

Miller: Okay.

Tanous: *You know that you're noted for having a wonderful sense of humor. There's a story, and I don't know if its true or not, but if it is I'd love you to tell it. It's about a speech you were supposed to give in Hamburg.*

Miller: Whether it's true or not, here is the story. I was traveling in Germany many years ago and a friend of mine, a German professor, arranged for me to give a talk to the finance faculty at the university in each city. I wanted to see all of the big cities in Germany, including Hamburg, but my friend said, I can't send you to the University of Hamburg because they're all communists there. There is, however, one school in Hamburg where the communists haven't taken over, and that's the high command staff school of the German army, the *Hochschule der Bundeswehr.* I'll set it up for you, he said.

So I went from Cologne to Hamburg on a military pass. I get into the *Hochschule der Bundeswehr* and, like he said, it's a military school. The students, all in uniform, went everywhere running at a trot, not only in the corridors, but up the stairs. Now the only talk I had for this trip was on a fairly technical subject of interest only to finance professors. So I looked down from the lectern at the rows of young uniformed faces sitting politely at attention in the high-tech auditorium, and the only thing I could think of to say was: "Gentlemen: Tomorrow we invade Poland!" *[Gales of laughter.]*

Tanous: *We're nearing the end of our talk, professor. I wonder if I might ask you, based on your experience, how do you think people should invest for the future, be it their retirement, or college education, or what have you? Should they buy index funds?*

Miller: Absolutely. I have often said, and I know this will get some of your readers mad, that any pension fund manager who doesn't have the vast majority—and I mean 70% or 80% of his or her portfolio—in passive investments is guilty of malfeasance, non-feasance or some other kind of bad feasance! There's just no sense for most of them to have anything but a passive investment policy. And I know people will say, yeah, but if everybody invested passively, who would discipline the corporations? Well, as I explained earlier, the few people who are willing to spend the money to do it. And they will get enough extra returns to compensate for their costs. But that's about it. Most pension fund managers cannot even reasonably hope to do any better than a passive fund. And, on a risk adjusted basis, they don't! I believe that data are quite strong on this.

Tanous: *In fact, Bill Sharpe thinks only "mad money" should be actively managed.*

Miller: That's based on the principle that, as long as you keep the amounts of active money reasonably small, the active managers won't do too much damage.

I'll tell you another story that will irritate your audience: The first time I made this point was in the '50s, when there was a guy at a pension fund who was explaining to me that he had five separate managers. At the end of each year, he'd see which manager did the best and which did the worst. He fired the worst and he brought in another one.

Tanous: *A fairly common tactic and theory.*

Miller: A common theory. Well, I always say that's like having a passive fund, all right. Only it's the most expensive way to do it. Because if you have five separate managers, you're going to wind up pretty much with the market average. So why not just go there in the beginning and stop all this style analysis nonsense. Some people, I'm sure, make a handsome living tracking styles and so forth. I'm very skeptical. If I were in charge of a pension fund, I would put it in passive management.

Tanous: *But the style thing does have relevance. The academics have demonstrated that styles of stock vary together. In other words, the growth stocks tend to perform similarly but, for example, the growth and the value styles don't perform the same way.*

Miller: Well, you know, I suppose if you take 50/50 growth and value, you get back to the market. How are you going to tell which one is due to take off?

Tanous: *You can't. The idea is that you allocate assets by style. One thing I find interesting is that the data show that value stocks outperform growth stocks.*

Miller: They show that they have over some period of time. As I said, I'm always worried that the last two hundred years, or whatever your sample period is, have been somewhat unusual. I take a very long view and I'm not convinced, yet, that simple passive investing isn't the best way to go for the vast bulk of all investors. Unless you can explain to me why some strategy that everybody could follow is superior.

Tanous: *Oh, they explain it all right. They explain it by risk. They say you get rewarded for the risk you take. Value stocks are riskier. Ergo, you get more reward with value stocks. Now, that's controversial.*

Miller: Yeah. But if it is risk that accounts for the differential, and it has to be if the differential is not just some random sampling fluke, then some day the risk will happen. And when it does, you give it all back. After all, our Dimensional Fund Advisors small-cap portfolio underperformed the S&P 500 for 6 or 7 years in a row. It's back up again now, but who knows when it will tank again? All you can say is that small stocks are part of total wealth. I should hold my share of them, not just the S&P.

Tanous: *Do you practice what you preach in your own investments, or do you secretly have an active manager on the side?*

Miller: No. I do read the papers. Sometimes I get intrigued by the idea of a drug company that has a drug for obesity, or something like that. I may take a flyer on some of those things.

Tanous: *Boy, am I glad to hear that!*

Miller: Yeah. But that's strictly recreational. It's not serious investing.

Tanous: *But for serious investing, I presume you invest in the market.*

Miller: For the equity portion of my portfolio, yes. But I made a mistake, probably along with many others in my generation who lived through the '70s. I had too balanced a portfolio—too much bonds, relative to stocks. Had I put more in stocks, I'd be wealthier today!

Tanous: *Many thanks, professor. That is no doubt worthy advice.*

Indeed it is! Stockbrokers rejoice! Here is the noted economist, Merton Miller, telling us he wished he had put more of his own money in stocks. And once again, we are exposed to the prevailing view among academics that those of us who try to beat the market are just wasting our time. Sure, some of us will succeed, just like a few of us will win the lottery or hit a slot machine jackpot.

I found it interesting that Miller's view of the efficient market hypothesis is not extreme. He allows that some people may be able to get information before others, á là Michael Price, and profit from that information. However, he believes that in the aggregate, the extra profits will only amount to the money spent doing the research. But, among those making those extra profits, there will be some who do very, very well. Our challenge is to identify these winners and observe how they do it.

As I reread Miller's comments, I was impressed by the elegance of his points, and the compelling explanations of his views on market efficiency. Miller is an historic figure in the field of economics. We asked him to stray from his normal field, the classic Miller and Modigliani theorem. But the journey was worth it. This wise man—I dare not call him old—not only shared insights and wisdom with us, he did so with humor.

FOSTER
FRIESS

If you do a little research on Foster Friess, the high-energy manager of the Brandywine Fund, you'll come across two or three stories pretty consistently. One has to do with pigs in a trough—we'll ask him about it. Another involves his distaste for staff meetings and how he handles them. And there's always the story about how Foster Friess behaves on airplanes. These are but a few of the anecdotes that herald the peculiarity of this very engaging, and very successful fund manager.

A look at a typical Brandywine Fund quarterly report offers a clue to Friess' management style. Rather than a dry statistical accounting of the last quarter's performance, his reports read more like a high school yearbook, featuring cheery profiles on employees, consultants, and even executives at the companies owned by the fund. ("Even with the hectic demands of planning her Autumn wedding, Nicole still manages to devote some of her personal time to various charitable organizations.")

The Brandywine Fund celebrated its tenth anniversary on December 31, 1995, having grown from a starting investment of $100,000 to a $4.2 billion fund, with more than 30,000, presumably very happy, shareholders. Average annualized return for ten years: 18.4%. We should be so lucky. As we will see in our entertaining and informative conversation with Foster, the performance does come at *a price. The price is, predictably, higher volatility than most other funds. You pay your money; you take your chances.*

If I had to pick the single most impressive statistic about Foster Friess and the Brandywine Fund, it would not necessarily be that he manages money for the Nobel Foundation in Stockholm, which he does. Instead, I can't help being impressed that the employees of Morningstar Inc., the premier firm in the tracking and rating of mutual funds, picked the Brandywine Fund as the leading invest- ment vehicle for their own 401(k) plan.

Tanous: *When did you first get interested in stocks?*

Friess: Hmm. I think it was when I took a University of Wisconsin business course on securities analysis. The professor was very high on a local Milwaukee stock. I cashed in a $1,200 insurance policy my father had bought me and wound up buying the stock two points above the published high. I lost so much money in it, at age nine- teen, that I was determined to get it back.

Tanous: *Nice answer! Your history is really interesting. In fact, one of my clients, a prominent Virginia cardiologist, is the one who first alerted me to Foster Friess. He's a very big fan of yours. Friess Associates started, I believe, in 1974, with one client. But it was one heck of an account: the Nobel Foundation of Stockholm. That's an impressive initial client.*

Friess: Our slogan, Peter, when we started in 1974, was even more impressive. Our slogan was: "Friess Associates, serving with honesty and integrity since 1974"! It lost its humor by 1976, so we stopped using it.

Tanous: *How did the Nobel relationship develop?*

Friess: I was with a family in Delaware that had a relationship with the Nobel Foundation. I worked with that family for ten years before launching Friess Associates.

Tanous: *Whatever happened to them?*

Friess: They're still doing what they've been doing. It was quite unusual how that relationship developed. The father of the fellow I worked for and his wife took a cruise to the Caribbean. On the cruise, they met a thirty-year-old-envoy from Sweden, named Nils Ståhle, who was stationed in New York. They became good friends and kept in touch. Twenty years later Nils Ståhle had worked himself up to be the director of the Nobel Foundation. He called up his long time friend and said, we're getting killed in these mortgages and fixed income vehicles. Can you invest in some American growth stocks? That was 1954. They started out with fifty or sixty thousand dollars in the '50s. Now it's well over $35 million, just in the Brandywine holdings they now have.

Tanous: *In researching your style and the way you operate, I was pretty interested in what seemed to be a network approach to gathering information on companies. Could you tell us a little bit about that?*

Friess: We think that having antennae tuned into the field to find out what is happening, rather than having all of our information coming from presentations that CEOs make at cocktail parties, gives us the opportunity to understand how the real world is functioning. So basically what we have done is put people in Phoenix, Jackson, and Wilmington, and augmented that by getting to know stockbrokers around the country in small regional firms, plus some consultants, who then create this network.

For example, in Phoenix, one of our researchers might take an executive out who knows something about what's going on in some of the data processing centers there. He knows which of the computers, like Amdahl versus IBM, might be better positioned to serve the needs of those major data centers. So it's just the ability to kick the tires on a nationwide basis. As we go forward, we hope to expand this network of consultants and brokers, and maybe even have additional offices.

Tanous: *That's interesting. You know, in this book we focus on process. What we're trying to do is find out what makes a very few individuals' performance so extraordinary. As I look at what you do, I think it's safe to say that yours is a growth, bottom-up style. But I wonder how accurate it is to call it momentum investing, which some people do, especially since you have such an aversion to high price-earnings ratios?*

Friess: That's well put. We kind of recoil at the description of us as "momentum" investors. Maybe we are that, but we don't like to be called that.

Tanous: *For instance, one of my interviewees, Richard Driehaus [page 53], is a momentum investor but, as near as I can tell, P/Es are a minor consideration in his case.*

Friess: They're very critical in ours. That's one of our key considerations.

One thought worth touching on is your question about how individuals have become so successful. I think the success of Friess Associates is not based on the individual. You're interviewing me because I'm the guy who was the first fellow on the job and have become part of the success. But I think the reason we've succeeded is because of the contributions of every single person here who is dedicated to doing a good job. Anyone knows that managing $9 billion is completely beyond the capabilities of one person. So the success that Friess Associates enjoys is not an individual success. It's much more than that. I think what we try to do is to create a culture where everybody realizes that, and is appreciative of one another. We try to encourage everyone, starting with the receptionist at the front desk, to treat the Pepsi delivery man with the same amount of dignity and respect as he or she would if the President of the United States came through the door.

Tanous: *I think that's a wonderful thing to say. But from where I sit, I've got to try to sort out how much of what you are saying is reality. You have a reputation for being an awfully nice human being and a modest one, to boot.*

Friess: I don't know. My wife would tell you I've got a lot of reasons to be humble!

Tanous: *How many stocks do you own, and what's your turnover?*

Friess: We have 220 stocks in our portfolio, with 180% turnover.

Tanous: *With that high turnover, I guess there's no getting away from a standard deviation considerably higher than the market's.*

Friess: We do not relate to most of those tenets of modern portfolio theory. Asking us about standard deviation would be like asking a plumber how many kilowatts he wanted to plug into a lamp. It just doesn't compute with us. The turnover, Peter, is a function of the fact that we have this pigs-in-a-trough displacement theory.

Tanous: *I was going to ask you about that. I'm glad you brought it up. Please explain it.*

Friess: The notion is, we always want to have the most dynamic companies in the portfolio. In our business, it's so easy to get to know a management, the product lines, get comfortable with everything we know about it, and know that it's doing well. You can fall in love with these companies and overstay. By creating this forced displacement idea, we are constantly looking for new ideas. When we find them, we force ourselves to displace some other company by limiting the number of companies that we can own.

This comes from the pigs-in-the-trough experience. I grew up in northern Wisconsin. I'd visit my friends on the farm. The father throws some food to the pigs. There are fifteen to a trough. Across the barnyard comes the sixteenth pig, who nudges himself on the trough. The fifteenth, the one that got displaced from the end, doesn't roll over and die. He isn't sick. There's nothing wrong with him. It's just that he's full, and content, and wanders off.

Tanous: *I guess he's just as happy as a pig in a trough, wouldn't you say? But isn't it possible, using this approach, that a perfectly good company will get nudged out of the picture?*

Friess: The companies that we're displacing are sometimes very excellent investments. Some could have a 20% to 30% upside, and would be considered a buy by many people. But we found one with a 60% or 70% upside. So the companies that we're selling *should* be good companies. If we're getting into a position where we're selling bad companies, then we're not doing our job. Every sale we make at Friess Associates should be of an excellent company, with good prospects. The only reason for selling is that we found something better.

Tanous: *I want to go back to a point you just made. You said you really don't pay much attention to the normal industry measurement tools like standard deviation, presumably beta, and some of the other things. Why?*

Friess: Because I don't think Andrew Carnegie, when he created his steel mill empire, thought about those. I don't think Christopher Columbus, when he came here to look for gold and treasure, thought about them either. We're that traditional.

Tanous: *Basically, that means you're much more focused on the fundamentals of what you're buying. You're more interested in the business than in whether or not the stock has moved around a lot.*

Friess: That's well put. We try to think of ourselves as businessmen buying businesses. We ask ourselves, what would this company be worth if the stock exchange closed down tomorrow and we suddenly had a private company?

Tanous: *I understand that approach. I also understand that you make it a practice to talk to the company's competitors before you buy the stock. Is that right?*

Friess: Not only their competitors; we talk to their customers, their suppliers, and sometimes that's how we come up with an idea. We'll be talking to a company and we'll ask: Of all the companies you're competing with, who do you see the most often? Who do you have the most respect for? Sometimes a competitor will reveal that; other times they won't.

Tanous: *You know, it's funny, when you say that it seems like such an obviously smart thing to do, but it's not something that comes up a lot when you're talking to money managers.*

Friess: It's due to our religion, so to speak, of focusing. We focus each day on how we are going to make money for our clients. We don't spend a lot of time finding out how other managers do that. We kind of prefer a monklike existence within the investment community. We don't have that much interaction with our peers unless we've been asked to speak on a panel or something.

Tanous: *This starts to get to some of the elements of your success. You know the word that comes up the most often among very successful managers, and it applies here, is discipline. It seems to me that discipline is important to you.*

Friess: We work very hard on inculcating discipline in the new people who join our firm. But before they come in, we want them to have those disciplines in place and then we fine-tune them. The people who have been successful at Friess Associates, each and every one of them, are, in their own right, very highly focused people. An example is, Diane Hakala, who is a stunt pilot. She qualified for the world championships twice. She was prevented from going once because her engine stopped at 700 feet and she ran her plane into a drainage ditch. She walked away with a broken ankle. The focus that you have to have to be a stunt pilot is dramatic. She takes that personality trait and puts that same degree of intensity and focus into the investment research process.

Tanous: *What does she do at your company?*

Friess: She is one of our researchers. In our company, we also have blurred the lines from those that traditional money managers might use. We don't use the term "analyst" and "portfolio manager." We use the terms "researcher" and "money manager." In our culture what we're trying to create is the highly trained, highly experienced, highly motivated, successful barracuda-type person in the trenches calling the companies and making the decisions as to which companies we are going to buy or sell. We do not have a system where a more junior researcher makes calls and reports to the sophisticated, gray-haired investment committee, who then blesses it, and then another senior type person puts it in the portfolio. What we've done is empowered the people who have the most cutting edge understanding of what's happening to the businesses. They are the ones who are pulling the triggers. We have a system of checks and balances, where we have a team leader who has to bless that decision before it finally comes to me for final blessing. But the way we're organized, very seldom do I ever have to interrupt any of those decisions.

Tanous: *What sort of people do you look for? What traits do you look for among people who are going to be outstanding in this business of finding and analyzing potential investments?*

Friess: First of all, a high degree of intellectual honesty. Second, a high energy level, an intense eagerness to win, an ability to interact effectively with people, and a natural curiosity. I like to have people with high energy levels, but who are called rather than driven. And there's a big difference.

Tanous: *Would you elaborate on that, please?*

Friess: Well, all of us have a need for significance. We all make decisions as to what gives us significance. I've found, in my life experience, that people who desperately need to prove themselves have high energy levels and are driven. There are, on the other hand, people who have the self-esteem and the significance already, who want to go out and manifest that for the benefit of others. They have the same high energy level. Remember the film "Chariots of Fire," about the Olympic runners? One man ran for self-aggrandizement and the other to honor God.

Tanous: *It almost sounds like a Calvinist culture, Foster.*

Friess: An old missionary once reminded me, "our lives are not to *earn* God's favor but to *return* the favor." I don't know that much about Calvin, but I will openly and eagerly try to share that the success that Friess Associates has enjoyed has come largely because both my wife and I are trying to embody the ancient Judeo-Christian traditions on which our country was founded. That includes the writings of Moses and David and Isaiah and Paul.

For example, these teachings declare that every one of us has weaknesses. Early on I learned that I have weaknesses and my teammates have weaknesses. Rather than beating them up and trying to change them, which I try to do, unsuccessfully, at times, it's much better to accept people's weaknesses and work around them. If one person is excellent at picking stocks, but he's not as effective as someone else with clients, then you design his job function so that he can manifest his strengths to the best of his ability, and not get bogged down by being in a situation where his weaknesses will impede him.

Tanous: *Most people, Foster, would just call that good management.*

Friess: Right. But I was a slow learner. I wanted each person to be capable of doing everything well. It's not too hard to figure out, if you have an analytical mind and you're analyzing stocks every day, that if you go out and see ten successful lives you might ask what makes them successful. And then you see ten dysfunctional lives and you ask what makes them dysfunctional. It doesn't take a brain surgeon to sort that out.

Tanous: *There seems to be a philosophy, even a deep faith, that permeates the discipline that you bring to picking companies. Is that right?*

Friess: Well, I think more importantly it permeates the culture. It's why a lot of good people like being part of this firm—because we take their intelligence and their creativity and we give them the chance to be forgiven when they screw up.

Tanous: *You should write a book.*

Friess: I'm talking about it. I'd like to put some of these ideas down. My wife, Lynn, suggested that if I do a book, I first ought to deal with the issues of investment theory and stock selection and secondly, as part of that, perhaps the notion of time management, another favorite topic of mine. What we're now thinking about is maybe we can come up with a book that says "Managing Your Time, Money and Life!"

A lot of people say, Foster and Lynn have this religious base to their lives. I always want to point out that every living human being on the face of the earth has a religion. It just might not happen to be the Judeo-Christian concept, or even one of the major five. But hedonism—eat, drink and be merry—is a religion. Materialism is a religion which says, gee, if I have all these toys and all these things, then that is what creates my sense of well-being and that is what makes me important. Every person has religion.

Tanous: *As I recall, the Calvinist issue is being very successful, in a monetary or other earthly sense, is a signal to your fellow man that God has already appointed you as one of the leaders. You have a straight path to Heaven, or something like that.*

Friess: I would disagree 100% with that notion, because the Jews taught that the rain falls on both the righteous and the unrighteous. In the Jewish tradition, you are taught to love your neighbor and be responsible for the poor and to be forgiving. As I said before, I believe that our lives are not to earn God's favor, but to return the favor.

Tanous: *You keep mentioning Jewish culture. I recall reading that you're a fervent Christian. What's the nexus between the two?*

Friess: Christianity is a Jewish religion. What people forget is that, for the first 70 years after Christ died, most of the people who knew about those incidents were Jewish. I guess it wasn't until Paul got on some boat and went to tell the gentiles about it, that it spread beyond the Jewish people.

Tanous: *Interesting point.*

Friess: What's so interesting in our culture today, Peter, is that because of the ignorance of this fact in our culture, we have a divisiveness that need not be.

Tanous: *Fascinating stuff, Foster. If we're not careful, we'll end up talking more about this than about stocks. Let's move on. Let's talk about your sell discipline. I confess that I was a little startled, happily so, when I read in your own literature that you describe your sell discipline as "harsh and aggressive." That gets to you.*

Friess: What we want to remember, in this forced displacement idea, is that we want to be very callous, if you will, as we evaluate all the pigs.

Tanous: *Which ones are full?*

Friess: Which ones are full and content and which ones are lean and mean and hungry. It's very easy to get emotionally attached to the one that is fat and happy. Remember, we buy companies where the recognition is yet to come. Therefore, we seek out companies that are in the process of changing their spots.

Tanous: *Can you give us an example?*

Friess: Sure. Going back to 1979, Tandy came out with their TRS 80, model 2, I think it was called, that was their little PC. Nobody really knew about it, because everybody looked at Tandy as a retailer of third-rate electronic products in those not-too-impressive Radio Shack stores around the country. Meanwhile, Apple Computer goes public at what, 30 × or 40 × earnings, as the perceived industry leader. IBM had not yet entered the PC market. So, what happens is you have a transformation, where suddenly people realize that the PC business at Tandy has gone from 9% of sales to 32% of sales. The multiple suddenly gets revised from a retailing multiple to a technology multiple as all the technology analysts figure out what they have.

Tanous: *But you had to see that.*

Friess: Right. And the reason we made fivefold on the Tandy investment while people who bought Apple were under water for awhile is that the public offering of Apple was so filled with euphoria. The high P/E on Apple created a bad investment with a good company, whereas Tandy was perceived as a less dynamic company than

Apple, but the P/E ratio and the changing perception made it a fabulous investment.

Tanous: *Conversely, Foster, what kind of companies do you* not *want to own?*

Friess: We typically do not like to own "concept" companies, like biotechnology, where they're going to lose money for the next three years, but this new drug is going to grow hair, or whatever, and it's going to earn $5.00 a share in 2001. We also have a hard time getting excited about utility companies because that's a politically-driven profit picture. You cannot grow beyond the demographics of a given area, except if you are able to get good pricing. If you start showing too much profit, the political process will take those prices away.

Third, we don't like to invest in companies whose fortunes are determined by a small number of decisionmakers. For example, if you have a peripheral company that only sells to IBM and two other major firms, the purchasing agent at IBM can do some damage to you. Conversely, a fast food operation is likely to have millions of customers every day. We are more eager to be in that kind of investment. We also have an aversion to some of the financial stocks, where the earnings are a figment of accounting imagination.

Tanous: *For example . . .*

Friess: When a company could, for example, sell insurance policies and spread the cost of the agent's commission over the life of the policy, using, (1) their guess as to what that will be; and (2) making a judgment as to what their losses are going to be, and, (3) creating reserves based on that potential loss. That, too, is a figment of their imagination and creativity, because you're selling a product for which you have no idea what the ultimate cost will be. There are some companies, where the accounting is very conservative and where the things they are doing are viable. So, despite these comments, we don't want to be so dogmatic that we aren't open to shooting fish in a barrel if we find such a company in one of these industries.

Tanous: *Your record, as you know, has been truly extraordinary. It's rare to find somebody who so consistently beats the averages, particularly at a time when 80% of fund managers don't beat the averages. I can find no other thing to say except that your discipline, your* *approach to investing, and the fact that there's a lot of hard work involved, seems to be treating you well. But why do you think your record is so much better than others? After all, Morningstar in according Brandywine its highest, five star rating for the past ten years, ranks you as the number one performing fund with no load or distribution charges currently available to the public.*

Friess: It gets back to the people that are part of Friess Associates. We've attracted an adequate number of people so that we don't have one person managing 80 or 100 different stocks, like some other firms do. We have divided up into small teams so that you might find three people following maybe 25 or 30 stocks. The ratio of investment professionals to the number of stocks we own currently is running 8 to 10 stocks per person, if you include as investment personnel our traders and the people who assist our researchers. Our "research managers" take the calls from the brokers and make sure that the information is forwarded to the researcher. If you take all 30 people involved in the investment process, you get a very nice ratio, focused on those 25 or 30 companies.

Tanous: *Looking at performance again, if we take the Lipper* [a mutual fund performance measurement service] *numbers, among the top ten U.S. growth funds for the last ten years, Brandywine Fund is number one for a single year, the last three, the last five, as well as the last ten years, for funds currently available to the public with no distribution charges or loads. Modesty aside, I think it's safe to say that Brandywine is the number one no-load growth fund.*

Friess: I think it would be accurate to say that, according to these numbers, we were the number one ranked U.S. growth fund still available to the public that has no load or distribution charges. That would be the accurate statement, I believe. There was one fund which was a couple of percentage points above us for ten years, but they are no longer available to the public.

Tanous: *I think the most impressive statistic about you is that the Morningstar employees picked your fund overwhelmingly for their own 401(k)s.*

Friess: We were flabbergasted when we heard about it. I was at a steeplechase on a Sunday, and a lady walks up to me and says, Gee, what a great article in *The New York Times.* I had no idea it was there, or that Morningstar had even selected us. That was the first time I heard about it.

Tanous: *You mentioned that one of the elements of your success is that you are a time management freak. Well, that may be too strong. But tell me about your attitude toward time?*

Friess: I'm very sensitive, now that I'm coming on 56 and have had a few friends disappear off the face of the earth, that we have a limited amount of time here. I'm also aware that, if you take out a pencil and say there are 365 days in the year, divided into 7 day weeks, of which five are typically work days, then you figure there are ten or twelve holidays nationally, and most people have three weeks vacation, that maybe two-thirds of the days, 240 out of the 365, are supposedly work days. If you assume eight work hours, that's one-third of the day. If you take one third of two-thirds, that's two-ninths. So, 22% of a person's life is supposedly in a work setting. But if you figure 22% is for working, you have 78% to eat, sleep, and be merry. You just want to use that 22% as effectively as you can.

Tanous: *What's your attitude about meetings?*

Friess: Well, you probably know the answer to that.

Tanous: *I admit I set you up with that question.*

Friess: We don't meet at Friess Associates if we can avoid it. When we do meet, we meet in a room with no chairs. We also believe that a meeting should never be used to make a decision and never used to transfer information.

Tanous: *I know you'd rather do it by e-mail, but why?*

Friess: When you transfer information in a written context you have something to refer back to. If I say to you, Peter, let's meet at Sugarloaf Cafe tonight at 6:30, you could say, I thought you said 5:30 or 7:30, or I thought you said Sweetwater. So the fact that you have the ability to make it clearer makes the communication dramatically better.

But what would be fun would be to take a sheet out of one of the magazines on your desk and read it and time it. Then read it out loud and time it. I read in one of these techie magazines, where they interview people like Bill Gates, that our ears process information at 30 kilohertz and our eyes process information at 30 megahertz.

Maybe some people are different, but I process information so much faster and more effectively with my eyes than with my ears. And if that is generally true, why don't we want to be in the mode where we are processing information more with our eyes rather than with our ears since we'll be more effective?

Tanous: *Well, let me answer that. When I have meetings with people, the face-to-face aspect conveys other things that are important to human beings, like emotion, degree of conviction, sincerity, forcefulness, and confidence. Things like that that are hard to put down on paper or on the computer.*

Friess: That's well put, and that is part of our strategy. The times that you *should* have meetings is when what you want to transfer is emotion. In our research process, when we ask a company about what they're telling everybody about future pricing of a product, we would much rather ask the question face-to-face. That way, we can get an understanding of body language. That's valid. But in terms of the day-to-day transfer of information like, "I'd like to go to dinner at 6:30 at Sugarloaf," that is better conveyed in written form.

You make a good point about the times you ought to have meetings. The meetings we have are to encourage people, to exhort people, to recognize people, and to build those relationships as part of the bonding process. Because we have this "fax vs. talk" culture, we therefore have the situation we're going to have next week, where we're taking 103 people to the Cayman Islands. We think by doing this, we also demonstrate that everybody in the firm is important. We don't just take the top ten hotshots. We take our company drivers who, although part time, are an important part of our success. We go to great efforts to make sure that people feel that everybody contributes. So everybody goes on the trip.

Tanous: *I hesitate to tell you this, Foster, but I've been told that when you're flying somewhere on a trip, you'll often get up and start talking to your fellow passengers, asking them what they do and how their company and industry are getting along. Forgive me for saying this, but do you realize that that sort of behavior could make you a frequent flyer's worst nightmare?*

Friess: *[Laughs]* I think I am! But, you know if a person keeps glancing back at his laptop to see if his battery is running low, you'd better move on to somebody else!

Tanous: *What do you get out of that?*

Friess: I get exactly what I want all our people to get. That is, to have their antennae tuned to companies that are coming up out of the weeds, that maybe haven't surfaced to become a Wall Street buzzword yet. You might be talking to some fellow in Minneapolis who you could ask about the significance of the Minnesota Mining restructuring, or what they were doing on some other things. What you get out of it is an insight from the day-to-day business person in the trenches about the trends that he sees evolving. It may be all kinds of things that may not have investment significance for 6, 8, 9, months, or a year. But you put that in your databank and you're alert to it when those opportunities do present themselves, because you know the background, and the context, and can judge whether or not it is important.

Tanous: *One thing you know, because you're in this business, is that the efficient market theorists say that everything that is known by your fellow passengers on the plane, or anybody else for that matter, is already reflected in today's price of the stock.*

Friess: That's what they believe, but think about it. If you think of some of the people who own IBM, they include a little lady in Des Moines, Iowa who doesn't read *The Wall Street Journal.* She's 82 years old. Does she know what's happening with the new memory products and if they are delayed or not? Does she know the plans for Lotus Notes?

Tanous: *The theory is that she, in particular, doesn't have to know it. The market in aggregate knows it, and all of that information is reflected in the price of the stock.*

Friess: If that's the case, why is Compaq Computer down 7 points today? Somebody didn't know that the PC market was slowing until today. That information was out there. These are things that can be discerned, if you talk to the supplier and talk to various people in the industry. They can tell you who is gaining market share. They can tell you that the pricing for Apple Computers in Japan is brutally awful. They can tell you that the new NEC computer is selling better in stores than the Hewlett-Packard computer. You go to lunch with some guy who is a clerk at a computer store and ask him, what's selling? Can you imagine if you owned a portfolio in an index fund and one of the stocks dropped 20% one day, and the client asks you why did you own that stock? And you say the reason I own it is because there's a group of young folks over at Standard & Poor's who decided to put it in the S&P index!

Tanous: *You and I are about the same age. I think about this and I expect you do too. Let's say you have another decade or two of very active involvement. What are the mountains that Foster Friess still wants to climb?*

Friess: Well, I want to continually work on becoming a better father and a better husband. Period.

That sounds okay, and it's a rather typical and predictable Foster Friess answer. The interview says it all. Here is a man who is not only uninfluenced by his success, he seems intent on bettering the lives of his employees and all those with whom he is associated. I think that Foster would have been just as content to spend the entire interview talking about Judeo-Christian teachings and the need for effective moral behavior in our daily lives. I was tempted to do that too, but we do have a mission, after all.

What did we learn from Foster Friess, who has one of the very best long-term records of success using the growth style? We learned that there is not just one way to select stocks in a portfolio. There is an inherent curiosity in his approach. Witness his seemingly peculiar behavior on airplanes, which is really very telling. You and I probably hide in our seats on a long flight, hoping that our seatmate wouldn't dare strike up a conversation. Not Foster. His behavior is driven by an intense curiosity, which is, no doubt, a principal ingredient to his success. Ask the right questions; you'll get the right answers.

Another memorable point: the pigs-in-the-trough theory is kind of cute in the telling, but let's not miss the wisdom of this tale. The "forced displacement" discipline creates a culture in which you are not just looking for new stocks to buy, you have to pick stocks to sell that you might not want to sell. Remember what he said: Friess might well sell a stock with a 20% or 30% growth rate, because it's going to be replaced by one with a 60% or 70% growth rate. That is an unusual approach for portfolio managers. Whatever you think of it, the evidence suggests that it works.

Another thing: Foster Friess spends most of his time at his home in Jackson Hole, Wyoming, another not-so-obvious financial capital. I mention this just in case you thought to be good at this business it was helpful to live within walking distance of Wall Street.

VAN
SCHREIBER

*Van Schreiber spent the bulk of his long career in money manage-
ment at C. J. Lawrence, which is now part of Deutsche Morgan
Grenfell. C. J. Lawrence was an old line Wall Street firm, the kind
we used to call "research boutiques." The firm was founded in 1864.
Not long after our interview, Van left his old firm to start his own
company, Bennett/Lawrence Management LLC, also in New York
City. (His former colleagues, W. David Wister and Robert Harris,
remained at C. J. Lawrence and plan to continue managing money
using the same general style and procedures at Deutsche Morgan
Grenfell.)*

*Van Schreiber comes across as a no-nonsense, let's-get-down-
to-business individual. I fully expect he seeks similar attributes
among the executives of companies he buys. If he were a doctor, he
would not score points for his bedside manner. A graduate of
Williams College with an MBA from New York University,
Schreiber has been managing money for over 30 years. We met in his
mid-town Manhattan office.*

*Over the years Schreiber's performance has been remarkable.
His style is exclusively growth, and his approach is disciplined. His
record, is computed back to 1987, shows gross annualized returns of
34.1% through the end of 1995. Moreover, there were no down years*

in the interim, although a few intervening quarters were real scary. This is the kind of long term performance that most of us can only dream of.

Tanous: *Tell us how you first got interested in stocks.*

Schreiber: I was eighteen years old. I was riding home in the car with my father, who was a cartoonist. I asked him what this stock market table in the paper was about. Incidentally, my job at that moment was unloading boxcars of heavy furniture, which came from the west coast. It was hot and hard work. I asked my father, what does this mean—IBM up 1/2? He replied that it meant that if you owned a share of IBM stock, you had made 50 cents that day. I thought about that for a second or two and I said: you mean this stock is worth 50 cents more today than it was yesterday, and you didn't have to unload a boxcar, or dig a ditch, or anything? He said, yeah, that's right. I decided this was the business for me. That is, literally, a true story.

Tanous: *Great story.*

Schreiber: Shortly after, I went to C.J. Lawrence and met with the managing partner. I had $1,000 and told him I wanted to invest it in Curtis Wright. Curtis Wright was developing a car that could fly. It's true; a car that could fly! What a great thing that would be, I said to this fellow, Alex Johnson. What a wonderful guy to put up with a naive kid like me. He dissuaded me from that so I bought some other stocks. A few years later, CJL hired me, after I finished graduate school. The point is that, I became an investor at a very young age and have always loved it. I became an analyst in the research department, visited companies, watched what was going on, invested actively, and made at least my share of mistakes.

In the process, I have come to certain points of view regarding what works, at least for me. I have also come to the view that there are some people who invest in completely different ways than I do and are wonderful at it. To say that their way is a good way, or my way is a better way, is not the point. You have to know what you are good at and do it. If you are a great rug merchant then be a great rug merchant. If you're a wonderful aerospace engineer, then be that. It is the same thing with the stock market. There are certain people who are great at it and that's what they should do.

Unfortunately, there are a great many impostors around who aren't good at anything but who like to wear the mantle of "I'm a growth guy," or "I'm a value guy," or whatever else because that sector has been on a roll in recent years. So they decide to be whatever it is that's hot. That's one of the tricks investors have to watch out for. Counterfeit people will hurt you worse than a bear market.

Tanous: *You know, Van, that there is a body of academic work that holds that the chances you, or anyone else, are going to beat the market over time are very slim. I don't expect you to agree with that, but it is an historical fact that a vast majority of portfolio managers don't beat the market. My analysis suggests you do, in fact, consistently beat the market, so the question is, quite bluntly, how and why?*

Schreiber: Your question is: Why have we been able to out-distance the market, when others haven't? I think the answer is, that we have a philosophy that is particularly appropriate for today's world. It is a philosophy we assiduously follow, and which is both pertinent to today's times, but is disciplined and adaptable. So, appropriateness and adaptability, I think, are essential elements. That's why I think the philosophy works. The end result is that we invest only in companies with extraordinarily high rates of earnings growth. But we don't always outperform the market. There are quarters when we don't. There have been six-month periods when we don't perform well, but, thankfully, they have been infrequent, and there haven't been any entire years so far, although one might always occur.

Tanous: *Could we talk a little about your growth investment philosophy, since this is the foundation of your management style.*

Schreiber: Yes. It's really so critical and so simple that a lot of times, people will say to me after they hear it, why doesn't everyone else do that? My answer is, I don't know why everyone else doesn't, but it sure works. The approach has two foundations. First is the idea that we are in an uneven and imbalanced economy in the United States. There are certain new trends, and forces which are having an extraordinary impact, and are spurring very substantial growth rates. These trends are literally changing the way we work and changing the way we live. These forces are going to propel high growth rates whether real GNP is up 1.8% or 2.1% or 2.6%; it simply doesn't matter. I think that our economy has been subject to this kind of change since the first energy crisis. I think we are in the middle of a technology revolution that future historians will label as significant as the industrial revolution. For now, it is a technology revolution, with technology permeating our lives and creating all sorts of trends and influences in its wake. Technology is not the only trend. Major changes are occurring in consumer spending patterns, and in the way businesses and governments conduct their affairs. We are very oriented toward finding those trends, and investing singly in those trends. Sure, they change over time. One must always be on the lookout for what's new and upcoming.

We don't believe in a diversified portfolio. If the aluminum stocks are bad, and the aluminum industry is adverse, we don't underweight aluminum, we have *no* weight in aluminum. Conversely, if telecommunications equipment is a strong market, because phone companies have to renovate 90 years worth of equipment to provide voice, data and video quickly and efficiently, that means the telephone companies are going to have to spend $100 billion to do the job. So, we're going to own a lot of telecommunications equipment companies. In terms of these trends, we really do get the wind at our back. It has been our experience that these trends—if you can get them right—really do have far greater impact than one would ever have thought at their inception. At any one time, we could be involved with 12–15 distinct themes. And they will change as the economy and world around us change. That's point number one.

The second idea is that of competition. We think that American businessmen are among the best and the brightest in the world. We think that United States industry at-large is intensely competitive. Our companies really battle it out, not just with foreign companies, but also with their domestic foes. We think that investors underestimate the payoffs for being with the competitively advantaged companies. They also underestimate the losses for being with the competitively disadvantaged companies. Big rewards accrue to the winner. No greater example exists than the Wal-Mart/Kmart matter. If an analyst for the last fifteen years had been recommending Kmart, because Kmart stock was cheap, the price-earnings ratio was low, and therefore Kmart was a buy, this analyst, for whatever reason didn't grasp the reason for Kmart's cheapness: Wal-Mart had Kmart in its sights and Kmart was a dead duck. I repeat, a dead duck! And it's been a dead duck for fifteen years. All it's been doing is wiggling around.

Tanous: *How does this Wal-Mart/Kmart example fit into your investment philosophy?*

Schreiber: What I'm saying is, we will buy the company that we identify as being the one with the skills that will enable it to emerge as the competitive winner. We want the best-of-breed because we think the best-of-breed ultimately wins major league, and the least best-of-breed loses. Wal-Mart has pounded Kmart practically to death, and much money was made by those who saw this coming 10–15 years ago. This is going on throughout American business. There are countless other examples of this.

Tanous: *This sounds very bottom-up to me.*

Schreiber: It is bottom-up. What we're doing in this approach is combining both of these ideas. That's the beauty of it. We're taking the most fertile and powerful trends. We figure out the companies involved in those trends, and buy the company in the trend that can really capitalize on it. No kidding around. So, when you put both of those ideas together, it is certainly no miracle that what you end up with is companies that can grow very fast. That is what we do. We make no exceptions. It has to be both together.

Tanous: *Let's go through the selection process. How do you get from here to there? How do you identify those companies which are going to turn out to be your Wal-Marts?*

Schreiber: Good question. Sometimes we're wrong about that. We meet with the managements. We talk to the managements . . .

Tanous: *Every company you own?*

Schreiber: Yes. We've met every one.

Tanous: *You personally?*

Schreiber: Me personally or my associate, Robert Deaton. I've met them, talked to them, sometimes alone, sometimes in a group. But I have met the people who run the companies and made judgments about their adequacy. Sometimes those judgments are wrong, but at least we have made a judgment that these people are good, can be trusted, are innovative, have their own money at stake, that they are determined, and that they are not just playing games out there. The process starts with our assessment of management and then moves on to whatever it is that is important for that particular business.

Sometimes it's customer service, sometimes it's being the most efficient or the lowest cost producer, sometimes it's having the best distribution. Most of the time, however, it is the ability to come up with significant new products. Not always, of course, but if you had to pick one, it would be this, the ability to come up with new things that layer on chunks of additional revenue in future years.

Specifically, we try to judge whether the company has got what it takes in that particular business. We have not invested in airlines, but were we to, we would want the one with the most efficient fleet. If you're a credit card processor, you've got to make sure you have a lickety-split computer system that can do the job in milliseconds, not one that creeps along. So whatever it takes in that particular business, we try to make sure that our company has it.

Tanous: *I presume you start with industries you're interested in. Take aluminums. You mentioned that you don't want the most efficient producer in the aluminum industry, for example, presumably because you just don't like that industry.*

Schreiber: Other people might be able to successfully invest in the aluminum industry. By buying a turnaround situation, it might work. Other stocks, besides ours, do go up. It's just not what we do. But if we wanted to be in the aluminum industry, we would find the company in that business that we thought was the most efficient. It's been our experience that, as time passes, they're the one in that business that is going to come through with the biggest numbers. Some day, we might want to invest in aluminum, although it's a little hard to see now, and that's how we would go about it.

Tanous: *Let's talk about your sell discipline.*

Schreiber: Okay. But before we start talking about selling our stocks, let me say first that the way we make money in stocks is by identifying the themes, and the companies that can capitalize on the themes, then giving the companies a chance to do it. So our successful investments will be held for a year, or two, or three, or four. What will happen as these companies capitalize on these trends, and the trends themselves grow deeper, is that you'll get three or four years' worth of just absolutely supercharged earnings growth piling up on top of one another. That makes for magnificent stocks. We're talking doubles and triples. We don't buy a stock today and sell it if it goes up

15%. That's not how we make money. That's a prelude to the sell side. Now let's talk about the sell discipline.

There are three elements to our sell decision. The first is the notion that stocks do become over-owned, over-loved, even over-adored. When you invest the way we do, you can reach a condition where popularity breeds a crowd. Then the stocks become so successful that everybody owns them and loves them. When we sense that happening, it's time to move on.

Tanous: *There's nobody left to buy?*

Schreiber: Absolutely right. There's nobody left to buy. That's sell rule number one for us. Granted, it's very qualitative. There's nothing quantitative about it. It's just the sense one gets that there's no longer a discovery potential here. You must sell when the news is good, but the stock seems to be losing its responsiveness to good news.

The second aspect to the sell decision is when the industry we're investing in, or the theme we're investing in, begins to develop some blemishes—in terms of the competitors within the theme. We like it when the competitors to our company are doing great. Most investors dislike that. They want to have the only one that's doing well. I disagree with that. I think it's a wonderful, healthy thing to be in a trend where everybody's doing well.

Tanous: *How about some examples of this.*

Schreiber: Sure. First, let me go on to say that when everybody is doing well, it breeds a healthy industry with happy investors who want to invest. We like more money coming into our trends because it makes the stocks go up. Generally, it requires that industry conditions are good which, of course, increases the odds that your company is going to do well, too. The reverse also happens. If individual companies start to do poorly, it's telling you that the industry is beginning to deteriorate. Investor attitudes will not be far behind. Beyond that, something is beginning to happen in the business that is going to make earnings harder to come by. In all likelihood, it will come and get your company too. So we like a healthy industry.

The third sell decision is when we're just wrong—about the individual company we're investing in, when we've misjudged it, for whatever reason. Then we get out. We do not spend any time sitting around looking at our mistakes. How many successful businessmen do you know who sit around holding on to some product or inventory that the market didn't want? The smart ones put their mistakes behind them and get on with it. So do we.

Tanous: *Can you give me examples of the second point, companies that attracted a lot of healthy competitors with lots of them doing well for awhile before deterioration set in?*

Schreiber: Let's take the client-server computing area. It's been a wonderful area for us. We owned Sybase and we owned Oracle. We sold Sybase because it had violated rule number one. Amidst good news, the stock just would not go up any more, so we sold it. We kept our position in Oracle. Two months later, Sybase reported terrible earnings. At that point, we began to sell Oracle. Oracle's stock has subsequently gone up some, but other technology companies, in less crowded markets, have done better.

Tanous: *You've been in the business a long time. What is different now from the way you approached the business of investing ten or twenty years ago? If we were here talking twenty years ago, would your answers be the same?*

Schreiber: I don't think so. Fifteen years ago, I was not as disciplined as now, and I was a lot more psyched about price-earnings ratios. The virtuous way was the whole idea of value, and never paying up, etc. Sort of the Calvinist theory of investing—you have to suffer for awhile before you are allowed to make money. I spent time thinking that I was smart enough to see companies that were going to turn around, that I could anticipate this kind of thing much more than, in fact, I could. Back then, I wasn't nearly as wedded to these principles as I am today. I think my investing record has been much better than it was back then. Of course, we have been in a bull market, for the last six or seven years, so it's easy to look good when the market is strong.

There's a lot more to making money in the stock market than just figuring P/Es. We learned to divide when we were eight years old! We could have started making money then, if that was the whole deal, and someone had just told us about it. That would have beaten selling lemonade!

Tanous: *You know that we consultants often go crazy with statistics that analyze manager performances. Your Sharpe ratio* [a measure of excess return per unit of risk], *for example, is off the charts, indicat-*

ing that you give the investor tremendous value-added for the risk they are taking. But in terms of our classic risk measurements, like standard deviation, you're way up there. Your standard deviation is at least twice the market's, which means that your portfolio has double the risk of the market as a whole. But, so far, the investor who has been willing to accept that risk has been amply rewarded. What is it about what you do that makes your portfolio so volatile?

Schreiber: It's just that we own very few stocks. In a typical portfolio, we only own 25 companies or so, which is peanuts compared to other managers. We get portfolios that come into us all the time where the previous manager will have owned 70, 80, or 90 companies. From a capital gains point of view—and capital gains are our objective—owning that many companies doesn't work. People who come with us have to accept the volatility to get the capital gains. We tell people right from the beginning, don't give us every penny. We want the investor to be comfortable with this style and be able to take the reversals that, inevitably, we will have. We don't want you to flip out when we have a bad month, because we're going to have bad months.

Tanous: *Do you short stocks?*

Schreiber: Not in our separately managed accounts. We do have a private partnership, called Bennett/Lawrence Partners, which is a little more aggressive than our normal accounts. It can short stocks. When we short stocks, we just flip around the investment philosophy we've been talking about and take the mirror image of it. We short decaying companies in lackluster businesses.

Tanous: *Van, let's try to summarize your approach.*

Schreiber: When you push together the ideas and the approach we've talked about, what you end up with is a universe of companies for which the gains in earnings are exceptional—far above what the average company will achieve. Moreover, the accident level is low. This kind performance in earnings almost always drives share prices up big.

Tanous: *Why do you think you are so successful?*

Schreiber: I don't know why. Maybe because doing what we've talked about is appropriate for the world out there. If the world were to change, and everything were to go flat or become a gray world with no color and everything was the same, this approach would be a failure. But we're not in that kind of world. We're in a rapidly changing one. New ideas come quickly. We're in a world where men and women 23 years old can conceive of ideas that create the internet. Have you heard about the 23-year-old who figured out how to access the internet and created this thing Mosaic, which is now part of Netscape? It is is about to become one of the greatest public stock offerings of all time. The kid figures all this out at the age of 23! Unbelievable! That's the future in store for us. *[Netscape went public in August 1995 at $14 per share, adjusted for the subsequent split. It immediately rose to over $40. By June 1996, it had attained levels as high as $80.]*

We left Van Schreiber and strolled down Fifth Avenue, thinking about what he had said. I thought there were quite a few interesting points in that discussion. In essence, his is an earnings-driven approach to investing: Find the best industry, the one which is in the forefront of innovation; then find the best participants in that industry and buy those stocks. There were a few other points he made that caught my attention. We will tuck them away for later review, after we have analyzed the approaches of all the different managers we interview. I was particularly struck by his answer to the question about how his investing approach had changed over the years. Remember when he said that he was "a lot more psyched by price-earnings ratios then." I think this is particularly revealing of a certain style of investing. In fact, I too remember when the price-earnings ratio was the first and last thing you looked at to determine value. How interesting that Van downplays that venerable concept now.

One final point about Van Schreiber's style. Remember his comment: "We don't believe in a diversified portfolio." It is this lack of diversification that contributes to the high volatility of Van's style. By the same token, the lack of diversification is also what contributes to his superior performance. With Van Schreiber, you are buying his ability to pick stocks using the techniques he described to us. His investors took a higher risk than the risk of the market, and they have been well rewarded.

REX
SINQUEFIELD

Rex *Sinquefield works in an ideal environment. His large Santa Monica, California office has an even larger terrace, decked out with tables and chairs and an unobstructed view of the Pacific Ocean. Traffic moves quietly on Ocean Avenue just below, a Riviera-like setting with lanes of palm trees which parallel sandy beaches.*

Sinquefield is chairman of Dimensional Fund Advisors, a different kind of money management firm. What they do is rooted in an investment philosophy to which they adhere with religious zeal. This firm manages $18 billion using proprietary fund vehicles which emulate different style and size attributes of various securities markets worldwide. What this means is that he might have one fund that behaves like the S&P 500, another that correlates with just the value stocks in the S&P 500, and other funds might emulate the performance of all small-cap stocks, and so forth. The idea is to allocate funds among these different vehicles to create an optimal portfolio. No one does this better than Rex Sinquefield. Welcome to the world of passive investment.

Passive investment proponents like Sinquefield are passionate people. They believe, ex-cathedra, *that you simply cannot beat the market. As you will see, when you confront them with the truth that there are managers out there who do beat the market, they revert to*

257

distribution charts which show that there will always be some who beat the market, but you really can't predict who they are in advance. Thus, active investment is a waste of time. You are far better off, they say, spending your time, energy, and money deciding what types of stocks you want to buy, and then buying those index funds that correspond to the types of stocks you have chosen, thereby saving time and money. Don't try to reach for that brass ring because you won't get it. Convert to passive management and your problems will be over.

Beware: this is the take-no-prisoners philosophy at this firm, whose board includes some the best known academics in the investment field, not to mention a Nobel Prize winner or two. If you believe in active management, and that a good manager can beat the market, prepare to be just a little shaken: Sinquefield is very convincing. Judge for yourself.

Tanous: *Let's start from the beginning. When did you first get interested in stocks? Was it as a kid? There's usually an anecdote or two associated with people in our business who have been as successful as you are.*

Sinquefield: When I was studying to be a priest in the Diocesan Seminary at Cardinal Glennon College in St. Louis, I owned $200 worth of one stock. I would check it periodically in the newspaper. Now here I was studying to be a priest, so why should I even be interested in this? After three years, I left the Seminary. At that time I owned two stocks. I just got interested in the process, but I fell on wayward times. You see, I was dabbling with active management when I was a college student. So, there is no question that in terms of financial experience, I've had a sinful past.

Tanous: *Okay, Rex. As they say in the ring: "Let's get ready to rumble!" It's time to get into the active versus passive management controversy. I'd like you to start by defining active investing and passive investing.*

Sinquefield: It was originally just a question of, can you beat the market or can't you? Back in 1973 when the world was simple, the first index funds were started, one at American National in Chicago and one at Wells Fargo in San Francisco. These funds were designed to emulate the performance of the market. I was fortunate enough to be heading up the one at American National. Back then, you could use the word "passive" or "S&P 500" as perfect synonyms.

When our firm, Dimensional Fund Advisors, began in 1981, we started creating a variety of passive or structured portfolios, to go after a lot of different asset classes. *[The reason for having different asset classes is that different types of stocks, e.g. value and growth, or big and small, behave differently as a class.]* None of these are pure index funds. You can't buy every stock in an index and perfectly emulate the index. In fact, if you tried that, you'd get killed— because of trading costs and other restrictions.

We get back to the question, what is the difference between active and passive management? Passive investing generally refers to the idea that you are going to get market rates of return from whatever category you're investing in. *[If you are invested in stocks, you will do no better or worse than the market over time. If you limit yourself to, say, small-cap stocks, then your return, over time, will be no better or worse than the returns on the aggregate of small stocks.]* We believe that you're not going to be able to do much better than that because the market doesn't misvalue securities. The prices are right. If you believe in active management, you're saying that there are people who can make valuation judgments that are superior to the market.

Tanous: *We've set the stage for where you're coming from. Let's grant that markets are efficient—the hypothesis we are discussing. Isn't it reasonable to assume that some analysts are better at predicting factors that may not be in a given stock price at a given time? For example, the fact that this particular company may grow faster than most people think, the fact that the public may develop an appetite for a product, demand which is not widely anticipated. It could be Barbie Dolls, Hula Hoops, or Pentium chips?*

Sinquefield: Your question is, basically, are there some people who can systematically see the future? That's what it comes down to. The problem here is understanding how the market mechanism works. The central point is that no one person has very much information. In fact, regardless of how smart they are, or how informed they are, they have a tiny fraction of the information that is available to the entire market at any point in time. The markets are completely inter-related. Do you think it is credible that there is one person who systematically has more information than a dispersed market of six billion people? That's not remotely credible. But that's the condition that somebody has to prove. That there is such a person who has all this information—and the information changes second by second—who is so good that he or she is going to come to better conclusions than the worldwide market that is setting hundreds of millions of prices every moment? That's not plausible.

Tanous: *Let's put this in practical terms by talking about someone you know, a very successful active manager, Richard Driehaus [page53].*

Sinquefield: Yes, I know him. Before Richard Driehaus was on the DePaul endowment committee, the committee had raised the subject of hiring an active manager. That didn't happen in my tenure as chairman, although it's happened since then. At one point during my tenure, Richard Driehaus' name came up. I expressed my reservations and nothing happened. Then someone mentioned that Richard was thinking about giving a substantial sum of money to the University. It turned out he was going to give an amount equal to about half of what we were considering having him manage. So I said, not only is it an excellent idea to hire him, but I think that sets the appropriate standard for hiring any active manager. I have reminded them of that consistently, and I think all universities should follow that model.

Tanous: *No doubt that Richard Driehaus is the quintessential example of the active manager.*

Sinquefield: Driehaus is an unusual example because he has an exceptionally good track record. He is what we call an "outlier" as far as active managers go.

Tanous: *Rex, please explain "outlier" for some of our readers.*

Sinquefield: This is someone on the far right tail of a normal distribution curve. *[The classic bell curve, figure 1. Those on the far right tail have above average returns. Those on the left tail are also outliers, but their returns are below average.]* Richard has an incredible record but he also has, as he will acknowledge, an extremely high variance *[a measure of volatility or risk]* strategy. I've not seen a strategy with as

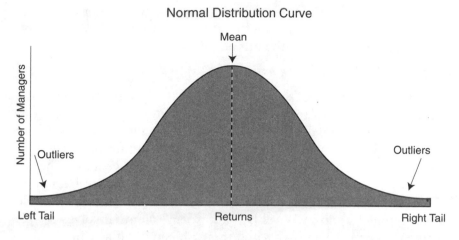

Figure 1

much variability as his. Nor with as high a return as his. It is not for the faint-hearted.

Tanous: *But my point is that there is a method to his success. Richard primarily seeks what he calls "positive earnings surprises."*

Sinquefield: I know. I've heard his presentation.

Tanous: *Perhaps his methodology works. Here's one of his examples. The Street is expecting XYZ company to earn $0.24 per share this quarter. The Street is wrong; the analysts are wrong; the company comes in with $0.38. All of a sudden the estimates start getting revised and now this stock is on a tear. They're doing a heck of a lot better than everybody had thought they were going to do. Now this is what Driehaus looks for, and this is how he makes his money. How does this differ from what you're saying?*

Sinquefield: Clearly, if someone comes up ahead of time with an expectation that is much higher than what is expected in current prices, and their expectation turns out to be right, then, in that particular case, the stock price will shoot up and they're going to look like a genius. There's no way we can explain those particular anecdotes, or gainsay them in any way, with any of the models or concepts of efficient markets. In fact, it's good to think about the difference between social sciences, like economics, and physical sciences in the nature of what they are able to predict. Physical science can make predictions about things in the physical world in great detail. Once they have figured something out, that prediction is always going to be true down to the nth degree.

Tanous: *They behave systematically.*

Sinquefield: In physical science, they've got to behave the same way all the time. It is as if they are subject to whatever new rule was discovered; there is no deviation from it. That's why predictions in the physical sciences can be precise and detailed. In the social sciences, like economics, predictions are going to be very general. They're going to be more pattern-type predictions. They will not be able to predict detail at all. The good social scientist or economist would never attempt to do so. Why? Because social science involves people who can change their beliefs and their objectives at any time. What is important one day may cease to be important the next.

So, when someone says, how can you explain this event or that event, the point is that the social sciences, including economic science, wouldn't even pretend to be able to explain a specific event by their models. It could be the case that Richard *[Driehaus],* or any other active manager, made a superior forecast and *ex post facto* the market was wrong. It could also be the case that it was just plain luck. There is no way to know for sure.

Tanous: *Let's talk about lucky people then. How do you explain the coterie of managers who appear to consistently beat the market over time? And I don't mean the guy who has one or two lucky years.*

Sinquefield: The answer to that is contained in your question. The guy that had one or two lucky years isn't the one we look at any more. We only look *after the fact* at those who ended up having a very good long-term record. We pull these people out from the right tail of the distribution. These are the most successful managers. How do you explain them? I could counter by saying how do you explain the three people at the left side of the tail, but we don't know who they are. They dropped out of the game. Table stakes were taken away from them a long time ago. In fact, there are probably many more of them than there are at the right end of the tail. So we have this huge problem of *ex post facto* selection bias when we look at these very successful people. We know 20 years from now, 30 years from now, there will be three or four or five other people. But we don't know who they are now. It would really be helpful if we could tell in advance. There have been loads of scientific studies looking for evidence that one can tell successful managers based on prior records. These studies do not meet with success. There is just no reliable evidence that there is persistence in professional manager performance.

Tanous: *I believe you have made the point in your writings that the burden of proof is on the active managers. Active managers must prove their ability to predict future price movements in a systematic way. Are you saying this has not happened?*

Sinquefield: It hasn't happened. Let's think about what would happen if someone was able to give a convincing proof that active management works across a broad sweep of managers. If so, what they're proving is that the *raison d'être* for the capitalist system is wrong. Market prices are wrong. But the study of market efficiency won't allow you to take a specific manager and prove whether or not he beat the market by skill or by luck. That's getting down to a level of forecast that is too precise and too detailed. All we can do is examine the vast array of managers and see if in aggregate, their performance conforms to a model that says, yes, it seems that market prices behave with uncanny accuracy.

Tanous: *What does that mean, "Market prices behave with uncanny accuracy?"*

Sinquefield: The best assumption is that market prices are always right. Yes, they fluctuate, but that's because there's constant news coming to the market.

Tanous: *This is important. You're saying that the changes in market prices are nothing but a reflection of changes in circumstances?*

Sinquefield: Right. Every moment in time. The information that comes and affects a given company need not even come from the company. Let's take an American drug company. We can see the price fluctuating and not understand what is going on. But perhaps there was a development made by a drug company in Europe that is going to have devastating consequences for the American drug company. As a result, people over there are taking action on the price. You don't know where the information is going to come from. But the market will impound it quickly as long as somebody acts on it.

Tanous: *Let's get into that. Let's talk about some of the studies that back up your thesis. Let's start with market efficiency.*

Sinquefield: Start with the two big experiments of the twentieth century. You have the consistent success of what we today call capitalism, and capitalist societies survived. But without exception, we witnessed the failure and collapse of systems, like communism, that are organized around the idea that you don't need free market prices. That's one very general and repeated experiment in mankind's history. I don't know how many civilizations there have been, several hundred or several thousand, but it's that many versus zero. It all goes one way.

Then we have all the work in the academic world for the last forty years. Nobody has been able to find that traditional managers have been able to out-guess markets by anything more than you get by chance. If all of these funds had been run by orangutans, we would get the same distribution of returns.

Tanous: *You mean we'd still get a Warren Buffett and a Peter Lynch?*

Sinquefield: You'd get Warren Buffett; you'd get Peter Lynch. And they'd probably work for less. In fact, they'd probably work for peanuts! All of this research suggests that you just can't find any evidence that active managers do well.

From a practical point of view, investors are probably better off if they just assume that markets are efficient. It will save them the distraction of wondering whether this fund manager is better than that one. There's huge risk in buying an active portfolio. The average investor is not able to assess all of the risks of an active manager. Suppose this active manager suddenly starts holding a concentrated portfolio and it falls 60%. Well, I hope no one has a serious amount of money in that portfolio! That kind of risk isn't going to happen to a marketwide portfolio. It's always possible that the entire market will fall 60%, but that's a much different event than an individual portfolio falling 60% because the managers have concentrated positions. Investors can have a much simpler life if they say, okay, I'm just going to assume that markets work. Now I'm going to think in terms of asset-class portfolios or index funds. What I really want to think about is how much risk I want to take. *[An investor who wanted to take market risk could just buy an index fund that emulated the market. An investor who wanted to take less risk than the market might put a portion of his assets in the market index fund, and the rest in a fund that emulated short-term interest rates, for example, since that is less risky than the stock market.]*

Tanous: *How do I configure my portfolio using asset classes?*

Sinquefield: Current research looks at three dimensions. How much do I want to have exposed to equities? Within equities, how much do I want to have exposed to companies that are really struggling, i.e., value stocks? How much to small stocks? The person who wants equities that will earn more than market returns over time, and recognizes that it entails above market risk, has only two avenues to pursue, based on current research, value and size attributes. *[That's because research shows that value stocks have higher returns than growth stocks and small stocks have higher returns than large stocks. But both value stocks and small stocks are riskier than the market as a whole.]* And, you can go domestically and internationally with both. There are lots of index funds available to do this. Those are the dimensions from which investors must choose.

If an investor decides to think in these terms and makes choices using asset class portfolios, life suddenly gets real simple. He doesn't have to burn the midnight oil figuring out what stocks to buy or what fund to buy. He doesn't have to buy all of those reports that list mutual funds; he doesn't have to read publications or listen to programs that are void of substantial content. I like to refer to this as "investment pornography."

Tanous: *Let's move to another discussion, which I know is dear to your heart; that is, the style question. Let's say that the world now agrees that the efficient market theory is correct, that over time it's pretty hard to beat the market consistently. If there are people out there who predict the future, we're not sure who they are or whether they're just lucky or not. That's the thesis. Now, once we decide to invest in the market, we still have some choices to make. Asset classes are the choices. Let's start there and move on to growth versus value.*

Sinquefield: Okay. It's one thing to say that markets are generally efficient. We have to add a second thing which is that, in any well-functioning market, the only thing investors get compensated for is taking risk. If people need to lay off some risk, they are going to have to compensate the people who will take that risk. It turns out that research over the last ten or fifteen years has really enriched our understanding of the types of risk that are in the market and that are priced accordingly.

There are lots of risks in the marketplace, but if the market doesn't reward them, then the investors will stay away. People can take all sorts of foolish risk, but the market won't reward them for doing that. What seems to emerge, in the equity markets at least, are three types of risk. There's overall market risk. Then there's value-type risk, which is a poor choice of words but we're stuck with it. This refers to the risk in companies whose current and future earnings are not going to be very good. The market seems to correctly assess who those companies are. That risk factor is at one end of the spectrum. At the other end, are the growth companies, those companies that are having fabulous earnings and will continue to do so. So we have this value/growth dimension.

Another dimension is the big/small dimension. Small companies seem to be similar to value companies in that, on average, they're going to have future earnings problems. That's a source of risk. The market doesn't like that. So, small stocks and value stocks seem to be associated with higher rates of return. But it's really a cost of capital question. The value companies are struggling, and because they have this type of risk, they have to pay more for equity capital. The high cost of capital for the firm means a high rate of return for the investor. Investors should not look on that as a free lunch. They are simply getting compensated for risk that they are bearing.

So getting back to your question, the choice is that, if I am going to buy equities, I still have to make decisions as to which classes of equities I want. Then I have to say, do I really want to take a lot more risk than is contained in the market in general to go after above market returns, or would I be happy with just marketwide risk? As we know, marketwide risk has provided returns on the order of 10% per year since 1926. There are now studies that go back much farther.

Tanous: *In fact, Jeremy Siegel, in his very well received book:* Stocks For The Long Term, *goes back much farther.*

Sinquefield: There were also two professors, Wilson and Jones, at North Carolina State University, who some years ago came out with a paper on studies of rates of returns from about 1870 to 1925. Their subtitle could have been "The World Before Ibbotson and

Sinquefield." What surprised me was their finding that the average inflation-adjusted return and the distribution of real returns on stocks was virtually identical to what Roger *[Ibbotson]* and I had found through the seventies. This was remarkable. It would suggest that now that we have over 100 years of data, the market says it wants about a six to seven percent premium over inflation for marketwide risk. So investors can think in those terms. I can buy a CD or a Money Market Fund. Or, if I am willing to take marketwide equity risk, I get another six or seven hundred basis points per year on average with acceptable risk.

Conversely, an investor could say, you know what? I want the higher returns of equities, but I want to be much safer. Then that investor can choose the growth stocks; stocks with high earnings. Those stocks will have lower returns, on average, because the companies have low cost of capital. They don't have to pay a lot to raise equity money or to borrow money. This is very counterintuitive. It goes against everything we were raised on in the markets. This is the essence of the three factor story which I'll explain later. What Fama *[page 167]* and French were able to show very well was, that when it comes to companies with high earnings growth, the market knows who they are. Companies that are shooting the lights out in terms of earnings do not have high costs of capital. They are not risky. So, why should they provide unusual rates of return? If they're going to provide a 25% per year return on equity, that's not the same as saying their cost of capital is 25%. They're the safest companies around. It's the companies that are struggling, hanging on for dear life, that should have to pay 25% for their equity capital. That's the essence of the story.

Tanous: *Yeah. But, the other side to that—the side we were all brought up on—is that the safe thing to do is to buy a value stock because it's on its back and it's going nowhere. It's selling at a discount to its book value, and the downside risk is real low because it's already flat on its back.*

Sinquefield: Right. That was part of the story. But you left out a part. If it's flat on its back, it's in the intensive care unit. You forgot to mention that, for a lot of people in the intensive care unit, the next stop is the cemetery.

Tanous: *Okay. Let's talk about value. The concept that's going around is the value stock thesis based on book value, Warren Buffett's approach.*

Now you wonder whether or not, in the new economy we are experiencing, this approach still has merit. The real value of many corporations in the technological age is not in hard assets. We're not talking steel plants or automobile manufacturers any more. We're talking about technological developments and software, the Microsofts and the Sun Microsystems. Doesn't this change the way we value companies in terms of their assets or the nature of their assets?

Sinquefield: Some things might change but that's no reason to think that the three-factor model will. Even in an industry that doesn't have a lot of plant and equipment, you're still going to have a ranking of, say, book-to-market ratios. The companies with the lowest prices relative to their book values are probably those in trouble. And those with the highest prices relative to their book values are those that are having great earnings success and are going to continue to do so. Typically, we don't find a wide dispersion within an industry because companies in the same industry, to some extent tend to thrive or struggle together. The time periods covered by many of these studies also witnessed changes of many types. Accounting variables are also subject to changes which pose problems.

Tanous: *The point here is not so much that we will still rely on high book-to-market ratios alone. The question is, how do you value the assets today in the new technological age? Aren't you convinced that the economy has changed enough so that the way we value assets ought to change? That is, the basis for book value.*

Sinquefield: I don't know because I'm not an accounting expert. Book-to-market is not the essence. That's simply a measure that helps us spot prospective success or failure. Other, better, measures may emerge. The driving force is really the fluctuation in the price. All the news being equal, a falling price is a market statement that this company is in trouble and, if they want to raise money, either equity or debt money, they're going to have to pay a lot for it. That's the same as saying that you investors, you have a high expected return if you buy this company, and there's a reason you have a high expected return. It's because you're taking a lot of risk.

Tanous: *Let's get down to the investor. You obviously have a value bias. This might be a good time to examine the value versus growth conundrum.*

Sinquefield: Sure. Let's rank companies in terms of size, breaking them arbitrarily into large and small. First, we rank the New York Stock Exchange companies in terms of market capitalization *[that's the stock price times the number of shares]*, from large to small. Companies larger than the median size NYSE company we consider large; the rest are small. American Stock Exchange and NASDAQ companies are then assigned to these two size groups. We create index funds like this, using the different size groups.

Tanous: *I presume you do this because the largest 50%, say, behaves differently from the smallest 50%.*

Sinquefield: Right. The smaller companies have a higher return, on average, and more risk. The next cut is book-to-market. We use the same ranking, from lowest to highest. Now we have a sort based on book-to-market, which separates value from growth *[the companies with a low book-to-market value are the growth companies; those with a high book-to-market ratio are the value companies]*. We also have a sort based on size *[large companies versus small companies]*. Now we take the intersection of these. Any company that is both a large company and a value company will be in the large value strategy and any company that is a small company and a value company, will be in the small value strategy. Same is true for the growth strategies. Now let's look at the returns.

When we do these combinations of value and growth, large and small, *[see figure 2]* you can see that value stocks outperformed both the overall stock market, represented by the S&P 500, and also large growth companies, by substantial margins.

Tanous: *This is particularly counterintuitive. The difference in these returns is staggering. The annualized compounded rate of return for the large value strategy is 14.57% per year for 32 years, versus 10.92% for the S&P and only 9.97% for large growth. Who would have thought? And interestingly, and I suppose this is just a coincidence, the standard deviation for the marketwide value strategy is almost the same as for the large growth strategy.*

Sinquefield: That's a coincidence. But the way you read this is that the standard deviations are about the same. The point here is that the additional return in large value strategy doesn't come at the cost of higher variance *[risk]*. It doesn't mean that it doesn't come at the

Investment Dimensions: Size of Company and Financial Strength

Historical Returns
Quarterly Data
January 1964—December 1995

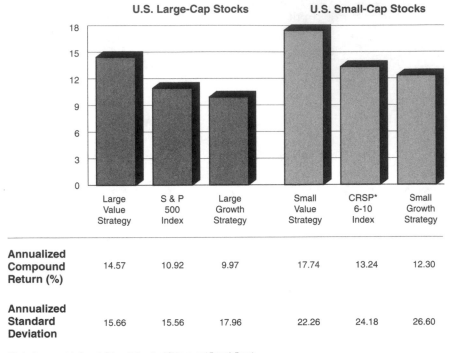

	U.S. Large-Cap Stocks			U.S. Small-Cap Stocks		
	Large Value Strategy	S & P 500 Index	Large Growth Strategy	Small Value Strategy	CRSP* 6-10 Index	Small Growth Strategy
Annualized Compound Return (%)	14.57	10.92	9.97	17.74	13.24	12.30
Annualized Standard Deviation	15.66	15.56	17.96	22.26	24.18	26.60

*Center for research in Security Prices, University of Chicago, and Fama & French.
Stocks ranked by size deciles. 6-10 deciles are the lower (smaller) half of companies
traded on NYSE and equivalent size companies on AMEX and NASDAQ.

Standard & Poor's data courtesy: Ibbotson, Roger and Sinquefield, Rex
Stock, Bonds, Bills, and Inflation Historical Returns
Dow Jones Irwin 1989
Updates by Ibbotson Associates yearbook

Figure 2

cost of additional risk. It's just that the risk isn't in the form of higher variance.

Tanous: *I'm afraid you need to explain that.*

Sinquefield: It goes back to the old model that the market portfolio is the only source of risk. Portfolios that were more variable relative to the market were deemed to have higher expected returns; those that were less variable were deemed to have lower expected returns. The working assumption is that variability is the only source of risk. When you have a world with multiple risk factors, it need not be the case that variability is the only source of risk. In fact, it need not be the case that variability is a risk factor at all.

Tanous: *If I follow you, Rex, you're saying that variability, or volatility, in a stock is a source of risk, but not the only source of risk. Another kind of risk you take when you buy stocks is the size risk, because small stocks are riskier than large stocks. You also take style risk, because if you buy a value-type stock, you are adding value risk to the portfolio. Can you give me an example of assets that have different returns but the same risk, measured in terms of variability, or volatility?*

Sinquefield: Sure. Long-term corporate bonds have higher returns than long-term treasury bonds both *ex post* and *ex ante*.

Tanous: *That's hardly surprising. Corporate bonds are considered riskier than U.S. government obligations, so you should get paid more for them.*

Sinquefield: Yeah, but they have the identical standard deviations, and that's over 70 years. Or pick any sub-period and it's the same.

Tanous: *Is the reason they have the same standard deviation that they react to one common external factor—changes in interest rates? The risk is clearly different, since the risk in corporate bonds is higher than in U.S. government-issued treasuries.*

Sinquefield: Right. But that doesn't show up as additional variance. Yet it's definitely a risk.

Tanous: *Okay. Then, how do I measure these other risks?*

Sinquefield: A simple way to do it is to look at a portfolio's overall price-to-book ratio, or book-to-market ratio. In general, stocks that have high book-to-market ratios are these value-type companies, and growth companies are those that have low book-to-market ratios. The only industry that seems to be an exception to this are the highly regulated utilities. They look like they are value stocks, but they really aren't. They have below market rates of return. This is the story in the large-cap arena.

The same kind of story holds in the small-cap arena. Small value stocks have much higher rates of return than small growth stocks, and higher returns than the overall small stock universe. And in this size universe, the standard deviations are basically the same.

Tanous: *But here again, the standard deviation of the small value strategy is lower than the standard deviation of the small growth strategy* [figure 2]. *So, simplistically, that suggests that small value is less risky, but still provides higher returns.*

Sinquefield: I wouldn't make much of that. The difference is not significant. Now these numbers, the standard deviation of the S&P 500, at 15.6, and the standard deviation of the *CRSP 6-10 [Small-Cap]* index, at 24.2, are indeed significant. We also see the well-known size effect. Small value has much higher returns than large value, small market higher than big market; and small growth higher than large growth. Incidentally, what makes us confident that this is a risk story, and a story that is going to continue, is that when we go to an independent arena, the international markets, we find portfolios that are formed the same way as they are in the U.S. and have the same kinds of premium relative to the overall market.

Tanous: *Could you demonstrate the value versus growth thesis?*

Sinquefield:: Look at this graph *[figure 3]*. This shows the return on assets *[1964-1992]* for value and growth stocks. You can see that the return on assets for value stocks was pretty low compared to the return on assets for growth stocks. But for the same set of firms, the return on their stocks was very high for value stocks, and comparatively much lower for growth stocks. That's the essence of the story.

Tanous: *That's quite convincing.*

Sinquefield: That's why it's a cost of capital story, relating to earnings success or distress. What Fama and French did was tie all this together and say that there is a rational market explanation for all these differences. That's why it has gotten so much attention.

Tanous: *Now may be a good time to explain the three-factor model.*

Sinquefield: "The three-factor model" is the term we use in contrast with the "one-factor model." The one factor model is, of course, the famous capital asset pricing model *[CAPM]* developed by Bill

Earnings Performance of Companies (Return on Assets) vs. their Stock Market Performance

Company Earnings vs. Stock Market Returns

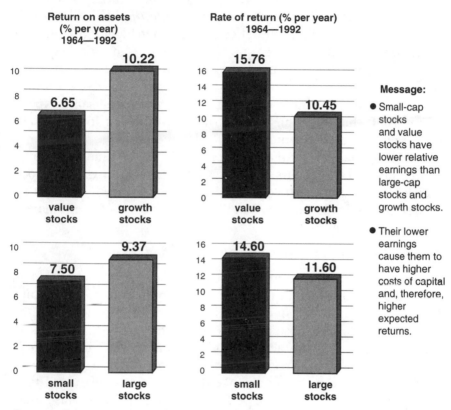

Courtesy: *Dimensional Fund Advisors Inc., Fama & French.*

Figure 3

Sharpe *[page 89]*, Jan Mossin, and John Lintner. This is the concept for which Bill Sharpe shared the Nobel Prize in 1990 with Merton Miller and Harry Markowitz. In fact, Sharpe's work was a direct off-spring of Harry Markowitz'. Sharp produced this very simple model that asked, under certain assumptions, how are securities priced in the marketplace? So it was called CAPM, the capital asset pricing model.

What Sharpe basically said was that, the return on a security or a portfolio—makes no difference— is directly related to the volatility of that security or portfolio relative to the market. *[Remember that the market has a beta of one. So if a stock, for example, has a beta less than one, that stock is less volatile than the market. A number higher than one means that it is more volatile than the market.]* To oversimplify, the CAPM model concluded that higher volatility, or beta, constituted higher risk, and that is what an investor expected to be rewarded for. The market is the one factor that drives the return on securities. If a portfolio has the same relative variation/volatility, or beta, as the market, it's going to have the same expected return. If the beta is higher, then the portfolio has got more variation/volatility and it's going to have higher returns.

Unfortunately, the theory didn't work. Over time, it suffered from empirical onslaughts, but it was an absolutely invaluable tool. Academic work in the field would not have advanced without that model. It was developed in 1964. Much of the early efficient market work used that model.

Tanous: *I suppose that leads us to the three-factor model.*

Sinquefield: The CAPM model said that you would get more than the market return in your portfolio if your beta is greater than one. If your beta is less than one, your expected return was less than the market because you chose to take less than market risk. This was an elegant theory, but in practice it didn't always work. The alpha *[a measure of return in excess of market return]* was a measure of returns that you got over and above that due to risk-bearing. This is what was used to measure the performance of portfolios. This model was very important academically and professionally, for a long time. But, as I said, it eventually gave way to the three-factor model.

The three-factor model, and the CAPM, which is a one factor model, have a common factor, the market factor. But the three-factor model has the two additional factors, the size factor and the value factor, hence the three-factor model. As a result, this model allows us to measure the sensitivity of whatever portfolio we're testing to the size factor and the value factor, in addition to the market factor which was the single factor in the CAPM model. So, if I have a portfolio that is marketlike, I have a beta of one *[one representing the market]*. When all these factors are present, the betas on nearly all diversified equity portfolios become one. They all have about the same amount of exposure to market risk, which is a new finding. But these diverse portfolios will differ from one another by their exposure to the *other* risks, value and size, and the three-factor model is the method by which we can evaluate that additional risk.

Tanous: *You say that the value and size risks may be greater, but at the end of the day, that has to be reflected in the market risk, doesn't it?*

Sinquefield: No. The reason that these betas differed from one in the old model was that the value and size factors were excluded. So the risk that they were contributing to the portfolio *looked like* additional market risk, but the fact is that the real causes of the variation

A Style Map of Popular Indexes

Based on Data for January 1979—December 1995

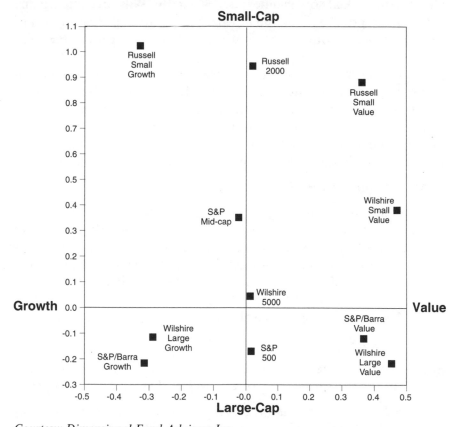

Courtesy: Dimensional Fund Advisors Inc.

Figure 4

were the size and value dimensions. Do you want to see where various indexes fall on the style map? Look at figure 4. Are the indexes growth, are they value, are they big, are they small? Anything to the left of the vertical dividing line is growth, anything to the right is value. Anything below the horizontal is large and anything above it is small. *[The hash marks measure the sensitivity of an index to value/growth along the horizontal axis and to large/small on the vertical axis.]*

Now look at the overall market portfolio at the crosshairs. This refers to all ten size groups we use. The S&P 500 is down here *[below the crosshairs]*. So you see that the S&P 500 is neutral on value and growth *[it's right on the vertical line]* but it is biased away from small companies and toward larger companies, so it's going to have returns slightly lower than the market due to the underweighting of small stocks. But look at some value indexes like the Wilshire Large Value index. It's off to the right, and down a bit, because it's biased toward large companies. But it's much more value-oriented than the S&P 500.

In terms of expected returns, based on years of data, each hashmark that we move to the right or the left is worth about 50 basis points a year in expected return difference. Along the size dimension, each hashmark up or down the chart is worth about forty basis points. So if you're moving on a 45 degree line up the page, you're picking up both size expected return and value expected return.

Tanous: *In other words by heading toward small-cap value . . .*

Sinquefield: You're picking up a lot of expected return, but you're also picking up a lot of extra risk. You're adding size risk. If you have a portfolio comprised of small companies that have high book-to-market ratios *[low price-to-book ratios]*, the chart tells you that you've got a lot of size risk, and a lot of value risk, in addition to one full scoop of market risk. And, because you're taking those three types of risk, you should have above market expected returns.

Tanous: *So basically, there is no free lunch.*

Sinquefield: No free lunch at all. That's the essence. There are ways to get higher returns and lower returns but they all come at a price.

Tanous: *I was hoping that the graph you showed me* [figure 4] *indicated that the market risk was the same for small-caps as for the mar-*

ket, even though small-caps had higher returns than the market. I guess that's not what it said.

Sinquefield: It does. If you invest in small-caps, you're taking as much market risk as someone who buys the S&P 500, but you're also adding a lot of size risk.

Tanous: *Let's talk about your firm. Say I'm a potential client. All this sounds interesting in an academic sort of way. But how does this, or you, help me make money?*

Sinquefield: The thrust of Dimensional Fund Advisors is to take what we believe is the best theoretical and empirical work that the academic world has produced and turn these into products that are useful for our institutional investors and advisors. The various specialized asset class portfolios are meant to be used only by professionals. The reason we don't sell to the general market is because these products should say: "to be used under adult supervision only." We have intentionally made them rather strong, high octane. They're also designed with all the other pieces in mind. So they are designed to fit together. You can combine them in whatever proportions you want, based on how much risk you want to take. That's the general thrust.

We've created about sixteen different asset class portfolios around the world, along the dimensions of size and value. We have domestic large value, domestic small, international large value, international small, etc. Some have regional modules.

Most of our clients are institutional and come to us for particular asset classes rather than to run their whole fund. But some clients do give us all their money. Fee-only advisors typically use us for all of their clients' assets. Were you to ask us how to go about running balanced portfolios, we would say that, if you're going after above market expected returns, then here's how we would do it. Parenthetically, let me add that, if you're going after market returns, it's very simple. You can hold an equity index fund and a short-term fixed income fund, and that'll do fine. That simple 60/40 portfolio compares rather favorably to all of the balanced funds in existence since 1976. It beats more than half of them. As simple as it is, it really works.

But, suppose somebody says, I want to go for above market returns, how do I do it? Okay, the only way to accomplish this reliably is to take additional risk. Based on the research, we know the avenues to go down to get that risk. They are the value avenue and the size avenue. We're going to do that domestically and internationally. The equity portion of the portfolio would be split something like this: We would put about 30% of the equities in the international markets, 70% domestically. The domestic would be roughly 40% large-cap and 30% small-cap; the large would be split equally between growth and value; the small would be split the same way *[equally between growth and value]*. The international arena is similar, except that we would not hold a plain market portfolio, like an EAFE *[an index of international stock markets]* fund, internationally. There seems to be no benefit to U.S. investors by doing that. Instead, we would split our allocation between value stocks and small stocks internationally as well.

Tanous: *To wrap it up, here we are in a world of thousands of mutual funds, all competing for investor attention, all touting extraordinary records. Go through* Forbes, Money, Worth, *see page after page of marvelous records—28% per year . . . 32% per year . . . 18% per year. All these geniuses making extravagant claims in an attempt to get our money so that we can enjoy these wonderful results for the next ten years, like those who got rich over the past ten years. Now, I'm sitting here with you, looking out your window at the Pacific Ocean, and you're telling me that it is all bogus. If you really want to make money in the market, you might say, don't try to beat the market, join the market. Is that fair?*

Sinquefield: I'm saying that you're only going to get paid for risk-bearing. You can expose yourself to various asset classes that vary in their risk, and that's what you're going to get paid for. If markets work, that's all you're going to get paid for. The reason we see all these people advertising these fabulous records is that the only ones who can afford advertising are those who have had fabulous records. You would be a fool to go out and say, "hire me, I'm the worst manager in past ten years." Equity returns are inherently variable, so there will inevitably be a wide range of returns, even among highly diversified portfolios. That's why we can get some people advertising fabulous numbers. We also know that there are people at the other end of the spectrum, none of whom choose to spend advertising dollars right now. They have nothing to sell.

Having left Rex's posh offices in beautiful Santa Monica, I couldn't help but realize that this interview wasn't exactly easygoing, and for that I apologize. Nevertheless, we are dealing in some really important concepts that we have to try to get a handle on.

The notion of risk in the market is important. Bill Sharpe, et al.*, won a Nobel Prize in economics for their work on the CAPM model, which introduced* beta *as a measure of volatility, as well as other ways of measuring risk important to the financial world. In the three-factor model, that approach is refined. It says that market risk is just one kind of risk. There are other risks. One is style—that is, value versus growth stocks. The other is the size component—that is, small companies are riskier than large companies.*

So what? You might say. Well, isn't it nice to know that in putting together a portfolio you are able to determine with reasonable accuracy the kind of risk you are taking, based on the kind of stocks you are selecting for your portfolio? It does make sense, and it is important to have some knowledge of these principles which are at the cutting edge of our ever-growing knowledge about investments in stocks.

As to Rex's position on market efficiency, his position is as dogmatic as it gets. He believes markets are efficient. Period. He allows little room for individuals who can predictably outperform the markets over time, claiming, as he does, that these "outliers" are only identifiable after-the-fact, or ex post facto. *In other words, the battle lines are drawn. As we hear other voices and engage other discussions, we will have an opportunity to judge for ourselves who is right and wrong on this important subject. Our opinions should and will influence our attitude toward stock market investments from now on.*

JOHN
BALLEN

John Ballen has managed the MFS (Massachusetts Financial Services) Emerging Growth Fund since 1986. To look at him, you might guess that MFS, the institution which gave birth to the mutual fund back in 1924, had decided to entrust him with this responsibility while John was a sophomore or junior in college. That wouldn't be totally accurate, but you might want to ask to see his driver's license anyway. Ballen ascended to Guruhood in the simplest manner possible—he outperformed his peers over a very long time. Indeed, his MFS Emerging Growth Fund has achieved a growth record of 30.5% a year for the five years ended 1995 and 20.3% for the ten-year period. Any questions?

This young man is not your ordinary portfolio manager. A graduate of Harvard, with an MBA from Stanford, his first love was academia. Strange that this fellow, who has consistently beaten the market by a wide margin, might have joined the bastion of academics who claim that people like him barely exist. In this interview, we examine his views on the active versus passive controversy and delve into the criteria that contributed to his extraordinary success as an investor.

This interview took place in MFS' offices on Boylston Street in Boston. Not once did Ballen feel compelled to leave the room or be interrupted by the market, which was roaring ahead the day we met.

281

Tanous: *How did you first get interested in stocks?*

Ballen: I didn't really have a background in the stock market. My parents came from pretty modest backgrounds. My father is a lawyer, my mother a school teacher. I became interested in the markets in business school. At the time the job of analyzing stocks seemed like something I might be good at. I had an academic bent myself and I had almost pursued a Ph.D. program *[Ballen was accepted in the Ph.D. program at Harvard.]* I had won a Fulbright scholarship, and completed a master's in economics. But, analyzing stocks seemed like a pretty thoughtful business, in which you could be creative, and maybe think a little ahead of the next person. So, it was a combination of a career that looked pretty interesting and something I might be good at. Besides, there was a pretty good investment management program at Stanford at the time.

Tanous: *You did some other interesting things. It certainly looks like you didn't have to worry about what your "safety schools" were when you were applying to college. You went to Harvard for your bachelor's degree and got your MBA at Stanford. What in the world possessed you to continue your education in Australia?*

Ballen: I wasn't sure what I was going to do in life and I was interested in academics. A Fulbright is a very academic thing to do and the Fulbright got me to Australia. There was no specific reason, other than that it seemed like a fun place to go and spend a year.

Tanous: *John, your investment record is phenomenal. You've been managing the MFS Emerging Growth Fund for almost ten years now. According to my records, over the last five years your compounded annual return has been over 30%, and over 20% over the past ten years. As you know, this book focuses on methodology and process, which is a fancy way of saying, how do you do it? Let's talk about your process of selecting stocks—what you look for.*

Ballen: For us, making sure we are early in the process is key. That makes ours a very research-intensive process. Wall Street is good at recommending things that have done well, but not necessarily good at recommending things that will do well. We do our own research and, hopefully, get into situations before they are all played out. We tend to stick to growth-oriented situations. We don't want to be dependent on cycles that go in and out of favor. We want to find companies that will grow. Eventually, size attracts other people. If you buy a small company that grows to become a large company, it gets recognized by others.

Part of the investment picture is that you want to be right, but you need other people to follow you fairly quickly. You don't want to be right and be proven right ten years later, when it's too late. In the investment process, you don't want to be too early, and you don't want to be too late. You want to be just on time. Given that you're looking at growth companies, eventually companies that get larger get recognized. If they don't get recognized by everybody, they get bought out by larger companies. I try to find companies—sometimes I say "I" but in the mutual fund sense we normally say "we," so I can just use them interchangeably—anyway, I look for companies that have a competitive advantage in the marketplace. Going back to some of the academic examples, there are different strategies that companies can follow—there's a low cost strategy; a high-value-added strategy; and we also try to find companies that can carve out a competitive advantage and go for the longer term. If you look at some representative aspects of that strategy, you'll notice that our fund's turnover is very low.

Tanous: *I noticed that your turnover is under 40%, which is unusually low for a small-cap growth strategy.*

Ballen: Actually, our turnover was 20% in 1995.

Tanous: *Yet yours is a high variance strategy, and your standard deviation is quite high compared to the market as a whole. I was fascinated that the turnover was so low, given this strategy. I still have trouble reconciling that.*

Ballen: Well, the positive to the turnover is, if you're a taxable investor, your after-tax returns are much higher. I think we're either the highest returning fund, or the second highest returning fund, on an after-tax basis over a ten-year period. But you asked why the turnover is so low. Well, one reason is the longer-term focus. We try to find companies that we want to own for the long term. If we find those companies, we stick with them. If you look at the top holdings in the fund, there are companies that we've owned for as long as five to ten years.

Tanous: *Please name a few.*

Ballen: HFS is the largest holding. *[HFS is a motel franchiser.]* We bought that company on the initial public offering in December of 1992. By the way, a lot of people ask, why do you buy initial public offerings? Is it just for the initial pop? HFS was a six million share deal. As a firm we got one hundred thousand shares on the offering. It went up two bucks—16 to 18—so we made two hundred thousand dollars. We then bought a million and a half shares in the after-market. In the ensuing four years, that stock has gone from 18 to 180. So, yeah, we made $200,000 on the IPO, and we made $250 million to $300 million since. That's the reason for trying to be early, for seeking out some of these companies as soon as they come out. HFS went up ten times in three years and we've held it since then.

Our second biggest holding is Oracle Systems. It has its ups and downs, but the initial position, when we bought the bulk of the stock, was one dollar a share on an adjusted basis. This was back in 1990. The company grew tremendously for five or six years. The stock had gone from 3 to 35, something like that, and it hit the wall—bad accounting, aged receivables, and so forth. We went in, looked at the technology, looked at the company, and basically made the decision that they were going to survive and, after a transition, do well on the other side. We've pretty much stuck with the stock since the time we bought it. The stock is about 40 today. We continue to own it.

Our third largest holding—let's see—that's probably United Healthcare. We've owned United Healthcare since 1988, and we've added to it at various times. They are the leader in health maintenance organizations. We have believed that cost containment is very important to the future of health care, and that HMOs are going to be the way that the government, corporations, and individuals are going to achieve it. The managed process is going to win. We stuck with these companies in good times and bad. There's a good example. United Healthcare has had a lot of volatility, as has Oracle. If you believe in the long term and stick with a position, that adds to your short term volatility.

Of course, if we were smart enough to get in and out of the stocks at the right time that would help, but I'm not sure we're smart enough to do that. You see, sticking with the companies as they go up and down contributes to higher volatility in the portfolio, but if you pick the right companies, you get the returns.

Tanous: *Just hearing about those three stocks makes me want to get right back to the question of process. We're talking about pretty different types of companies. Health care, technology, lodging, yet you've picked stocks from all of these industries, right? You said that you're looking for early stages of growth, but that's the investment equivalent of motherhood and apple pie. Everybody wants that and nobody will disagree with that approach. Yet the fact is that you are unusually successful at finding the early stages of growth. So I want to delve a little bit more into what John Ballen looks for in a health care company, in a high tech company, in a lodging company, and see if we can identify what he finds that others don't.*

Ballen: In all three of those companies, and I haven't really thought about this until you asked that question, there is a similarity. If you look at the business model of all three of those companies, I think you'll understand what attracts me to them. HFS is a franchiser, they don't own any real estate. They get a four percent royalty from Howard Johnson's, Ramada, Super 8, and from other lodging brands. And they are, basically, not using any of their own capital. It's a superior business model, if you can grow it, because it doesn't require a lot of capital and it throws off great cash flow. That's an almost infinite return on equity. The same thing can be said of United Healthcare. They don't own any hospitals, they don't have any capital invested—an infinite return on equity. It's basically a marketing machine with networks and information, and so is HFS. They are not asset-intensive businesses at all. The third one, Oracle Systems, is the same story. It's not a hardware company, it's a software company. There's no capital employed so there is an infinite return on equity. You're leveraging off the brand name equity. All three of these stocks, which have been tremendous investments in the market, have that similarity. Their business model is not flawed.

Why do I do it this way? I guess the story I would tell is this: There were two companies that started about the same time in technology. I think people would have argued that both these companies would be really successful back in the mid-'80s. The two companies were Microsoft and Sun Microsystems. Sun was going to lead in workstations and was going to make the next generation PC, while Microsoft was going to become the leader on the software side. Now what happened is that both companies have grown to about the same size. They both grew to $4 billion, $5 billion, $6 billion *[in rev-*

enues]. But Microsoft has been a much better stock. The reason is that Sun is in a capital-intensive business with much lower return on equity, or return on capital, and the return to the investor has been much less. So while there is a place for investing in capital-intensive businesses, if you really look at the great stocks in the last ten or twenty years, they have been those companies that have been able to leverage themselves successfully.

Tanous: *That's very interesting. So one of the things you look for is a franchise, in the broad sense, which you identified as the business plan, and a system that almost has cookie cutter applications. If you run one hotel or hospital successfully, if you do one right, chances are you're going to do the others right. Is that it?*

Ballen: That's for sure. In all these ideas, you want to make sure they are expandable. The franchise element is the most important thing. You're getting paid for something in addition to the capital you're putting up. It's not so much a commodity-type business. You can go into commodity businesses, but you have to recognize it's a different type of investment. You want to find a company that's going to become the largest company. It's going to have the best economies of scale, the lowest costs. It's a whole different business model. It requires access to capital as well. Obviously, if you have a lower return on equity, you're going to need to raise capital.

Tanous: *How else might you characterize your selection criteria?*

Ballen: I categorize the types of stocks I buy into four categories. (1) Growth at a reasonable price—that's where the value guys and the growth guys sort of agree. (2) The second-chance stocks—where all the facts are on the table, but people choose to ignore them, and there's a turnaround coming—like Oracle Systems. HFS would be a growth at a reasonable price example. (3) Traditional growth stocks—once you're in some of these stocks, you might be early, but if you follow, as you said, a cookie cutter approach, they roll out the growth and you hang on for dear life and make ten times your money. For example, in the Office Depots of the world. (4) The non-traditional growth stocks—sometimes the most opportunistic, like the HMOs and whatnot. These are companies that are not perceived as exciting companies, but something is changing out there, and you are one of the first to recognize that something is different in the industry. HMOs have been around 30 years, but it's only been in the last ten years that the emphasis on cost changed the industry. This became an exciting growth industry even though it had not been before. Seven years ago a light bulb went off in Detroit that said, you've got to lower costs to compete with the Japanese. So, if you are clever enough to buy auto part suppliers, and you figure out that the big companies have to outsource and give business to these other firms, you succeed. If you can be early, a lot of times these companies are selling at very low multiples with very little growth, and then they take off.

Tanous: *Let's take another example and again focus on methodology. Take Office Depot. When did you first buy that stock?*

Ballen: We bought it around when it went public, in '86 or '87. We've owned it since. It's gone through three separate periods. In the first period, there were four major companies in that field that went public—BizMart, Office Depot, Office Club, and Staples. We actually bought all four companies. We liked the industry; they all had about 20 stores. At that point, you couldn't tell who was going to be successful and who wasn't; who was going to get the capital and who wasn't. In this case, you really had to bet that the winning companies were going to win enough to offset the losing companies.

Tanous: *Did you have equal holdings in all four?*

Ballen: Initially, we probably did have fairly equal holdings in all four. Over time we sorted them out; we learned more about them. Two didn't work out. BizMart didn't work out because they opened seven out of 35 stores in Houston. Those were bad. They didn't get access to capital, and they eventually sold out to Office Max. Office Club stumbled a little bit, although not as much as BizMart, and they sold out to Office Depot. Staples and Office Depot sort of vied for the winning position.

Tanous: *What happened to Office Max?*

Ballen: Office Max was a division of Kmart, so you never got an opportunity to invest in it. But, as I mentioned earlier, the investments in these companies went through three stages. We held on through all three stages, and added at various points. In the initial stages, all four companies were growing and doing well. Then they started to compete against each other and against a bunch of other non-public competitors. There was a shake-out period, and you made very little money in the stocks from 1989 to 1991. After 1991, once you got down to three or four players, they leveraged their costs and expanded their margins, and it became a great industry.

If you were really clever, and we weren't clever enough, you would have sold Office Depot after the initial pop, waited the two-and-a-half years during the shakeout, and got back in. I think the problem with being so clever is that you might miss the buying points. It's very difficult to sell at the top and buy right at the bottom. We held during that time, and added to our position, because we kept saying, it's going to happen, it's going to happen, over and over again. Then you made ten times your money from 1990 to 1996. You had plenty of time to get in.

Tanous: *Back in 1986 you saw a new industry being born, and something about it, something about your analysis told you that the idea of these chains of stores that catered to offices was going to really catch on. Right?*

Ballen: We knew it was a big market. You just knew it was a $100 billion market. You knew it was served by inefficient dealers who had poor selection, poor prices, but, nevertheless, some service. And you knew it wasn't being served by the Home Depots, the Wal-Marts, and the other big box *[large store]* retailers out there.

Tanous: *So you bought them all!*

Ballen: We were the largest investor. We probably owned 5% to 10% of all four. We had owned Home Depot and made a lot of money; we had owned Costco and gone through different cycles before. We learned from our experience what to look for. There have been a lot of other big box industries that haven't taken off.

Tanous: *I want to guess at something. Would it be accurate to say that there were other fund managers back in '86 who felt as you did that this was going to be a great industry? Is it fair to say that you are one of the few who believed hard enough to stay with the stocks through the shakeout?*

Ballen: I suspect that a lot of people saw the shakeout coming but got smart and sold the stock—and never got back in. A lot of managers never look back or revisit an old holding. They have an absolute sell discipline.

Tanous: *In your case, though, there is a history of revisiting or staying through and maintaining confidence in your original decision. As part of that, do you pay a lot of attention to the management of companies? Do you want to talk to them?*

Ballen: Yep. We try to do as much of that as we can. We're active in doing that. In a lot of the investments we hold, we're the largest shareholder the company might have. So they talk to us on a very proactive basis. Of course, you want to keep your objectivity as well.

Tanous: *So you don't want to play golf with them.*

Ballen: You don't necessarily want to play golf with them. Let me tell you my Jiffy Lube story. This was a company in the fast oil change marketplace. It came public in the '85-'86 time period and did very well. We tripled our money and sold it. We bought it back after the crash *[in 1987]*. The reason we were interested in that market was that we observed the number of gas stations declining. The *EPA [Environmental Protection Agency]* was taking a dim view of people throwing that stuff in their back yard after they changed the oil. It seemed that a service business, like Jiffy Lube, made sense. This was a royalty-type business, a good business model, a franchise with a 40% market share in the U.S. for oil changes. We invested, but it didn't work out. We ultimately sold our stock after we lost half our money. So this wasn't a good story to tell you.

The reason we lost money in the stock was twofold: (1) We misperceived what the larger players were going to do, the Mobil Oils and the gas stations of the world. In order to get your repair business, the gas stations were willing to really discount the oil change business. So no one was destined to make money in that business. (2) Management didn't prove capable. I realized that things were not going as well as they could be. They started to lend money to franchisees who couldn't pay it back. That was the biggest problem. They eventually sold out to Pennzoil at a dime a share. Basically, they went bankrupt. So I'm sitting one Saturday morning, talking to the president of Jiffy Lube, and he answers all my questions. I hang up. On the surface, everything was okay. I felt better. He assuaged my fears.

Then, on that Saturday morning, I sat back and said, gee, I'm calling him on Saturday morning and if this is what it takes, maybe there's something wrong here. What was wrong was, if you have an investment where you need to be calling the management on a daily basis to find out how the business is, that's probably not something you should be investing in. You should have enough confidence in the longer term promise of the investment. You shouldn't really care about this year's Christmas sales. You should be investing in companies where if Christmas is bad, you would be thinking, that's a wonderful opportunity to buy more stock. But my investment premise then was that Christmas was bad, and I'm going to sell the stock. Something was wrong.

I try to seek out companies where it isn't mandatory to be quizzing them daily, where the longer term trend is powerful enough to overcome a few short-term setbacks that may come along. If you find yourself feeling that you really want to call a company on a Saturday morning because you need another daily update, you probably shouldn't own the stock. Monday morning, I came in and sold the stock. It went to zero.

Tanous: *John, that sounds awfully intuitive. Is there something more there—a seat-of-the-pants or gut feeling?*

Ballen: It combines many elements. One is a vision of the future and how the company will fit in it. That may allow you to disregard, or put less weight on a particular event, like this year's Christmas sales. Some people don't think you should be talking to managements at all, since they always put a cheery spin on things. The important thing is the valuation of the stock relative to the future of the business.

Tanous: *But do you think there might have been something intuitive about the decision to sell Jiffy Lube? I mean, as you tell the story, I get the feeling that you put down the phone on that Saturday morning and you said, you know, something doesn't feel right.*

Ballen: I suppose you're right. That speaks to the intuitive nature of the business. There are just so many inputs that you can't put into the computer, ranging from the extracurricular activities of the CEO, to how the management treats the employees. There are so many different inputs that don't fit models. That's why you can't just put data into a computer and expect it to spit out buys and sells. There are too many variables with different weightings. In rare cases, the CEO is a crook and you may not be able to see that. Can you sense that? Sometimes you can and sometimes you can't. That part

becomes intuitive. In some aspects, that's why the business is structured the way it is. In our firm, and in most firms, you have analysts
and portfolio managers. The analysts are meant to be very factually
oriented and know the day-to-day data. Hopefully, the portfolio
managers are a lot more experienced and endowed with intuition.

Tanous: *So back to Jiffy Lube. You sold the stock and took a loss.*

Ballen: Lost half our money. We could have lost it all.

Tanous: *Do you believe in maintaining cash reserves? Do you worry
about the market as a whole?*

Ballen: You can't ignore the larger picture. You want to know when
the market is going to gravitate toward your types of companies,
because that's when you're going to be rewarded. More important, I
think, is to focus on the fundamentals and make the assumption that
the market will eventually reward your investments. I focus on the
fundamentals, make sure the growth is in the companies. At the end
of the year, I check to see if we came through with what we thought
we would. I pay a lot less attention to the overall market.

Tanous: *Do you ever go into a substantial cash position? How big is
your portfolio now?*

Ballen: Close to $4 billion.

Tanous: *Might you close it again?* [Ballen closed his fund for a period from January 1994 to January 1995.]

Ballen: Let me answer the first question about the cash. I use market timing or what's happening in the market as a whole. For
instance, a recent example is the technology stocks, which have been
out of favor from the fourth quarter of 1995 until a few weeks ago
[early January 1996]. There are a lot of investments I wanted to add
to. But they're out of favor and you wonder when it's going to turn.
There are a lot of companies that we don't own here at MFS that,
frankly, we thought were going to have poor earnings. We figured
the poor earnings would come out before the good earnings. So that
gave us a time line. The company is going to report disappointing
earnings through March, so when is the batch of bad earnings going
to be released?

There's one story we called almost perfectly. We figured that
Motorola was going to be the last bad earnings report. We said that,

on this date, these stocks had a chance of turning. Believe it or not, we were right there to the hour, aggressively buying on the Motorola disappointment. You know, we're a $4 billion fund, so we're not going to turn the whole fund on. These are things we do on the margin.

Tanous: *In fact you had cash reserves and you used them.*

Ballen: You have reserves. You recycle some money from other industries. We're not omniscient, but when the market had done very well from 1991 to 1993, we got to the beginning of January 1994 and made a list of stocks we wanted to buy. It was a very short list. We thought the valuations were fully reflected in the fundamentals. We closed the fund on January 15, 1994. Our signal to investors was, we're going to close the fund. Existing investors can reinvest but we're not going to market the fund, because we don't think the opportunities are there. That proved to be a good decision. We kept making that list up religiously for the next four quarters. We got to the fourth quarter of 1994, a difficult year, and saw the list grow and grow. About then, we decided that the opportunities were there again. So, we did a big road show, did some promotion, and reopened in January of 1995. And 1995 was a great year. So that proved to be good timing for everybody. We didn't get people in and disappoint them.

Tanous: *How's your list look today?*

Ballen: Our recent list is ample. There's no reason to close again now. Given where valuations are, we see some good times ahead.

Tanous: *John, let's switch focus a little bit. Something that is of great interest to me is the "great debate." The academic community, which has contributed tremendously to our understanding of how invest-ments work in the modern world, is pretty much of one mind about one important thing. They maintain that you can't beat the market over a long period of time. One reason I'm here in Boston talking to you is that you are one of the people who seemingly disproves that widely held contention. Let's talk about that. The academics are, of course, aware that people like you exist, but to them you are the out-liers on the distribution curve. The question is whether or not there are people like you, who can systematically beat the market, or whether or not they just got lucky. Many academics think that you're just a lucky guy. How do you answer that?*

Ballen: The first thing I'd say is, look at my background. I worked at the National Bureau of Economic Research, I published some articles on economics for them, I'm an economist by training, I studied econometrics, at Stanford Business School, I studied the Sharpe models and all the rest and was about inches away from becoming an academic. I was accepted in the Harvard Ph.D. program in economics.

Tanous: *That is interesting. Just think, John, you could have been one of those very same people who don't believe in people like you!*

Ballen: I was pretty close to being one of them! So I fully appreciate where they are coming from. The other thing I'd say is, it has gotten easier to beat the market, not harder, over the last five years. The reason is that, in some sense, the market has gotten more irrational and random. There are a lot of new players out there, especially on the momentum side, who create great disparities and huge volatility in the market. You can notice that, with stocks up 50% or down 50%, in one day. Those become opportunities. From volatility emerges opportunity.

I would contend that, in a lot of sectors, the market has become a lot more volatile. I don't know how you measure it, but I believe that the volatility has added to opportunity. I know a lot of the people you're interviewing. There is a good correlation that the people who outperform year-in and year-out seem to consistently outperform, and the people who underperform continue to make the same mistakes year after year. All the academics will say, if you look at the models, and there is a stringent view and a non-stringent view, that if you have information that other people don't have, that is a reason for outperforming. It's not necessarily inside information or non-public information; some of this information involves the experience level of the person who has dealt with the investments before, as well as all the research that that person may or may not be doing.

Tanous: *So, basically, what you're saying is that you don't believe at all in the efficient market hypothesis—that all of the public information is in the price of the stock at any given time. What you're saying, and there are other examples of this, is that there is a body of information out there, available only to a select few people who are (a) smart enough to get it, and (b) smart enough to analyze it. Is that a fair statement?*

Ballen: I think the information is out there but people choose to ignore it. The information is 90% out there, but most people don't know how to interpret it or use it. There is 10% that is just hard-sweat work. But the information is out there.

Tanous: *So it is not, therefore, reflected in the price of the stock now if most investors have not used the available information fully or properly.*

Ballen: Exactly. The information is not being used properly. That's why you see the volatility. I can give you case after case where, when you look back, you'll say, of course, how could we have missed this?

Tanous: *How about an example?*

Ballen: Let's go back to United Heathcare, one of our largest positions, a company that dominates the health care area. They sit right in the middle of the trend toward lower costs, HMOs, health care maintenance, Medicare, Medicaid, and negotiating with hospitals, etc. I don't think anyone would deny that. Last year, on the margin, you had a slight uptick in medical costs and a flattening in their premiums, so they missed the quarterly earnings that Wall Street was hoping for. Not once, but three times in a row. These were small misses. What happened each time was that the stock went down, down, and down. When the stock got down to $34 a share, they had $17 of cash per share on the balance sheet.

Previously this company had grown 25% to 30% a year. It was selling, at an adjusted basis for the cash, at 8 × earnings—half the multiple for the premier company in a growth industry with 25% growth going forward. But it still went down and down. Wall Street deserted it. There wasn't an analyst on Wall Street who was recommending it so far as we knew. The market felt that, with each disappointment, it must take the stock lower. Even though these weren't big earnings disappointments; these weren't big disasters.

I'd say that most people looking at that situation then would have said, that stock is a buy. Why did it get so low? Because people sold it because of the disappointment. They said there's another disappointment in earnings coming, so it's got to go down, no matter how low it is already. It became a self-fulfilling prophecy. Stock's going down, I have to sell . . . Stock's going down, I have to sell . . . But they ignored the fact that the slightest bit of positive news, even if it was minor news to the company, could just change the psychology tremendously.

The company didn't change, but a piece of positive news comes out and the stock goes from 34 in, probably, June of 1995, to close to 64 in early 1996. Up almost 100%. The mistake we made is that we started buying too early. We started at 40 on the way down to 34. We got more aggressive as time went on and built a large position. We are one of the largest shareholders in United Healthcare. Presented in retrospect, most people would say that the stock never should have got down to 34, but, at the time, people were selling it because there was another piece of bad news. "It must go down; it has to go down . . ."

Tanous: *Your point is that all of the available information at the time suggested that the viability of the company was not affected just because quarterly earnings were a few cents off; that everything about the company suggested that it was going to continue to be successful, despite the little setbacks. Did you become a value investor all of a sudden?*

Ballen: We had no incremental information that wasn't readily available to anybody. It was all out there. People did not interpret it. They chose to ignore it.

On the other point, I find that the value guys and the growth guys are looking for the same thing. I feel best when I have the same stock in the portfolio that Michael Price *[page 33]* has. I feel we both have a successful investment because I have a valuation that makes sense to me, and I've got the growth, and he's got a valuation that makes sense from his point of view. So I'm always very comfortable when I see that we're owning the same types of stocks together. Too much is made of the differences between value and growth. The goals are the same. No one wants overpriced securities, and no one wants companies that aren't growing. Basically, we're all looking for growth at a reasonable price.

Tanous: *Except that the value guys are buying cheap assets, at least to them.*

Ballen: Hoping that there will be growth from those assets or the earnings will be recognized, or that value will be created.

Tanous: *The academics maintain that the value stocks are riskier than the growth stocks.*

Ballen: I believe that. One of the riskier things about the value stocks is they tend to go out of investors' minds quicker, and therefore, when they're out of favor, they go really out of favor. Especially the small ones. The other factor is that you have no salvation from the companies themselves, because they're not growing out of their problems. With growth companies, as long as the growth is still there, there is always a market for those particular securities or even for the companies themselves. So we have investments that, if they don't get recognized, tend to get bought out. We have several buyouts in our portfolio every year. Managements get frustrated that the value of their company isn't being realized in the market, so they sell the stock to another company for a higher price.

Tanous: *When you buy a stock, you are generally buying a large position. Are there any industries, or theories, or ideas, that are completely excluded from your consideration? Are there industries in which you are inherently not interested?*

Ballen: One of the exercises I like to go through is to ask, is there a comparable company or a comparable industry that has been a successful investment? There are some industries and some companies where, frankly, it's a lot more difficult to make money, where the business model doesn't make much sense. There are some very capital-intensive industries where it is very difficult to have sustainable returns over the longer term. So, we're not going to say you never can make money in a particular industry.

One of the things that made HFS a great investment was the fact that the motel and hotel industry was out of favor at the time. People concluded that it was an industry you never wanted to be invested in. The reason was that, from 1985 to 1990 the companies went bankrupt. Prime Motor Inns is a good example. A high flying growth stock hits the skids and goes bankrupt. They owned a lot of real estate; the cycle turned on them; they had a lot of debt; the company goes under. That gave a big black eye to the whole industry. No building in the hotel and motel industry, no investment, everyone had written it off.

Comes HFS in December 1992, and there hadn't been any hotel building for five or six years. No lending, low occupancy, low prices, but the industry was about to turn. One of the things that propelled that investment was that it came out just as the industry was about to turn. On top of that, because it was such a bad industry, when they went public, you were able to buy it at 13 × earnings, a very low multiple. So a double effect—of getting the company just when the industry was turning, and the valuation was low.

Tanous: *What mistakes do investors make?*

Ballen: One of the mistakes people have made over the last four years is not investing in the stock market, because they thought the economy was weak. The recovery, since 1991, has been the weakest recovery in the last 40 years. Yet it's the second best profit period. It is exemplified by companies like AT&T laying off 40,000 workers. It's been the second best profit period because corporations are outsourcing, downsizing, and right-sizing. So the mistake people have been making recently is saying, I'm not going to invest in the stock market, because the economy is just so-so. This story *[outsourcing, downsizing, right-sizing]* may be a book in itself, because the U.S. is doing it and the rest of the world is behind. That's the reason the U.S. markets, I would say, are doing as well as they are. As Peter Lynch *[page 111]* said, most money has been lost, not by people buying the market and having it go down, but people not buying stocks and having them go up. The reason some people have not been investing is the economy, but the companies are doing great.

Tanous: *This is a question I probably won't ask anyone else in the book. I'm posing it to you because you are probably the youngest person I'm interviewing. It's the old job interview question. What do you expect to be doing 10 years from now?*

Ballen: Probably working on the 20-year record. The business moves quickly. In some sense, you might conclude that it has become a more difficult business. You see a lot of successful people retiring early. Peter Lynch is an example. I don't think there's anything else for me that provides the day-to-day stimulation. This is a tough business. It's a game of inches. While it's easy to tell stories of owning stocks that have worked out for years, the fact is that you are looking at these companies every day. There's a lot of pressure and hard work. People burn out.

On the other hand, it's hard to imagine doing anything else. It's so exciting and you learn so much every day. When we interview people, what we look for is not someone who knows everything on day one, but people who will learn from their mistakes, who will learn from their Jiffy Lubes, and apply what they learn to other companies; people who aren't destined to make the same mistakes over again. If you stop learning, you have probably outlived your welcome in the business. It won't be me who decides not to stay in the business. It's such a hard business that, once your performance turns down, for whatever reason, either the firm or the investors will vote with their feet, and you go on to something else. A lot of people chose to get out at the top. A lot of people burned out. A lot of people have been asked to leave. It's a tough business.

This meeting gave us quite a bit to think about. Ballen shared his approach to picking successful stocks, which revolves around what he calls the "business model" of his prospective company. Return on invested capital is the key to his interest in a company. Microsoft versus Sun Microsystems was a good example of two very successful companies where one, Microsoft, has been a much more successful stock, primarily, according to Ballen, because Sun is a capital-intensive business and its returns have been lower.

As to his other selection criteria, I found his approach to selecting the stocks within a market segment he likes fascinating. After all, if you are prescient enough to see a new, high-growth industry emerging—like mass market office supply—which company in this emerging industry do you bet on? Simple. Ballen bought them all. Then, as the competitors slugged it out, he waited and concentrated his bets on the survivors. I think his "business model" approach has a lot going for it. Once again, it involves the discipline and intelligence of the manager, as well as his skills in evaluating the information at his disposal.

Interesting, wasn't it, that Ballen almost became an academic? His keen intelligence and methodological approach to his craft reflect his training and professionalism. We're not talking about gunslingers or wild market traders here, just a strong commitment to the nuts and bolts of investing. And it really pays off.

I believe that Ballen shed some new light on the efficient market theory. He said that, in his opinion, the market had actually become more irrational and random over time. He thought that the information is indeed available to investors, but how they interpret it varies; presumably some are better than others at doing that and the ones who are more successful will have better returns.

Personally, I think his insights are visionary and we will discuss them in the final chapters of the book as we move toward a conclusion on how best to beat the market, if beating the market is even possible.

ROGER F.
MURRAY

C lose your eyes and let your mind wander back, way back to the Great Depression. We are now in the early '30s. Young Roger Murray has just graduated from Yale with high honors, and he is fortunate enough to be one of the very few members of his class, or any other graduating class, to get a job. He will rise to become the youngest vice president in the history of Bankers Trust Company before, eventually, deciding on a career in academia. He is recruited to be an associate dean at the Columbia Graduate School of Business where he audits the class taught by Benjamin Graham. When Ben Graham retires, his class will be taught by Professor Roger Murray. We are there at the birth of value investing. We are there with the masters themselves, Benjamin Graham and David Dodd, and their successor, Roger Murray.

If you have already read my interview with Mario Gabelli (page 77), you know that Mario, in his shy, retiring manner, quietly suggested that maybe, just maybe, I had not interviewed the right academics. So, armed with his gentle suggestion, I sought out Roger Murray, who is now retired. What a discovery! Professor Murray was not only the successor to the most famous value instructor of all time, he is the co-author of the most recent edition of Graham and Dodd's Security Analysis. *Believe me, no one in the world of invest-*

ing risks excommunication by referring to this book as the bible of investing.

Do you happen to have an IRA account? Thank Roger Murray. He originated the concept and saw it to fruition in Washington when it was enacted as part of ERISA. In 1993, he was the recipient of the prestigious Nicholas Molodovsky Award, which has been conferred only eleven times, to individuals who have made contributions of such significance as to change the direction of the investment profession. Benjamin Graham was a previous recipient of the award, as was Nobel laureate Bill Sharpe. Now sit back, open your eyes again, and treasure the words of one of the masters.

Tanous: *How did you get interested in stocks?*

Murray: As an undergraduate at Yale, after taking my first economics course, I did a summer project for my instructor, who then gave me some extra credit for Economics 101. I did an analysis of several companies and their equity securities. This gave me a chance, in the summer of 1930, to do my first analysis. Fortunately, no one was relying on my conclusions! Although the Harvard Economic Society had informed us that the decline in economic activity had run its course by the middle of 1930, we found out later that it was only the beginning.

Tanous: *You said this was in 1930. So we're talking about a few months after the 1929 crash?*

Murray: That's right. But in the spring of 1930, there was a widespread view that the market crash was behind us, and now that it was over, we would resume long term economic growth, and all was well.

Tanous: *Is that scary?*

Murray: The market rallied in the spring of 1930. What happened in 1931 was that the British went off the gold standard, and the German banks collapsed. These events had not been foreseen.

One of the securities I analyzed was Missouri Pacific convertible preferred stock. It was a very good exercise in understanding and analyzing the conversion feature. The only trouble was that the conversion feature was quite irrelevant—the stock was wiped out in the subsequent bankruptcy of Missouri Pacific. That's how I got my first experience in the market.

Tanous: *Even though you are very well known as an academic, Professor, you didn't start out that way. In fact, you had a pretty illustrious career in business before you turned to academia, didn't you?*

Murray: Yes, I did. In the spring of 1932, if you had any hopes of getting married, you had to go to work. That is, if you could possibly find a job. Happily, I was able to do that. That enabled me to save enough money to get married in 1934. I was working at Bankers Trust Company. In those days, you started at $25 a week, and they assured you that you were being grossly overpaid because they really didn't need your services very badly. They were carrying old time employees out of a sense of loyalty, but they did venture to take on three trainees in June 1932, instead of the usual 30, and I was, happily, able to get one of those spots.

Tanous: *At this point you had just graduated from Yale, correct? And with obvious academic distinction, since you were one of only three trainees hired just as the depression was about to start. That, in itself, is quite an achievement.*

Murray: Well, I was certainly very hesitant when I asked the senior officer in the bank if it would be all right if I took two days off after graduation before I reported for work. I didn't want to appear casual about starting to work. He assured me it was all right.

Tanous: *A lot of your classmates didn't find work, I suppose.*

Murray: That's right. One of my very good friends, a very fine-looking colleague, who had been very active in drama and the arts at Yale, was selling neckties at Macy's. Whenever I visited Macy's, I'd make sure that I didn't go through the necktie department. I didn't want him to see me coming by because he hardly needed recognition in that kind of position.

Tanous: *Perhaps you could tell us about your transition from banking to academia.*

Murray: Well, I had earned my graduate degrees and worked my way up the ladder. I was the youngest vice president in the history of Bankers Trust, and I had a very fine career there. But, for many years I had known Courtney Brown, who had become the dean of

Columbia Business School. He had been a colleague in my early days at Bankers Trust Company. One day he invited me to become associate dean, to be the inside man to his outside dean responsible for fundraising. I, of course, would have to endure the experience of teaching a class for thirteen weeks. As we all know, you can't deceive yourself; if you don't do well in the classroom, you know it.

I went to Columbia Business School as an associate dean. I managed budgets, and faculty recruiting, and curriculum design, and those kinds of things, on the condition that I could teach one course. I had already signed up to teach the seminar which Benjamin Graham had taught for many years. He was retiring to California. I had sat in on the seminar with him, and I enjoyed it immensely. But that wasn't the same as teaching a class. That was just a fun experience—watching and listening to one of the masters of the field.

I had two-and-a-half years to find out the answers to the two questions. Could I teach? And, did I really like it, and find it rewarding? When the answers turned out to be affirmative, I stood for tenure. I had done a lot of writing as chief economist for Bankers Trust, so I could meet the publication standard and gain the recognition of colleagues in the field.

Tanous: *It's staggering to think that we're sitting here talking about taking classes with Benjamin Graham. What was Dodd's role at the time?*

Murray: He taught the Security Analysis course. He had done that for a couple of decades right from the text. That textbook was an interesting joint product. Ben Graham was not addicted to writing a serious text. He was full of ideas, loved to chat, loved to think out loud. Dave Dodd sat in on Ben's classes and took copious notes. Then Dave Dodd would go dig out and verify the examples that Ben had used. That's how the first edition of *Security Analysis* came about in 1934.

That year, the conventional wisdom was that bonds were the only investment outlet. Stocks were nothing but speculation, pure and simple. So the mission that Ben and Dave had in writing the first edition was to say, now really, there is such a thing as investing in common stocks, contrary to what the standard textbook on investment in those days said. The standard textbook then was by Chamberlain and Edwards. They made it absolutely clear that stocks were speculation, and bonds were the only avenue that could be called investing. After the devastation of the securities markets, nobody, except for Graham and Dodd, was prepared to stand up and say, now just a darn minute. When those prices get low enough, even what you might think of as speculative securities do have investment quality, because you are paying a price that provides you with, to use their term, a big margin of safety.

Tanous: *That presumably is the value stock thesis.*

Murray: That's right. The value stock thesis.

Tanous: *As I understand it, you taught the course after Graham and Dodd retired.*

Murray: When Dave Dodd retired, after I'd been at Columbia for three years, I took his class. From then on, I taught the Security Analysis course.

Tanous: *You're also the co-author of the most recent edition of that famous book,* Security Analysis, *right?*

Murray: That's right. I started teaching with the edition of the '50s. For the 1962 edition, I was the publisher's advisor. So when Ben Graham and Sidney Cottle were doing that edition, I had the fun of being the arbiter of debates between them.

Tanous: *You mean, you were the kibitzer!*

Murray: Yeah. I was the kibitzer for McGraw Hill. So I stored up lots of ideas from that experience and from my teaching, and had the opportunity to develop them further in 1988, when I co-authored the fifth edition.

Tanous: *I can't resist asking you what Graham and Dodd were like as people.*

Murray: Ben was just exactly the way he was pictured—a man who read for background, a fine classical scholar, a man with an idea a minute. He had a wonderfully agile mind. Dave Dodd was a wonderful gentleman. One of the finest people I have ever met anywhere. He could listen to Ben all day long, but he retained a healthy skepticism, and when Ben would launch into one of his ideas, which came along about every 30 seconds, Dave would quietly just sit down and say, that's an interesting idea, Ben. However, do you believe that the facts really support that strong a conclusion? Then he'd get to work on the serious analysis.

Tanous: *So these guys would sit around and come up with investment ideas?*

Murray: Sure. They just loved to talk about their experiences with stocks. They were early investors in GEICO. They were always kind of interested in insurance companies, because insurance companies had portfolios of assets.

Tanous: *This reminds me of another investor who went to Columbia and also likes GEICO.*

Murray: Of course. Warren Buffett. Warren generated his assets in the insurance business. We think it's Berkshire Hathaway, but, most of the time, it's one of their insurance companies that owns a large part of that portfolio. Again, this lends itself to financial analysis because insurance companies manage large amounts of capital.

Tanous: *I'm curious about how, from a value investing point of view, you deal with underwriting risk when you buy insurance companies. You know, three or four hurricanes might hit, something you can't predict.*

Murray: In its most extreme form, Buffett deals with it through reinsurance.

Tanous: *I see. You lay off the risk by selling or syndicating it?*

Murray: Yes. You can systematically analyze levels of risk and exposure, but it doesn't mean you end up with certainty. The idea is that, if you do your homework, this business is just like managing a portfolio with a margin of safety. That term "margin of safety," shows up frequently in Graham and Dodd.

Tanous: *By reinsuring, you're basically laying off the risk onto someone else.*

Murray: Right. You control your exposure.

Tanous: *Did you run across Warren Buffett at Columbia?*

Murray: He had come and gone before I got there. I didn't meet up with him until later. One of the good sessions he and I had was when we were both on the SEC Advisory Committee on Corporate Disclosure, which was a fun enterprise. Dave Dodd originally introduced me to Buffett, but on our committee, we had the opportunity to sit around the table and really discuss things at length.

Tanous: *Have you had any other relationship with him?*

Murray: He comes back to Columbia on occasion. When I taught the class in value analysis year before last, he was one of our guest speakers. You heard about that class, didn't you?

Tanous: *Remind me, please.*

Murray: We did it out of the blue. We decided to give a value investing course, limited to 75 kids, although we had upwards of two hundred applications. You discover now that in our wonderful world of quantitative methods and financial economics, students don't have much opportunity to explore areas like this.

Tanous: *Why not?*

Murray: It's interesting. I'm serving on a group for the CFA *[Chartered Financial Analyst]* institute. We're examining the kind of training a specialist in equity investing should have. The students have finished the CFA, they are still actively engaged in equity security selection and portfolio management, what should we offer them beyond what is covered in the CFA program? It's fascinating. There are about a dozen of us working on this; two of us paying attention to accounting and corporate finance, and what are the rest of them focusing on? Valuation! I always come back to something Ben Graham said to me. He said, if you give me a reliable estimate of the earning power of a company, I'll value it on the back of an envelope.

Tanous: *I think even growth managers would agree with that. Now, it's time to put the boxing gloves on. I'd like to focus our discussion on one of the principal features of this book.*

Murray: Okay.

Tanous: *What we're doing is talking to a lot of active managers and also to some academics all of whom, except for you, happen to be efficient market theorists. It was Mario Gabelli who suggested that I was talking to the wrong academics. "You should talk to Roger Murray!" he shouted at me. I said, I'd love to talk to Roger Murray. So, thanks to Mario, I'm here.*

Here's our conundrum. These efficient market guys snicker when you talk about analyzing companies and figuring out which ones have hidden values that the market hasn't uncovered. To them, of course, there are no hidden values! Everything about that company is reflected in the market price. So please help me out, Professor.

Murray: To use the Graham and Dodd terminology, we're talking about the difference between intrinsic value and market value. Market efficiency purists will tell you that, fundamentally, the only real expression of value that exists is what you read in the marketplace. And it is the best expression, absent inside information, of the significant events that are occurring and are about to occur. That's saying that market price is the best estimate of economic value.

Now, let's turn to the concept of "intrinsic value" in a Graham and Dodd sense. This is the value of an enterprise, not a stock certificate. This is the value of a company based on its earning power. What do we mean by earning power? It's what we have a valid reason to expect in terms of the volume and profitability of this business, and the characteristics of this line of business. If we can identify those underlying characteristics, we can reach some reliable conclusions about what may lie ahead in terms of growth, consistency, and levels of profitability. If we can do that, we don't have a problem on valuation, since all the elements to arrive at a valuation are there. We don't need to refine that estimate of value to three decimal places. What we're looking for is under and over-valuation, recognizing that we've inevitably got a margin of error in framing our expectations—because we're talking about a future about which we only have vague knowledge and guidelines.

Tanous: *But absent the ability to predict the future, the efficient market theorists say that all of the information that leads to a valuation comes to rest at one spot—the price at which the security trades. To them, there's no such thing as overvalued and undervalued, because there is no such thing as mispriced securities.*

Murray: Which, obviously, is a silly statement. How can you say there is no evidence of securities being mispriced? Let's look at our most recent history of the most efficient market. Let's start on January 1, 1995, and all those securities are efficiently priced. And at the end of 1995, they trade at prices 35% higher.

Tanous: *Okay. That's new information coming into the market.*

Murray: New information? Was it really? Look at the underlying information. We had a very good year. Was it 17%, depending on what measure you use? If you want to talk about new information you could say, well, on average, we get only 7% per annum increases in earnings, and this year it was 17%, so the new information was the differential of 10%, right?

Tanous: *Okay.*

Murray: How do you relate that to a 35% rise in stock prices?

Tanous: *I don't know. How do you?*

Murray: If stocks were priced efficiently at the beginning of the year and they were also priced efficiently at the end of the year, that would tell us that a normal growth in the value of American industry is in the range of 35%, which was the rise in value of stocks. Any different answer about the trendline value of American industry leads us to the conclusion that the market was inefficient at the beginning of the year or at the end of the year.

Tanous: *That's clear. What you're saying is that earnings may have gone up 17% in 1995, but they sure didn't go up 35%, which is what the stock market went up.*

Murray: Right. And that that's not my idea of efficiency! And it isn't yours either, if you sold out on the first of January. The other thing that happened, to your amazement, is that what securities you had in your portfolio made a difference. If the market is efficient, diversification shouldn't matter. You don't really need to diversify. You want to avoid extreme economic and political factors, but, generally speaking, if General Motors is priced efficiently it doesn't matter if you buy General Motors or you buy Ford.

Tanous: *But then you don't have the benefit of diversification.*

Murray: Okay, I don't want to stake my whole future on the automobile business, so I will own General Motors or Ford. That way, I will not have more than five or six percent of my portfolio in the automobile business. But now we're talking about diversifying economic and other factors. These are all elements subject to the analytical process. That being the case, how can market prices be so inefficiently determined in such a highly developed market system?

Tanous: *Good question. What's the answer?*

Murray: For securities to be efficiently priced, there must be a disciplined analytical process by which those prices are reached. That disciplined analytical process takes a lot of hard work by trained and experienced people. But most of us would rather not do that much work. We'd rather find an easy answer if we could. One easy answer is that I buy stocks because they're going up. That's now called momentum investing. Some will say, now, that makes sense to me. Those securities that show the best momentum will, of course, have the most promising future! Ask yourself, what kind of reasoning is that? Momentum analysis means that you will miss every turning point in the course of a company's history.

Tanous: *So when you ask the question, how can market prices be so inefficiently determined in a fully developed market system, the answer you just gave is, they aren't efficient because, for them to be efficient, people would have to do all this work all the time. They don't.*

Murray: That's right. It is a disciplined, even burdensome undertaking. You really want to have the capacity to identify corporate change, departures from the past pattern. One thing you know about the past pattern of published financial statements is that companies have a chief financial officer who monitors the value of the enterprise. He knows how to do that. One of his functions is to smooth out as many of the financial bumps as he can, and provide as much continuity in the pattern of growth as he can. Now, we're talking about people who obey the law, we're not talking about fraud. We're talking about the techniques within the range of generally accepted accounting principles that permit you to change the timing of the recognition of gains and losses. That's neat. Now you can fuss around with this stuff, but eventually the whole story will show up in those financial statements.

Tanous: *This presumably is the hard way. You have to do the work to find the true underlying data to make a good investment decision, right?*

Murray: Exactly. Think of that financial statement as a published photographic portrait—the financial guy has touched it up, taken out the blemishes. He's removed the worry lines, and gives you that lovely, smooth picture. That's what the chief financial officer's assignment is. That's what he wants you to see.

What I have said for years and years, until I'm tired of hearing myself say it, is that every large corporation should have on the payroll a highly skilled security analyst. Put him to work, give him full access to all of the financial information being generated. Have him do a very down-to-earth careful analysis, where you don't have any of the sugar coating, or painting out of blemishes. Have him work in secret. You, as the chief executive of this company, keep his analytical results locked in your bottom desk drawer. Look at them instead of what those wonderful financial people are saying, what the investor relations people are saying, and what your public relations people are saying. You would make very much better decisions for your company if you see it as it really is, instead of as it's been touched up.

Tanous: *Well, what's the role of the auditor in all this?*

Murray: The auditor? He has no basis for complaint. You're still within the range of generally accepted accounting principles. Just think of the financial statements we have been reading in the last five years. This is after one of the great inflationary periods in American economic history. This is after a major change in price levels has had an opportunity to work its way through the system. Under these circumstances, we should be looking at huge amounts of realized capital gains on capital assets. What do we read instead? You don't find any unusual gains realized. All you read about is unusual capital losses.

Tanous: *Well, the assets are valued at cost, right. And if they're not sold, they're just there on the balance sheet.*

Murray: They're just there, and if you do sell them they should show a big profit. Yet you and I look at those restructuring write-offs, and now we have this new one about how you write down long-lived assets that seemed to have lost value, and that creates a huge write-off. What does that tell you? It tells you that we have had a huge overstatement of corporate earning power.

Tanous: *Why is that?*

Murray: Because there has been a totally inadequate level of depreciation, or even the expiration of, economic value. We have failed to recognize the reality that sometimes we don't have to use up capital assets, they simply lose value because of obsolescence.

In determining the intrinsic value of an enterprise, we must try to get at the real earning power. Not reported earning power, but the actual economic value of a company, which the market may or may not perceive correctly. We can say, with a high degree of certainty, that the market is going to be right in lots of valuations of lots of companies.

One of the things that the trained security analyst has to do is to develop a willingness to throw away his work. For example, you go to work and you think you have uncovered a scent of undervaluation. You immediately do all your work and, after all that effort, your best conclusion is, no, it's not undervalued. In fact, it's fairly valued in the marketplace. And now you say, I just learned something, but isn't this terrible! You and I know that a lot of analysts who come up with that answer won't admit it. Instead they'll say, you know, I must have missed something in my analysis.

Tanous: *I know. They can't accept that all that work went to waste, so they look for a reason to recommend it anyway!*

Murray: Absolutely!

Tanous: *Let's look at investing from an individual investor's point of view. After a year like 1995, when most of the mutual funds and money managers did not do as well as the market, the investor might just throw in the towel and say, you know, what the hell, why don't I buy an index fund, or a combination of index funds, rather than try to do all this myself. What advice would you have for this investor?*

Murray: I would say, go ahead and buy that diversified index fund portfolio. Make your choice about the type of asset allocation you want. Focus on asset allocation, because for most of us, the big difference in returns will come from asset allocation decisions, unless you have real investment skill and you're really ready to work.

Tanous: *So you're saying it's okay for an investor to buy markets rather than stocks or managers?*

Murray: Yes I am. I think that because, on a part-time basis, those people don't have the time or the expertise to make informed choices.

Tanous: *Good point. But, on the other hand, I interviewed Peter Lynch and he says, do a little research, keep your eyes open, and you might find a great company.*

Murray: What Peter says about that makes perfectly good sense. This is one of the oldest dimensions of security analysis. Where do you begin your security analysis? By looking at the company, what its competitive position is, what the costs of entry are, all of those factors. But that doesn't take you the last mile. Suppose you go through that kind of process, and you say to yourself, I've studied retailing intensively and I believe that the discount store is here to stay. So, I'm going to make my long term investment in Kmart.

Tanous: *Yeah. Bad choice.*

Murray: Now I did everything right up to the point of analyzing Kmart versus Wal-Mart.

Tanous: *Okay. Let's say I'm the investor, professor, and I really appreciate your advice. You're right. My odds aren't too good out there since I'm not a professional investor. Maybe I should just buy these index funds. But I really am prepared to do the work. I'm really into this! Give me some advice on beating the markets and selecting and buying some of those undervalued securities.*

Murray: Okay. First, you sit down and think about identifying your universe. You've heard Warren Buffett say many times, I don't make my choices in fields I don't understand. That's very good advice. Stay away from activities that are unfamiliar to you and will continue to be unfamiliar to you. That's the first level of advice. The second level is that by the time a company has its highest level of recognition and popularity, you can be pretty darn sure that the market valuation has run well in excess of the intrinsic value of the company. It's that well-known and that well-liked.

Tanous: *So, you've got to find the undiscovered ones. Is that the idea?*

Murray: You've got to find the undiscovered ones. Look at a field that makes good sense on business and economic grounds. Then pore your way through the whole battery of information on companies that are in that field, and which have gotten themselves established, to some extent. Next, sit down and do an old-fashioned spreadsheet comparative analysis. Look at all the companies in this field, and narrow it down to six established companies. Next, sit down and put them though your ratio analysis. That starts to give you some insights, assuming that you're satisfied with the data you're using and it is comparable enough so that your comparisons have a chance of being meaningful. Go down there and see rates of change in sales and earnings, levels of stability in the underlying earning power of these companies. Then, narrow yourself down from six to two.

Tanous: *Instead of picking just one, how about buying them both?*

Murray: You may do that. Having narrowed them down to two, you may decide that it is too close to call, so you put half your money in each.

Tanous: *I want to ask you about your role with the Individual Retirement Account.*

Murray: I was Gene Keogh's expert. He was a member of the House Ways and Means Committee from Brooklyn. He was a fairly senior guy on the Ways and Means Committee. When he called the chairman of Bankers Trust Company and said, I need an expert to support me against the Treasury's contention that the Keogh Act will result in too great a revenue loss, the chairman said, I know just the guy you want. His name is Roger Murray. So, for ten years, each year when the bill would come up—one year in the House, one year in the Senate—I would go and give my testimony stating that the Treasury estimates of revenue loss were absolutely unreal and outrageous. Anyway, we finally got it passed.

By then, I was over at CREF *[College Retirement Equities Fund]* thinking about pension benefits that were completely portable. One of the greater assets of academia is that you can change jobs and your retirement benefits will move with you as long as you are in TIAA-CREF *[(Teachers' Insurance and Annuity Association College Retirement Equities Fund) Virtually all teachers and college professors in America are participants in this retirement program, which is one of the largest institutional pools of money in the U.S., with over $160 billion under management for 1.8 million participants in 5,800 schools and non-profit educational institutions.]* That's because you own the policy from day one.

So I looked around the landscape and said, we've got a fine organization here that covers academia, and others are covered by their company or their union. But the people in the workforce who don't have a comparable opportunity are those who have a lifetime of work, where their economic asset is their skill and professional ability, but who do not have continuity of specific employment. What we ought to do is fill that gap by having an individual retirement account, where an individual could sign up with a financial institution and have a part of his pay go into a lifetime savings account. It would then be possible to make it tax deductible, just as it is for everybody else.

The beauty of this is that it becomes a wonderful asset for financial institutions, and they will promote it because they will gain a long term depositor. Furthermore, here is the ideal place for people to buy stocks and make long term equity investments, because they will have locked themselves into this program. The one thing we know about stocks is that if you give me 15 or 20 years, I'll give you a superior rate of return, which is what you need for your retirement savings.

Tanous: *How did you get from cogitating about this idea, to the IRA as we know it?*

Murray: There was a hearing in Washington. They were kind enough to invite me to come and talk about retirement income. I gave what I thought was expert testimony, but nobody gave me the time of day. I got nowhere. However, the Hunt commission was appointed to study our financial institutions, and they invited me to write a position paper to address fiduciary standards for the protection of pensions. I said, I'm delighted, and I'm just the right guy to do that. But, curiously enough, as you get about two-thirds through the paper, there is a slight departure. We talk about the gap in the availability of pension plans for the individual who is not part of a significant group. The potential remedy for this is something called the Individual Retirement Account. They said, hey, you've really got something! You're absolutely right!

Out of the Hunt Commission report comes the Employment Retirement Income Security Act *[ERISA]*. Where do you find a tax benefit for the self-employed? Answer: in ERISA. It's ERISA that provides your deductibility for a contribution to your IRA. We got this in a bill that has to do with the careful inspection and auditing of pension plans. Never happened before. The magic here was that this could happen, not in ten or twelve years like the Keogh Act, but in three or four.

Tanous: *So we have you to thank for it.*

Murray: We got it in the side door.

Tanous: *Tell me, Professor, the coincidence of the signing of this bill, just as we came to the end of the '73-'74 bear market, is a bit striking, don't you think?*

Murray: It's a sheer coincidence. I had done work on pension reform way back in the '60s. The appointment I had was when Kennedy was in office. I worked on one of the task forces that addressed pension reform. But it took a long time, and a series of hearings.

In September 1974, while we were preparing the annual report of the Common Fund *[a large mutual fund and investment group which addresses the specific needs of educational institutions],* we had had discussions about the fact that colleges were withdrawing their participation in the equity fund and putting the funds into high-yield bonds. We decided we had to do something like write a statement *[in defense of equities].* My colleagues said, Roger, you write the first draft. I wrote the first draft. We had a meeting of the investment committee. They said, gee, we like this and we kind of agree with it, but we think you're taking too strong a position. My position was that this was an opportunity of a lifetime to buy equities.

Tanous: *This is in 1974?*

Murray: September 1974.

Tanous: *Talk about timing!*

Murray: They all wanted to tone it down. I listened patiently and said, I'll tell you what. I've got a deal you can't refuse. I'll write a disclaimer and say this is not really an expression of the Common Fund. We observe freedom of thinking and speech, which is common to academia. This is one man's opinion, not necessarily endorsed by the trustees. My offer was that, if this turns out to be right, it will be the Common Fund's statement. If it turns out to be wrong, it can be Roger Murray's statement.

Tanous: *Did it work?*

Murray: It worked. I went back to my original draft and didn't have to modify the conclusions. It was illustrative of the conventional wisdom. I never had more invitations to speak than I did in the fall of 1974. They couldn't get anybody else to constructively talk about buying equities. I had never spoken at the Chicago Analysts Society and I got an invitation to talk to them. I said I'd be delighted. That was the only time I ever used the word "never." The old saying is never use the word "never" in relation to equities. And I used the word by saying you'll *never* have an opportunity to buy stocks as cheap as they are now. I said it and I meant it. On an analytical basis, there was no question about it.

Tanous: *You're making it irresistible for me to ask you what you think about buying equities in mid-1996?*

Murray: In mid-1996, they are overvalued. The case is not as extreme as in 1987, but it's only not as extreme because we do not have the interest rate factor as strongly positioned as it was in 1987. In 1987, I got every one of my pension asset management clients to cut their equity exposure by 20% to 25%.

Tanous: *What would you do today?*

Murray: Today, I would get back to the minimum part of your range. My typical pension fund range is 50% to 75% in equities. You don't rebalance unless you cross 80%. But if that's really your range, you ought to be down close to your minimum. Of course, my minimum is higher than most people's.

Tanous: *Some of our readers are going to want to know how you pick stocks. How do you do it for yourself, for example? What's your advice to others who aspire to wealth through common stocks?*

Murray: Do intensive analytical work on a limited number of companies, where you have an opportunity to get a real good understanding of what decisions are being made, and what is going on in those companies. That's why I have never owned a lot of stocks in my portfolio. I would rather have, and I will get better results, from a dozen companies that I really understand, and that I know well enough so that I can make an informed decision on whether I should continue to own those companies. That affords me a basis on which to judge the quality of the important decisions that management makes from time to time in a variety of circumstances.

Tanous: *I think that is sound advice. I really get upset at those books that purport to tell you how to beat the market without mentioning the hard work you have to put in to do it.*

Murray: One thing I'm sure of is that, in the market, there is no such thing as a free lunch—as Milton Friedman always says. As the old saying goes, you build your wealth the old-fashioned way, you earn it.

Tanous: *One last question, Professor. Some people might find it surprising that someone who witnessed first hand the 1929 crash and lived through the Great Depression, would emerge so bullish on equities.*

Murray: The answer is, if you went through that period and you were, as I was, an MBA and a Ph.D. candidate, immersed in those financial markets and in the economic environment, after you had been through that, the kinds of worries and concerns that baffled investors and market-makers in the '50s, '60s, '70s, '80s, and '90s are trivial.

I am certain Roger Murray is right about that. It is interesting indeed to hear an investment perspective that covers not just a decade or two, but every important period in the history of the American equity markets. To have that perspective, from the viewpoint of someone who worked on Wall Street and subsequently became a well-known academic, is truly invaluable. I enjoy conjuring up mental images of young Roger Murray and his colleagues, Ben Graham and Dave Dodd, teaching security analysis to thousands of eager students. And what was that fellow Warren Buffett thinking about in class?

Let's take a quick look at the main points. Professor Murray gives us a different viewpoint from the other academics with whom we spoke. He doesn't believe in efficient markets, at least not perfectly efficient markets. Did you catch the difference between market value and intrinsic value? Graham and Dodd, and Murray, seek the intrinsic value of the company as a business by poring over financial data and applying ratios. Is all that intrinsic value reflected in the price of the stock at all times? Murray doesn't think so, and neither do any of the value managers we talked to. Of course they don't. Their raison d'être *is finding undervalued securities.*

I also found the notion of redoing the financial statistics—in a way that is not designed to put the best foot forward—interesting. That, presumably, is what you and I are supposed to do as part of our financial analysis. And financial analysis is how we attempt to discover those undervalued stocks.

That leads us to his investment advice. Are you inclined to listen to hot tips and great stories? Then you would be better off, as Professor Murray suggested, buying a combination of index funds and staying out of trouble. That's the easy way and, incidentally, with that advice he joins with our efficient market theorists, who don't think you can beat the market in any case. Are you prepared to do all the work necessary to make an informed investment decision? Then go for it! But don't forget to do all the work. Good advice, Professor. And by the way, isn't that what Peter Lynch told us to do?

ROBERT B. GILLAM

B ob Gillam is a very successful money manager in a most unlikely place: Anchorage, Alaska. His firm, McKinley Capital Management, Inc., was started in 1988. Gillam actively manages investment portfolios incorporating modern portfolio theory, with quantitative computer models. Alaska is awesome by any standards. Bob Gillam, a lifelong resident, will tell us about this State, which is more than twice as big as Texas. I visited in early summer, when the weather is near perfect and the scenery beautiful beyond description. Alaskans are rugged people, and proud of it. My hotel resembled a hunting lodge complete with intimidating stuffed bears—which looked 20 feet tall. In fact, it seems like almost every public place in Anchorage has a trophy bear. I vividly recall trying to sleep at 10:30 P.M. and having to close the curtains in my room to keep the sun from streaming in. Such is summer in Alaska.

Gillam's success is not only a testimony to his intelligence and skill, but also to the dizzying advances in communications and electronics. After earning his B.S. in economics from Wharton, he received his M.B.A. from the Graduate School of Business at UCLA. He started managing individual and institutional accounts in 1970. Sitting in Anchorage, he gets information as fast as anyone on Wall Street. He needs to. His style is a combination of both quantita-

tive analysis and momentum. Both judgment and instant reactions are the keys to success.

Gillam's performance record proves that he is doing something right. For the 12 months ended June 30, 1996, his portfolios were up 42%. For the trailing 6 years ended June 30, 1996, his clients enjoyed annualized returns of 31%. Let's find out how he does it.

Tanous: *How did you first get interested in stocks?*

Gillam: I've been interested in the stock market since my earliest memory, probably going back to when I was 12 or 13 years old. I started looking at the financial page, which at that time, here in Alaska, was a week old. I was fascinated by stocks. My fascination with stocks is even stronger today.

Tanous: *You grew up in Alaska?*

Gillam: My father was fortunate enough to come here just before the start of World War II. He came here on an adventure. When the war started, the War Department found out that he had been a West Point cadet. That was it. They drafted him on the spot and put him in charge of freight coming into Alaska. The freight was transshipped to Kbarask, in Russia. The U.S. supported the Soviets by shipping war material through Alaska. We put it on the Alaska railroad and shipped it to Fairbanks. From there, the cargo was loaded onto DC 3s, which made over 25,000 flights to Russia, then onto the Trans Siberian Railroad and across to the front with Germany. After the war, my father stayed here. That's how our family ended up here.

Tanous: *So, you were born here.*

Gillam: Yes, I was.

Tanous: *Your company, McKinley Capital, has a phenomenal record, which we'll get to in a minute. One thing I noticed in looking at your style, is that you don't fit neatly into nice style boxes—value, or growth, and so forth, the way most managers do. How do you describe your style?*

Gillam: First of all, the people who designed the styles, value/growth, large/small, apparently didn't know much about the market. We are in the business of finding the stocks that go up. We are not in the business of fitting ourselves into a category. Our business is generating excess market returns with controlled market risk. It doesn't matter to us whether it's a $300 million stock or a $30 billion stock. It's irrelevant. My client doesn't call me at the end of the year and ask: Tell me how you beat the index? Did you buy small-cap or large-cap? Value or growth? It doesn't matter to them. We are a value manager when that's the thing to do, we're a growth manager when that's the thing to do, same for large-cap and small-cap.

Tanous: *So you're not what we call style-specific.*

Gillam: Absolutely not.

Tanous: *In that case, let's find out how you do it. Let's talk about methodology. Since whatever it is you do transcends specific styles, what common elements allow you to make money in all these different categories?*

Gillam: First, we look at the market as a whole. We let the market lead us. At any time the market will reward certain industrial groups with "excess" returns. We invest in market leadership. Our database contains 13,000 stocks from which we choose our portfolios. Each week, every Saturday, we rerun the numbers on the entire universe of stocks. For every security in the universe, we calculate an alpha value *[a measure of excess return]* and a risk value, which are two very important numbers to us. Remember, there's nothing we can do about the stock market's moves up or down.

Tanous: *Do you also use something like the Sharpe ratio?*

Gillam: Not exactly. Our alpha is a straight linear alpha. We use a base index which could be the S&P 500, the Over-the-Counter Composite, it doesn't really matter as long as the base is constant for the entire regression. When we come up with a stock's alpha value, we compare it to all other alphas in the universe. We want alphas of our stocks to be in the top 6% or 7% of the continuous universe—a very select group of stocks. Assume that the S&P 500 has been going up at one percent a week. If your company has an alpha of one, that means that you've been going up at two percent a week.

Remember, there's nothing we can do about the stock market's ups and downs. What we can do, however, is buy the stocks that have positive alphas. People who buy companies that have a big negative alpha *[meaning they have been returning less than the market]* might as well believe in the tooth fairy. You are trying to buy something cheap. But there is nothing cheap in the market. Nothing! The market knows! We never bottom fish.

Tanous: *I suppose the next thing you're going to tell me is that you are an efficient market theorist.*

Gillam: No. There are inefficiencies in the market every day. Our experience suggests that about 9% of the universe is inefficiently priced on any given day. There is a series of studies I used when I did graduate work at UCLA that dealt with stocks which make new highs and with those making new lows. This has now been popularized in America as "momentum investing." My research at the time showed that, if your stock makes a new high on any given day, the probability exceeds 70% that it will make yet another new high in the next 90 days. That was true then, and it's true today. What was also true, at the time, was that, if your stock made a new low, the probabilities exceeded 65% that it would make another new low in the next 90 days.

Tanous: *That's momentum investing, all right.*

Gillam: Exactly. So clearly, all you have to do is buy the new highs, right? The trouble with that approach is that, at the end of the year, you've got hundreds of stocks that you own long, and hundreds that you shorted, and you have no way of getting out, because there is no sell signal for any of them. The second problem with this approach is that it doesn't tell you why highs breed highs and lows breed lows. But the fact is that they do.

What that really means is that excellence breeds excellence. Here's how we get to it. Assume we know that the alpha value of a market index is zero *[by definition]*. We wish to own those sectors and stocks that are now demonstrating superior performance. We'll relate the outperformance to real earnings later. Why don't we divide the market, so that we can figure out which stocks have a positive return, above the index? It doesn't matter how much the index is up or even if it's flat. Remember, our objective is to earn excess market returns. The market might be down 20%. If I'm down 10%, that's excess return—because we beat the index. On a relative basis, we did better using our long style only. Our hedge fund, however, seeks absolute returns, and that's not the same. *[A hedge fund shorts stocks as well as buying stocks and holding them. Hedge funds are generally considered aggressive.]* But for most of the money we manage, we try to develop a return above an index.

So, start with the companies that have positive alphas above the desired index. It turns out that the stocks that have a positive alpha *[above the market]* comprise only 20% of all the stocks in the universe. Some 15% - 20% of stocks will earn *all* of the excess returns after commission and fees! We run the data every Saturday to stay current with the tides of the market. Now, what you really want to have is a stock that is making more money than the market. But someone will say, gee, I don't want to buy it because it just made a new high. Well, the typical stock that we owned in our portfolio in 1995 made 50 new highs over the year. So, if the first time it made a new high you said, gee, I don't want to buy that because it's too high, you missed the next 49 new highs.

Tanous: *Are we back to talking about momentum investing?*

Gillam: You could call it momentum investing, but we have gone further and have discovered and explained mathematically why companies make successive new highs. We think that, more often than not, companies whose share price is doing well *[versus an index]* exhibit a common trait with other stocks that are also doing well; namely, the earnings growth rate is expanding. We've discovered, we believe, that excess market returns occur in a stock for somewhere between one and five quarters. Market inefficiencies never last. The market does catch up. Let's assume that we can calculate a market risk number for every single security. If we can do it, we could then optimize the risk/reward ratio. We calculate risk by taking the standard deviation of the string of returns *[for each stock]* over the time periodicity.

Tanous: *Hold it, Bob. We've got to get back to speaking English.*

Gillam: It's not as hard as it sounds. What we do is calculate a risk number, which is based on the standard deviation of a string of returns. Look at this list. *[We pore over a computer run of alphas.]* This column shows the stocks that have an alpha of, say, 2 or better. These are the stocks you want to own.

Tanous: *So this list represents most of the market?*

Gillam: Right. You don't buy something that has an alpha of zero. Why not? Because by the time you get through with commissions, spreads, and inefficiencies, you wind up with a return less than the market. That's not our business. *[Gillam points to another set of stocks that have alphas close to zero.]* So, what this means is that you don't buy these.

Tanous: *So this is a distribution of returns, and you're saying you want to buy the outliers, which are the star performers.*

Gillam: Yes. But the return, in and of itself, is not enough. Suppose you have an alpha of, say, two. It only means something when it is related to everything else. Now, you could just buy the high alphas. There are fellows who do that. They're called momentum investors.

But here's what you really should be doing, in my opinion. Take an alpha value of two, which is desirable. Ideally, we also would like to have risk below the market's. I was sitting in Denver a number of years ago, looking at managers because I had a hand in the managed money department of Boettcher and Company. We had managers whose performance was all over the chart. We would look at their risk and return, and we'd hire the manager with the right characteristics for the particular client.

What we do at McKinley is look for the stocks whose risk/reward characteristics are optimized, based on our guidelines. Our formula calculates not the theoretical risk, but the actual market risk of a specific security compared to all other securities. *[Risk is often calculated using standard deviation, or the volatility of the stock compared to the volatility of the market.]*

Tanous: *I think what you're doing, is segregating and identifying the high alpha stocks with lower risk from all the others. That gives you potentially higher market returns with acceptable risk.*

Gillam: That's almost right. We can use our understanding of risk to optimize return at a given risk level. Two years ago one of our clients asked us to create a portfolio with a risk characteristic similar to, and no more than, the S&P 500, but earning a higher net return. We did that by identifying the market risk, holding it as a constant, and optimizing alpha. We've been able to earn 50% or so more than the index, with similar risk to the market.

For the first five months of 1996, our large-cap portfolios are up 19% to 20% versus the Russell 1000, which is up 9.8% or so. In our aggressive portfolio style, where we buy small and large-cap stocks, we're up about 35%, while the Russell 2000 has gained about 15% for the same period. In fact, our aggressive equity portfolio has averaged twice the index return over the last six years or so, after fees and commissions.

Tanous: *That's extraordinary. Is this unhedged?*

Gillam: Unhedged. Straight long.

Tanous: *If we use standard deviation as a measure of risk, it seems to me your standard deviation is about three times that of the market.*

Gillam: Not true. The fact is, we run several different styles. My mid- and large-cap portfolio is designed to have a standard deviation about the same as the market. And it does, we think. In our aggressive growth equity style, the one you have the numbers on, we calculate our standard deviation a little differently than others do. The price you pay for "excess returns," however, is occasional excess volatility.

Tanous: *Let's summarize before we go on. You're saying that the alpha is the excess return of that particular security compared to an index.*

Gillam: Could be any index, as long as you are consistent. What we want is relative alpha value. The alpha and the standard deviation, combined as a fraction, create what we call the OR index. It's a measure of the risk and reward. What McKinley requires is that the alpha value be positive, and for every additional measure of risk we assume, we demand more return.

Some people look at stocks differently. They might say, I'm going to be a value investor. I'm going to buy this particular stock because its book-to-price ratio is high, or it has a large cash flow. A correlation analysis of this approach shows little relation to stock performance. Think about it. The fellows who buy value, what do they believe in? You might say it's book-to-price.

Tanous: *That's fairly classic.*

Gillam: Okay. Others say value is cash flow per share. My point is that there is no definition of value. If the stocks that have low price-to-book ratios do outperform over time, by definition, they will be the stocks that have positive alpha values. We would own them at that time, and not before.

Tanous: *There is a definition of value stock. It's high book value to market value.*

Gillam: That's not true. I know guys who say that value has to do with cash flow per share. I'm a value investor. Every value investor I have ever known has different views of what value is. The ultimate value is to optimize the equation of alpha versus risk. We're in the business of excess returns. We're not in the excuse business. We are not going to try and excuse poor performance by saying that our "style" is now out of favor.

Tanous: *Let's go back to excess returns.*

Gillam: Once we do our analysis of the 13,000 companies in our database, we screen out the top 5%, say 650 or 700 stocks that exhibit the highest OR score, or risk-reward ratio. These stocks are often inefficiently priced because the earnings growth rates are accelerating, which creates a lag between market expectations and earnings performance. The next question is, why do these companies typically have excess returns for one to five quarters?

Tanous: *That's the question.*

Gillam: It's taken me 20 years to get the answer.

Tanous: *Okay. What's the answer?*

Gillam: The answer is that these companies have a positive value for the second derivative of the earnings growth rate.

Tanous: *Hold it right there. I just heard the sound of ten thousand of my books slamming shut. We have just lost all the readers, including me.*

Gillam: Okay. Let me explain it this way. If a company has earnings growing each year by 15%, and has had such growth for years, then the market's level of uncertainty is very low; everybody knows! What if the growth rate itself is growing? Then, not everyone knows, and, indeed, uncertainty is high. When earnings growth *exceeds* market expectations, excess returns often occur as the market adjusts to the new reality, usually very quickly. The typical performance of McKinley stocks during earnings *[announcement]* seasons, four times a year, is such that almost two-thirds of our holdings report earnings above the *highest* earnings estimate on the Street, and much higher than the mean estimate. Those stocks are inefficiently priced!

Tanous: *That's a lot better.*

Gillam: It doesn't have to be some Silicon Valley stock. Suppose you had a company that, five years ago, grew earnings 3%; four years ago they were growing at 6%; three years ago, 11%; two years ago, 14%; and now it's 22%. That is acceleration of the growth rate, a better circumstance than a company whose earnings are up a constant 15% a year. In the latter circumstance, the market knows and expects 15% and the stock is priced to anticipate 15%. It's in the first case that you have the opportunity for excess returns. It's not the growth in earnings. It's the growth of the growth rate of earnings. We want companies where the rate of growth is intensifying.

Tanous: *Even so, some of these companies won't always do well. Some will have problems and their stocks will do badly. How do you identify those, or don't you?*

Gillam: The most important thing about making money in the stock market is to realize that you're hunting with a shotgun. That means you'll have outliers. If you're wrong, you're wrong. So we sell immediately if our expectations are incorrect. We follow the dead-cat-bounce rule.

Tanous: *Excuse me?*

Gillam: The dead-cat-bounce rule. If a cat jumps off the top floor of a skyscraper, when it hits the pavement, it will bounce a little bit, and on that first bounce we sell. We're out. If you're wrong, get out. If we buy a stock at 50 and something goes wrong and the next trade is at 33, the first trade at 33 is me. I'm out. The price you pay for holding a loser is that you allow the loser to occupy a spot in the portfolio that could otherwise be occupied by a winner! Selling is much harder than buying.

Tanous: *We haven't talked about fundamentals in this process.*

Gillam: There are a lot of fundamentals. After we have done the risk/reward work, the second thing we do is balance sheet integrity analysis. We do not want any embarrassing events for our clients. Remember, we narrowed our search from 13,000 to 650 companies based on a risk/reward analysis. Our next set of screens narrow the potential portfolio picks even further. We don't buy anything below $10 a share. We don't buy anything unless it trades a minimum of 50,000 share a day. These two screens eliminate a lot of little companies that don't trade very much. Next, we look at the balance sheet. We have a maximum leverage allowed on the balance sheet, depending on the specific industry. Steel stocks have a different number than, say, communications stocks.

Tanous: *So you do classic balance sheet analysis.*

Gillam: Yes. We use our company designed screens to do this analysis quickly. We do it every week. Red flags can appear abruptly. If we own it and the numbers change, we sell it. We look at the quick ratio to be sure a company has enough cash to pay its bills. *[The quick ratio, or acid test ratio, is: current assets, excluding inventory, divided by current liabilities.]* The definition of corporate bankruptcy is not zero net worth, it's that you don't have the cash to pay the bills when they're due. Two-thirds of our 650 stocks will be eliminated by the balance sheet, liquidity and pricing tests. There are only three rules that count: safety, liquidity, and rate of return. Is there anything else?

Tanous: *How about what the company does?*

Gillam: It doesn't matter, as long as the business is legitimate! It could be hula hoops, widgets, or steel bars. It doesn't matter. We will not, however, put more than 20% of our clients' money in any one sector. We do know what they do, and we follow the research of every analyst that follows the company. Our quantitative data ranks every stock's earnings acceleration and growth rate, on a scale of 1 to 99. That's our E rank *[E is for earnings]*. We rank growth rate acceleration *[or deceleration]* into a 1 to 99 grid. These rankings are recompiled daily from data garnered around the world by our computer system. An E ranking of 1 means that your earnings growth rate is accelerating more than 99% of all stocks in our universe. It's a comparative value, not an absolute value. All of our holdings must be in the top 20th percentile, or better, to be included in one of our portfolios.

Tanous: *You track earnings estimates, presumably.*

Gillam: We try to use all the data services that provide earnings intelligence.

Tanous: *I presume that if earnings come in above the estimate, you've got to be pretty quick to take advantage of that.*

Gillam: Actually, we try to own stocks *before* good earnings are reported. That's the trick. Some of the data services such as I.B.E.S. *[Institutional Brokers' Earnings System]* track the pre-earnings announcement chatter. They have a database of pre-announcement information that we use with our other quantitative systems. The theory is that, if a company is going to put a spin on a bad number, it does it as early as it can. So, for a number of days before a company actually reports, we do a ratio of the percentage change *[in estimates]* over the number of days. Then we can assign a probability that the company is going to hit the expected earnings number or go over or under the expectation.

Tanous: *I see. Some talk about earnings revisions long before the actual announcement might be a harbinger of bad news. Who prepares that?*

Gillam: I.B.E.S. and others. We blend all the sources into our final ranking. Market intelligence comes from many, many sources these days.

Tanous: *What's an example of a pre-announcement?*

Gillam: Say the company announces a charge in the first quarter of $6 million. I.B.E.S. puts it in the database, and we adjust the earnings estimate immediately. But we do it intelligently. Suppose the company had a terrific quarter and was going to earn, say, $0.30. As a result of the charge, their earnings might now be down $0.06, but that was only a one-time charge. The quarter was actually very good. The prior quarter was $0.20 and the Street was looking for $0.24 this quarter, but they did $0.30! It's very important to know that. Sometimes the Street is fooled by looking at a reported number and doesn't look behind the number. You've got to keep your databases current if you expect to outperform. We try to follow every analyst live.

Tanous: *From Alaska?*

Gillam: Right. The proper use of technology today is to gather vast quantities of data from every spot on the globe and distill it quickly into usable buy and sell decisions. Communications systems know no geographic boundary. McKinley portfolios regularly own the superior stocks in the leading groups; technology keeps it that way. It's not, what *we think is going to happen*. It is *what is actually happening*. We are in the reality business. Technology keeps us informed and realistic. While a guru may forecast future events, we try to be pragmatic about what is happening now.

Tanous: *Tell me more about your E rank system of 1 to 99.*

Gillam: There are five sub-components of the score. It's not only earnings, it's the quality, the size, and the speed of change. The SUE index *[Standard Unexpected Earnings]* is an important subset of the E rank. We give you a score much like Value Line does, only theirs is 1 to 5 and ours is 1 to 99. If we give you a score of 10, it means that, based on all of the numbers and comparisons we are looking at, your company's earnings growth rate is accelerating and that acceleration exceeds that of 90% of the universe. That stock would be a desirable holding if it meets all our other screens.

Tanous: *This sounds a lot like momentum investing.*

Gillam: It's not. Momentum is stock price. We're talking about accelerating growth rates. We will also go through the Graham and Dodd methodology—the balance sheet and liquidity tests—and it's all very important. We pay attention to leverage, and quality of earnings. If a company has too much leverage on the balance sheet, we drop it from consideration. Leverage creates bankruptcies. Our stocks all have a ranking of earnings growth rate of 1 to 99.

Tanous: *Can a stock have all your desired characteristics and still be too expensive?*

Gillam: Yes. If a stock's price-earnings ratio, on estimated earnings for the next year, exceeds the projected growth rate, we won't buy it.

Tanous: *That's very interesting as well as very fundamental. You're saying that if the company is growing by 30% and the price-earnings is, say, 35 × earnings, you don't buy it because the P/E exceeded the growth rate.*

Gillam: Right. It might even be a sell signal. That's why we sold IBM after we had a double. That's why we sold Microsoft. That's also the reason we don't buy new issues—in our system we can't assess risk levels without a history of trading.

Tanous: *What's a good summary of your investment philosophy, Bob?*

Gillam: An acceleration in the earnings growth rate will often lead to excess market returns. An example of this is McDonnell Douglas, a low risk stock where acceleration has worked magic. It was one of our largest holdings last year. It had less risk than the market and a great return. Why? Because McDonnell Douglas reinvented itself to reflect smaller military budgets. The company had been misunderstood. This company reported earnings above estimates for several quarters recently. The result was a stock price that doubled in the last five quarters. Earnings growth rates are everything. McKinley stocks regularly beat the Street estimates. Excellent market results occur when your holdings perform above expectations.

Tanous: *How does your investment theory work in a down market when the market is not paying as much attention to earnings? How does your philosophy pan out in a bear market?*

Gillam: In down markets earnings acceleration is much less important than capitalization. We try to keep our returns within the market range when markets decline.

Tanous: *This sounds like a very disciplined investment philosophy.*

Gillam: Exactly. Our disciplined structure led us to Cognos Inc., one of my largest holdings. At the end of last year, this was a $40 stock, now it's almost $70. The four or five analysts that follow this company have been between 10% and 30% low on earnings for the last three reporting periods. Cognos has surprised us with good news. These were estimates for the first period of 1996 *[Gillam shows me a list].* They reported $0.73; that's three cents above the high estimate. Now, if you look carefully, they reported on the 10th of April, and the stock was about 60. The stock ran from 60 to 69 on that news. Excess market returns. This is typical of a McKinley stock.

Tanous: *The question is: How did you know that this stock was going to report better earnings than the Street expected?*

Gillam: The E rank, 1 to 99. If you're 99, you're near death. You want a company like Cognos, with an E rank of 4.

Tanous: *Does 99 mean that it's underperforming the estimates?*

Gillam: It means a deceleration in the growth rate. Your products might be outdated, Somebody came up with a better gizmo than yours. Your technology is lagging. That sort of thing.

Tanous: *What does a 50 mean?*

Gillam: Fifty means you're the median. It means that out of any number of stocks, say 100 in this case, there are 49 above you and 49 below. What we would like is for all of our stocks to be up near the top. Here's another one with a very high E rank, California Amplifier. In January *[1996]* the stock was 15. The stock is almost 40 today. The median return is 4.25% . . . per week! I've got a six figure position in that stock. As long as the company stays on track, we'll stay with it. Another great stock the last several quarters is C-Cube. Look at McAfee and Ascend. Great stocks.

Tanous: *We talked to a few of people who own Ascend.*

Gillam: We own a boat. A full boat is a full allocation. That means 3% of my portfolio is in this stock. Here's another one, CDN *[Cadence Design]*. The high estimate was $0.38; it came in at $0.42. HBOC *[HBO & Co., a health maintenance company, not the cable TV company]* was a blowout! The high estimate was $0.39; it came in at $0.46. It gap-traded up 14 points on the next trade. Our stocks do that. Here's Raychem. The high estimate was $0.97, and we had a big run in it; it came in at $0.89. So we were wrong. Next trade: we're out.

Tanous: *That is certainly consistent with what you've told us.*

Gillam: Earnings are everything. It's not the growth of earnings, it's the growth of the growth rate. So we have built a big computer system here. We've got 21 employees and we've got 50 computer systems. Those satellite receivers you see on the roof are ours.

Tanous: *You haven't fully answered my question about how all this works in down markets.*

Gillam: Our objective in down markets is to do no worse than the market. If the market pulls in 10% and we're down 9% or 10%, please don't fire me. 1994 is a prime example. We were down 3.2%. The S&P was actually down a little over 1%, if you take out dividends. So we were in the hunt. Now, if in a down market you are able to do no worse than the market, but in an up market you can do double or triple or better, then it's just a matter of time.

Tanous: *Let's talk about performance. Your numbers are amazing. For the last five calendar years, based on the numbers I have, your composite was up over 31% per year net. That's pretty impressive. What is your portfolio turnover?*

Gillam: Sometimes low, sometimes not. For example, if you take our top ten holdings at the end of 1995, at the end of March 1996, we owned all of them except one. But there are times when the market rotates and leadership changes. We will be concentrated in the seven or eight leading groups. When you get a change in one of the leading groups, we can have a huge turnover. For example, on November 7, 1995, the semiconductor analyst at Merrill, who has been following the industry for years, had a conference call. During the call, he made the comment that he thought that D-RAM chip prices would be down 40% in the next one to five quarters. While he was speaking, we retrieved the data on Micron from our computers and we discovered that the pre-tax net was 47%. So, let's see, 47% minus 40% is . . . not very much! Of my top seven stocks at that time, five were semiconductor stocks—LSI, Altera, etc. Before the call was over, I had sold every single semiconductor stock we owned.

Tanous: *That's funny. When I was in Richard Driehaus'* [page 74] *office, we were walking around the office and he decided to sell his entire position in Altera.*

Gillam: We sold 100% of our chip stocks in less than ten minutes. We were able to do it because of our internal system which we call BFG 9000 *[don't ask]*. You know, some analyst comes up here and I know right off if they're a prop head. In Alaska, if you're a computer whiz, you're called a prop head. Down in Texas, you're called a gear head. It's a language thing. When we get these people to come in here and look at us, we know immediately if they're prop heads. We show them our trading system, the BFG 9000, and if they know what it is, they're prop heads. If they don't, they majored in English. All the prop heads know you have to have a system that allows you to move on a dime. If you're a mutual fund, you don't need it. You only have one account to manage, the fund. But if you run several thousand individual accounts, like we do, it's different. Our BFG 9000 allows us to do that.

Tanous: *Now, in the case of the D-RAM chips, which you just told us about, a good part of your decision was related to your confidence in the analyst. I suppose that's an important factor.*

Gillam: We rate analysts on a scale of 1 to 5. If you're a 1 analyst, and you change an estimate big time, up or down, I listen to you. If you're a 5 analyst, you're just a freshman. You have no track record. But guys who can move the market, you pay attention to. I pay attention.

Tanous: *How are your accounts divided? When new clients come in, what style choices do they have?*

Gillam: Our primary product, the one that made us famous, is our growth equity style with what we call an "anything" capitalization portfolio. We could have an IBM right next to a Cadence Design. The stocks in the portfolio have an average capitalization of about $1.7 billion. These are all separately managed accounts.

Tanous: *That's not that small. So you're not buying really small companies, presumably because your screens require a minimum amount of market liquidity.*

Gillam: Sure. We don't buy anything below a market cap of $200 million. And for the client who says I really want excess returns, but I want less volatility, we accommodate them, too. As I mentioned, a client once asked us for a portfolio with a standard deviation about the same as the S&P 500 with optimization above that. So we created it. We run this for several large institutions.

Tanous: *Can anybody have access to this?*

Gillam: Anybody. That's our mid- to large-cap portfolio, which some clients call the "Blue Chip" portfolio.

Tanous: *So it's not a small-cap product. What has the performance been like?*

Gillam: It's a mid- to large-cap portfolio. The average capitalization is about $8 billion. It's presently up 20%, after fees, for the first five months of 1996. We use this identical style in the international markets, which also beats the relative indexes by 75% or 80%. So we have three portfolios: One is an "anything" cap, which has more risk than the market; the second, the mid to large-cap, has the same risk as the market; and the international portfolio is the third.

Tanous: *The "anything" cap, by definition, let's you buy almost anything. How has it done?*

Gillam: The "anything" cap, as I mentioned, is also our growth equity portfolio. Even though we can buy almost anything, we insist on liquidity. This portfolio is up 34% in the first five months. That compares to 15% for the Russell 2000.

Tanous: *Very impressive. How about your international portfolio?*

Gillam: That's up 17% this year, after fees. The EAFE *[Europe, Australia, and Far East Index created by Morgan Stanley Capital International]* benchmark is up around 4%.

Tanous: *You also have a hedge fund, I believe.*

Gillam: Yes. It's called McKinley Select Partners, and we also have an off-shore version for foreign investors. The minimum in the domestic partnership is $500,000 and $2 million for the overseas version. It's a partnership, so we can take a standard performance fee, and we can also employ a short strategy. The fund is up 72% this year *[through May 1996]*, before taking our performance fee.

Tanous: *Sounds like you earned it! What is the total amount you now have under management?*

Gillam: About $750 million.

Tanous: *How can a relatively small investor access you?*

Gillam: One of our business areas is what we call the carriage trade—individual accounts, which a lot of firms won't do. I do it because I get to meet exceptional people. So I like that business. But we have certain requirements. The account has to be in a wrap fee environment, so that commission brokers don't overcharge the clients. *[So-called wrap fees are offered by many of the larger brokerage firms. They combine, or "wrap," all commission charges and manager compensation in one annual fee, which can sometimes be as high as 3% of the amount invested.]*

Tanous: *But wrap fees can be pretty expensive too, you know.*

Gillam: They are if the manager doesn't trade, like value managers, who in my opinion trade much less often than someone like us. The reason most people don't achieve excess returns is that they're lazy with the time they devote to their investments. If you take an hour-and-a-half train ride from Stamford down to the Street, think of the transportation time. And are you going to go to the office on Saturday to put in more time? No way. Notice that today is Saturday and our staff is here.

Tanous: *Back to the minimums.*

Gillam: We take certain wrap accounts at $150,000.

Tanous: *Presumably, you have to go through a large brokerage firm to get that. Who do you deal with?*

Gillam: Smith Barney, Piper Jaffray, Dain Bosworth, A. G. Edwards. We like firms with a low cost to the client. We also deal with commission brokers, but only if they charge rock bottom commissions. We don't want our performance penalized at the client's expense by high commissions. Our minimum institutional account is now $10 million. I remember when we were featured in *Money* magazine. The guy said, you'll now get 500 calls from 500 people who want to invest 500 dollars! He was right.

Tanous: *Before we conclude, I have to ask you about where you live. I just made my first trip ever to Alaska to meet with you. I'm here in your offices, in the distance we can see Mount McKinley, which is 180 miles away. That tells you something about the environment around here! Yet in this modern office, which is as high tech as anything I've seen, we're here on a Saturday and you've got a lot of people working.*

Gillam: Our staff usually gets in before 4 A.M. and they start running the quant stuff. We sit around and talk strategy. The kind of people who come here must have some frontier spirit. If the only way a person is going to be comfortable in his environment is riding a subway, he's not going to make it here. Most of the people here live within 15 minutes of the office. I live on a lake, where I park my float plane in my front yard. It's ten minutes to the office. The king salmon will start coming over the dam in the next ten days and I can stand on my dock and catch king salmon. The market closes at noon. I go jump in my flying machine. It doesn't get dark till 11:30 in the summer. I can land on some lakes and rivers and fish and have a great time. There are a lot of fun things to do here. I have more snow machines than cars. There are virtually no taxes in Alaska. Why pay state taxes and high sales taxes if you don't have to? We're the same distance to Tokyo as we are to London, which is great for an international player. Our specialty products, the hedge funds in particular, have big participations in Europe and Asia. We make money and we have fun.

Tanous: *It speaks to the technological advances in communications that you can be here in Alaska and get exactly the same quality of information on the same timely basis as somebody in New York City.*

Gillam: When we started, we figured we were able to do it because of this new, incredibly fast computer called the 286! We originally bought six of them. They used to take 13 or 14 hours to do our quant runs. We now can run them in 35 minutes. Our pricing comes down via satellite. We don't use phone lines—they're unreliable. It's all part of our philosophy to generate excess market returns. Everyone here is motivated by fear and greed. Those are the perfect reasons for someone hiring us. We're not motivated by anything other than performance. I've never had an employee leave. Why? Because we pay them extraordinary amounts of money.

Tanous: *What are your personal plans for the future?*

Gillam: I'm going to be 50 in a couple of months. I intend to do this for ten years. I will see to it that almost every one of my employees gets rich, if they perform. If they get rich, I will have done pretty well for myself, too. There is nothing in the world that excites me more than coming to work and seeing that we beat the index yesterday, last week, last month, and last quarter—by 2 or 3:1—for our clients.

I dare say that beating the index by 2 or 3:1 would excite me, too. And Bob Gillam has done it. His performance record proves the validity of his methods, although we haven't yet seen how he will do in a really sloppy market. Interesting that he comes right out and tells you that his goal is not absolute, but relative performance. If the market is down 10% and he is down only 9%, he figures he's doing his job. That is a perfectly realistic approach, given his style.

Bob Gillam is clearly a product of his surroundings. Perched amid the towering terrain of the Alaskan frontier, you might think of him as the John Templeton-of-the-North, although the pristine beaches of Nassau (where Templeton works) are definitely not his style. Gillam is as rugged as the environment in which he grew up. His personality is fully reflected in his style of investment management. I keep remembering Rex Sinquefield's (page 257) admonition about this style of investing: "Not for the faint-hearted." Yes, indeed.

You may also have been struck by the stark contrast between the style of someone like Bob Gillam and other types of managers— value managers, for example. You and I may see the benefit of both growth and value styles; Bob doesn't want to hear about it. But his singlemindedness does underline the contrast between different styles and the importance of considering style in your choice of investment managers and funds. For those who seek excess returns and are comfortable with his style, there are few, if any, better practitioners than Bob Gillam.

DAVID E. SHAW

When you enter the offices of D. E. Shaw & Co., you immediately know that you are not in a typical Wall Street firm. That's perfectly all right, since D. E. Shaw is the antithesis of what most of us expect of an investment firm. Bathed in secrecy, D. E. Shaw is spoken about in financial circles in whispers, as if the mere mention of the name portends the discussion of classified material with its deep, dark secrets. Shaw's name is little-known to the general public. But the firm, and its founder, David Shaw, have acquired a growing reputation in financial circles as the king of the quants. Shaw is the smartest, most successful, and his firm is the most secretive of those that employ higher mathematics, and the most powerful computers, to create trades and arbitrage situations that make good money.

I promised you that our interviews would not be with money managers who used exotic techniques that none of us could hope to emulate, but rather with managers who buy stocks and make a great deal of money doing it. I also promised there would be one exception. David Shaw is that exception. D. E. Shaw's offices are futuristic and stark, perhaps a harbinger of the future of money management. The dress code appears to be jeans, polo shirt, and a Ph.D. in math. The office space has been cited in Architectural Digest, *and pictures of it have been displayed at The Museum of Modern Art. The design is meant to focus on the intersection of finance and technology.*

Prior to meeting the firm's founder, I took a tour with Trey Beck, Nick Gianakouros, and Marlene Jupiter. We visited what they call a "trading pod," which perfectly resembles the control room of a NASA space capsule. The press has reported that D. E. Shaw, on busy days, has accounted for as much as 5% of the trading volume on the New York Stock Exchange.

On another floor, a huge trading room, much like its Wall Street counterparts, houses dozens of young—dare I say?—rocket scientists. They work with proprietary software, designed in-house. The average age of the staff appears to be under 30. Most of them have graduate degrees in math and computer science. There are few, if any, MBAs. In a nutshell, the firm devises mathematical algorithms to create trading opportunities based on inefficiencies in markets worldwide.

Typically, the firm accounts for as much as 2% of the NYSE trading volume every day. The large number of trades results from Shaw's quantitative trading strategies which are designed to make tiny profits consistently, producing above average returns. How much exactly? It's hard to tell, but Shaw's investors wear big smiles. The estimates range from 20% to 30% a year.

Let's take a journey into the future: meet David Shaw.

Tanous: *How did you first get interested in stocks?*

Shaw: I was curious about them when I was quite young. My stepfather was a professor of finance at UCLA. He built part of his reputation publishing papers that failed to find any evidence that it was possible to beat the stock market! So I grew up with the random walk model *[which holds that movements in stock prices cannot be predicted]* and the efficient market hypothesis. I still believe that, to a first approximation, those theories are largely true. At our firm, we make our living by finding the rough edges in the efficient market, but it's remarkable how hard it is to use new information to beat the market. I grew up believing that there was probably no way to do what we now do, and there was a long period when I had nothing to do with any of this.

Tanous: *I assume this was during your time in academia.*

Shaw: That's right. I was trained as a computer scientist, and still really think of myself as a computer scientist, as do many of the people here. I enjoy that tremendously. I finished my Ph.D. at Stanford and was a professor at Columbia for a while, but was lured away by Morgan Stanley with two enticements. One was an economic one: I was able to make many, many times the salary I was making as a professor. I was thinking about having a family and knew I would need some sort of net worth if I wanted to feed and educate my children.

The other lure was that they were claiming to be able to do something that I had learned from my stepfather was probably impossible—to beat the market. That was a challenge. At first I was very skeptical. I asked a lot of questions of the people at Morgan Stanley, who were clearly very smart. But I knew how easy it was to fall for a statistical artifact and believe that you actually had something that worked when, in fact, you were just lucky. They managed to convince me, without telling me how they were doing it at that point, that there was no question they really did have something that was working.

Tanous: *This isn't the proverbial black box, is it?*

Shaw: I can't comment on anything that was done at Morgan Stanley, but our approach at D. E. Shaw & Co. is very different from what's sometimes referred to as the "black box" approach, for a particular mathematical reason. If you just plow through enough data, as long as your model is rich enough—by which I mean that it has enough parameters, enough different variables—you can always find patterns in the data. But the vast majority of the time, those patterns aren't useful. They are ones that don't have any predictive value. That's what's called "over-fitting" the data. It's the big problem that most amateurs at this run into. They get very excited; they think they've discovered something; but, if they do it by simply sifting through a lot of historical data, the patterns they come up with are generally not useful for trading.

Tanous: *Are you saying that they're forcing the conclusion?*

Shaw: That's basically right. You're in a situation where you will always find something, whether it's really there or not. The process of finding things that are real, that you can actually trade on, is unfortunately very difficult and extremely expensive. It requires a huge amount of research. We have done that through a scientific process—we formulate hypotheses about how the market works, and then test them rigorously. The vast majority of our hypotheses turn out to be false. Probably 90% of all the research we do leads nowhere.

Tanous: *That's fascinating. Can you identify what it is about the 10% that works, that makes them work?*

Shaw: Unfortunately not, or else we wouldn't do the other 90%! That's the reason we now have 350 employees around the world, and why, at the core, we are really a research organization. We have virtually no people here who study companies and decide whether the products that they make are good products, or whether the CEO is a good CEO, or whether the market they're attacking is a good one, although those are all very important things. In fact, although I think in many ways we are a model for the future of a big part of Wall Street, it's worth keeping in mind that, for much of what Wall Street does now, not only are we not good at it, we don't do it at all. I believe that many of those functions will always be important, like analysts studying companies and understanding industries—there's an important reason for such activities. But in our case, with the exception of the computer industry and other information-related industries, which we have to understand very well, we have no expertise at all in the traditional investment research area.

Our particular niche involves understanding the mathematics of the market. The service we provide is that we make the markets more efficient and more liquid. Unfortunately for us, by doing that, we also reduce the number of profit opportunities for ourselves. That's why we can't simply take what we're doing now and scale up from our present capital *[about $800 million]*, and just take ten times as much money, and make ten times more profit. It wouldn't work.

Tanous: *Is that because, after the first $800 million, efficiency comes back?*

Shaw: That's exactly right. We tend to make the markets efficient by making our profit as a low-cost producer of market efficiency.

Tanous: *I want to go back to your 10% that works. I'm fascinated by that. The efficient market hypothesis holds that whatever pattern you find has no predictive value.*

Shaw: Right.

Tanous: *So, you're telling me that, that's true most of the time, but, guess what? There are some patterns that we have been able to find that do have predictive value. Is that what you're saying?*

Shaw: That is true, but they *[the patterns with predictive value]* are also generally very small. We trade in enormous volume. It's been accurately reported in the press that on occasion we've accounted for more than 5% of all the New York Stock Exchange volume.

Tanous: *That's incredible.*

Shaw: That does include our customer transactions as well as trading for our own account. It's very large, but in many cases we're making unbelievably small profits, on average. In fact, in a given strategy, we might only make a profit 51 times out of 100; 49 times out of 100 we lose. It's like having a very, very tiny house advantage in an enormously large casino with a huge number of customers.

Tanous: *Could you give me an example that most people would understand of a "10%-type-thing" that works?*

Shaw: I've been asked that before. First of all, even if we could, we probably wouldn't describe it publicly, since we'd be giving out very valuable proprietary information. But the fact is that almost all the things we do are so complicated—and there's a good reason for that—that it would be very hard to encapsulate the basic idea succinctly. The vast majority of all the straightforward, obvious, easily explainable things that even a highly-trained mathematician might try simply don't work. That's probably because people out there have already taken advantage of the simple arbitrage opportunities. So, in fact, most of what we do is difficult to describe, highly complex, and very hard to find. We've spent many tens of millions of research dollars to discover all the subtle things we now know about the markets, and our job gets harder, and our results get more complex, every year.

Tanous: *Tens of millions on research?*

Shaw: It's a very expensive proposition, and it's not a one-time thing.

   If we were starting today, which we aren't, I'm not sure we would even go into this business, just because the barriers to entry would be so high. When we started we could find a few effects that were big enough for us to make a profit on, and that paid the bills while we went on and tried to find more. But at this point, none of those individual effects are really that large. Typically, you have to have a number of them to make a profit. Without a critical mass of research results you would actually lose money—a lot of it, and fairly quickly—after accounting for transaction costs.

Even with extremely low execution and clearing expenses, every time you buy something you push the price up a little bit, and every time you sell, you push the price down a bit. In our case, this effect is unusually small because we've done a huge amount of research on minimizing transaction costs and market impact. Nevertheless, even with our transaction costs—which we believe are probably the lowest in the industry in many of the world's largest financial markets—if we found only one or two of these inefficiencies, they typically would be too small for us to make money. They wouldn't be as large as costs of making the transaction. So every time we might make a trade, we'd actually lose money. But if you have a number of inefficiencies and you can find a way to combine them properly, in some cases, several of the inefficiencies will all point in the same direction, and the sum of all of those inefficiencies will be greater than the transaction costs.

Tanous: *But is that the principle? I mean, if you had to summarize most of what you do, is that it?*

Shaw: Yes. Most of what we do, with a few exceptions, does have this characteristic. We'll typically be looking at 10 or 12 different sources of inefficiency, each of which was monstrously difficult to find, and each of which is very small. Occasionally, they'll combine and surpass our transaction costs. Even then, we're just barely able to break through the transaction cost barrier, do our trading, and move on to the next set of inefficiencies.

Tanous: *David, could you give me an example, using types of securities, so that we can get an understanding of what a transaction might be?*

Shaw: Well, that part is easy enough to describe. The vast majority of our strategies are working in many of the instruments in a given country. So we might be trading in stocks, bonds, options, futures, warrants, convertible bonds—a large number of different instruments. Our technique is to look at all of them, all at once. There's no one single trade. By way of contrast, the early approaches to quantitative trading might involve buying one thing and then selling short some related security.

Tanous: *Exactly. That's my old-fashioned idea of arbitrage. You have a convertible and you calculate that the convertible price is out of whack with the price of the underlying stock, so you short one and buy the other. That's my simplistic view of arbitrage.*

Shaw: That's actually a fairly sophisticated view, since most people don't understand how that works. Using that classical type of arbitrage, where you might buy a convertible bond and then short the underlying stock, you actually could make money 10 or 15 years ago. Back then, the state-of-the-art was represented by trading groups like Princeton Newport Partners, co-founded by Ed Thorpe, who made his early reputation using quantitative techniques to beat the blackjack dealers in Las Vegas. That was a time when you could make money with a single trade in a couple of instruments. These days, it's a lot harder to find a simple trade like that, so we're forced to search through a huge universe of securities looking for trading opportunities that are much more complex, that often involve a large number of different positions in a lot of different instruments. We now collect data in real time from over 100 exchanges and over-the-counter markets around the world. The data is pumped into our ethernets, our local area networks, and the computers that execute our trades in various parts of the world can look at the data and find disparities. These disparities typically involve many different instruments.

Tanous: *Doesn't a disparity, by the nature of what we're talking about, refer to a disparity between two different things?*

Shaw: It's usually between many different things, but at least two. The unfortunate part is that the original two-thing disparity approach doesn't work well anymore. For that reason, our optimizer typically has to look at a huge number of different things.

Tanous: *What exactly is an optimizer?*

Shaw: The purpose of a portfolio optimizer is to trade off risk and return in some predefined way, and to try to come up with a portfolio that's as close as possible to optimal in terms of those risk/return criteria. What's optimal for any given investor depends on his or her risk-versus-return preferences. The optimizer knows about things like transaction costs, the hedging of various risk factors, and the principles of diversification. So it constructs a portfolio that is nearly optimal with respect to some risk/reward criterion, and then it modifies it continuously as new data come in.

Tanous: *What does the optimizer look like? Is it a computer program, an algorithm, what is it?*

Shaw: It's both of those things. We design optimization algorithms, and then we realize them by writing a computer program. An algorithm is an abstract thing which you make concrete by writing a program. As an example of what such a program might do, the optimizer might find that one security looks under-priced relative to all these other different instruments, but if I actually bought that security, then I would have too much exposure to automobile stocks, and I would also tend to be short interest rates, because I know this company is sensitive to interest rates. I might also be making an implicit bet on economic cyclicality, and if the economy started to go bad, I might lose money that way.

Tanous: *I think I understand. If you find one thing that looks attractive, you can't just buy that. You have to hedge the new thing, so you determine what the different influences on it could be. It could be interest rates; it could be the economy; it could be competing industries. You establish positions in these other areas to hedge all the new risk. Is that right?*

Shaw: That would be a simple model, but in practice you never really look at an isolated trade. You have to look at the whole universe. We use an optimizer that takes into consideration all the factors we know about—which isn't necessarily all the factors that exist, but all the ones we've discovered—both for predicting profit and also for minimizing various sorts of risk. That doesn't mean eliminating them. It's the sort of thing you were describing, where you analyze the influences on a given stock, get information on all of the related stocks, bonds, options and so forth, and then construct a portfolio that tries to get as many of those risk factors as possible to cancel out. But it doesn't happen in a simple way. Everything relates to everything else. The idea is to find as many possible sources of predictive power as possible, to give yourself a very slight edge.

Tanous: *You explain this complicated business so well. There are two things that interest me about this. One is, if I'm a client, how do I quantify the risk I'm taking in this strategy?*

Shaw: Well, I think the first thing you should know is that we don't have clients in the usual sense. We have a private partnership that happens to do proprietary trading, but we're not what's generally referred to as a money manager. What we have is a big body of capital, most of which was provided by private investors who have been with us for years. We use that money not only to buy and sell securities, but to pay our salaries, to buy our computers, and to pay all our other expenses—just like IBM or Microsoft. We haven't broadened our investment base for a long time, and we're not looking for any additional capital. In short, we're not in the business of managing people's money. Our investors are able to review the financial statement of the firm, just as they could if they were investors in IBM. They know a fair amount about us, and about how we operate, but they generally don't try to understand all the details of our individual strategies.

Tanous: *Do they just pray a lot?*

Shaw: I think it varies. They tend to be financially sophisticated, but I think they also know that what's really important is understanding our methodology and our approach, the kind of scientists we hire, and so forth, rather than understanding how any given trade is actually working. In deciding to go into partnership with us, I think they probably evaluated us in much the same way they would go about choosing a physician. You probably wouldn't ask each doctor what medication he'd prescribe for each of a dozen different sets of symptoms, then try to analyze the biochemical basis for all his decisions. If you really wanted to maximize your odds of surviving, you might do better by trying to find out where each doctor went to medical school, whether she's board certified in a relevant specialty, where she has admitting privileges, and how smart, competent, and up-to-date she seems to be.

Tanous: *I think we've all gotten the picture that these are very complicated trades. Even if you capture the inefficiency that you seek, it's going to get corrected very quickly. Is it reasonable to assume that these trades don't last very long?*

Shaw: It depends on the trade, but very often that's true. The range of things that we trade on varies, from things that happen very quickly, all the way up to things that can last for years. They're all typically combined together within a common optimization framework.

Tanous: *So some can last for years?*

Shaw: Yes, some can be very long term.

Tanous: *Given the amount of capital, given the fact that the effect is, as you put it, small, if you have a trade on for a year, can I assume you're going to lose money?*

Shaw: Because of the cost of capital?

Tanous: *Exactly.*

Shaw: It tends to be sort of proportional. Generally, a long term trade would be something where the amount of return you get per unit of time might be comparable to another trade that you put on for a shorter period.

Tanous: *So built into the system is a feature, whatever it is, that factors in the cost of time.*

Shaw: That's right. Although I forgot to mention it earlier, the optimizer also knows about the cost of capital, and it's not likely to get very excited about something that would tie up a lot of capital for a long time.

Tanous: *David, you're what Wall Street people call a "quant." I'd love to know what your definition of a quant is.*

Shaw: I think, traditionally, that word has been used to describe people who use quantitative, or mathematical techniques—and these days that generally also involves computational techniques—to make investment decisions.

The key thing that distinguishes pure quants, which is what we are, from other types of investors, is whether human judgment is involved in finding profit opportunities. Now, a lot of human judgment is involved in what we do, but it's not in making the decisions about what to buy and sell. In our case, human judgment comes in during the research phase—discovering things, formulating hypotheses, testing them, and designing algorithms. Those are all very people-intensive activities. The other part that's intrinsically human, and very important, is watching for "real world" events that could increase risk.

If you're a pure quantitative trader, you're not using those human beings to say, I think this market is going up, or this looks like a good company. You are using them, if you're a good quant, to say things like, boy, this phenomenon could be explained by the fact that there's something here that the market knows about and that our computer doesn't. So from that human analysis, we may conclude that we don't want to have too much exposure to this because it could be very risky. Those are the kinds of situations where human judgment is needed in our business.

Tanous: *Your employees are different from those you normally see in a money management shop or a Wall Street firm. Tell me what you look for in your employees.*

Shaw: What we care about most is finding, literally, the very best people in the world for whatever the position is. Although what we're best known for is our quantitative research people, the same principle applies to everybody at D. E. Shaw & Co. We spend an unbelievable amount of money on recruitment, relative to our total operational budget. In particular, we spend a lot identifying the very best people in the world in whatever categories that interest us. In fact, we'll often start way before the point where we really need someone. A typical example might be to find out who the top experts in the world are in a particular aspect of Bayesian statistics.

Tanous: *What is Bayesian statistics?*

Shaw: I was actually just using that as an example, but the name comes from Thomas Bayes, an 18th-century mathematician who came up with a mathematical way of updating someone's prior beliefs to reflect any new data that might later become available. One of the main insights of the Bayesian approach is that, the more reason you have initially to believe that something is true, the less new statistical evidence you should ask for before deciding that it probably *is* true. This is relevant, for example, when we conduct a scientific experiment, since we'll want to make use of any information we might have had *before* conducting the experiment to decide whether the result we get *during* the experiment is due to pure chance or to the thing we're actually trying to study.

Tanous: *It's interesting because if I understood it correctly, what you described also applies to the efficient market hypothesis, doesn't it? In your example, you try to determine if the results are real, or simply a chance occurrence. Likewise with some of the successful investment managers who achieve great investment results. These managers believe that they beat the market because of their skill. Efficient market proponents believe that they do so by chance with only a very few exceptions. The two exceptional names that always come up are Peter Lynch* [page 111] *and Warren Buffett.*

Shaw: My guess is that in most cases, the efficient market crowd is right. It's hard for me, though, especially because I'm not an expert in the more traditional approaches to money management, to guess whether any given traditional, non-quantitative investment manager has done well because of skill or because of luck.

Tanous: *That's my job! This book will, I hope, help a lot of people make that judgment.*

Shaw: It will be interesting to read your other interviews. Even if the market is, for the most part, efficient, I don't think that rules out the possibility that there are some people, for example, who are able to find stocks that aren't well covered, research them, act on what they learn, and earn excess returns, while in the process indirectly providing the market with a little bit more information about the fair value of those stocks.

Tanous: *But when you tell that to the academics, they say, yes, in the aggregate, that is true. But the extra profit will exactly equal the amount it costs to do the research.*

Shaw: In principle, that's what should happen in any perfect competitive market, financial or otherwise, once it's reached the point of economic equilibrium. All free lunches should gradually get more expensive, until eventually they're fairly priced. What Wall Street does is to pay some people to go out there and investigate companies and tell us what they find so that the market can deploy capital where it can best be used. That's a very valuable function.

One thing that is important for me, personally, to try to get across to people is that, despite the fact that this isn't the way we at D. E. Shaw make our living, we should all be grateful that there are people out there who study products and companies and so forth.

That's a very valuable thing. Our markets are efficient, and our economy is robust, only because these people are doing their jobs all the time. We only do part of the job; we're definitely not doing the whole job. Arguably, the job that those other people are doing is in many ways even more important.

Tanous: *David, there's something else that comes up when you talk to a lot of the successful managers. Many of them, especially the ones who are clearly superior to their peers, may well have a sixth sense of some sort, in addition to their other qualities. Now they're all very smart, they're all very disciplined, they're all focused, but you wonder if there isn't an undefinable something extra at work. I suppose instinct and intuition don't apply in your business, do they?*

Shaw: I think you're talking about what I think of as a sort of "right brain" thought process. Although it might seem surprising, that sort of thinking actually is very important to us in the first phase of our work. That really is what makes it possible for us to generate hypotheses, to come up with ideas to test. It's definitely a non-mechanical process. It requires people who've developed a gut-level feel for the market models we've built up over the years with those tens of millions of dollars we've spent, and who take in new information all the time. They might say, here are some things I think might be going on in the marketplace. Let's look out there and see if we can find something. Most of the time there's nothing there, but every once in awhile we do find something. Usually it just leads to another series of questions; it's almost never a strategy, but sometimes it provides another clue.

What we do is similar to what a classical natural scientist does. You go out there and study some set of phenomena. Then, using that sort of experience-based pattern recognition and creative thought that's so hard to describe, you formulate a well-defined hypothesis about what may be going on. Then, as you discover things that don't quite fit your theory, you formulate a new hypothesis, and you continue to test. One thing I think is often misunderstood, not just about our type of business but about the nature of science in general, is that the hardest part, the part that really distinguishes a world-class scientist from a knowledgeable laboratory technician, is that right-brain, creative part.

Tanous: *Really?*

Shaw: I think so. You explore, you learn, you get a feeling for the stuff that's out there, and with any luck, you eventually develop a sense for what might be worth testing. The left-brain part is your knowledge of the rules of the game. You've learned how not to get fooled by data. You've learned how to make sure that you're not falling victim to mass psychology or scientific fads, which is very easy to do. That left-brain part is essential for making the slow, steady progress that moves science ahead. But the creative part is extremely important. That's what really drives it all.

Tanous: *Can you give me an example? Can you think of a case where that process you just described might have led to something?*

Shaw: That gets tougher because of the proprietary nature of what we do.

Tanous: *Good! You mean it's a secret. That's even better!*

Shaw: That part is. The places where the promising hypotheses come from tend to be something that we jealously guard. But I can tell you that the creative part is different in every case. It generates a wide range of ideas, most of which don't work.

Tanous: *One of the people I interviewed, whom I like a lot, is Bill Sharpe [page 89]. One of the things he's interested in is efficient markets. I said, Bill, I know you're an efficient market guy, I know what you believe, but look, if you had to invest money actively, what would you do? He said, my favorite active strategy is a "long/short" strategy, which to me means "market neutral." And of course, that is kind of what you do. What's your definition of market neutral?*

Shaw: Okay. The way we define it, and it has been defined in other ways, is that it means we're not trying to make money by predicting the direction of the overall stock market, or for that matter, of things like the level of interest rates, or the slope of the yield curve, or what's going to happen to the economy. Those are all effects that we're not able to predict. If we could do that with a high degree of reliability, we would bet on it. So it's not that we have a religious commitment to the notion of market neutrality. It's just that we haven't found a formula to predict the overall direction of the market, and we aren't very optimistic about finding one worth betting on in the future. The chance that we're really going to find something with enough explanatory power to give us a statistical edge by looking just at the market strikes us as really unlikely. So we just don't focus on that. Since we don't know how to predict the market, and since exposure to the market is risky, we try to avoid market exposure, which is why we're called market neutral.

In practical terms, what market neutral means to us is that we try to hedge out market risk, and, more generally, all of the different sources of risk that don't give us a predictive edge. That means that, at any given point, we'll have almost no exposure to the direction of the stock market or interest rates, or to any of those variables I mentioned. It's usually not exactly zero, because if you insist on having literally *no* exposure, you wind up paying too much in transaction costs. You waste money making a lot of very small transactions, and that turns out to be a bad idea. Typically, what you are trying to optimize—and this may be too mathematical to include in your book—is something like $\mu - k\Sigma^2$ where μ is excess return, the amount of return you expect to get over the risk-free rate of interest, k is a constant that reflects your own personal tolerance for risk, and Σ is the expected standard deviation of the value of your portfolio over time.

Tanous: *YIKES!*

Shaw: The thing that's relevant here is that, because the Σ part of this function is squared, a small amount of exposure to a given risk factor doesn't make much difference, but as the amount of exposure gets bigger, the danger grows really fast. To give a simple example, if you were to multiply the size of your risk exposure by a factor of ten, the pain you'd suffer—or more precisely, the number of dollars of profit you should be willing to pass up to eliminate that exposure—would go up by a factor of a *hundred.* What you really want is not a fixed risk limit, but an optimizer that knows how painful any given level of risk is, and that quickly, but smoothly, increases the penalty it charges for taking on more risk. That gives you an optimal tradeoff between risk and return.

Tanous: *Speaking of risk, how about October 1987. What happened? How did you do?*

Shaw: Well, I was at Morgan Stanley then, and I'm not at liberty to discuss their performance, but I can tell you that we don't spend much time worrying about stock market crashes at D. E. Shaw & Co. Once again, since we can't predict them, we don't bet on them. We tend to be pretty well hedged against them. We also can't predict market volatility, so we try to hedge that out also. Anything we can't bet on, we try to find a way to hedge.

Tanous: *Isn't the existence of quants a fairly recent phenomenon? Since there have always been great academics and great mathematicians around, is it because computers have gotten so powerful that the quant theories can be put to the test?*

Shaw: It certainly helps to have powerful computers. But I think a lot of this could have been done with the computers that existed ten years ago. Actually, there were a few quantitative traders ten years ago. Because the markets were less efficient, it was actually a lot easier to break into the business and make money as a quant at that point than it is now. Since that time, both the markets and the business of quantitative trading have matured. There's also been a lot of progress over the past few decades within the discipline of quantitative finance, including some extraordinary contributions in the development of modern portfolio theory, on the one hand, and also in the theory of option valuation, which was pioneered by Fischer Black and Myron Scholes.

Tanous: *You know, both of them were students of Merton Miller [page 213], whom I also interviewed.*

Shaw: They must have been great students. I was really upset when Fischer Black died. He was much too young, and a brilliant and wonderful guy. The contributions he made were just stellar. The Nobel Prize is only awarded to people who are living, which probably means that he just narrowly missed it. He would almost certainly have gotten it within the next couple of years.

Tanous: *Let's talk about secrecy. I've read the very few articles that have been written about you. You seem to shy away from talking, not only about your methodology and volume, but also about performance. The articles I read had to speculate about your performance. But I'd really like to know about your performance. Can you talk to me about it?*

Shaw: No, I'm afraid I can't.

It's true that we've kept our returns private, but part of the reason for that is that we've simply never had much *reason* to talk about them publicly, since we weren't trying to raise money. The limitation for us wasn't how much capital we had, but how much new capital we could put into a strategy before the returns started to seriously degrade. Whenever we found a new strategy, we could go to our investors and say, we could use another $50 million dollars, and they would generally write a check right away. So we really didn't have the problem of raising money, which is the main reason that most traders like to publicize their returns.

Tanous: *How long have you been operating?*

Shaw: Since mid-1988. We started trading in January 1989.

Tanous: *That makes for a nice seven-plus-year record. I think I understand your reluctance to disclose performance figures, but let's give it a shot. Have you had any down years?*

Shaw: Even that's not something we discuss outside of the firm.

Tanous: *If I wanted to pick a benchmark to compare your performance against, let's start with a fairly easy one for you, the S&P 500. For the last seven years or so, the S&P has done about 15% per year. Are you over or under that?*

Shaw: Again, I can't comment on that. That's just our company policy. We declined to tell *Fortune* what the numbers were for the same reason, so they tried to get the information elsewhere and it came out wrong.

Tanous: *They said your record was 18% a year.*

Shaw: They were wrong, although I really don't think that was the writer's fault. The information that's out there about us can be confusing if you don't know how to interpret it. Since we don't help them, I really can't blame the press for getting it wrong.

Tanous: *I have this feeling that when you say it's wrong, it's wrong on the low side. . .*

Shaw: I'm afraid I can't confirm anything about our returns. We're a private partnership. We regard all performance information as confidential.

Tanous: *Are you a registered investment advisor?*

Shaw: No. We're not a mutual fund, and we're not an investment manager.

Tanous: *In your company profile, you mention that you've used your capital to hold a position for weeks or months while awaiting an off-setting order. Now, if you're holding a position for weeks or months, that position, one might assume, is subject to market risk. How do you neutralize the market risk over all that time?*

Shaw: Okay. Let me just back up to make sure you know the context for this. There are actually three parts to our business. We've been talking about the first part: our proprietary trading activities. The second part is our customer-oriented businesses. *[As part of their business, D. E. Shaw, and other firms, will, from time to time, bid on a large block of stock or even an entire portfolio that is for sale. In Shaw's case, they utilize their proprietary quantitative techniques to devise ways to make a profit on the stocks they wind up owning.]* There, we might acquire a position from a customer who wants to sell for whatever reason. If we have a big position that we've acquired from a customer, we're unavoidably exposed to that one issue, but we can still hedge the *market* risk, and usually various other risk factors. For example, if we acquired a long position in a stock, we could sell short a related stock or a whole bunch of related stocks so that we hedge out certain risk factors associated with the stocks we just acquired. Our optimizer would actually do something more complicated, but just as an illustration, if somebody had sold us a bunch of General Motors stock, we might short Ford and Chrysler. But maybe that leaves us with a net interest rate exposure because they have different balance sheets, so some other stocks in unrelated industries that have the opposite interest rate exposure might serve to hedge that risk. It all just gets thrown into this big pool which uses the same sort of optimizer that we use for our proprietary trading.

Tanous: *Let's move on and talk about some other areas of your activities. First, Juno. I think I know what it is. I've seen the ads for free e-mail service. It's out there. But what I don't understand about it is, its place in the nexus of your activities.*

Shaw: Juno is a project that comes out of the third part of our business.

Tanous: *The first part is the private partnership; the second the customer business?*

Shaw: Yes. The second is our various customer-oriented financial services businesses. The three parts of our business are connected in one important way, though, which is that they all take place at the intersection between technology and finance. That's our niche.

Tanous: *That's a pretty broad mandate.*

Shaw: Yes, it is broad. It's also important now because finance is going to be revolutionized by technology. Flipping that around, if you try to project the flow of capital into various business sectors, it's hard to imagine one where there is likely to be more action over the next few decades than in technology. Even within technology, we tend to specialize in information technologies, because that's what we understand. More than anything else, I think the reason that what might seem to be a superficially disparate set of businesses really hang together for us is that the people who do these different things are the same people.

We started to talk about our hiring policy earlier. We make it a point to hire the world's greatest computer scientists. We have a disproportionate share of all the greatest minds in the field of computer science and related quantitative fields, and also people who can do entrepreneurial things, or who have spent their time since they were kids dreaming up ways to do things like beating the horse races or the casinos. Others started their own businesses when they were very young. I myself started my first one when I was about 11.

Tanous: *I'll bet it wasn't a lemonade stand.*

Shaw: It wasn't a lemonade stand. It was actually a one-time proposition. We made a movie, a horror movie, with some of the kids in my neighborhood in West Los Angeles. We had a bit of an edge, since some of the kids' parents worked in Hollywood. One of them was in makeup, and I think someone else explained to us how single-frame animation worked, so we made a movie with faces melting and various objects moving around by themselves, and stuff like that. I don't think it could have cost more than $100 to make—we made it on 8 millimeter film—but that would have been a lot for a group of kids. The plan was to show it to the other kids in the neighborhood for 50¢ a show. What happened, though, was that the processing lab lost one of our rolls of film. That was my first and only experience with angry investors. I sure don't want to experience that again.

Tanous: *A lot of people have seen the ads for Juno and I admit to being surprised when I heard it was one of your companies. Juno is, as I understand it, a company that offers free e-mail service. I hear you'll send anyone who asks for it a free disk with the software. Can you tell me more about Juno?*

Shaw: First of all, we believe that the internet craze is for real—that this is an industry whose time has come. I've been using the Internet since its early days, more than 20 years ago, when it was still called the ARPANET. It was named after the Defense Department's Advanced Research Project Agency, which funded it. Back then I certainly wasn't the only one to recognize how important e-mail was bound to become, eventually. Pretty much all of my colleagues and friends realized, even then, that the way we were beginning to live— sending electronic mail to each other around the world, sharing a huge amount of information—was much more efficient than sending letters, or making repeated phone calls to people who were never at home or their offices. We could see that it was a very powerful medium, but the time wasn't right until recently. The timing was, in large part, because of the chicken-and-egg problem. If there's nobody to send messages to, it's not so interesting to be able to send messages. Now we're rapidly approaching critical mass. It still hasn't quite happened, but I think we'll soon see nearly universal penetration of the business community, in the same way that faxes have now become nearly ubiquitous. I think it will soon be unthinkable to not have an e-mail address. It seems inevitable that this will be one of the main ways people will communicate.

Tanous: *In fact, I notice that we're starting to see more and more e-mail addresses on business cards.*

Shaw: That's right.

Tanous: *Your Juno business got a lot of attention, because you advertise free e-mail service. Pretty cool! People like that. Obvious question: How do you make money?*

Shaw: On advertising, initially. But the bigger picture, for us, is that we believe that what's really going to be phenomenally valuable, in the long run, is simply to have as many people as possible stare at your screen for as many minutes a day as possible. Right now, we have this notion of shelf space in a grocery store, where if you control the shelves in the Safeway chain, you can use that to sell a lot of product. Obviously, people won't buy things they don't want, but if the product *isn't* on display, they'll never see it. The major difference is that you can drive to various stores and walk around. But, in the online world, you have people focusing for long periods of time on a single square foot of real estate.

Tanous: *Like a computer screen?*

Shaw: A computer screen. People who work in the information business, like you and I, spend a large part of their day watching that screen. So having contact with those people becomes extraordinarily valuable. How that contact can best be exploited is not entirely clear yet, because the industry is changing so quickly. At least it's not that clear to me. But it seems fairly clear that there will be many ways to extract value from this sort of "digital shelf space," whether by putting ads there, or providing on-line shopping, or managing people's financial lives, or whatever. However things evolve, we want to be involved.

Tanous: *Juno already exists. Now I have e-mail through America Online and Netscape. What's Juno going to give me that I don't already have?*

Shaw: First of all, if you're like me, and most of the time you spend online is spent reading and sending e-mail, you may not want to pay an online service for something Juno can give you for free. It's also much simpler to use than a full-blown online service. Here, I'll give you a copy of the software. *[David hands me a disk with the Juno software on it.]*

Tanous: *Thanks. I'll try it at home.* [You can get your free copy by phoning 1-800-654-JUNO.] *Now let's talk about FarSight, another of your creations.*

Shaw: The idea behind FarSight is similar, in some ways, to Juno. The basic notion is digital shelf space: Get the eyeballs on our screen. Here we're trying to tie all of the aspects of a person's financial life together. The goal is to allow the user to be able to do brokerage, checking, commercial banking, automatic bill-paying, and in the long run, probably a number of other things, through one integrated system.

Tanous: *I heard you spend a lot of time in Washington. What do you do there? Do you want to change the world or something?*

Shaw: I'd love to if I could, but one of the main things I'm learning is just how difficult and time-consuming it is to make changes within the public sector. I don't have a better prescription for how to design a government. As is often said, it may well be that this is a terrible system, but there aren't any better ones. My limited experience in government has made me more appreciative than ever of the freedom and the rapid pace of the private sector. All that being said, I was truly honored when President Clinton appointed me to the President's Committee of Advisors on Science and Technology a couple of years ago. It's really a very part-time job. We meet with the President occasionally, and by ourselves a bit more often. In between meetings, we review various things that are going on in government that have to do with science and technology.

I'm also now serving as chairman of the Panel on Educational Technology to advise the President on how computing and networking technologies might be used to improve the quality of America's K-12 schools. The President announced his educational technology initiative in the last State of the Union address, but we still have to come up with a more detailed picture of what ought to be done in that area. It's a terrific panel—two of the eleven members are Nobel laureates, and we've also got Chuck Vest, the president of MIT; John Young, the former CEO of Hewlett-Packard; Sally Ride, the former astronaut, who also happens to be a first-rate scientist; and several of the leading experts in the field of educational technology, among others. But even with all that creative brain power on board, I'm finding that it takes a lot of my time to serve as chairman, and I'm looking forward to sending our final report off to the President and getting back to having an occasional weekend or evening free.

Tanous: *Last question. What sort of advice would you have for the average investor who wants to make money in the stock market?*

Shaw: Because they generally don't have access to hedge funds, I actually think—and this is what I tell my own relatives—that their best bet is to keep expenses down and stay well-diversified. As for asset classes, even though there's no guarantee that the future will look anything like the past, there's a fairly widespread belief that the equity market is associated with excess returns. Over the long term, equities may be a pretty good bet. So I would probably recommend a fairly conventional sort of asset allocation, but with very low expenses. One good choice might be index funds, since they turn over infrequently, giving them some tax advantages, as long as you're not paying out too much in management fees. Management fees only make somebody else rich, somebody who's probably not adding any value—at least based on the available statistical evidence. I think that makes a lot of sense.

Tanous: *One of the theses behind this book is that I'm interviewing the very best minds in the business, people I believe have demonstrated predictability, like Peter Lynch, John Ballen, Michael Price, Eric Ryback, Foster Friess, Mario Gabelli, and so forth. Wouldn't you want to use this kind of person to try to get excess returns?*

Shaw: Maybe. The only thing I can say is that that's an area I have no special expertise in. My gut tells me that some subset of those people actually are skillful, not just lucky, and that there is something real there, but I'm not sure I could tell you which ones are which.

My visit to D. E. Shaw is something I still think about a lot. When you have spent over 30 years in the financial business, and you suddenly encounter something completely different, it can be a bit unsettling. Imagine. Computer scientists and Ph.D.s in math making money in the stock market. In David Shaw, we have met the acknowledged master of the quants. Welcome to the future.

David has an uncanny ability to explain complicated theories in a way that most of us can actually understand. That is an unusual talent. Of course, he was a professor at Columbia for some years, and I have a feeling he was a superlative teacher and must be missed there. Since you and I don't have Ph.D.s in computer science or math (or do you?), it's not likely we would understand the algorithms and methodologies he uses. But, not to worry. He's not going to tell us! David Shaw's secrecy only adds to his mystique on Wall Street. In fact, few people have actually met him. You and I are in rare company.

With his capital base of $800 million, and his huge trading volume, David Shaw is in the forefront of the computer and information technology revolution. And remember what he told us: the craze over the internet is real! Yet when you talk to him about the way most of us will make money in the stock market, his first bit of advice is to pay attention to costs. David knows how hard it is to beat the market. Adding costs, like management fees and trading commissions, can only make it that much harder.

In our discussion of investment strategies for most of us, he was leaning toward passive investments, like index funds, where the odds are greater that, with low fees and an intelligent asset allocation, we will do well. But then in his very last comment, he quickly opined that there probably are exceptional managers out there who do have something special, and who are skillful. "There is something real there," is the way he put it. Good advice to ponder as we contemplate our own investment programs.

Perhaps, some day, David will launch a fund that will allow those among us who can't write a $50 million check to have an opportunity to invest with him. Until then, we will have to satisfy ourselves with our visit with David Shaw, and our exposure to what may be the future of investing for those with the brains and the wallets to enjoy it.

PART THREE
THE ROUTE

YOUR ROAD MAP TO WEALTH

Our conversations are over. We have spoken to true investment gurus—investment managers with unquestioned records of success, managers who stand head and shoulders above their peers. We also had conversations with great academics in the investment field, whose accomplishments include winning the Nobel Prize in Economic Sciences and whose theories are still followed and form the basis of investment methods widely used today. In this penultimate chapter, we will distill the knowledge and insights we've acquired into a practical investment approach for all of us who want to build wealth to follow.

At the outset of our journey, I asked myself a series of questions, the great questions. The answers to those questions would provide the foundation upon which our ultimate investment program would be built.

Now that we have spoken with so many leading investment lights, we must focus our attention on those points and issues that have the greatest potential for our investment success or failure as individuals. Let me remind you of those questions:

- Is investing in stocks the most intelligent path to wealth for most of us?
- If so, is it possible to consistently beat the market?
- Which style of investing is best?
- What are the key characteristics of investment geniuses?
- What did we learn from the Gurus that we can use in our own investment program?

- How can we replicate the Gurus' success:
  a) when managing money ourselves?
  b) by finding Gurus to manage our money for us?

Once we have mulled over the answers, I will share with you my conclusions and fashion them into an investment strategy I believe we can all use to successfully enhance our future wealth. Don't worry, I'm not going to lay one of those boring and banal lists of dos and don'ts on you. You've seen them a hundred times ("Dollar cost averaging is the key to investment success . . . Remember to diversify your portfolio . . . Invest for the long term . . ."). I know this isn't the first investment book you've ever read and I don't want to insult your intelligence.

I want to share another important, and personal, comment with you. I mentioned early on that I have been in the financial services business for over thirty years. You might think that after all that time, I pretty much already knew, at least in a general sense, most of what there was to know about growing rich by investing. My experience in writing this book taught me otherwise. I was, frankly, amazed at what I learned. Had my education and knowledge, therefore, been lacking? I don't think so. I think instead that the experience you and I have had together, of sitting down and talking to some of the greatest investment minds in the world, inevitably led to discoveries that no one person is likely to have uncovered otherwise. Okay, I'll take a little credit for asking some of the right questions. There has to be some advantage to doing this for thirty years! But again, I learned a lot. If you feel the same way, you are not alone.

Let's take the easy question first.

Is investing in stocks the most intelligent path to wealth for most of us?

Yes. Next question.

Oh, if you have any doubts, please go back to the chart on page 8, the one I nicknamed: "The Chart that Hungry Stockbrokers Consider the Greatest Chart in the World." If that doesn't convince you that stocks are the way to go, there's not much more I can do to change your mind.

Is it possible to consistently beat the market?

This is the question that strikes at the very heart of the efficient market debate. We heard proponents of both sides. The top experts in their field. One group told us that we could not expect to beat the market except by chance. Other experts told us that they do beat the market. They do, in fact, seem to beat it regularly, and often spectacularly.

Let's review the arguments briefly. The efficient market theorists believe that the market is so efficient that everything that is known about a stock is reflected in the current price. To them, research departments, forecasts of earnings, newsletters full of advice, and all the rest of the stockpicking paraphernalia are a waste of time. "Investment pornography," Rex Sinquefield called it. Is it the equivalent of believing in clairvoyance? There are no mispriced securities, they say. So why do stocks go up and down, you ask? Because of new information coming into the market all the time. That new information, which may be good or bad, will have an effect on the price of the stock. Only you don't have that information in advance.

So, why buy stocks at all? Because, they say, over time and through history, investors have demanded at least some extra return on their money for taking the risk of stocks. That's pretty logical. If owning stocks only got you the same return as buying treasury bills, why would anyone take the risk? So equity markets, on the whole, reward investors for the risk they take.

Now you start to see the logic of the efficient market theorists. Since you can't really predict the future of a given stock, what you must rely upon is the overall return the market offers. More recently, the great academics, like Bill Sharpe and Gene Fama, have advanced our knowledge of how stocks behave by identifying the performance pattern of specific styles of stocks. We learned, for example, that value stocks outperform growth stocks, presumably because they are riskier, and you only get paid for the risk you take. Likewise, small stocks outperform large stocks because the small companies are riskier than the large companies.

So, if you want higher returns than the general market offers, just buy more small stocks or value stocks for your portfolio. You want less risk? Tilt your portfolio toward large growth stocks. Of course, you don't actually select what stocks to buy; you buy an index fund that emulates the entire market, or some size or style sections of the market. Your portfolio will have a mix of these different asset classes which match your own requirements.

That's the basic argument.

The active managers see it differently. Good research pays off, they say. The efficient market theorists are wrong. There are under-valued securities, undiscovered securities, and mispriced securities out there, and there are plenty of them. Hard work, good investment skills, a talent for investing, all these qualities will give you an edge. Remember what Peter Lynch told us: "I've always said that if you look at ten companies you'll find one that's interesting. If you look at 20, you'll find, two; if you look at 100, you'll find ten. The person that turns over the most rocks wins the game." That's the "hard work" thesis.

To this crowd, there is no question that a very good investment manager can beat the market. Of course, not all of them can, since all of them together constitute the market! But, as in every field, there will always be some exceptional performers who excel at what they do. Do you doubt this? They point to their records—I've beat-en the market consistently over the past (so-many) years. That's proof, isn't it?

Not really, say the efficient market theorists. That's just the effect of a normal distribution. There will always be outliers, those who do exceptionally well and those who do exceptionally poorly. Hey, Tanous, the people you interviewed are the outliers. The question is, will they be there tomorrow? Sure, everybody talks about Warren Buffett and Peter Lynch, but how many more of them do you think there are? They define "outlier." The word, my boy, is "persistence." Show me persistence and maybe you have a point. But all the studies we have seen suggest that the great managers of today are the has-beens of tomorrow. What good is great perfor-mance if you can't predict it in advance?

There it is, my friends. I hope I have adequately summarized the views of the two camps. Our moment of truth has now arrived. It's time to come to the conclusion that this book purports to draw, albeit in a completely unscientific way—not as a serious academic study, which it most assuredly is not, but as the observations of a pro-fessional in the investment industry, after conversations with some of the industry's leading managers and academics.

Have you reached a conclusion yet? I suspect you have. Let's see how your conclusion compares with mine.

To begin, I found the arguments on both sides very compelling. The passive investment proponents, the efficient market theorists, offer a tempting alternative when they say, why waste your time picking out stocks and managers? You are taking a lot of risk when you do that. Buy markets, or styles, or size of securities and you'll have a much better idea of what you will get. And think of all the time and fees you'll save! In this, they are right, of course. And we will take this point into account when we talk about our recommended investment strategy in the last chapter.

But did the efficient market theorists prove their case—that great investment performance comes only by chance? I don't think so. I kept a very open mind about the subject as I traveled across the continent researching the question. And lest you think that I might have a bias based on my work as an investment consultant, let me tell you straight out that, in my firm, we recommend both passive and active investment strategies and will continue to do so based on the requirements of the client. So I have no turf to protect or be influenced by.

Here's the point: We interviewed some of the top investment talent in our country. I don't pretend that these are the only great investment minds out there, because surely there are others. But I think that our Gurus proved the point without a doubt. The efficient market theory is flawed. There are simply too many examples of stocks that were discovered by a great manager before anyone else knew what was going on. A vivid example is the Michael Price story about tantalum. He picked Kawecki Berylco and Molycorp and International Mining because he did his homework. Go back and reread our conversation. There were many other good stock picks recalled by our Gurus.

Does that mean that the market is inefficient? No. Here is the conclusion I have arrived at: The market is not perfectly efficient at all times. However, the market is *constantly in the process of becoming efficient*. By that, I mean it takes time for efficiency to be achieved. The notion that information is reflected in stock prices instantaneously just doesn't seem to hold up. We have run up against too many cases where thorough, painstaking research combined with seasoned investment judgment have given the investor an advantage. I do not believe that these examples can be dismissed as anecdotal blips. There are too many of them. In time, the information that the Gurus uncover gets reflected in the price of the stock and the stock price moves up or down toward that "intrinsic value," or true price. Hence the market is constantly becoming efficient; it just isn't instantaneously efficient. Great managers see these changes coming, not through clairvoyance, but through skill. Remember Richard Driehaus. He combines skill with uncanny investment abilities to take advantage of "positive earnings surprises" before the surprises are reflected in the price of the stock. But the real skill is his ability to identify and stay with the winners and quickly shed the losers.

What about the "persistence" issue? The efficient market theorists claim that our Gurus are the Gurus-of-the-Moment, if you will. Next year, there will be another, different set, they say. I don't think so. For one, we made damn sure that those we chose had that quality of persistence. Nobody becomes a Guru in this book with just one or two years of hot investment performance. Here's the test. Go back three, four or five years. Look at our Gurus from that vantage point. How did they look then? For the most part, very good. A decision five years ago to invest with almost any one of our Gurus, based on his or her track record at the time, would have resulted in a sound investment decision. The persistence was there. Persistence persisted.

My conclusion: you can, in fact, beat the market. If you put in the time and the work you have a fighting chance of doing it. I think your odds are better if you spend your time finding the right Guru to do it for you, although only you can assess whether or not you are prepared to do what it takes to succeed. That does not mean that you should shun the passive investment strategies altogether, and we will discuss ways to use passive strategies later.

Which style of investing is best?

Many of you reading this book learned about style differences in securities for the first time. Others were already very familiar with them. We learned, among other things, that different styles of stocks have different performance records. We learned, for example, that value stocks have outperformed growth stocks over time. Why this has happened is somewhat more controversial. Rex Sinquefield told us that this occurs because value stocks are riskier than growth stocks, and you get rewarded for the risk you are willing to take. Others made the case that value stocks aren't riskier, citing studies that showed that, since the end of World War II, value stocks outperformed growth with no discernible increase in risk. We also learned that small-cap stocks outperformed large-cap stocks over time. Here, the idea that smaller is riskier was not challenged as much. So what's the answer to the question?

If we were looking for a single answer, it would probably be that on a long-term, risk-adjusted basis, value stocks are the way to go. But that's not the best answer. The right answer, in my opinion, is to diversify your portfolio as much as possible in different styles and classes of securities with different risk components. You want to use, as much as possible, noncorrelating asset classes. That is a fancy way of saying that you want stocks that don't all go up and down in lock-step. Remember what Peter Lynch told us about style: "If value funds are out of favor, Mario Gabelli and Michael Price can't be expected to perform as well as a growth fund, if growth is in favor." As usual, he is absolutely right.

Value and growth stocks, small and large stocks, tend to do well at different times in the market cycle, although both possess market risk as a common element. Reread the Sinquefield interview for this discussion.

In our chapter on portfolio construction, we will take these characteristics into account to suggest a portfolio structure that combines the best elements contributed by the investment academics, along with the experience of the Gurus we interviewed.

What are the key characteristics of investment geniuses?

You may have developed your own list. Compare it to mine, based on our interviews with the Gurus:

DISCIPLINE ▼ Every one of the Gurus had this. No wishy-washy investment approach that changes with the times or the current state of the market. Some of their philosophies may have evolved over time, but they don't vacillate. They stick to their guns. It reminds me of successful bowlers. I learned this early on when I was first learning how to bowl. Professional bowlers always throw the exact same shot. They practice just one move. It's like a pitcher who only throws one pitch, and it always goes the exact same way. That's what bowlers do. In order to hit the pins they want to hit, all they do is move the position and starting point of the ball's trajectory. But it's always the same shot. Discipline.

FOCUS ▼ This is a corollary to discipline. Keep your eye on the ball. And they do. Our Gurus just don't get distracted by the fad of the moment. They are seasoned professionals who know what works for them and they stick with it.

INTELLIGENCE ▼ We heard that a lot, didn't we? Yes, you have be very smart to succeed at this business. That shouldn't be surprising, but to many, it is. I suppose it's because so many people look at the stock market like a big casino where some lucky gamblers win. Not true. It does take smarts. I trust this point came through in the interviews.

HARD WORK ▼ This doesn't come as much of a surprise, I hope. We saw countless examples of the amount of work these people put in to identify companies that are worth buying. As in so many of life's endeavors, you get out of it what you put in. It's that basic.

THE GREAT INTANGIBLE ▼ Let's face it. Some of these Gurus have something "extra." Problem is, the "extra" is tough to put your finger on. I remember occasions during our talks when phrases came up that alluded to that something extra. Eric Ryback saying that he'll hold a stock until it "starts looking at me funny." Driehaus deciding instinctively to sell his position in Altera while we walked around the trading room. Scott Johnston came right out and said it: I have a sixth sense. All great managers have a sixth sense, he added. These are examples of instinctive behavior. What is it? Where does it come from? I don't know. Perhaps there really is a sixth sense. If it is there, the real question is how much does it contribute to performance? Can you be a Guru without it? I tend to think you can. If that something extra does exist, I suspect it is not the predetermining factor that makes for great investment success. We saw too many other criteria that do.

What did we learn from the Gurus that we can use in our own investment program?

I hope you developed your own list along the way. I would like to share some of the highlights of mine with you. I can't really mention all of the good advice we got here because I'd almost have to rewrite the entire book. Along the way, specific comments stuck out. Here are some of my favorites. These are sometimes one-liners, other times specific investment ideas, all of which, I believe, we should use in our own investment programs, be they picking stocks, buying mutual funds, or selecting investment managers.

I was intrigued by a strategy that Bill Sharpe talked about and realized long after the interview how much sense it made. Remember, this Nobel laureate is not a proponent of active management. But he did outline his favorite active management strategy which, he told us, he dubbed: "a modest proposal to revolutionize the investment management industry." He may be right.

Let's go over it again. He finds a great manager who specializes in, say, growth stocks. Then he tells him to identify the ten very best stocks he knows and buy them. Then he says, pick ten of the very worst stocks you know and short them. In so doing, he has taken out of the equation one of the most important risks the investor faces: market risk. Why? Because even if the market goes down, he is hedged by being long and short different stocks. Likewise if the market goes up. That means that he is only paying for *selection,* the manager's ability to pick the stocks most likely to go up and the stocks most likely to go down. In fact, that is really all we should ever pay for, since we can't predict the direction of the market. This strategy is sometimes known as "market neutral," but be really careful, since different managers' definition of this strategy vary widely.

I was equally fascinated by Peter Lynch's approach to finding great companies. Peter wrote about much of this in his own books, but the advice is enduring. You start by observing. You see what companies are doing well in your own backyard. You notice what products are being talked about. Then, if you're really ambitious, you get information on these companies and see if you can make a case for buying them early. You just can't argue that this makes sense. I do, however, question your and my ability and patience to do all the work that must, inevitably, go with this strategy. Another bit of advice from Peter: Great companies make great stocks. Simple, but telling.

While we're talking about doing the research ourselves, it might be useful to re-read Professor Roger Murray's advice on the kind of research you need to do before buying a company. He spelled it all out: pick an industry, analyze the companies in it, do spreadsheets, do ratio analysis, narrow your field down from six to two companies, and start all over again. I admit that this doesn't sound like a lot fun, but have I convinced you, at least, that finding great investments involves work?

Here's a quick quiz: can you recall one particular phrase that kept coming up in our interviews with both active and passive managers? Time's up. The one I remember vividly is: "There's no free lunch." Seems to me there was always somebody trying to beat that notion into our heads. For good reason, of course. The money isn't lying around waiting for you and me to pick it up just because we read a nifty article on investing or a new theory that works every time (on old data, of course). We're back to doing the work.

We also learned a few things from the momentum investors. I immediately think of Richard Driehaus and also Bob Gillam. Buy companies that are going up, not down. Duh! But do we do that? No. Because we get scared when we see a stock hitting new highs every day. We think maybe we missed that one, so we look for something else. But those other stocks are going up and that's why they're hitting new highs! So these guys look for accelerating earnings trends, positive earnings surprises, and stocks headed in one direction. This, too, makes a lot of sense, but it is, as Rex Sinquefield observed, not for the faint-hearted. Problem is, you may have to get out just as fast as you got in if something changes. Best leave this approach to the pros.

How about the value crowd? We spoke to a number of them, including Mario Gabelli, Laura Sloate, the indomitable Michael Price, among others. This is the Graham and Dodd approach to investing. It requires research and study to find those hidden jewels— companies that have not been discovered or that have hidden assets not yet recognized by the market. This approach makes sense for some industrious investors because, in this case, you just might have some knowledge that others do not yet possess. For example, you might work in a field that gives you special insight into an area. You could use your privileged judgment and understanding (although not inside information, of course) to invest ahead of the crowd.

There are also geographic advantages. Here's another Peter Lynch quote from our interview: "I wish Home Depot had started here in Boston instead of in Atlanta." What's he saying? Just that you may have an edge if you see a great company or concept starting to take hold in your own backyard. Okay, it's a bit of a stretch to call this value investing, but the point here is that we are looking for hidden assets. Finding them early is always a good idea.

Here is another important lesson we learned from the Gurus: there are many different styles of investing and successful investors generally choose one and stick to it. Laura Sloate buys value stocks. Period. Likewise Michael Price. But can you imagine Richard Driehaus picking a value stock? It's almost funny. This point will come up in our next discussion

Replicating the Gurus' success: can we do it ourselves, or should we find Gurus to manage our money for us?

I am reminded of the interviewer who asks the candidate: do you consider yourself a decisive person? The candidate responds: well, yes and no. My sentiments exactly.

There are only a handful of Gurus in this business. You met a great selection of them. There are some things we can learn from them to help in our own investment programs. Let's start by looking at the steps we need to take to pick stocks ourselves and construct an intelligent portfolio.

ALLOT THE TIME ▼ First, if you set about picking stocks yourself, allot time to do the research. I realize that your broker may call you with some nifty story, and presumably he, or his research department, did the work, but ask a lot of questions anyway. If you are going to rely on someone working for you, at least make sure the work was done. Ask questions. You will find out quickly how thorough your broker or advisor is.

I remember a time, years ago, when I trained institutional brokers by role playing with them before they pitched an investment story to a client. I would pretend to be the client, listen to the story, then ask questions. Some of these fellows had spent hours learning the intricate details of some new medical technology and were primed to discuss this new found knowledge in great detail. But when I asked what the company's sales had been for the last two years, I often got a deer-in-the-headlights reaction. If your broker doesn't know basics, like the company's revenues, you can't trust him with the rest of the data. For starters, keep a list of questions to ask your broker or advisor when he or she comes around to pitch the next Microsoft to you.

Questions to ask your broker about any recommended company:

- Revenues

  What are the company's sales?

- Growth rate of revenues

  How fast have sales been growing?

- P/E

  What is the price-earnings ratio of the company based on its anticipated earnings? How does that compare with other companies in its industry?

- Market cap

  What is the market capitalization of the company. Is it too small (or too large) for my portfolio?

- Gross margins

  What are the company's profit margins? How do they compare to those of peer companies in the industry?

- Debt ratio

  How much debt does the company have? How does this company's debt ratio compare to its peer group?

- Management

  How long has senior management been with the company? Have you (or your research analyst) spoken/visited with them? How recently?

- Competition

  What are the barriers to entry into this business? Who are the major competitors? Has the analyst spoken with the competition?

- Timeliness

  What was the price of the stock when the brokerage firm first recommended it? (It should be on the report. You don't want to be the last person on the list that he called.)

  If your broker knows most of the answers to these questions, then you can probably take him/her seriously.

Here are other criteria to guide you, based on the advice of the Gurus.

Pɪᴄᴋ ᴀ sᴛʏʟᴇ ▼ This is very important. As we have seen, almost all of the Gurus have chosen a specific style of investment that he or she is comfortable with. They don't bounce from style to style, each chose one and stayed with it. You should do the same. This is a very personal choice. It depends on the type of person you are. Did you identify with any of the great managers in the book? Do you see yourself as a latent Michael Price, Mario Gabelli, or Laura Sloate? Then you should probably go the value route. Did you like the approach of Foster Friess, Richard Driehaus, Bob Gillam, and Scott Johnston? You are probably more oriented to a growth or momentum style, but if you go the momentum route, be prepared to spend a lot of time at it. How about Eric Ryback? His is a nice safe approach with a value orientation. Perhaps you identified with the way he operates.

Then there are the academics, and for our purposes, I will lump Rex Sinquefield in with them. Did they make sense? In that case, forget about selection entirely; save your time, and buy index funds. (More on this in the next chapter.)

Fᴏʟʟᴏᴡ ʏᴏᴜʀ sᴛʏʟᴇ ▼ Did you pick growth? Here are the attributes to look for in the companies you select:

- Attractive industry fundamentals
  Growing industry
  Dominant or emerging position in the industry
- High rate of earnings and sales growth
  Industry growth twice as high as the economy's growth
  Company's growth among the highest in the industry
- Reasonable price-earnings ratio
  P/E should not be much higher than the growth rate, e.g. if growing at 20%, than a stock price 20 × earnings is okay.
- Strong management
  Demonstrable accomplishments either at this company or a prior one.

Perhaps you felt more comfortable with the value approach. Here are your selection criteria:

- Low price-earnings ratio (or no price-earnings ratio if the company isn't making money)
- Left behind by the market

    A neglected or cyclical industry that may be on the verge of a turnaround.

    A company with a troubled past that now has new management, new capital, a new product, or a nice combination of these.

- Sells at a discount to book value
- Hidden assets

    Perhaps the company owns Manhattan, which it acquired from the Indians, but, following good accounting practice, is carrying the purchase on its books at cost, $24.

- A catalyst factor that will cause the stock price to rise.

You must also choose your size parameters. Are you more comfortable with small stocks? Large stocks? Small stocks are more exciting, but they entail greater risk. You'll have to decide that.

A final word about picking a style. If you are going to pick stocks yourself, let me at least get you to agree to one thing. You won't become an expert in all the different styles. That is one of the great fallacies of most of the investment advice you have read. The authors expect you to be good at picking all kinds of stocks—growth, value, large and small. Now why is it that they expect you to do something that most of the Gurus don't even try to do? Don't even try to become an expert in everything! If you are going to pick your own stocks, at least find out what you are likely to be good at, and stick to it.

But that creates another problem. If you become expert in one area, you aren't likely to wind up with a style-diversified portfolio, something that I recommend you do. Given the choice, I would much rather you own both growth and value stocks, and also small-cap and large-cap stocks. It is this diversification that will see you through difficult market periods while allowing you to participate in the growth of equity values over time. So how do you solve this problem?

Pick the style that you feel you are most likely to excel with, given your personal preferences and talents, then turn to outside help for balance and diversification. Don't try to do it all yourself.

In the next chapter, I will suggest specific asset allocations for specific types of risk. Whenever possible, we will use the actual funds managed by the Gurus we have interviewed.

When do I sell?

Most professional investors will tell you that deciding when to sell a stock is much harder than deciding when to buy it. For that reason, many Gurus use formulas, or benchmarks, which virtually take the decisions out of their hands. Perhaps that's why the factors that go into a sell decision are often referred to as the manager's "sell discipline."

For some managers, selling based on a formula makes the task a lot easier. Certain small-cap managers, including a few of our Gurus, sell when a company becomes too big to be considered a small-cap company. Other managers and investors set specific price objectives. They may, for example, decide that a 30% increase in the price of a stock over a defined time period is ample reward and that any objective beyond that would be greedy. Conversely, these managers may have a discipline to limit their losses. If a stock declines by a certain percentage, they're out. Momentum managers, on the other hand, will stay with a stock as long as it is moving in the right direction—up!

As you can see, there is no easy answer to the question about when to sell a stock or even a mutual fund. In order to arrive at our own intelligent sell discipline, let's start by applying the process of elimination.

First, let's agree that we are all investing for the long term, that is, a minimum of three to five years. This is important for a very simple reason: no one has yet come up with a consistent way to predict stock price movements. Yes, one or more prognosticators will get lucky and call a major turn in the market, like the crash of 1987, but how many do you know who have been able to do that two or three times? Don't even bother looking. Thus, the first sell idea we should eliminate is market timing. We are not going to sell our stocks or funds because some market prognosticator decided that the market was headed for a slide. Even if he or she is right, will they be there to tell us when to get back in? Not likely. The advice you have heard to stay invested is good advice.

When do we sell? Is it wise to set a specific investment gain objective and sell when it is reached? You can't go broke doing that. On the other hand, you will miss those ten baggers Peter Lynch talks about, stocks on which you might make ten times your money.

Here's the soundest advice I can give you about selling. First, in the case of a mutual fund, you should consider selling if the Guru who manages your fund, and who might have been the reason you bought it in the first place, decides to change jobs or go fishing for life. The manager might possibly be replaced by another good one, but you won't know that right away. You might want to sit on the sidelines and observe for a while.

Another reason to sell a fund is if its objectives change. If your growth fund starts to act like a value fund because the manager decided he likes value stocks, then you no longer have a growth fund! Find another one. Finally, if the fund's performance over time (one year or more) deteriorates below both the fund's past performance and a suitable benchmark (S&P 500 for a market-like fund, a growth stock benchmark for a growth fund, etc.), it may be time to part company and find a new fund.

For stocks, my favorite sell discipline is to apply the same criteria I used to buy the stock in the first place, only in reverse. Have the fundamentals of the company changed for the worse? Is the price of the stock no longer reasonable based on the criteria I used to buy it originally? Is the business still sound? Has the competition caught up to my company? In other words, if I can no longer find good reasons to buy the stock, at its present price, then maybe it's time to sell.

This technique also applies to the decision to sell at a loss. There are two ways to look at a loss. First, you might decide that if a stock declines 15% or more, no matter what the reason, you want to get out and cut your losses. I prefer to use a less mechanical approach. Once again, I evaluate what may have changed to cause the decline. If the stock is going down because the market is declining, that is not a reason to sell it. But if new factors have cropped up, and you would not buy the stock at its present price, consider getting out, even at a loss.

It amazes me that some investors make sell decisions based on whether or not they have a profit or a loss. These investors will simply not sell a stock at a loss. They just don't want to admit they made a mistake. Don't be like that! Whether you have a profit or a loss is immaterial to your investment decision. Behave rationally! This advice notwithstanding, and human nature being what it is, even if you devise your own sensible sell discipline, you will probably do what most of us do: the day after you sell that stock or fund, it will be the very first name you look up in the paper the following morning!

Should we invest in stocks ourselves or let someone else do it for us?

Well, if you are an investor who wants to select your own portfolio, you may not like what I am about to say. Should you, or should you not, pick stocks yourself? I know there's a lot of helpful advice out there. There are thousands of stockbrokers eager to get some of your attention, and a lot of your money, in order to share with you the combined wisdom of their own "expert" views plus those of their research departments. The research budgets at top Wall Street firms exceed $50 million per year, so you'd think they must be doing something right. I wish I could be sure of that, but I'm not, although, some research departments are better than others.

If you don't want to listen to some broker with a good story, there are always the newsletters where, for a paltry hundred bucks a year on average, you'll benefit from the wisdom of their top picks. These often come from some of the top seers in the business.

And don't forget the books, the countless books which purport to show the true path to investment wisdom along with a nearly foolproof way to pick stocks. How good are these books? Probably as good as the last diet book (or investment book) you bought. Hey, if they worked, we wouldn't still be buying them, would we?

Remember Driehaus' story about the piano virtuoso? To become a virtuoso, and have people pay to listen to you play, you have to be very talented, to be sure. But you'll never make it to Carnegie Hall without a strict and grueling regimen of practice, practice, practice. I know you'll agree with that.

Let's take another example. Let's assume you are a very smart person, a fact which I do not doubt for one minute. Suppose you, and someone just about as smart as you, decide to become, say, jet pilots. Your friend, however, decided to keep his job as a nuclear physicist and you chose instead to give up your lucrative heart surgery practice and devote all of your time to learning to fly. You went through every course, every training program, flew eight hours a day and also most weekends. Your friend did the minimum coursework, flew whenever he had the time, and barely managed to get his license. After a year or so, who would you rather go flying with?

Now let's bring the analogy home. You follow the market, you like to do some research on companies, although admittedly it's pretty basic research, and from time to time you decide to buy a stock, either because you uncovered it yourself or someone sold you a great story about the company. Do you believe that your likelihood of investment success is going to be as good as someone who is just as smart as you (or dare I say, smarter?) who spends all of his or her time managing money? The amateur versus the professional? Forgive me, but I don't think so. It's hard enough to be good at this business, which is why this book features only a handful of Gurus out of tens of thousands of *professionals*. Sure there are other Gurus, but the point is the same, isn't it? I'm sticking with the odds.

Does that mean you can't possibly do well on your own? Of course not. It's just a question of how much time and effort you are willing to put in it. And you must be honest with yourself about this. I proffer this advice with some trepidation. For one, whether or not you agree with me, at least give me credit for not pandering to you the way some other books and articles do so shamelessly. They will make you believe that you, the amateur investor, are going to have as much success investing as some of the top professionals. And even if you do invest yourself, what are your odds of winding up in the top tier of investment manager performance? What if, instead, you tried to find those investment managers or mutual fund managers who might be likely to wind up in the top tier? It's your money.

So, my recommendation is that you not take up part-time jet airplane flying, that you not manage the bulk of your assets yourself, and that, in both cases, you get professionals to do the job for you.

Did I hear you say you still want to invest for yourself? Okay, let's talk.

I realize perfectly well that some of us invest not only for profit but also fun. Nobel Prize winner Merton Miller, who is basically an efficient market theorist, told us he, too, takes fliers in stocks. It's just something we enjoy doing, a process of investigation, discovery, and ultimate reward through profit. If I haven't discouraged you by now, well, you are probably destined to go ahead and do it, so do it right! All I ask is that you do it with a limited percentage of your total assets.

My contribution to the exercise is to provide the guidelines for you to follow. Refer to the Gurus as often as you can. Repetition helps. As you continue your quest for the next stock on which you'll make ten or twenty times your money, read through some of the summary criteria we learned from the very best of the managers.

Here's my bottom line: you will succeed if you are serious about putting in the time and effort. Please remember, there are no shortcuts. It's about work, not luck. If you're a lucky person, play the lottery.

CRAFTING AN INTELLIGENT PERSONAL INVESTMENT PLAN

I used the word "intelligent" in the title of this, our last chapter, for a reason. I want you to distinguish what you are doing from the investment blather and hoopla from so many other sources. Forget all those promises of instant wealth from stocks, thousand percent returns, and tempting penny stocks that will make you a fortune, and all the rest. I don't have to tell you where all this comes from. You probably know as many sources as I do. By now, you also know what *doesn't* work. Our job, yours and mine, is to concentrate on what does. Our objective is to create wealth intelligently, with all the odds in our favor.

The next thousand years is just around the corner. All of us will retire by some time in the first century of the next millennium. The quality of our retirement years will directly depend on the investment choices we make along the road. For many of us, our material well-being long before retirement will be a function of the financial choices we make at different life stages. Whatever your age, there is a wonderful opportunity staring you in the face. You now know that throughout recent history, the stock market has delivered the best investment returns of all asset classes. You learned new techniques for analyzing risk and returns from the Nobel Prize-winning economists who devised them. You visited with investment Gurus who deliver top-of-the-class investment results.

Now it is time to put what you have learned into practice.

Before we apply our investment crafting tools to a specific portfolio, we must establish some basic parameters. The first two are your age and your time objective. Of course, at some point in our

387

lives, we will be putting aside money for retirement, the earlier the better. But retirement is not everybody's immediate objective. There are homes to buy, children to educate, fantasies to indulge, and they all have one thing in common: they cost money. If you are young and have small children, you already know how expensive it is going to be to put those kids through college. Personally, I am staggered when I read about the costs of educating our children. When I went to Georgetown, it cost something like $2,000 a year for everything. Two of our three children have since graduated from that same school. The cost was recently running about $25,000 a year. So, if your kids are young . . . it's frightening, isn't it?

Before you even think of retiring, perhaps your shorter term goal is a red Ferrari, an oceanfront home in Florida, or a lodge in Aspen. (Let's skip your other fantasies for the moment.) We both know that your passbook savings account isn't going to get you from here to there. The good news is that you are young and the really good news is that you have just received advice from perhaps the greatest investment minds in America. Remember, your investment time frame is an important component to your investment strategy. The longer you have, the higher the odds you will achieve your goal. So if the kids' college days are ten years in the future, you may want to invest more aggressively than you might otherwise. If your son or daughter is in high school, I hope you already have a nest egg for college. In this case, you may need to invest that money more conservatively, because you will be spending it in a few short years.

Retirement money, in your 401(k) or IRA, should be approached the same way. Are you in your forties or fifties? When do you plan to retire? At 59, 65, or later? Most of us know individuals who enjoyed first-rate pension plans throughout their lives. They managed to retire with the very same incomes they earned while working. I hope you are one of them. Today, we view such plans as both a bonanza and an oddity, since there are precious few of them around any more. In the future, your wealth —retirement and otherwise—will probably be a function of your skill and foresight in planning your own investments, more than likely through your IRA or 401(k) plan. Alas, the era of lifetime employment and munificent pensions is over.

But the news needn't be all bad. If you start your investment program early enough, you will be faced with a pleasant dilemma— whether or not to retire at a very early age, continue your present career, or embark on a totally new activity, secure in the knowledge that a comfortable nest egg will ensure financial viability for the rest of your years. Look, I know that if you are under 50, the idea of retirement seems so remote that you don't even want to think about it. Okay, don't think about it. Just think about building wealth to use any way you want while you're still young enough to enjoy it.

The point is, no matter what your age, now is the time to get started. What better way to embark on a new or revised investment program than after having enjoyed the advice and wisdom of some of the greatest investment minds of this century?

Your risk tolerance is another parameter. This is really tricky since many of us *think* we know what our risk tolerance is, but don't really. I can't count the number of times in my own business that a client told me his or her risk tolerance was high; they were investing for the long term, after all, and we all realize that short term market fluctuations are unpredictable and unavoidable, so just please find me some Gurus who make 20% a year consistently. Please.

You know what happens, of course. As soon as one of their managers has a bad week, the phone rings off the hook. *What's wrong with him? Didn't you tell me how good he was? Do you think we're going into a bear market? Why did my manager sell XYZ at a loss?* Hello? Remember our discussion about the long term? So it goes. Clearly, risk tolerance assessment is better performed by a psychologist than an investment advisor. But we try.

My advice to you is that you be brutally honest with yourself about risk. It's amazing how no one seems too concerned about risk when stocks are going up. Our memories are very short. Can you really stand a paper loss of 15% or 20% or possibly higher? That's quite possible with an aggressive portfolio, you know, including the one you might put together yourself. The bottom line is that you must settle on an investment strategy you genuinely can live with. If you can't live with it, it won't work. Period.

In this chapter, we utilize the knowledge we garnered from the Gurus to arrive at guidelines which will give direction to your future investment decisions. These are practical, sensible, time-tested guidelines which you should follow seriously. You may have heard some of this advice before. That's good. It means that some of the advice you got wasn't all bad. But as with fine cuisine, it is not just the ingredients, but the combination of ingredients, that creates great dishes. Likewise with your investment portfolio.

In this chapter, we will construct some sample portfolios using the methods employed by the most sophisticated institutions to maximize return and manage risk. We will make use of the Nobel Prize winners' techniques, as well as some time-tested performance enhancing techniques employed by the great investment Gurus we encountered along the way. To make the examples more vivid and practical, whenever they fit our framework, we will use the actual mutual funds managed by the Gurus with whom we spoke. We will not recommend those Gurus who are private money managers because most of them have minimums that are so high, few readers will be able to employ them directly. (Laura Sloate, however, is available through Smith Barney's consulting division, with a $100,000 minimum.) For those fortunate few, the same principles of selection we use to select funds can also be applied to the great money managers.

We illustrate both conservative, and more aggressive, strategies. Most importantly, the strategies can be tailored to your specific risk tolerance and needs using the very same funds, but in different combinations. This will be clear in a few minutes.

An important point. You no doubt know that many long term portfolios consist not just of stocks, but of stocks and bonds. We didn't talk much about bonds, did we? In fact, the only Guru we encountered who was interested in fixed income securities was Eric Ryback of the Lindner Fund. Our primary reason for ignoring bonds is that we spoke with investment Gurus who are equity managers. That's where the performance is.

Historically, bonds were used by portfolio managers in bank trust departments to create ballast in a portfolio. The idea was that your bonds would provide stability and income, and help you weather any storms in the stock market, or so the theory went. My, how times have changed! While there are still an awful lot of portfolio managers who believe that conservative accounts should be invested 60% in stocks and 40% in bonds, most modern managers are aware of the new realities of the marketplace. In recent years, long term bonds have proven to be as volatile as most stocks, causing gyrations in market values that would get a momentum manager's attention. In 1994, for example, the "long bond" (30-year treasury bond), declined over 17%. Even after you take into account the income you received from the bond, you were still down over 10%. That's safety? It is often said that more money was lost in bonds in 1994 than in stocks in the 1987 crash.

What does this mean to modern portfolios? Just this. If you want fixed income for stability, for God's sake, don't buy long term bonds! Buy short term (up to five year) instruments. Shorter maturities don't fluctuate as much with changing interest rates, since you get all of your money back as soon as they mature. We will show a few examples of portfolios with some fixed income securities.

Frankly, there is an interesting case to be made that you shouldn't use bonds at all in any portfolio, even a conservative long term portfolio. No one has made this case more brilliantly than guru Peter Lynch. In the September, 1995, issue of *Worth* magazine, Peter wrote a cover story entitled "Fear of Crashing," which offers compelling evidence for staying in stocks through thick and thin. In my opinion, it was a superb piece of analysis. Check your local library or call *Worth* magazine in New York to get a back issue.

Another important point. We didn't speak with any international equity managers this time around. However, I believe that it is important for you to consider including some international stocks in your portfolio simply because, today, almost two-thirds of market capitalization is outside the United States.

An important reason to own international stocks is our FANCY-EXPRESSION-OF-THE-DAY: Non-Correlating Asset Class. Try that out at the gym. As you might expect from all we have learned, you will want your portfolio to be diversified by style (growth versus value) and also by size (large-cap versus small-cap). In so doing, you will achieve intelligent diversification along those areas of risk which have been identified in the market.

But there is yet another way you can diversify risk, and that is by owning foreign stocks. Stocks in foreign countries tend to behave differently than American stocks. In other words, their performance does not *correlate* with the performance of American stocks. Back to our fancy expression, non-correlating asset class. You diversify risk if your types, or classes, of securities do not correlate well to one another. That means, to put it very simplistically, whatever makes your American growth stocks move one way, is not likely to move your foreign stocks. Thus, having a group of stocks in your portfolio that behaves differently from other classes ought to give you another element of stability.

By combining great managers with our heightened knowledge of how markets work, we should go a long way toward having a truly intelligent portfolio that delivers what we expect with a minimum of surprise.

By now, you ought to be asking whether I'm going to come down on the side of the Gurus who recommended we go passive, that is, not even try to beat the market, since so few managers do. Or will I opt for the Gurus who have proven that over time they can, in fact, beat the market? I'm going to recommend both.

Did I just hear the word "cop-out"? Harsh, my friends. Hear me out. The fact is that it is indeed very, very difficult to beat the market over long periods of time. We happen to have identified some of the greats who have done so, and who, we expect, will continue to outperform their peers. But we also ought to play the odds a little bit. How? By having a portion of our assets in intelligently diversified passive funds whose performance over time has been more predictable than that of any specific active manager. How much will we have in passive investments, you may ask? That is, in part, a function of your risk tolerance.

Likewise style and size. Do we want to bet the ranch on growth? Or maybe small-caps? I don't think so. What we want to do is to participate in all of these styles and size attributes since they tend to do well at different times and at different stages of the market. That is intelligent diversification. Having 50 growth stocks is dumb diversification.

Let's get started.

The way we are going to approach portfolio construction is to use the best data available to us to "back-test" different combinations of strategies and see what works and what doesn't. Why do we back-test? Because unlike so many of the great prognosticators on Wall Street, on TV, and in newsletters, we admit to a humbling failing. We cannot predict the future. Given this handicap, we will analyze what works, at least historically. In so doing, we will be able to select great combinations with the advantage of hindsight. No losers here! So please always bear in mind that in making recommendations in this manner, we are benefiting from what is known as "*ex post* bias." Put another way, it's real easy to win at the races when you already know which horses won.

Why do this at all? Because history tells us some interesting things. We know, over periods of time, how certain classes of securities behave, the longer the time period the better we are able to assess the pattern. We have also spent time identifying those rare investment managers, the Gurus, who have something extra, that something that allows them to consistently beat the market. Here again, the longer they've been able to do it, the better. This becomes our learning laboratory. These are the people we want to analyze and emulate. These are the Gurus we want to use.

I mentioned we would use a combination of active and passive strategies. Passive management means more than just buying a market clone, like an S&P 500 fund. But we will use that index as a benchmark. Today, passive strategies are very sophisticated. Remember the interview with Rex Sinquefield? His firm, Dimensional Fund Advisors (DFA), offers dozens of passive funds from which interesting combinations of asset classes can be created. We will use some of them. I should point out that DFA funds are only available through financial planners and advisors, but there are plenty of those around. For readers who prefer to do it themselves, we will also use some Vanguard index funds in our examples. These funds can be purchased directly and are very cost-effective.

For active funds, we will use the mutual funds of our Gurus but, of course, other funds can also be used.

Let's start on the passive side of the street. Look at figure 1 (a Table of DFA Strategies). Here we have stocks and bonds broken down by size (large-cap versus small-cap) and style (growth versus value) going back a full 20 years—a good sample. Also included in this table are international funds and bond funds. Now suppose you built your portfolio by buying index funds representing these different classes of securities. Look at the 4 strategies (plus the S&P 500 index as a benchmark) and breakdowns here and you will see how your investments might have performed using these different combinations of passive strategies. Note that the different portfolios are in order of ascending return. (Annualized compound return, at the bottom of the table.)

Remembering what we learned about standard deviation (which represents the risk of a particular grouping of securities), you might expect that the standard deviation would tend to be higher as the return increases because we know that to get higher returns we generally have to incur higher risk. But wait a second. Look at Strategy #3, a diversified portfolio that is 80% stocks and 20% bonds. Those results are very good at 17.50% annualized with a standard deviation of only 10.40! Remember: the S&P 500 over the same 20-year time period had a return of 14.59%, and a standard deviation of 13.65. Hmm. Let's see. If this diversified portfolio gave me a return of over 17% a year, which was more than the stock market as a whole returned, and it did it with less risk, (i.e., lower standard deviation), that's starting to sound an awful lot like a free lunch to me! Look at Strategy #4. Here we have a high annualized return of 19.52% and a standard deviation about the same as the S&P 500. (But stay skeptical a little longer. Hindsight is wonderful.)

PEFORMANCE FOR BALANCED STRATEGIES

Annualized Compound Percentage Returns
January 1976-December 1995

Portfolio	S&P 500 Index	DFA 60/40 Normal Strategy			
		1	2	3	4
S&P 500 (U.S. Large Stocks)	100	60	10	14	17
U.S. Large Value Stocks			10	14	17
U.S. Small Stocks			5	14	17
U.S. Small Value Stocks			5	14	17
EAFE Index (int'l. large stocks)					
International large value			10	12	16
International small stocks			10	12 .	16
Long term gov't./corp. bonds		40			
Short term corporate bonds			40	20	
Annualized compound return (%)	14.59	12.89	16.01	17.50	19.52
Growth of $1	15.23	11.31	19.50	25.14	35.38
Annual standard deviation	13.65	10.35	8.47	10.40	13.04

U.S. Large Value, U.S. Small Value and U.S. Small Stocks courtesy Fama-French and CRSP.
EAFE courtesy Morgan Stanley.
Int'l. Large Value: live and simulated DFA International High BtM.
Int'l. Small Stocks: live and simulated DFA International Small-Cap Strategy.
Long-Term Corporate/Government Bonds courtesy Lehman Brothers.
Short-Term Corporate Bonds: DFA One-Year Fixed Income Strategy.
DFA 60/40 Normal Strategy Invests 10% in Five-Year Income, 20% in One-Year Fixed Income and 10% in Global Fixed Income.

Courtesy: Dimensional Fund Advisors.

Figure 1

Now look at figure 2. Column 1 shows our benchmark, the S&P 500, over a 10-year period from 1986 to 1995. As you will see, during that period of time, the stock index returned 14.84% annually, one dollar invested grew to $3.99, and the annualized standard deviation was 13.83. So this will be our return and risk benchmark when we compare different strategies to the market as a whole. Now let's look at some different allocations during the same period.

PERFORMANCE FOR EQUITY MIXES

Annualized Compound Returns
January 1986-December 1995

Portfolio	Strategies								
	1	2	3	4	5	6	7	8	9
Brandywine		20				35	30	25	25
DFA Normal Balanced Strategy		60	40						
Gabelli Value							30	25	
Lindner Dividend		20	30	30	20				
MFS Emerging Growth			30	30	20			25	25
Mutual Shares						35		25	50
S&P 500 Index	100					30			
Vanguard Growth Index				20	30		20		
Vanguard Value Index				20	30		20		
Annualized compound return (%)	14.84	14.53	15.64	16.15	16.16	16.42	16.39	17.47	17.55
Growth of $1	3.99	3.88	4.28	4.47	4.47	4.58	4.56	5.00	5.04
Annual standard deviation	13.83	8.54	10.42	14.53	14.97	12.87	13.94	14.05	14.22

Gabelli Value Data from 10/89.
MFS Emerging Growth data from1/87.
Vanguard Growth & Value Indexes from 12/92.

Courtesy: Dimensional Fund Advisors.

Figure 2

At this point, we're going "active/passive," choosing Guru-managed funds, and passive funds, both intelligently diversified. We will now zero in on several strategies from figure 2.

After doing the requisite homework, our investor decided to invest the portfolio into three funds (Strategy 2). First, DFA Normal Balanced Strategy (a diversified, passive allocation all by itself) for 60%, and then add The Brandywine Fund for growth and as a more aggressive investment (20%), and Lindner Dividend Fund, for income and stability (20%). This investor has put most of his assets into a balanced, passive strategy, but added growth and balance with an income and value-oriented fund, plus a growth investment. We'll call this Moderate Strategy "A". How did he do? His overall return for the 10 years was about the same as the S&P 500, but his standard deviation was only 8.54 compared to 13.83 for the S&P 500. That tells us that this strategy gave us the same return as the market, but with considerably lower risk than we would have incurred just by investing in the market as a whole!

MODERATE STRATEGY "A" (January 1986 - December 1995)		
PORTFOLIO	ALLOCATION %	
DFA Normal Balanced Strategy	60%	
Brandywine Fund	20%	
Lindner Dividend Fund	20%	
		S&P 500
ANNUALIZED COMPOUND RETURN	14.53%	14.84%
GROWTH OF $1	3.88	3.99
ANN. STANDARD DEVIATION	8.54	13.83

Suppose instead we wanted higher returns with lower risks. (Remember the northwest quadrant?) Now we need a combination of the Gurus. Look at Figure 2, Strategy #3, which we will highlight as Moderate Strategy "B" in the chart below: 40% DFA Balanced, 30% MFS Emerging Growth, and 30% Lindner Dividend Fund. This allocation returned somewhat more than the market (15.64% versus 14.84%). And what about the standard deviation? With a standard deviation of only 10.42, this allocation was about 25% less risky than the market.

MODERATE STRATEGY "B"
(January 1986 - December 1995)

PORTFOLIO	ALLOCATION %	
DFA Normal Balanced Strategy	40%	
MFS Emerging Growth	30%	
Lindner Dividend Fund	30%	
		S&P 500
ANNUALIZED COMPOUND RETURN	15.64%	14.84%
GROWTH OF $1	4.28	3.99
ANN. STANDARD DEVIATION	10.42	13.83

Okay. Let's get more aggressive. Perhaps you are relatively young, and your investment time horizon is years in the future. You also are the kind of person who is comfortable with greater than average market fluctuations. Here is a more aggressive strategy from figure 2, Strategy #9.

AGGRESSIVE STRATEGY
(January 1986 - December 1995)

PORTFOLIO	ALLOCATION %	
Brandywine Fund	25%	
MFS Emerging Growth	25%	
Mutual Shares	50%	
		S&P 500
ANNUALIZED COMPOUND RETURN	17.55%	14.84%
GROWTH OF $1	5.04	3.99
ANN. STANDARD DEVIATION	14.22	13.83

Note that in our Aggressive Strategy, we have significantly outperformed the S&P 500 (17.55% versus 14.84% over ten years) and, interestingly enough, we did not assume a great deal more risk as measured by the standard deviation values (14.22 versus 13.83 for the S&P 500). In the process, we also retained both style and size diversification by splitting the portfolio 50/50 between growth and value strategies. MFS offers us exposure to small to mid-cap stocks, and to some extent, Brandywine does as well. Our value component is represented by Michael Price's Mutual Shares.

Now it is your turn.

Using what we have learned, you should now be prepared to construct an intelligent portfolio for your own use, one which reflects your personal risk tolerances, goals, expected returns, and time horizon. Your portfolio should also reflect the latest advances in academic techniques to make money in the stock market, and the wisdom of the Gurus.

Before building your personal portfolio, we need to review and establish the criteria upon which our investment foundation will be built. Let's quickly review a checklist of desirable features for our intelligent investment portfolio.

- Choose both active and passive investment strategies to increase the likelihood of consistent investment performance
- Use non-correlating asset classes to reduce volatility:
  Use both growth and value stocks or funds
  Use both large and small-caps in all but conservative strategies
  Use international stocks, emphasizing funds for this purpose, to get geographic diversification
- For the active portion of the portfolio, use the Gurus, or the best talent available to you, or even your own stock picks, by applying the criteria we used to select Gurus in the introduction.
- Consider your time objective to be a minimum of 5 years and preferably 10 or more.

Remember: Our strategy is to use passive and active allocations to increase the odds of success and to maximize our returns. We expect excess profits from the active managers, but since we know how hard that is to do, we want to use only the finest talent available (or your very best stock picks using the Guru methods) for the active portion of the portfolio.

Let's consider three basic strategies, conservative, moderate, and aggressive. These will be generic in nature, allowing you to select your own stocks, funds, or managers, within the defined categories. We will "fine tune" your portfolio with a few subsequent adjustments to match your personal criteria as perfectly as possible.

First decision: Which strategy is right for you, conservative, moderate, or aggressive? Perhaps you already know. The answer is a function of your time horizon and risk tolerance. Look, if you have 15-to-20 years to go to retirement, you should lean toward the aggressive approach with your 401(k) and IRA strategy. On the other hand, what is your emotional tolerance for market swings? Will a decline in your portfolio gnaw at you mercilessly? The reason this is important goes beyond concern for your emotional well-being. The danger is that if you get upset about market swings, you may make some untimely, and possibly very bad, investment decisions. Of course, you, and perhaps your spouse, are in the best position to evaluate your risk tolerance. Be very realistic about it. I can't second guess you on this subject.

On the other hand, if you have some gambling instincts, and you elect a super aggressive strategy even though your time investment horizon is only a few short years, take a deep breath and count to ten. It is just plain foolish to try for aggressive growth, with its accompanying risk, *unless the odds are in your favor.* It is time that tilts the odds in your favor. And, at the risk of beating this point to death, I want to instill in you that we are stacking the odds in our favor with our approach to wealth. We know what works and we know what doesn't. By taking the known factors and the latest academic advances on historic stock performance and combining that information with outstanding Guru performance and strategies you can use, we will do as much as we can to tilt the odds our way.

Here are the three basic strategies you can use:

CONSERVATIVE STRATEGY

PORTFOLIO	ALLOCATION %
Passive 30% Vanguard Growth, 30% Value, 40% Short term Bond Index *or* 100% DFA Normal Balanced	50%
Growth stocks *or* Growth stock fund	20%
Value stocks *or* Value stock fund	20%
International stocks *or* International stock fund	10%
	100%

This allocation will have the highest percentage of passive funds and will include some short term bonds to reduce volatility. The passive funds give us the highest degree of confidence that our performance there will be in line with the historic performance of the markets we are trying to clone.

MODERATE STRATEGY	
PORTFOLIO	ALLOCATION %
Passive	
40% Vanguard Growth 40% Value	
20% Short term Bond Index	
or 100% DFA Strategy #3	40%
Growth stocks	
or Growth stock fund	20%
Small-Cap (diversified growth and value)	10%
Value stocks	
or Value stock fund	20%
International stocks	
or International stock fund	10%
	100%

The differences between the conservative and moderate portfolios are subtle. You will quickly see that the principal difference is the introduction of the small-cap style. For our purpose, we will not try to allocate the small-cap portion by value and growth as that is hard to do, since most small-cap managers are, in fact, growth managers. A diversified small-cap fund, or your own small-cap picks, will do fine. We also lowered the passive allocation in the moderate strategy as we will be trying for higher than market returns to a greater extent than with the conservative strategy.

The aggressive strategy reduces the passive allocation to 25% of the portfolio. Even so, note the DFA passive Strategy #4 (figure 1) is actually quite aggressive, having shown returns over 19% for 20 years. (This is not your father's passive strategy!) We've also done away with the bond portion altogether. It's not stability we're after, it's high octane performance. Our small-cap allocation is up to 30% of the portfolio. And note the subtle tilt toward value stocks (value

AGGRESSIVE STRATEGY

PORTFOLIO	ALLOCATION %
Passive	
50% Vanguard Growth, 50% Value	
or 100% DFA Strategy #4	25%
Growth stocks	
or Growth stock fund	10%
Small-Cap (diversified growth and value)	30%
Value stocks	
or Value stock fund	15%
International stocks	
or International stock fund	20%
	100%

allocation is 15% versus growth 10%), since we know that value out-performs growth over time. Whether or not it does so with more risk is still controversial. This portfolio will provide an intelligent higher risk, higher reward trade-off.

Now we must tinker with our basic portfolios to adapt them to your personal circumstances. You say, look, I know I want the conservative strategy, so what else do I need. What's to tinker with?

Here's what I mean. We need to fine-tune the allocations within the strategies to adapt not only to your risk tolerance, but also to your age, the time frame of your expected returns, and even the purpose of the funds. (Some things are postponable, i.e. that Ferrari you think you need for your midlife crisis; others are not, like the kid's college education.)

CHANGE   ADJUSTMENT*

	CONSERVATIVE	MODERATE	AGGRESSIVE
Time frame objective 3-5 years	1	3	2 *or* 6
Time frame obj. over 10 years	2	4 or 5	No change
Greater risk tolerance	2	4	7
Lesser risk tolerance	1	3	2 *or* 8

*ADJUSTMENT KEYS

1 Increase passive allocation by 10% to 15%. Reduce small-cap allocation by same amount.

2 Consider basic moderate strategy.

3 Consider basic conservative strategy.

4 Decrease passive allocation by 10%. Increase small-cap allocation by 10%.

5 Consider basic aggressive strategy.

6 Increase passive allocation by 10 to 15%. Add short term bond allocation of same amount.

7 Decrease passive allocation by 5%. Decrease value stock allocation by 5%. Increase small-cap allocation by 10%.

8 Increase passive allocation by 10%. Decrease small-cap allocation by 10%.

REBALANCING ▼ In any portfolio, the asset allocation is likely to change over time. That's because each of the asset classes you chose will perform differently over time. For example, if the small-cap portion of your portfolio has a terrific run, your allocation will tilt toward small-cap because there are now more dollars in small-cap as a result of your gains. Your original 10% allocation may now be 16% because it has gone up so much in value. What should you do?

What most portfolio managers do to correct these situations is that they periodically "rebalance" their portfolios. You should do this too. The process is simple enough. You sell the asset classes that have performed too well and increase those that have underperformed. Huh? You mean, we're selling our winners and putting the money with the losers? It seems counterintuitive, doesn't it? Well, maybe. But if your original asset allocation had a purpose, and it did, you should stick to it.

How often should you rebalance? Most portfolio managers set parameters. For example, whenever your allocation changes by more than 5% *of the total portfolio,* you rebalance. For example, if your growth allocation is 20% of your portfolio, you would rebalance if growth got to 25% or more of the portfolio. That could be because your growth stocks did very well or your passive stocks did poorly. It could also result from another allocation doing particularly badly. In the latter case, the first thing you want to do is make sure that the underperformance wasn't due to a problem with the fund manager or with your particular stocks. If that is the case, first take care of the problem. If the underperformance is simply due to a group being out of favor, then you proceed with the rebalancing by selling growth stocks, or shares in your growth fund, until the percentage is back to 20%, the original allocation. The money from the sale would be added to those areas where the percentage allocation had declined, and the reason for the decline was explainable and acceptable.

SEMI-ANNUAL REVIEW ▼ At least twice a year, look at your portfolio critically. Perform the sort of review we investment consultants do. Ask these questions:

- Have my investments performed in a satisfactory manner?
- Were the appropriate benchmarks matched or exceeded? (In other words, did my equity portfolio match the performance of the S&P 500? Or did my small-cap portfolio keep pace with an appropriate benchmark, like the Russell 2000?)
- If an investment underperformed, what was the reason? If it is a mutual fund, was there a change in fund managers or fund objective?
- Does the portfolio need rebalancing?

These portfolios show how combinations of excellence can result in superior performance. What's more, you don't have to rely exclusively on the Gurus. A combination of intelligently chosen passive and active strategies can do the job, too.

To construct your own portfolio, you need to follow some of the basic guidelines we learned from the Gurus. By all means, use the funds managed by the Gurus we interviewed. They have been around and they will continue to be around, God willing. They have passed the test of time.

Here's the bottom line. Since you and I know that we can't predict the future, and since we also know that most superior investment performance occurs by luck, not skill, we must learn to distinguish true investment genius, the Gurus, from the rest. Our conversations with the Gurus gave us insight into the qualities that set the Gurus apart. These are valuable lessons to learn.

In real estate, they speak of location, location, location. The investment equivalent is persistence, persistence, persistence. In the absence of a working crystal ball, we must make use of what has worked in the past. Persistence means track record, and with track records, the longer the better. Three, four, or five years of good performance may not be enough. Ten years gets interesting, and twenty years even better. The Gurus have passed the test of time. Passive strategies have also passed the test of time, and, as we have seen together, the academic advances in this area have been impressive. We can capitalize on this knowledge by using combinations of active and passive strategies, tailored to our specific circumstances and risk profiles.

Using these examples as guidelines, you can see how it is possible to tailor a specific portfolio to your individual circumstances. Now that you know about style and size diversification, and the importance of standard deviation to measure risk, you can confidently construct a personal portfolio. You know how to measure return against the risk you are willing to take. So, having determined all these parameters, you can start the building process by style, size, geography (international versus domestic) and risk. Armed with this knowledge, you may wish to seek the help of a financial advisor or broker to assist you. Among other services, these individuals can help you with standard deviation data, which is not easy to calculate and often not readily available.

For my part, I truly hope you enjoyed and profited from the time we spent together and especially our visits with the Gurus. There were no secret recipes, no magic formulas, no miracle 10-step plans, just sound advice from the greatest minds in the investment business. What more could we ask?

Thanks for coming along. I hope our paths cross again.

INDEX